I Am Brian Wilson

i am Brian Wilson

a memoir

BRIAN WILSON

CORONET

1

First published in Great Britain in 2016 by Coronet
An imprint of Hodder & Stoughton
An Hachette UK company

A CIP catalogue record for this title is
available from the British Library

Hardback ISBN: 9781444781335
Trade Paperback ISBN: 9781444781328
Ebook ISBN: 9781444781311

Printed and bound by
CPI Group (UK) Ltd, Croydon, CR0 4YY

Hodder & Stoughton policy is to use papers that are natural,
renewable and recyclable products and made from wood grown
in sustainable forests. The logging and manufacturing processes
are expected to conform to the environmental regulations
of the country of origin.

Hodder & Stoughton Ltd
Carmelite House
50 Victoria Embankment
London EC4Y 0DZ

www.hodder.co.uk

To Melinda—
God only knows what I'd be without you

Contents

Overture

Royal Festival Hall, London, 2004

It's been hard and it's been easy. Mostly, it's been both. My friend Danny Hutton from Three Dog Night recorded a song, "Easy to Be Hard," that I sing to myself in my head sometimes: It's easy to be hard, it's easy to be cold. It's cold now. It's the winter of 2004 in London, and I'm getting ready to go onstage at the Royal Festival Hall. Some of the songs I'll be singing are about the sun and the beach. There's not much of either of those in London right now. But there's water—the Royal Festival Hall is right on the river—and some of the songs are about that.

When I got here I was walking around and heard someone mention that the hall was originally built in 1949 but redone in the fall of 1964. That was a big year, 1964. It was the year of everything. The Beach Boys toured around the world. We were in Australia in January with Roy Orbison and all over the United States in July. They called that tour Summer Safari, and we played with people like Freddy Cannon and the Kingsmen. When we weren't touring, we were recording: "Fun, Fun, Fun" and "The Warmth of the Sun" at the beginning of the year, "Kiss Me, Baby" at the end of the year, and more songs than you can count in between. We put out four records—three studio albums (including a Christmas one) and a live album. And that was on the heels of 1963, which was almost as busy—three albums and constant touring, too.

I don't go back and listen to that old music very much. But I do think about it, and I try to imagine what was in my head back then. I can't always get a clear picture. Sometimes it's pieces of pictures. It's hard to get back to where you were, you know? Over the years I've played new music and I've played old music. I've played both here at the Royal Festival Hall—my band and I came in 2002 to play *Pet Sounds* straight through, and people loved it. That was in summertime. Tonight is different, though. Tonight is the moment I have been dreading for months, and imagining for years. Tonight, in the second half of the concert, we're playing *SMiLE*, the Beach Boys album that never was, for the first time. What the hell was I thinking? Why in the world did I think this was a good idea? *SMiLE* was supposed to be the follow-up to *Pet Sounds* back in the mid-'60s. It fell apart for so many reasons. It fell apart for every reason. Some of the songs that were supposed to make up *SMiLE* came out on other records over the years, but the real album went underwater and didn't surface for decades. Finally I got back to it and finished it up. In my sixties I did what I couldn't do in my twenties. That's what has brought me to London this time.

I'm sitting out in the theater. Everyone's getting ready. What brought me here to London? It's hard to keep my train of thought. There are so many people going back and forth, so many musicians. I hear them tuning up or trading licks, but I also hear them talking, both the musicians here and other musicians from the past. I hear Chuck Berry, who was one of the first artists to turn boogie-woogie into rock and roll. What would Chuck have thought about all these strings and woodwinds? He probably would have walked right past them and gone onstage with a pickup band he hired when he rolled into town. I hear Phil Spector, who did all those great records in the '50s and early '60s. Phil's voice is scary, always challenging me, always reminding me that he came first. "Wilson," I hear him saying in my head, "you're never going to top

'You've Lost That Lovin' Feeling' or 'Be My Baby,' so don't even try." But maybe he wants me to try. Nothing is ever simple with him, not when he's in my head. Simple isn't what he's about. People say that we named *Pet Sounds* partly as a tribute to him: check the initials. I also hear my dad in my head. His voice is louder than the others. "What's the matter, buddy? You got any guts? Is this all about you? Why so many musicians? Rock and roll is two guitars, a bass, and drums. Any more than that is just about ego."

When I hear those voices, I try to shut them out. I'm just trying to get a feel for the room and how the songs will come alive inside of it. I'm also trying to get a feel for where I fit into all of this. Back in the old days with the Boys, I never liked going onstage. People used to write about how I seemed stiff. Then they started writing about how I had stage fright. It's a weird phrase, "stage fright." I wasn't afraid of the stage. I was afraid of all the eyes watching me, and of the lights, and of the chance that I might disappoint everyone. There were so many expectations that I could figure out in the studio, but they were different onstage. A good audience is like a wave that you ride on top of. It's a great feeling. But a crowd can also feel the other way around, like a wave that's on top of you.

There are other voices, too, along with Chuck Berry and Phil Spector and my dad. The other voices are worse. They're saying horrible things about my music. *Your music is no damned good, Brian. Get to work, Brian. You're falling behind, Brian.* Sometimes they just skip the music and go right for me. *We're coming for you, Brian. This is the end, Brian. We are going to kill you, Brian.* They're bits and pieces of the rest of the people I think about, the rest of the people I hear. They don't sound like anyone I know, not exactly, except that I know them all too well. I have heard them since I was in my early twenties. I have heard them many days, and when I haven't heard them, I have worried about hearing them.

My whole life I've tried to figure out how to deal with them. I've tried to ignore them. That didn't work. I've tried to chase them away with drinking and drugs. That didn't work. I've been fed all kinds of medication, and when it was the wrong kind, which was often, that didn't work. I have had all kinds of therapy. Some of it was terrible and almost did me in. Some of it was beautiful and made me stronger. In the end, I have had to learn to live with them. Do you know what that's like, to struggle with that every single day of your life? I hope not. But many people do, or know someone who does. Everyone who knows me knows someone who does. So many people on the planet deal with some type of mental illness. I've learned that over the years, and it makes me feel less lonely. It's part of my life. There's no way around it. My story is a music story and a family story and a love story, but it's a story of mental illness, too.

London is part of that story. I have often said that this city is my spiritual home. London audiences really appreciate my music. The *SMiLE* show is part of that story. It's a way of bringing something back that looked like it would stay in the past. To calm myself, I try to meditate my way into the music. Music is the solution. Music takes what's inside me and puts it into the world around me. It's my way of showing people things I can't show any other way. Music is in my soul—I wrote that once, and it's one of the best lyrics I ever wrote.

I remember what I was thinking about: the past. Resurrecting *SMiLE* is both past and present. When we didn't finish the album, a part of me was unfinished also, you know? Can you imagine leaving your masterpiece locked up in a drawer for almost forty years? That drawer was opened slowly. It came open a little bit at a Christmas party at Scott Bennett's house, where I played "Heroes and Villains" on the piano, and then a little more when David Leaf told me to play it at a tribute show at Radio City Music Hall. And then it was pulled open almost completely by Darian Sahanaja. Darian is a singer and songwriter, just like me, except that he's much younger, which meant that he loved the music we made but also had a new way of looking at it. He plays keyboards in my band and acts like a kind of musical secretary. At the Radio City show, which came a little after that Christmas party, my songs were performed by other people, like Paul Simon, Billy Joel, Vince Gill, and Elton John. Some were the big hits, but two were songs we had recorded for SMiLE, done the way we had originally imagined them. Vince Gill, Jimmy Webb, and David Crosby played "Surf's Up" and the audience gave them—and the song—a long standing ovation. I couldn't believe it. I was shocked. I was sitting on a stool at the side of the stage and David Crosby came off and said, "Brian, where did you come up with those fucking chords? They're incredible." I shook my head. "You know," I told him, "I said good-bye to that song a long time ago." Then I went out and played "Heroes and Villains" for the first time in more than forty years. I had promised at the party. The ovation was huge. The great George Martin introduced Heart, who played "Good Vibrations." I couldn't believe what he said about me, then and later on: "If there is one person I have to select as a living genius of pop music, I would select Brian Wilson. . . . Without *Pet Sounds*, *Sgt. Pepper* wouldn't have happened. . . . *Pepper* was an attempt to equal *Pet Sounds*." The producer of the Beatles said that about me—it was hard to even imagine. I was so honored.

After that, people started to ask if I would ever think about per-forming the whole album. I said yes. I was happy to say yes, but there are times, like now, when I'm not sure I was right to be happy.

I am sitting out here in the theater, meditating but not quite meditating. I'm aware of everyone going back and forth. At least a few of them want to stop and remind me about the way tonight's show will work. I feel like I've been over it a hundred times. I know it backward and forward. We'll start out with an acoustic set, then some material from my solo albums, then some early Beach Boys hits, then a few songs from *Pet Sounds*. Then there will be an intermission, and then the moment everyone has been waiting for—*SMiLE*, finally.

A guy stops near me and clears his throat. I look up. It's Jerry Weiss, who has been my road assistant for years. "Hey, Brian," he says. "They're opening the doors now. Let's go backstage."

"Thanks," I say. "Where's Melinda?" Melinda is my wife.

"She's in your dressing room. Let's go there." But I want to go to the band's dressing room instead. That's what you're supposed to do before a show, at least after you try to find the vibe of the room. You're supposed to be with the musicians and talk about the thing you're about to make. I ask Jerry where the band's dressing room is and he looks disappointed for a second but leads me to the band's room anyway.

Darian is the first one I see. "Hi," I say. "Do you mind if I sit here with you guys for a few minutes?"

"Of course not," Darian says. "How are you feeling? Are you ready?"

"I'm ready," I say. But because he asked, I tell him the truth also. "I'm a little scared and nervous. Do you think people will like it?"

"More than that. They are going to love it. You won't believe how much. And then . . . "

Darian has crossed the room now and I can't quite hear him. I am almost completely deaf in my right ear. It's been that way since I was a kid. A professional musician who can't hear on one side of his head? It's funny but not funny. Over the years I have learned how to make it work in the studio, but it's harder onstage, where you have to know what's going on all around you. It's hard to stay on key when you can't hear everything that is being played. The sound up there can be overwhelming and I have only one monitor, to my left. It has to be positioned perfectly, just right, or all I can hear is noise. And of course there are these voices in my head. Sometimes they come with me onto the stage. Sometimes in the middle of a song I lose concentration because they are getting louder. Every time, I get through it. But then the next time, I'm not sure I will.

We're ten minutes until show. Jerry tells me there are lots of people I know in the audience tonight. I ask where everyone is sitting. I want to be able to see them from the stage. That helps me with my nervousness, to know that the audience isn't one big wave but lots of faces I already know. Melinda is sitting in the center, right in front of me. I will be able to look straight ahead and see her and feel her support. Jean Sievers, my manager, is right next to her; she helped get me here, too. Van Dyke Parks, who worked on *SMiLE* with me, writing lyrics, is also down in front with his wife, Sally. Roger Daltrey got to the theater early and came backstage to say hello. Wix and Abe from Paul McCartney's band are down there. George Martin is down there. I'm thinking of all their faces and trying not to let the stage fright get to me. It surges and then goes back down. If I get used to the rhythm, I can make sense of it. Someone says something I can't quite understand on my right side, and I turn so that my good ear catches it. "Time to go," the voice is saying. "Time to go." The lights go down and I hear the sound of the audience coming up.

CHAPTER 1

Fear

There's a world where I can go and tell my secrets to
In my room, in my room
In this world I lock out all my worries and my fears
In my room, in my room

—"In My Room"

Mornings start at different times. In summer I wake up pretty early, sometimes as early as seven. It's later in the winter—when the days are shorter, I sleep longer. I might not get up until eleven. Maybe that happens to everyone. It used to be worse. I used to have real trouble getting up in the winter, and even when I did, I might stay in bed for hours. These days it's a little easier to start the day, no matter what the season.

When I wake up these days here in my house in Beverly Hills, I head down the back staircase to the den. That's where the TV is, and also my chair. It's a navy-blue print chair that's been there forever. It used to be red. It's been covered and recovered because I have a habit of picking at the upholstery. That chair is where I go when I come down from the bedroom. It's my command center. I can sit there and watch TV, even though the set is at a little bit of a weird angle. I love watching *Eyewitness News*. The content is not very good, but the newscasters are pleasant to watch. They have nice personalities. They also give you the weather. I like game shows, but I am getting tired of watching *Jeopardy!* It's the same bullshit every day. I like *Wheel of Fortune.* I like sports, too, mostly baseball, though I'll also watch basketball and football. I get more interested toward the playoffs.

But the TV isn't the only thing I can see from my chair. I can see into the kitchen and almost everywhere else. I can turn and look out the window and see into the backyard, which has a view of Benedict Canyon. The whole city's stretched out there if you go and look. And there's a touch-tone phone right next to the chair so I can call whoever I want. I don't use a cell phone. I have had a few over the years, but I don't like them. I love being in the chair. If I'm in Los Angeles, I'll end up there 100 percent of the days. If I come into the room and someone else is sitting in it, I just stand nearby until they clear out. When I go on the road, I take another chair with me, a black leather recliner, so that I can have the feel of home. I have them set it up on the wings of the stage and I sit there instead of in the dressing room.

Some people reach for coffee first thing in the morning. I don't. I'm not a coffee drinker. That doesn't mean that I'm alert on my own all the time, though. My nighttime medications make me drowsy, and it's hard to get started. There's a little hangover from the pills. When I get to the chair, I'll sit there for half an hour or so. Then I'll go out to the deli for breakfast. Breakfast has changed over the years. When I was less concerned about my weight, it might be two bowls of cereal, eggs, and a chicken patty. These days it's a veggie patty and fruit salad or a dish of blueberries. Most mornings Melinda will come into the room, and she only has to take one glance to tell what kind of mood I'm in. She's been with me long enough to know what the good moods look like, and what the other moods look like.

She doesn't say anything in the mornings usually. She lets me sit. If the mood lasts until afternoon or evening, she'll ask me about it. "What's bothering you?" she'll say. Usually it's that I really miss my brothers. Both of them are gone—Carl for almost twenty years, Dennis for more than thirty. I can get into a space where I think about it too much. I wonder why the two of them went away, and where they went, and I think about how hard it is to understand the biggest questions about life and death. It's worse around the holidays. I can really get lost in it. When it gets bad, Melinda sits near me and goes through the reality of the situation. She might remind me that Carl's been gone for a while, and that even when he was alive, we didn't spend so much time together. Toward the end of his life, we saw each other maybe once a year or so. "Of course you miss your brothers," she'll say. "But you don't want to miss them so much that it puts you on a bummer." And she's right. I don't.

Other times it's something else. Maybe it's the voices in my head. Maybe it's one of those days when they're telling me terrible and scary things. If it's one of those days, Melinda goes through the reality of that, too. "The voices have been saying they're going to kill you for years," she says, "and they haven't done it yet. They're not real, even if they seem real to you." She's right about that, too. On days when Melinda's not here to talk to me, I try to remind myself of what she might say. I always remember to take a walk. That clears my head. I can usually get myself calm with a good walk.

Today, in the chair, I'm in a pretty good place. Things don't seem so heavy and nothing's getting me down. There's a special event coming up. There's a screening of a movie. It's called *Love and Mercy*, and it's a movie about my life. Not my whole life; it doesn't go as far as this chair or this book. It's a movie about my life and my music and my struggles with mental illness, both in the '60s and later on. The movie covers thousands of days. Some of them were good days. Some were great. And good days grew out of bad, which is one of the main points of this movie and my life—much of it is about the love story between me and Melinda, and how she got the ball rolling to get me out of the hellhole that Dr. Landy had created for me. Melinda and I had been working on the movie for years, off and on, trying to get one made that told as much of the truth as possible. It took almost twenty years to finally get it done. Can you believe it?

The screening for the movie isn't today. It's soon. But today is a regular day. I'm going to get cleaned up, comb my hair, and go out for breakfast. There's a stoplight on the way to the deli that stays red forever, almost nine minutes. Later I might go see my son Dylan play basketball. He's eleven, and he's a great little player. I used to see more of his games; it's gotten harder since I had back surgery. Dylan also plays the drums a little bit. That helps him get tension off his chest. It might be a good idea for me to teach him piano.

∽

When I wake up in my house in 2015, I am happy to be here. When I woke up in my house more than two decades earlier, I wasn't sure how I felt. The doctor had just gone out the door. The doctor was Eugene Landy. The patient was me. "I am leaving because I lost my license," he said. "Bye, Brian."

I didn't say anything. I was glad to see him go. His back, moving away from me, was like a tide going out. Dr. Landy's leaving was my freedom. Through history there are stories about tyrants who control entire countries. Dr. Landy was a tyrant who controlled one person, and that person was me. He controlled where I went and what I did and who I saw and what I ate. He controlled it by spying on me. He controlled it by having other people spy on me. He controlled it by screaming at me. He controlled it by stuffing me full of drugs that confused me. If you help a person to get better by erasing that person, what kind of job have you done? I don't know for sure, but he really did a job on me.

∽

Sometimes memories come back to me when I least expect them. Maybe that's the only way it works when you've lived the life I've lived: starting a band with my brothers, my cousin, and my high school buddy that was managed by my father; watching my father become difficult and then impossible; watching myself become difficult and then impossible; watching women I loved come and go; watching children come into the world; watching my brothers get older; watching them pass out of the world. Some of those things shaped me. Others scarred me. Sometimes it was hard to tell the difference. When I watched my father fly into a rage and take a swing at me, was that shaping or scarring? When I heard voices in my head and realized that they weren't going to go away anytime soon, was that shaping or scarring?

When I sit in the chair in my house, I try to watch everything. I have always been that way. I try to listen to everything also. I have always listened to sounds in the studio and sounds in the world, to the voices in my band and the voices in my head. I couldn't stop myself from taking all those things in, but once they were in me, I couldn't always handle them. That was one of the reasons I made music. Music is a beautiful thing. Songs help me with my pain, and they also move through the world and help other people, which helps me, too. I don't know if that's the whole story, but it's part of it. The struggles I have faced—from the way my dad was, to the arguments in the band, to the mental health issues that have been around as long as I can remember—are all things I have tried to deal with in my own way. Have I stayed strong? I like to think so. But the only thing I know for sure is that I have stayed.

∾

I'm thinking of a picture. It's a picture of a picture, actually—me in the early '70s, lying in bed, looking at the cover photo of the Beach Boys' *Sunflower* album, which came out in 1970. The album's photo of the band—of me; my brothers, Dennis and Carl;

my cousin Mike Love; Al Jardine; and Bruce Johnston. It's the whole band, but not just the band. My daughter Wendy is there, too. Mike's kids Hayleigh and Christian are there. Carl's son Jonah is there. Al's son Matt is there.

The photo was taken at Hidden Valley Ranch, which was Dean Martin's place near Thousand Oaks. We were all out on the golf course, goofing around. Ricci Martin, Dean's son, was the photographer. He was a cool guy, and good friends with my brother Carl. Eventually Carl produced an album for him called *Beached*. It was a really nice record. Dennis drummed on it. There's a beautiful song on it that Carl wrote called "Everybody Knows My Name."

For the cover photo of *Sunflower*, we dressed mostly in red, white, and blue, and over the photograph there was a banner with the group's name and then the title of the album in a rainbow. I was all in white: white shirt, white pants, white shoes. I was looking down, partly because Wendy was in my lap, wearing pink. I was in pretty good shape at that time. My weight was good. I look calm. Maybe not happy, but sitting right in the middle of everything. *Sunflower* was the first record the Beach Boys made for Brother/Reprise Records, after recording for Capitol Records for a decade.

Photographs can be misleading, and the cover photo of *Sunflower* sure is. I was the center of the band in the photo, but by the time that record came out, I wasn't at the center of the band anymore. Some people will say that I pulled away from the center. Some people will say that I was pushed away. Maybe it was a little bit of both. I'm not sure. What I'm sure of is that all the guys in the band had different ideas about what kind of music to release, how to go onstage and perform our songs, when we should repeat ourselves and when we should try new things. Because *Sunflower* was our first Reprise record, I wanted to go all the way with being new. I even had the idea that we should change the group's name to the Beach, because we weren't boys anymore. I told the rest of the guys that and they didn't like the idea. They thought it would confuse the people who bought our records. We had careers to protect, which meant we had sales to protect.

Not only wasn't I completely in control of the group, but I wasn't completely in control of myself. How do you know when a problem starts? Did it start in 1964 on an airplane to Houston, when I freaked out and decided that I couldn't tour with the band anymore? Did it start in the '40s when my father whacked me because he didn't like how I was acting? Did it start in the '70s with drugs or long before that with the beginnings of mental illness that no one knew how to handle? What did it matter when it started? What mattered was that for a while it wouldn't end. I was scared at the time *Sunflower* came out. I felt like the band was slipping away from me. I felt like I was slipping away from myself. The time in my life when I had complete control and confidence in the studio was behind me, and I didn't know what was ahead. I didn't know how to get that control and confidence back. I once called it "ego death." I didn't know if anything would ever come back to life.

I couldn't have known that almost fifty years later I'd be in a mostly stable and happy place, still dealing with those things but having learned so much about how to do it. I also couldn't have known that before things would get better, they would get worse. A few years after *Sunflower* it was much worse. I was worse. My body was filled with drugs and alcohol, and my brain was filled with bad ideas. The bad ideas came from the rest of it and caused it, too. Back then, like I said, mental illness wasn't treated in a straightforward way. People wouldn't even admit that it existed. There was shame in saying what it was and strange ideas about how to deal with it. Back then, I wasn't going anywhere most days, and when I was in the house I didn't even move around much. I felt stuck because I was depressed, and that caused me to gain weight, and then I felt stuck because I had gained weight. I got up to over 300 pounds. I wasn't going onstage with the group. I could write songs, but I did it less and less. I needed help desperately, and people close to me were desperate to get it for me.

And so the doctor came. My wife at the time, Marilyn, called for him. It was right around the United States Bicentennial and everything was red, white, and blue like the *Sunflower* album cover. It felt like Independence Day all year. But Dr. Landy didn't believe in independence. He wanted me to get the weight off and develop healthier habits, and the way he decided to do that was to put himself in the middle of everything in my life. He called it twenty-four-hour therapy. There weren't any more hours in the day. When friends came to see me, Dr. Landy interviewed them to make sure they passed his inspection. When I was allowed to see friends, it was never on my own. Dr. Landy always sent someone to monitor me, sometimes more than one guy. He wanted to make sure that the people weren't bringing me drugs or anything else unhealthy.

It would be a lie to say that he didn't get results. He took the 300 pounds and brought them down to about 185, which is the weight I should have been. I was a football quarterback in high school and that was what I weighed back then. I hadn't appeared with the band onstage in about a decade, except for a few shows—I did a pair in Hawaii in 1967, one at the Whisky in LA in 1970, and a few shows in Seattle a little after that. But mostly I just couldn't get on the stage. In 1976, after a few months with Landy, I managed to come on for a few songs in Oakland and then did a whole night in Anaheim for a show being taped for TV. I only sang lead on one song, "Back Home," which was coming out on an album we were just about to release, *15 Big Ones*. That was the message: back home.

Dr. Landy's stay with me was pretty brief in 1976. He got some results, but then he went too far. He was getting too involved, and then I found out what he was charging. I confronted him about it. I was pretty angry. No one was happy to be talking. I threw a punch and he threw one back and that was the end of it—that time, at least.

Things were better when he left. We put out some pretty good records, not only *15 Big Ones* but also *Love You* in 1977. But then there were bad years again. The worst of them, 1978, was one of the worst years of my life. I went into a mental hospital in San Diego and then called Marilyn and asked for a divorce. I couldn't control my thoughts and I couldn't control my body. It wasn't the first time I had felt like that, but in some ways it was the worst because of what I did to deal with it. I drank Bali Hai wine and did cocaine and smoked cigarettes and my weight went higher than ever; at one point I tipped the scales at 311 pounds.

There were so many costs. One of them was the music. Record labels kept asking us for new albums. Maybe "asking" is a polite word. They expected them, and didn't expect anything but yes for an answer. So we ended up making records, but they were records that showed how the band was being pulled in many different directions at once, albums like *M.I.U. Album* in 1978, *L.A. (Light Album)* in 1979, and *Keepin' the Summer Alive* in 1980. Most fans of the band don't like those records. Some fans don't even know about them. There are only a few songs on those records that I like when I think about them, like "Good Timin'" and "Goin' On," but mostly they aren't worth thinking about too hard. I didn't do much on those albums. I wasn't in any shape to do much. The same was true onstage. In March of 1979, a day or so after I got out of the mental hospital, I flew into New York for a concert at Radio City Music Hall. I was about as unprepared as possible in every way. I lasted for one song, "California Girls," and then split to the side of the stage. On one tour I was playing bass, and I spent almost the entire concert back there perched on an amp. The amount of singing shrank and shrank until it was just the middle eight of "Surfer Girl" ("We could ride the surf together"), the first verse of "Sloop John B," and not much more than that.

There's one show I remember from 1982. It was at the Westbury Music Theatre in New York, and there was a stage that circled around like a lazy Susan. We were playing "Do It Again" and all of a sudden I started laughing. I couldn't stop. I had cigarettes on top of the piano and I managed to grab them. We took intermission, and then I came back and perched on the corner of the stage as it rotated and I smoked. I was laughing, but nothing was funny. I was coughing, and I couldn't come up for air. A few weeks later I was given a letter that told me I was out of money and fired from the band. The first part wasn't true. The second part was, in a way. Everyone's patience for the Bali Hai and the drugs and the cigarettes and the giggling had come to an end.

⁓

This time it was the Beach Boys who called Dr. Landy. It was a group decision, except for Dennis. I don't think they knew what else to do. At first Landy took me right to Hawaii. When we were there, he started me on an exercise regime, no more drugs, no nothing. I had to kick it all. It took me about a week, but I did it. That week cleaned me up, but it was hard. I was rolling around in bed. I was screaming, clutching at the sheets. I never felt so fucked up.

When Dr. Landy came back, he had the same idea as the first time around, which was that the people near me were part of the problem. That meant that everyone had to go. Caroline, my girlfriend at the time, was one of the people who had to go, even though she was doing nothing wrong. It was sad. But soon I was pumped so full of what Dr. Landy was giving me that my memories of her just faded away.

The first time through, Dr. Landy had succeeded a little bit. His method was never perfect, but it gave me relief. The second time through, there was no relief. Relief would have been a kind of freedom, and he didn't believe in freedom. He gave me more and more pills and called them vitamins. He sent girls to keep me company. He played games with me where he put his hand on my leg to see if I had feelings for anyone. He had barbecues at my house, but instead of inviting my friends or family, he invited his family and other doctors. He made big plans, like going back to Hawaii and then to London, but then the plans disappeared without explanation. He let me have a margarita every once in a while. He screamed so loud it made me cry.

⁓

Sometimes I worked up the courage to confront Dr. Landy just a little bit. "Gene," I would say, "why are you here?" He wouldn't answer me. Instead he would ask a question back: "Did you eat at the wrong time?" or "Why aren't you clean?" I didn't know why I wasn't. There was food on my clothes. I wasn't cutting my nails regularly, and no one else was either. I couldn't focus because of the medication, but I also didn't want to focus because I was ashamed and afraid. So many days during that time were just a waiting game from sunrise to sunset, to the moment they would end. I must have run into old friends or talked to people in my family who thought they weren't getting any real part of me, and they were right.

Gene didn't want any other people around me. He wanted me to depend on him for everything. His methods could be violent. Sometimes that reminded me of my dad, which seemed wrong. It was wrong for him to feel like a father when he was worse in every way. He was angrier. He was more unfair. I had no idea if there was any love to go along with the anger. With dads, you struggle to get independent. You push against them and sometimes they push back. With Gene, it seemed like he never wanted me to push. He hired a woman named Gloria Ramos to make me food. Gene told me about Gloria before she came. He told me that she was working for him. He told me that she was going to cook for me and buy some groceries. There had been another woman before her named Deirdre, but she didn't stay long.

I wasn't sure about Gloria at first because she was working for Gene. That made me afraid. But I watched her and decided that she wasn't like his other people.

Gloria didn't speak much English, but I spoke a little Spanish so I could talk to her. There was a song called "¿Cuando Calienta el Sol?," which means "How hot is the sun?" I would sing that and also play some piano for her. For a while, she was my only friend. I loved eating frozen yogurt but Gene wouldn't let me, so Gloria would order it for herself and share it with me. Other times she watched TV with me, and still other times I didn't feel like watching TV so I asked her to close the drapes and blinds and just leave me there in the dark. She wouldn't do it. She said she had to leave the door open. I wanted it closed for lots of reasons. I told her one: mosquitos could get in, and they could make you sick. She told me that they had medicine for that kind of thing, but I didn't know if medicine would work.

Sometimes I would explain the whole picture to her, as a way of explaining it to myself. I would tell her that I was famous because of the Beach Boys, and that I had made things that people loved, and that I was worried I wouldn't be able to do that anymore. She would say that no one cared about that. Not in a bad way. She wasn't saying that people didn't like my music. She was saying that no one cared about that when they weren't around me, and that being a healthy person was just as important. That made me cry. She asked me what I wanted her to do and I just didn't know. I wanted her to stay because I felt safe.

⁓

Finally Gene left. There were lots of reasons why he left. But the final straw was when I started seeing Melinda and she got enough looks into my life to see what Gene was doing, and that even if he had helped me once, he wasn't helping me anymore. Thanks to Melinda calling my mom and brother and helping them get the goods on Landy, Carl and his lawyers started working on freeing me from the situation and I started feeling more courage. Still, even after people figured out that Gene was doing nothing good for me, he was around for a while. He got into my music. I remember one real fight with him. He had started out charging me something like $25,000 a month for treatment. I don't remember the exact number. But there were so many other expenses. He was living in my Pacific Palisades house and remodeling it with my money. He was taking his family to Hawaii for a month and sending me the bill. And the monthly expense kept increasing. In the late '80s I looked once and it was $30,000. In the early '90s I looked again and it was $35,000. I couldn't stay silent. "What is this bill here?" I said to him. He looked at me like he didn't understand the question, but he understood it fine. "I thought I'd charge a bit more," he finally said. I lost my temper with him. That helped me see that his days were numbered.

When Gene finally left that second time, I tried to get back on my feet. In some ways, I was happy. It felt like a tremendous weight was gone from my shoulders. My steps were easier. Still, there were days when I was too depressed to do anything. I couldn't go to a restaurant or to the movies. I could deal with it by getting angry, but I wasn't sure what was making me angry. I could throw a can in the air or kick something, but that didn't solve the problem really. I slowly got back to being me. It took me a while. After all, it was nine years of bullshit.

◡◠

Or was it thirty years of bullshit? I said that I don't know how far back to draw the line that led to Landy, but I do know one point the line passed through. That was in 1964, at Christmastime. I was with the band on an airplane going to Houston to play a show at the Music Hall there. Just a few days before, we had returned to Los Angeles from Tulsa, where we played their new arena. In the airport I started to feel like I was slipping away a bit. At first I thought it was about my marriage. Just a few weeks before, I had married Marilyn. I was a young husband, only twenty-two, and she was an even younger wife, just sixteen. I was happy we were married, but I was worried, too. My thoughts about love and romance were all confused. How do you ever know if you're the right person for someone or if someone is the right person for you? A few months before, we were all hanging out and I noticed her talking to my cousin Mike Love in a way that I thought was a little too friendly. That night I couldn't stop thinking about it.

"Do you like him?" I asked.

"Sure," she said. "He's a great guy."

"No. I mean do you *like* him?"

"That's ridiculous," she said.

"Is it? Be honest with me."

She tried to calm me down and eventually did, but the thought was still there at the airport.

But that was only a small piece of a bigger puzzle that was falling apart faster than I could put it together. The band was huge. We were more than famous. When we hit number one in Sweden with "Surfin' Safari" back in 1962, we laughed about it. Number one in Sweden. But "Surfin' Safari" also went Top Twenty in the US, and then it seemed like there were Top Ten hits all the time: "Surfin' USA," "Surfer Girl," "Be True to Your School," "Fun, Fun, Fun." It was hard to get any higher than that because of the Beatles. They were on *Ed Sullivan* in February of 1964, and in April they had all five of the top spots in *Billboard*. That week we were at thirteen with "Fun, Fun, Fun." In May we released "I Get Around," and that went into the Top Twenty when songs by the Dixie Cups ("Chapel of Love"), Mary Wells ("My Guy"), and the Beatles ("Can't Buy Me Love"), still, were at the top.

Then in July something changed on the chart. The top song wasn't by the Dixie Cups or Mary Wells or the Beatles. It was by us. "I Get Around" was number one, right above "My Boy Lollipop." I couldn't believe it. It wasn't just Sweden anymore. "I Get Around" was also our first gold record. And it wasn't just how many people were buying our records. It was how people were talking about our records. They made us out to be the next great pop act after the Beatles, though we had been putting records on the charts for years. And some people were saying we were even better, that our songs were more interesting or sophisticated or created more positive energy.

When we played "I Get Around" and "Wendy" on *Ed Sullivan* in September, that cinched it. We were in striped shirts and white pants, an outfit that would become kind of like our uniform. It was the Beach Boys' equivalent of the Beatles' mop tops. That's how we were remembered. The stage was a trip. Someone had the idea of putting roadsters next to us. We played around them. I couldn't really absorb any of it then because I was performing, but I have seen it since. I've always loved the way the girls screamed when they showed a close-up of Dennis at the drums. And Mike had a funny little dance that he broke out when Carl was doing his guitar solo on "I Get Around." We did four more songs at the T.A.M.I. Show a month later, which was really an amazing concert: not just us but the Miracles (with Smokey Robinson, one of the greatest singers and songwriters ever), the Supremes (with Diana Ross), Marvin Gaye, Lesley Gore, Jan and Dean, James Brown, the Rolling Stones, and even Chuck Berry. Can you believe a lineup like that? And we were right in the middle of it.

It made me happy, but it made me dizzy also. When I started, I just wanted to make music with my brothers and my friends and leave the business to my dad, who was managing us. We were a family band in every way. But that year we got big, things changed. It was scary for me. We got going really fast. I was kind of a dumb little guy. I didn't really acknowledge we were famous. Every now and then I would, but I was so busy cutting records, writing songs, and going on tour that I didn't have a chance to sit down and think about it. So instead there was just this exciting feeling that was sort of sickening. We were climbing, but what was up there when you went even higher? And what if you fell? That made me nervous and afraid, and I closed my eyes and tried to feel brave.

That December, at the gate in the airport before we flew off to Houston, nothing was working and my bravery was gone. "I don't want to go on that plane," I told the band.

"I don't know how else we're going to get to Houston," Mike said.

"I can't be on it. I won't be on it." I called my mother and told her to come pick me up. She laughed a little and told me not to worry. But that worked about as well as closing my eyes.

We boarded. The plane went faster and faster down the runway, lifted off, and started climbing. What was up there when we went higher? I heard the other guys talking. Dennis said something about a girl he was supposed to call back. Carl said something about the harmonies on "I Get Around." Then my thoughts swarmed and I blacked out. To me I blacked out. To everyone else it looked like I was screaming and holding my head and falling down in the aisle.

When we got to Houston we went straight to the hotel. In my room I quieted down, which didn't mean that I calmed down. Mike and Carl visited me. I stared straight at the window like it was a wall. I had so much going on inside my head, but I couldn't make sense of any of it.

The next day I flew right back home to California while the rest of the guys went and finished the dates. Glen Campbell replaced me the next night in Dallas, and then they went on to Omaha, Des Moines, Indianapolis, and Louisville. When they came back to LA, I called a band meeting. "I'm not going to play with the band anymore," I announced.

"You're quitting?' Carl said.

"No. I just mean that I'm not going to play onstage. I want to stay home and write songs."

The guys didn't believe it at first, but I said it enough times for them to eventually believe me. Glen pinch-hit for me a little while longer, but soon he wanted to do his own solo trip, so the band hired a guy named Bruce Johnston. Bruce was a staff producer at Columbia Records who had played in a group called the Rip Chords. He had a similar falsetto to mine.

I stayed at home and wrote. At first it was great. I had some songs I was working on that I thought would really stretch what music could do. Those songs turned into *The Beach Boys Today!* and *Summer Days (And Summer Nights!!)*, and then they turned into *Pet Sounds*, and then *Pet Sounds* turned into *SMiLE*, and then *SMiLE* turned into nothing. Along the way the pressure started to pile up again and the blackouts happened again. The voices in my head happened, too, more and more often. I was trying to make this amazing music, and the band was rehearsing all the time, and I couldn't handle the pressure. I couldn't always figure out how to balance the time by myself thinking of songs and the time with other people playing them. I knew that I couldn't do it on the stage, but then there were times when I thought I couldn't even do it in the studio.

I didn't know who to talk to. I didn't really tell the other guys in the band. I might have said a word or two, but I could tell from the way they were listening that they didn't really understand. Once I told my dad and he narrowed his eyes and said, "Don't be a pussy. Don't be a baby. Get in there and write some good songs."

And that's what I did. I wrote some good songs. But through the whole thing, I was sinking. Later on, much later, I would have a support network to help me figure out what to do when I was sinking. I didn't have that then. I had problems instead. People would look at what I was doing and look past it. It was "Brian— he's an eccentric guy" or "That's just Brian being Brian." But no one ever really tried to look into what was happening with me and my mind and get me out of there.

∼∘

When Dr. Landy left, he left me to my freedom. I can't say that I knew what to do with it right away. I had been on a routine for a while, and being off the routine was relaxing in lots of ways. I was kind of in a holding pattern, but not a bad one. I hung out with Melinda mostly. We would go to lunch and drive around. We would go to Hollywood Boulevard and the movies almost every night. Melinda used to laugh because I would spend hundreds of dollars on souvenirs like I was a tourist or a junk-aholic. We listened to the radio sometimes. K-Earth 101. It's an oldies station in

Los Angeles with a huge broadcasting range. People can hear it as far south as San Diego and as far north as Bakersfield. When we were just starting out, they called it Boss Radio. It began broadcasting in 1941, just before I was born. It broadcasts from Mount Wilson in the San Gabriel Mountains. I'm not named after the mountain and it's not named after me, but it's a happy coincidence. At night Melinda and I would listen to artists like Johnny Mathis, Nat King Cole, Randy Newman, and Kenny G.

Music circled me as an idea. One of the first people I called when Landy left was Andy Paley. Andy had a great history in pop music. He worked with lots of people and worked with me on the first solo record. If Landy was the bad part, Andy was the good part. When I started to get that feeling again about making music, I called him. "Let's write some new tracks," he said.

We wrote a song called "Soul Searchin'." We wrote a song called "Desert Drive." We wrote a song called "You're Still a Mystery." We wrote them with the Beach Boys in mind because Don Was, the producer and bassist, wanted to do a Beach Boys record. That didn't pan out because Carl didn't like the songs—I don't know why. Then Sean O'Hagan, from the band the High Llamas, was going to do it. That didn't happen either. The whole project just weirded out. Anyway, when we were writing, we didn't use a big professional studio, and usually we didn't even use the four-track in my house. We just sang and played and recorded on a boom box. When songs got better and they were ready to be picked off the tree, then we booked studio time for me. I would call friends like Danny Hutton, who sang with Three Dog Night, and he would come in and help flesh things out. It felt the way it sometimes did in the old days, and that was freedom. But it was hard to imagine doing any of it alone. I needed Andy there with me, or at least someone I trusted who would keep me encouraged. I was scared as hell to go and make new music. It was always a combination of scared and excited for me. I didn't see it as an album yet. I was never really sure where it would all end up.

Sometimes I would play the new music for Dr. Marmer. Steve Marmer—he was the doctor I went to after Landy left, and he was one of the people who helped me get my balance back. They say there are three things that matter when you are dealing with mental illness: finding the right support network, finding the right medication, and finding the right doctor. Dr. Marmer was definitely the right doctor. Dr. Landy had bullied me about music. He had bullied me about everything. Dr. Marmer talked to me about it. If I said I was thinking about music, he told me that he thought it was a good idea. If I played him a new song or part of one, he was supportive. And even though sometimes we talked about my thoughts and feelings, sometimes we just talked about music. And not my music, even—classical music or singers that we both liked. Lots of the things I was thinking and feeling then, or trying not to think and feel, came out only when I talked about music. Later on, Dr. Marmer came to see a show of mine and he was so happy. He couldn't believe that the onstage me was the same me in his office. He couldn't believe that I could be in command that way. The truth is that I will never really be comfortable up there, but I know how to tough it out and get through it. And whether I'm comfortable or not, it's a place where I can be what I am.

⌒

In late 1993 I got a call from Van Dyke Parks. I hadn't really worked with him since the late '60s, on *SMiLE*, but we worked on "Sail On Sailor" together in the early '70s. Van Dyke called me up and asked me to sing lead on a track of his. He had a song that he thought would be a perfect fit for me. It was called "Orange Crate Art." He wrote it because oranges were such a part of the California experience, and also because people say that nothing rhymes with *orange*. I said I wasn't sure if I was up for singing on the song, so he came to visit to convince me. I wasn't busy with anything else, and it was obvious. I was just sitting in my bedroom watching the TV set. I don't mean I was watching a show or anything. It was just the set. I liked thinking about all the things that used to be on it, all the shows I had ever seen.

Van Dyke came in and convinced me to come record with him. When I got to the studio, the equipment was kind of like the TV. I liked thinking about all the things that used to be on it. But I wasn't sure what I was going to do with it. "Why am I here again?" I asked him. He laughed. "Because I hate the sound of my own voice."

I sang on that song, and I ended up singing on a bunch more. That wasn't what I thought was going to happen, and sometimes it made me so nervous I felt sick, but we ended up with an album. The album had the same name as the song, *Orange Crate Art*. The whole thing was ready for me, thanks to Van Dyke. He wrote out all the lead vocal parts on charts and I came in and sang them. Then I arranged and sang my harmonies, stacking my vocals to add the Brian Wilson vibe to the record. The songs were about his ideas of California, the history of the state, and the myths that change the way people see history. At the very end, he even added a Gershwin piece, "Lullaby." That was completely his idea, but it was an idea I liked.

∼

Around the same time there was another project. This one looked backward, over my shoulder. I was still a little scared to look forward. Don Was had talked about making a record with me—instead, he decided to make a documentary about my life after the Beach Boys. He had the idea to name it after one of the songs from *Pet Sounds*, "I Just Wasn't Made for These Times." We came up with an idea for the soundtrack, which was to take some of our old songs and make them young again. I don't listen to Beach Boys music that often. Sometimes it brings back some bad memories, you know? But there are times when I'll go back and hear records and try to think about them—not what I was thinking when I made them but what they are as music.

For the soundtrack, Don Was cut the instrumental tracks himself with great musicians like guitarist Waddy Wachtel and drummer Jim Keltner. Don is a great bass player himself. Then I came in and sang on them. We did "Caroline, No" again, one of the most beautiful songs from *Pet Sounds*. We did "The Warmth of the Sun." We did songs from my solo album like "Love and Mercy" and "Melt Away," and when we did those songs, we took Landy's name off the credits, which by then was my legal right. I even cut a version of "Do It Again" with my daughters Carnie and Wendy. We all sang my original high part together. It's a great version of that tune, worth checking out. Wendy came with me to *The David Letterman Show* to play it, which was nerve-racking but fun. I sat at the piano and she was in boots next to me. Billy West, who does voices on TV, played guitar with me for that performance. He got the solo.

The soundtrack ended with "'Til I Die," a remake of a song originally on *Surf's Up*. It was one of my saddest songs, and also one of the best Beach Boys songs where I wrote all the music and all the lyrics. I remember when I wrote it. I was walking out by the water and thinking about how big everything was and how small I was, how insignificant I was—and not just me but how insignificant everyone was. Did people even matter? Life flashed by so quickly you couldn't even grab hold of it, but people spent all of it trying to find meaning and purpose. I went to the piano and tried to capture the melody in my head, and then I wrote lyrics trying to explain all the things I was thinking and feeling.

> *I'm a cork on the ocean*
> *Floating over the raging sea*
> *How deep is the ocean?*
> *How deep is the ocean?*
> *I lost my way*
> *Hey hey hey*

I'm a rock in a landslide
Rolling over the mountainside
How deep is the valley?
How deep is the valley?
It kills my soul
Hey hey hey

I'm a leaf on a windy day
Pretty soon I'll be blown away
How long will the wind blow?
How long will the wind blow?
Ohhhh

The lyrics go way down and then the "hey hey hey" picks them back up and then the lyrics go down again. Those are the waves, the raging sea. There's a lyric that Van Dyke wrote on *Orange Crate Art*, in a song called "Palm Tree and Moon," that has the same idea: "When a comet comes out to fall / Why on earth do we feel so small?"

I was happy with the records I was starting to make again. They weren't about people moving in all directions at once, like some of the Beach Boys records from the '70s and '80s. They were records by people who were all trying to do the same thing. But when I went out to talk about the documentary, I wasn't comfortable. I didn't like questions about why I had been away. I didn't think I had been away. I had been right where I was all the time. Maybe my band moved away from me. Maybe audiences moved away. But I hadn't gone much of anywhere, which was part of the problem. I was sure I needed to get started again, but I was also afraid to get started again. One of the hardest things was overcoming the fear that I would never make music the same way again—not that I wouldn't know how, but that people wouldn't let me. Around the same time I wrote some new songs with Tony Asher, who wrote many of the lyrics on what was probably the most famous Beach

Boys record, *Pet Sounds.* In the '90s, after not working with him for years, I got back together with Tony and we made some new songs. We weren't sure when they would come out. I wasn't sure if I was going to make a normal record. I wasn't sure if I could.

As it turned out, I couldn't quite do it yet. We made a song called "This Isn't Love" that came out without Tony's lyrics on an instrumental album, and then with lyrics in a Flintstones movie, with Alan Cumming singing it. Later on I released it myself on a live record. Another song we wrote, "Everything I Need," was really nice to make. I remember cutting the track for it and how comfortable it felt. Hal Blaine was there, drumming. Carol Kaye was there, playing bass. Tony Asher was there. I scored a cool vibe those few days in the studio, a real sense of the old days. When it came time a few years later for the song to go on an album—one by my daughters Carnie and Wendy, who were recording as the Wilsons—things changed. I was going to record and produce the album with them, using some of the new songs I had written with Tony. But the girls were young. They wanted a vibe and a feel that I couldn't deliver. I got the idea I should just wish them good luck and bow out. And when I bowed out, things changed. Things changed with the songs I had written. There was a day when they were overdubbing strings. When I got there, the string players were already cutting. They weren't using my arrangement. I had a twinge, remembering how it felt to have my music taken away from me. "I don't want it to happen again," I said. I wasn't sure who was listening. I put my foot down, but I was unsteady on it.

CHAPTER 2

Family

When I grow up to be a man
Will I dig the same things that turn me on as a kid?
Will I look back and say that I wish I hadn't done what I did?
Will I joke around and still dig those sounds
When I grow up to be a man?

  —**"When I Grow Up (To Be a Man)"**

Much of what I see from my chair on the first floor of my house is kids. Melinda and I have five of them. Daria, the oldest, will turn twenty in 2016. Our second daughter, Delanie, is two years younger. When we first adopted them back in the '90s, it was a new family for me, but also a reminder of an old family. I had two little girls once before, Carnie and Wendy, back in the '70s, two little angels who came into my life. They grew up into wonderful women, but once they were little girls. I remember looking at them and loving them so much. I also remember looking at them and wondering what family meant.

After Daria and Delanie, Melinda and I adopted three more kids—Dylan, Dash, and Dakota. Late in my life, I got a big family. I see and hear it from my chair. Kids slam doors. Kids fight with each other or leave clothes heaped on furniture. Kids don't do their homework on time. Kids go to games and the other kids go sit and watch and cheer them on. I sit there, mostly quiet, but I see all of it. My chair is the command center. Sometimes at night I'll ask Melinda questions about something I've seen. "Why didn't you make Dash pick up his jacket?" I'll say. "Why didn't *you* make him pick up his jacket?" she'll say, laughing.

When there's a big deal, Melinda will tell me that she needs my help. I know what she means. She means that it's time for me to talk to the kids. When those times come, I'll call them down and give them a little lecture. I'm stern. I never get mad or mean. But the kids know to listen. They know that if I'm talking to them about something, it's important. I remember once a few years ago, when Daria came home from boarding school for Christmas break she left her suitcases out in front of the house. Not in the front hallway but outside on the lawn. It was driving Melinda crazy. She said something about it to Daria the second day and the third day, too, but the suitcases were still out there. "Brian," she finally said. "You have to do something about this." I did everything about it. I called Daria down to the first floor. Sometimes when I call her it's to ask her a question or have her score me some carbohydrates from the refrigerator, but this time I said her name loud enough that there was no confusion. I told her to bring the suitcases inside. I said it real clear. The suitcases came in.

After I did *Orange Crate Art* with Van Dyke and *I Just Wasn't Made for These Times* with Don Was, I started to get the idea of making my own record, for real. I was still working on some stuff with Andy Paley. We still had songs like "Desert Drive" and "Gettin' in Over My Head," and we had more songs, too, like "Chain Reaction of Love" and "Soul Searchin'." There were record companies sending out good signals about signing me. The Beach Boys had just made a country record in Nashville with stars like Toby Keith and Lorrie Morgan and Willie Nelson. We took our old songs and performed them as duets with the country singers. Lorrie Morgan did "Don't Worry Baby." Toby Keith did "Be True to Your School." It was a weird deal because there were so many moving parts to that record, and only some of them were me. The record was listed as being produced by me, but I can't remember being as hands-on as I would've liked. I mostly coproduced. The one track I worked hard on was "The Warmth of the Sun," with Willie Nelson. What a great voice he has, and what a thrill it was to work with him. I think I produced the hell out of that track. The record came out; unfortunately it didn't do very well.

The coproducer on that album was Joe Thomas. Joe was a big guy with a good tan and his hair brushed back. He had been a professional wrestler at some point when he was young. With his muscles and his hair, Joe looked like he should have been from LA or maybe Miami, but he wasn't. He was from the Chicago area. Eventually we started spending time there, too. How that happened was almost funny. Even though the country record did not score so well on the charts, I started to work with Joe. He was around, and he seemed interested in helping me make new music. Joe and I were hanging out and we decided to build our own studio. We had been recording in a place called River North in Chicago that was really popular. I think it was the biggest studio in the city. I went there to work with him on some new tracks. We mostly weren't using the songs I made with Andy Paley. We were writing new songs, and that was fun. Melinda became friends with Joe's wife, Chris, and one day Chris asked Melinda to go with her to look at a new house they were thinking of buying. It was in a city called St. Charles, which is about an hour away from Chicago. Right next door to the house Chris picked, there was another house for sale. "Let's take it," Melinda said to me.

At first I wasn't sure what she meant. She told me that it was the right size for us and the kids, and it had a basement that looked like a perfect place for a recording studio. We'd keep the Los Angeles house, obviously, but when we went to Chicago we could be near Joe and Chris, both for fun and to have an easy way to work.

We bought the house and started to put in the studio. It wasn't easy. We dug the basement down an extra six or seven feet and put in three recording rooms and a mixing room. I made sure the walls were covered with fabric for sound control. If you talk to enough musicians, you always hear stories about creating perfect environments. Musicians have ideas about what will give them the best sounds on record. Guys at Columbia Records' studio on Seventh Avenue in New York used to hang microphones from the top of the stairwell, ten floors up, and use the whole stairwell for reverb. I wasn't trying for ten floors, but I wanted to have a space in St. Charles that worked for music. That was one of my requirements if we were going to get that house.

⁓

There are houses and there are homes. Burt Bacharach wrote a song about the difference between the two. A house is a building. A home is a feeling. With the dug-out basement and the fabric on the walls, St. Charles was a nice house, but it was never really a home. It was a house away from home. I grew up in a home in Hawthorne, California. It's not there anymore. When the Century Freeway came through in the '80s, the place got torn down. Eventually politicians put up a monument there about the birth of the Beach Boys. A monument is nice, I guess. But it's even less than a house, which is less than a home.

The home was at 3701 West 119th Street. I grew up there with my brothers, Dennis and Carl. It seems weird to say that. It seems obvious. But there was nothing obvious about it at the time. The same way that Carnie and Wendy came into a family in the '70s and Daria and Delanie came into a family in the '90s, I came into a family in the '40s. My parents had me first, in the summer of 1942. Dennis came along two and a half years later, at the end of 1944, and then Carl two years after that, at the end of 1946. Every new boy that came along had to go into the same bedroom with me. There just wasn't any more room than that.

One house, three kids, two parents: my father, Murry, and my mother, Audree. My mother was gentle, kind, and loving. She was nice to me whenever I needed it. If I was hiding under the sheets on a school day, she would call my name and tell me it was time to wake up. A few minutes later she would call me again. She always spoke kindly. Later on I wrote about the way she used to wake me up in a song called "Oxygen to the Brain." The opening line of that song, "Open up, open up, open your eyes . . . / It's time to rise," that was my mom in the mornings. One of the first things I remember is her putting me in my crib. I don't have a picture of it in my head, not really. If it were a picture, I would be remembering from outside myself. I remember it from inside myself, just the feeling of it, hands lowering you down but a face staying above you to protect you. For a while I was the only kid and she favored me. When Dennis and Carl came along, she spread out her love. No one can ever say that she didn't try to love all her kids the same. But I think Carl probably ended up the favorite. He was the baby, and in some ways he was the easiest to love.

Mostly my mom worked. She didn't go to a job, but being at home was the hardest job in the world. She cleaned up after us and did lots of laundry. Dennis got dirty all the time, rolling around on the ground. He was a wrestler in school—and in the rest of his life, too. If you walked by Dennis on a normal day, just tried to go past him to get to the other side of a room, there was a good chance that you'd end up involved in a wrestling match. My mom was also in charge of food. She didn't have to go far to buy the groceries. There was a market only a few minutes down the street. She cooked all the time, and cooked well: porterhouse, roast beef, roast chicken. Back then there was no such thing as a vegetarian, not really. Meat was how you knew you were eating a good, full meal. People still remembered the war and the idea that all the good living could be taken away from them, so meat was America. The roast beef she made was my favorite thing, and it came with my other favorite thing, mashed potatoes. Food made the house smell great. Between meals there were snacks and treats. One of the things I remember is this sweet vanilla condensed milk, Eagle Brand. My mom would boil it until it turned brown and tasted like caramel. That was a great dessert.

My mom also drove us where we needed to go, because my dad was at work. Every morning she would make us brush our teeth and comb our hair. "Now get dressed," she would say gently—the big thing back then was pink-and-black socks and trucker boots. Then she would drive us to school. In the afternoons and on week-ends, she took us to the beach and to relatives' houses. She turned us on to games around the house, like Monopoly. We used to love playing Monopoly, all the boys.

Mom didn't discipline us much, except to warn us that our dad might. If we were doing something bad, she would stand back a little bit and put up a finger. "You'd better watch out," she'd say, "or your dad is going to get you." She was right about that. My dad was different from my mom. If he wanted us to wake up, he would stand in the door of the bedroom and say, "Hey! Get up!" Even when he was speaking softly, his voice wasn't soft.

My dad worked in a company that sold lathes, but he loved music. It was something that was as important to him as his job, and then more important. He was the one who steered me and my brothers toward singing and playing, and who made it easy for it to be more than a hobby. He converted the garage into a music room—he didn't dig seven feet beneath it and put fabric on the walls for sound quality, but he made a music room for Hawthorne the way I made a music room for the place in St. Charles. He sang with my mom when we were little and then tried to get the whole family to sing together. He even wrote songs himself, and not as a total amateur. He had some songs that did something in the world.

But there were other parts of his personality that were as bad as his love for music was good. There were days with my dad that I wish never happened, and not just a few of them. They added up to months or even years, and they had a big effect on almost everything that came later—every friendship, every decision I made about people, probably even every decision people made about me. I said before that there are parts of my life that are hard to talk about. Lots of the things that happened with my dad are in that category. It's not that I can't talk about them. It's just that I don't want to talk about them before I talk about other things, because it's easy to misunderstand them, even for me. The things with my dad happened almost from the beginning, but I'll talk about them later. They happened later, too, but I don't want to talk about them now, at the beginning.

∽

What was life in Hawthorne like? It was like life. I didn't know anything else. My brothers and I went to school. We hung out in the house. Other kids from the neighborhood dropped by to hang out in our garage, or we went to their yards and played. We weren't rich, but I never felt like we needed money. We got plenty of presents for Christmas. I got a Babe Ruth watch one year. Another year I got a train. My dad, always looking for ways to bring music into the house, bought us a Wurlitzer jukebox and stocked it with records by Les Paul and Mary Ford, Perry Como, Rosemary Clooney.

Rosemary Clooney was the first singer I remember hearing. She wasn't the first singer I heard, but she was the first one I remember really hearing in an important way. She had a song, "Tenderly," that came out when I was about ten years old. Listening to it was like a dream. There were these strings that came in at the beginning, and then a whole orchestra, though it was done so subtly. I think it was Percy Faith who was in charge of her orchestra. But the real star of "Tenderly" was Rosemary Clooney. She just came sweeping in with everything, and her phrasing was perfect: when she said the evening breeze caressed the trees, you could see the trees moving. You could understand why she was singing about them, and how she was like a tree herself. I hadn't really heard a song like that before. I feel like I learned to sing from that song. I used to sing it to myself on the way to school, or when I was up in my room. My brothers sometimes told me not to sing and that it was annoying, but mostly they seemed to like it.

The other big member of the family was the television set. Maybe that's true for all kids who were my age. The TV came to us around 1950, when I was eight years old. At first we watched whatever was on, all in black and white. There was wrestling and roller derby and game shows, and there were also kids' shows, like *Time For Beany*. That was a show that aired in Los Angeles about Beany, who was a boy, and his sidekick, Cecil the Seasick Sea Serpent. It was a great show.

California had great weather most of the time, so when we weren't listening to records or watching TV, we explored our neighborhood. There was a tunnel that ran from one side of the town to another. Kids said it was a storm drain, but I wasn't really sure what that meant. One afternoon my brother Dennis and my cousin Steve Korthoff told me to come with them and walk in the storm drain. It was fun to walk in the tunnel for a little while, and then it was less fun, and then it wasn't fun at all. I started to get a headache. I didn't like being underground that way. I kept saying, "I'm going back." Steve and Dennis tried to convince me not to go. I was the oldest so I felt like I should be the leader, but I couldn't be a leader if they wouldn't follow me. I turned and went home, and on the way I slipped and cut my hand on some glass. Dennis and Steve kept walking, got bored themselves, and climbed up out of a manhole cover.

You wouldn't think this, but I almost never went to the beach as a kid, even though it was only a few miles away. The first time I ever went to the ocean I couldn't believe it. My dad took us, and I was so scared at the size of the ocean. Also, I had light skin that burned easily and I didn't like squinting against the sun for hours. Once I went with my friend Rich Sloan and I kept my jeans on so the sun couldn't get to me. And there was barely any surfing either. I tried once and got conked on the head with the board. So Los Angeles and California were more about the idea of going in the ocean than they were about actually going in the ocean. I liked to look at it, though. It was sort of like a piece of music: each of the waves was moving around by itself, but they were also moving together.

～

When I went to the house in St. Charles near Joe Thomas, there was no ocean. I missed it. I missed looking out at it. I had written so many songs that were inspired by the Pacific Ocean and the idea of the Pacific Ocean, and here I was two thousand miles from it. I know the miles because I asked someone to look it up. There was water, though, in St. Charles. We were right on the Fox River, and you could see it driving through town. The river was mostly pretty quiet. It was like a mirror. It didn't send ideas out like the ocean.

The more I saw the river, the more I liked it, but the more it got me thinking about California. It was water just like the ocean. And thinking about California made me think about *Holland*, an album the Beach Boys made in 1972. That album was made in Holland, like its title said. The whole band went over there, all the Beach Boys, because Jack Rieley, a great guy and songwriter who was managing us at the time, saw that I was struggling in Los Angeles. I was exhausted from being separated from the group, from making music in the studio while they were out touring with it. There were problems with my weight. There were problems with cocaine. Jack wanted to give me a new start and new inspiration. We went over to Baambrugge to record. Rather than dig down seven feet and put in a new studio, we had a studio sent over from Los Angeles and rebuilt in a barn in the Netherlands.

I liked the place. I liked the food and the cobblestone streets. I liked the environment. But we were there half a year, and that was too long. We got homesick. What ended up happening is that we kept writing about California. I was smoking marijuana and listening to Randy Newman's *Sail Away* album, which put me in a very spiritual mood and inspired me to write. I wrote *Mount Vernon and Fairway*, a ten-minute-long piece with six different sections. I named it that because I wanted Mike to think it was about him, and it was in a way. That was where his house was in Baldwin Hills when he was a kid.

My first concept of the piece, which I thought of as a fairy tale, was much more ambitious. The six sections would be linked by a fairy-tale theme, and I wanted to cut new arrangements of some of the songs we used to hear on our transistor radios in the late '50s, like "A Casual Look." They would be interspersed throughout. It would be a whole trip about the group. I even had my imitation of Mike's dad in there, yelling at Mike's brother, Stan. But when I ran it by Carl, he said, "What?" That shook me up and I backed off and stopped recording it. I am not sure to this day if he thought it was too creative or too ambitious or if he just didn't like it. In the end, Carl was the one who ended up producing the whole fairy tale with the pieces I already had. We put it on as an extra for *Holland*, as an EP.

Mike and Al put together something they called the California Saga, which connected two songs, "California" and "Big Sur," with a poem by Robinson Jeffers. I didn't know much about Jeffers except that he had died a few months before we wrote "Surfin' Safari." But his poem "Beaks of Eagles" was great. It said some of the same things about people that I said in "'Til I Die," that individual people can change but people overall never really change, that history is so much bigger than us all. And Al's lead vocal on "The Beaks of Eagles" might be my all-time favorite Al lead ever. There are some great songs on that record. "Steamboat" kicks ass. I really like "Only with You" and "Funky Pretty," too. It's a damned good album no matter where or how we made it. The cover photo of the record has a picture of a canal that goes right through the middle of town.

If you look at the songs on *Holland*, it seems like we were writing and singing about a California we were remembering, but the truth is we were writing about a California we were imagining. When we were home in Los Angeles, at our own houses, we thought mostly about the things that were in front of us. When Jack took us away, we wrote more with our imagination. St. Charles wasn't as far away from Los Angeles as Holland. Holland was 5,500 miles away. I had someone look that up, too. But it was still far enough away that I had to write with imagination rather than memory. That's probably why I named that album I made with Joe Thomas *Imagination*.

Imagination was the first record I had made in ten years, the first real one. I had done *Orange Crate Art* with Van Dyke, and I had done *I Just Wasn't Made for These Times* with Don Was, but this was different, a real record with a title and just my name—an actual Brian Wilson solo record. I don't know what gave me the courage. Maybe time did, maybe waiting did, maybe medication did, maybe Melinda did. I also had a visit from George Martin. He was in Los Angeles for a documentary, and he came by the studio and we listened to "God Only Knows." He remixed parts of it right then and there, and I was just amazed at how much better he made it sound. I told him he scored a better mix than I did on the original. It was a lesson from a brilliant man and producer. I loved what he did with the Beatles. I loved what he did with "God Only Knows" in the studio in 1997. And I loved him as a person. We got along great. When he passed away in March 2016, I was really broken up. He was one of the true greats, you know?

When Joe and I started *Imagination*, we had a routine down. I would wake up at ten thirty or eleven and call Joe, and he would walk over from his house next door. We would do a few hours in the studio, and then we would take a break for lunch. I did mostly the same thing for lunch every day—I ordered whitefish from a place called ZaZa. I loved the whitefish from that place. Then I would nap and relax and watch TV and Joe would go golfing. When he came back, we would all go out to dinner at a place called Mill Race Inn, which was about fifteen minutes away in Geneva. Then we would come back to my house, meaning the studio, and work for a few more hours. The record got made that way. Most weekends, though, we went home to Los Angeles.

At times it felt like a new family was growing there in St. Charles: me and Melinda and the kids, Joe and Chris and their kids. It felt like an extended family stretched over two houses. But it was also different from anything I had ever done. When I went to Holland, I went with the Beach Boys. That was my old family, stretched over two countries. I knew all the strange and great and sometimes less great ways that we worked together. I knew which songs of mine Mike would pull back from, and when I would have to fix up someone else's songs by building a little piece of music to put between two other pieces: a bridge to get over a canal.

In St. Charles the record was being made mostly by two of us, and it was the first time I'd had that kind of working relationship. I had written songs with people before. I had worked on lyrics with people. But when I worked with people in the old days, whether it was Tony Asher or Van Dyke Parks, I mostly made the songs and then worked with them to get the lyrics right. When I made songs with Andy Paley, he helped out by playing great and keeping track of all the ideas we were having, and I have had other people in my life I felt so lucky to work with, from Jeff Foskett to Darian Sahanaja to Scott Bennett to Paul Von Mertens. If people make great music their whole life, they have to be smart about knowing it's at least partly because of the people working with them. Music starts in your mind, but it ends up always being a collaboration. There are too many sounds happening all at once for it to be only one person.

With Joe, the creative relationship was a little different. He would say that he was going to take a basic track that we had cut and get it into shape, which usually meant adding instruments. Then I would add the vocals. I loved singing into a microphone. The microphones there were Telefunken, and they got a good clear sound. But that also meant I had to share some things I wasn't used to sharing. Joe brought a certain vibe to the record. He knew that the people buying my records were getting older, and he wanted a record their ears would like. I wasn't always sure about the direction but Joe was, and that was how things went on that project. There's a lyric on "Your Imagination," "I miss the way I used to call the shots around here." I don't think I wrote that lyric. Joe did. But sometimes I felt it.

☙

The way I used to call the shots around here:

Up in the bedroom in Hawthorne when I was a kid, we all started to sing. When I was ten or eleven, I went through a phase where I tried out some instruments. My dad encouraged it. I learned both the ukulele and the accordion. They were small instruments that were easy to have in a house where three kids shared a bedroom. I even played some shows for kids in school before I got sick of it. That was it for those instruments mostly.

When I got a little older, I switched over to piano and started picking out the melodies of songs I heard on the radio. I picked out the melody to "Tenderly" and played along with myself while I sang it. I learned to listen and sing, and then I learned how to teach others to listen and sing. Dennis and Carl and I had a little trio going, and I started bringing songs to the group. I brought songs by the Chordettes and the Hi-Lo's and Nat King Cole. I brought "Ivory Tower," which was a hit for Cathy Carr and Gale Storm when I was fourteen or so: "Come down from your ivory tower / Let love come into your heart." And I brought so many songs by the Four Freshmen, who started out as a barbershop quartet in Indiana and designed more and more sophisticated ways for their voices play off each other. I tried to understand the way their voices were working, to take their songs apart like they were clocks and then rebuild them for me and Dennis and Carl. I'd listen to them until I understood the main melody and the harmony vocals above and below it. Then I would teach the harmony parts to my brothers. For three years we sang those songs and songs like them.

Later on with the Beach Boys, I had to learn that not everyone understood everything at the same time. Sometimes I would explain a song and Mike would take longer to understand what I was saying. The same thing happened when I was a kid. When I taught my brothers harmony parts, Carl got it right away, and he got it beautifully. He was our main man for vocals. Dennis took longer. I had to be patient with him. He had other things going on—different friends, different sports. He sang with us sometimes in our bedroom. But he didn't like when we would try to tape our singing, and he wasn't as interested in sitting at the piano with me. Carl was always on tape and at the piano. He was also the one who turned us on to R&B. We used to lay awake at night and listen to stations like KFVD and KGFJ. There was one show called *Huntin' with Hunter* where the DJ was a guy named Hunter Hancock. He had come to LA from Texas in the '40s, and he was one of the first white DJs to play R&B. Carl loved the records he would play: Johnny Otis, the Penguins. We had never heard anything like it. They were just as sophisticated as the Four Freshmen but different. We tried to imitate those harmonies also.

When I was twelve or so, I really got into that music along with the vocal groups, and I kept going on the piano. My uncle Charlie taught me to play the boogie-woogie like it was done on those Johnny Otis records. There were other players I learned about also, like Ivory Joe Hunter and Pinetop Perkins. I went to my piano all the time and did it. I ended up calling that kind of playing Uncle Charlie's Boogie. When you look at a recipe, it lists ingredients before it tells you how to cook them. Those were my ingredients: beautiful songs by singers like Rosemary Clooney, vocal harmonies from groups like the Four Freshmen, and the boogie-woogie. Those are the sounds that started moving around in my mind.

We lived about two miles from Hawthorne Municipal Airport, and all day long there was nothing but airplane noise. I didn't really like airplanes, even then. My mom's dad, who was also named Carl, flew planes. We had Carls in every generation. My grandfather

Carl was in the Shriners and always smoked a cigar and had a sword in a case with rubies all over it. He also had a pilot's license and learned to fly small planes all around Los Angeles. When I was ten or eleven, he took me up with him. I was excited but very scared. "Don't worry, Brian," he said. "It's okay." It was comforting to hear him say that, even though I decided I didn't want to keep flying with him. Planes were a problem even if you weren't up in them. The noise got in the way of our singing. We had to shut the windows to keep it out.

But when we got to a certain point in practice where we thought we had a nice version of "Ivory Tower," we would call my parents in and sing for them. My dad was interested not just in music but in how it was recorded, so he would buy us recording equipment sometimes, and we started putting our songs down on tape.

～⌀

Music was starting to be everything, but it was still all about family. I was singing with my brothers. I was learning piano from Uncle Charlie. I was getting my ideas down on tape machines my dad was bringing home.

And there was more family around, too. My dad's brother Wendell and his wife, Billie, lived near enough that we would visit there often. They had two kids, Wendy and Mike (both are names that came up over and over again in the extended Wilson family), who were about the same age as me and my brothers, and when we were there, we played checkers or Monopoly with them. Wendell collected strange things and always had surprises. His house was the first place I ever saw a theremin. I was fascinated with it. I knew you could make music with human voices or pianos—and, I guess, with ukuleles and accordions—but the idea you could invent new musical instruments was something I had never thought about.

My dad's sister Emily, who everyone called Glee, married a guy named Ed Love, who was in charge of a sheet-metal company. They had money because of that, more than us, and six kids. The oldest was Mike—another Mike. This Mike, Mike Love, was very friendly and very funny, and he made me laugh. I really liked him. We hit it off real well, and soon enough he was almost a fourth brother. When I was fourteen, the two families went Christmas caroling together; we sang "Hark the Herald Angels Sing" and "O Little Town of Bethlehem." As soon as Mike and I could drive, we started driving over to each other's houses to hang out. Hanging out meant watching TV sometimes, or it meant talking about school or girls, but it also meant singing—the same way I taught harmonies to Dennis and Carl, I taught them to Mike and his sister Maureen. We also did Everly Brothers songs. I loved "Dream." They were the best duet singers I ever heard. I don't even know how they did what they did.

I remember back in the winter of 1963 when the reservoir up at Baldwin Hills gave out and a big flood knocked down hundreds of houses. People drowned, too. I took Carl in the car and we drove over there. The cops were standing at the head of the street. "You can't come in here," one cop said.

"But my cousin lives up there," I said. Carl, in the passenger seat, nodded and tried to look worried. They waved us through. The funny thing is that I don't even know if they lived in Baldwin Hills anymore. I think they had moved to View Park. But I wanted to see what happened with the flood.

As time went on Mike did more than carol with us. He became part of the whole Wilson music project. We started singing up in the bedroom and then went to the garage to sing and play some more. Mike played the saxophone, sort of. He played, but he wasn't really a player the way some guys were. But Mike could sing. He had a deeper and rougher voice that worked really nicely with the rest of us. When you build up harmonies, lots of it is teaching people parts, but some of it is listening to the sounds they're already making and building something out of that. Later on we added in one more singer and player, Al Jardine, who was a guy from the neighborhood who played guitar with a band called the Islanders and was deep into folk music. Al was also in a band called the Tikis back then, and he had already been making songs, sort of; in junior high he recorded a version of a Longfellow poem called "The Wreck of the Hesperus" with some of his own music, and also wrote a song called "Steam from the Washing Machine." That was more of a teen song. And Al could also play stand-up bass.

＊

As a kid I was a real athlete. My dad took me to a park near the house and showed me how to hit a baseball with a bat. He held the bat in his right hand, floated the ball up there with his left hand, and then swung the bat. It went *whap!* and the ball flew as far as I could see. Then he made us do it. Of all my brothers, I was the best. I was the oldest, but I was also the best. Carl wasn't much of an athlete. He didn't take to it. Dennis was a good athlete, but he was more into things like wrestling. At team sports, I was the best. In baseball I could run the bases in seventeen seconds, go all the way around. And I had a great arm, a Willie Mays arm. I was a lefty, and I could bring the ball all the way in from center field to the catcher. When I was seventeen, I thought I would be a major league baseball player. Then I got into the music business, and it got into me. I think it probably worked out for the best. My high school uniform is in the Rock and Roll Hall of Fame in Cleveland. It has the grass stains. They never washed out.

It was a big time for California baseball back then. We got our first team in the mid-'50s, the Dodgers, who came from Brooklyn. I wasn't really a Dodgers fan. I was a Yankees fan. I played center field myself and wanted to play center field for the Yankees, though Mickey Mantle already had that job. I also loved the Red Sox—they had Ted Williams and Johnny Pesky and Dom DiMaggio, Joe DiMaggio's brother. There was a third DiMaggio, Vince, who was also a center fielder. They were a brother act, too. I remember listening to Buddy Blattner doing the game of the week on ABC. I remember listening to baseball on the radio and sometimes switching over to hear music. Andy Williams came on all the time, singing his early hits like "Canadian Sunset" and "Butterfly."

I had a great arm, but that was about as far as it went. Even though I could smack the ball far when I threw it up in the air the way my dad showed me, I batted under .200 in games. I think it was .169. I couldn't hit a curveball for shit. I had only one home run. Can you believe that? I also played football. That's what kids did in California. I started playing as a junior in high school and lasted about a year. I was the quarterback, and I was pretty good at it. I could see the field and time it so the ball got out to the receivers. I could also really throw. Once I was with some friends and we had a contest to see who could throw the farthest. I put it up in the air, and someone down the way measured where it landed and said it went sixty-five yards. I guess I had the arm.

Al Jardine played with me. He was a back. During one game, I called for a pitchout. I told him I was going to pitch to the left. But I got mixed up and looked right. Al was standing out there all on his own and three guys hit him, high and low, and his leg just snapped. I had to hear about that for years. "You know, Brian," Al would say, and I knew what was coming next: "You're responsible for my broken leg." He tried to make a joke about it, tried to be sarcastic, but it has come up too many times over the years for me to think he doesn't still hold a little bit of a grudge. And then I got hit myself. During practice one afternoon I got knocked on my back and the corners of my vision started to fade. I felt like everything was going black. It scared me half to death. I went right up to the coach and told him I wanted to quit the team. "Fine," he said. "Go to the showers." That was the end of my football career. Back to music.

⌇

Time jumps around. One day you're hearing a song on the radio. The day after that you're bringing other guys into your family's house so you can complete the puzzle and make records of your own. My dad helped push us toward being a real singing group. He thought it was a great idea for me to bang around on the piano until I had a song of my own.

Time jumps around so much that it's hard to remember exactly what happened. Plus, it's been written about so many times that it's almost like a story someone else is telling me instead of a piece of my own life. I was noodling around at the piano. Dennis came home and told us that all the guys were getting into surfing. Dennis was the real surfer of the group. He thought that if we wrote a song about it, it would be cool, and we might be cool along with it. I started fooling around and singing just that one word, *surfin'*, trying to make a song out of it. Mike was around that day, and he added in some bass notes, *bom-bom-dit-dit-dit*. I added some more chords. Mike added words. I cooked up harmonies. If you look at a recipe, those are the ingredients of a song.

Surfin' is the only life
The only way for me
Now surf, surf with me

We fooled around with the song. We sang it a bunch of times and wrote more words for it and took out some of the words we had already written. We practiced harmonies until they sounded right to us, and then changed a few notes around to make the sound more exciting or unexpected. It was just a family thing then. It was playing for the family, and playing in the family. It was the fall of 1961 and I'm not sure that any of us thought it would go much further than that.

But we tried. The first step was to get a name for the group. You couldn't have a record if your group didn't have a name. We tried a bunch of names, like Carl and the Passions and Kenny and the Cadets. Eventually we ended up naming ourselves the Pendletones. I don't remember whose idea it was, maybe Mike's, but it came from the same place as the song. It was part of the package.

Pendletones was a name about the way surfers dressed—plaid Pendleton shirts over white T-shirts and khaki pants. Real surfers put a layer of Vaseline under the shirts to keep warm, but we weren't real surfers. We were real singers.

My parents went to Mexico on vacation and left us money to take care of ourselves. Instead, we went and rented instruments and rehearsed "Surfin'." When they got home and found out, my dad was really pissed at what we had done. He threw me up against the wall. But when he heard what we had cooked up with the song, he calmed down. He thought we sounded pretty good. He was proud of us, even, and that made us so happy that we decided to do more with our music. Dad knew a music guy named Hite Morgan who had an office on Melrose Avenue, and he piled us into Hite's office and we sang "The John B. Sails," a folk song that Al knew. Hite Morgan liked what he heard. He said so and Dad kind of smiled, not a full smile but enough of one for me to tell that he was really happy that Hite Morgan liked us. But Hite Morgan wasn't sure about the song. He told us we needed a song of our own. Someone piped up—I think it was Dennis—and said we did have our own song. I had to speak then and say it wasn't finished. "Well, come back when you finish it," Hite said.

That's what we did. We went into Hite's studio and that was our first real recording session. We worked on "Surfin'" all day. I wanted it to sound a certain way, and I kept everyone there with my questions. I didn't like the way that people's voices were falling in the mix. I wanted to rethink it. After a bunch of takes, my dad wasn't sure what we were doing was working. He said something about how we were kids—and it's true. We were. He thought he had a better idea of how to make it sound the right way, how to bring the guitar up, how to make sure all the voices could be heard. He said he wanted to produce the session, and we let him.

When we were done, Hite Morgan said he was going to make it into a record. He went off somewhere. We didn't know where. It turns out he went to a guy named Herb Newman who owned a label named Candix Records. It wasn't until the crates were unpacked that we saw the label had changed our name from the Pendletones to the Beach Boys. A guy at the label named Russ Regan didn't like our name. He changed it. We were in my car the first time we heard the song on the radio. There were three or four songs by local bands and listeners had to pick their favorite. We went crazy. I ran up and down the street yelling. Carl felt sick from excitement. There's no feeling like being a new band and hearing yourself on the radio, except maybe when that band is your family. The story has been told a thousand times by a thousand different people, but that doesn't mean it didn't happen exactly that way.

⌇

When I was a kid, I made music with my family. As I got a little older, I made music with other people who were part of our inner circle. By the time I was in my forties, I was making music with lots of people. My musical family was constantly growing, and every new person I worked with taught me something. I hope I taught them, too. Families can be the strangest, most wonderful things.

During the *Imagination* sessions we took a trip down to the Florida Keys to write a song with Jimmy Buffett. "You know, Brian," Joe said on the plane. "We're going to be close to Kokomo."

"Really?" I said. "Kokomo" was a song the Beach Boys did without me. My cousin Mike wrote it with a few friends of the band, all great music guys. One was John Phillips, from the Mamas and the Papas. One was Scott McKenzie, who wrote "San Francisco (Be Sure to Wear Flowers in Your Hair)." And then there was Terry Melcher, whose mom was Doris Day and who worked with so many people back in the '60s like the Byrds and the Rising Sons. The Beach Boys had known Terry forever. He had been in a group with Bruce Johnston, the Rip Chords, before Bruce joined our group.

Terry was also the guy in the middle of the situation with my brother Dennis and Charles Manson. Dennis, who knew two of the girls in Manson's group because he had picked them up hitchhiking,

introduced Manson to Terry and tried to get the two of them together on a music or film project. It didn't work out well. Terry
and Manson didn't get the right ideas about each other and they
stopped being friends. A little after that, Terry moved out of the
house on Cielo Drive where he was living with Candice Bergen and
Mark Lindsay, the lead singer from Paul Revere and the Raiders. And
a little after that, Manson came to the house. He wasn't let in because Terry wasn't there anymore. The people who were there were
Roman Polanski and Sharon Tate. The Manson people came back
one more time and killed Sharon Tate and four other people. For
years people tried to figure out if the Manson family was looking
for Terry or if it didn't make any difference to them who was in the
house. Families can be the strangest, most horrible things.

It's weird that "Kokomo" has anything dark in its past because
it's such a light song. It's a feel-good party song. When Mike and
John and Scott and Terry finished writing it, they told me they were
going into the studio to cut it, but they told me too late. I couldn't
make it to the session. Mike and Carl sang lead. Bruce Johnston and
Al Jardine sang backup. It was a huge hit. I think it went to number
one. The first time I heard it on the radio, I loved it, though I didn't
even know it was the Beach Boys. When someone told me who was
singing, I couldn't believe it. It had such a cool sound and such
great harmonies, and the lyrics were nice and relaxing.

When Joe told me that Jimmy Buffett's place was near Kokomo,
I got excited. "Can we go there?" I asked.

"Sure," Joe said.

"That's cool." I mentioned it to someone else on the plane,
one of the musicians, and he looked at me strangely. I turned back
around and Joe was laughing. "What's the joke?" I asked.

"Kokomo's not real," Joe said.

"What do you mean?"

"It doesn't exist."

Now everyone was laughing, and I started laughing, too. I wasn't
against jokes. I played jokes all the time when I was a kid. Once

my friend Rich came over to the house. My mom was sitting in the music room and I introduced them to each other. Then I said to my mom, "Rich thinks you're fat and need to go to Vic Tanny's." That was a gym. Rich looked like someone punched him in the stomach. But my mom didn't mind. "I know my son," she said, laughing. After that, Rich and I went into the kitchen and played a game with a funnel. You put a penny on your forehead and then leaned forward and tried to drop it in the funnel. I missed once or twice. Rich told me to lean back to get a better angle. When I did he poured a glass of water into the funnel. It got the front of my pants all wet. I was so mad. I threw the funnel down on the ground.

I got mad pretty often. Once I hit the wall in the kitchen. It was a good thing I didn't get the stud. But with the funnel, I wasn't that angry for long, and when I thought about it I wasn't sure I was angry at all. Other pranks I did to make people feel better. One of my cousins, Sherry Ann, got hurt. She banged her head bad. She was in St. Vincent's Hospital, and I went up to see her and wrapped my head in toilet paper so I looked like a mummy. I wasn't really a mummy, but I wanted her to think just for a second that I was so that she wouldn't think about her own head and how it hurt. It was an escape.

That's how I felt about Kokomo. It didn't matter to me if it was a real place or a fake place. Even a fake place, if it's made up of real ideas, can be real for a second. The song we ended up writing with Jimmy Buffett, "South American," proves it. It was a kind of fantasy about fame and attention. The guy in the song has lunch with Cameron Diaz. But there's also an escape:

> Got a letter from a long-lost cousin of mine
> Who owns a little piece of heaven in the Argentine
> It's a different planet, it's a different place
> He calls it out of this world without traveling to space

During *Imagination* Carl started dying. He was barely fifty, but he was sick with lung cancer. Carl had smoked since we were kids, which people never believed; he had such a pure singing voice that it didn't sound like he had ever touched a cigarette. That summer the Beach Boys were out touring without me. Carl was too sick to stand for most of the concerts. He sat on a stool.

I wasn't following the progress of the disease too carefully. We didn't have a very close relationship toward the end, and that was hard. Whatever was happening with the Beach Boys at that point, we were brothers. We had started out listening to the radio in our room, and we had been through forty years of being together in the same band. Carl had helped get Dr. Landy to leave the second time, and I was grateful for that. Through 1997, our mom was in bad shape. We were a little closer for a little while, Carl and I, but his health was failing, too. It's hard to talk about the way people's health goes. It's the life going out of them in a way that's very hard to understand.

The last time I saw Carl was at his house off Benedict Canyon. Carl hadn't met Daria yet. He kept saying that he didn't want to meet her until he was better because he didn't want to scare her. We got a call from Gina, Carl's wife, that she wanted to have a small Super Bowl party and that Carl finally wanted to meet Daria, who was a little more than a year old then. When we got there, Gina met us. "Carl's sleeping," she said. Lots of family was there at that party. Gina's mom was there. Carl's son Jonah was there. We sat with everyone, and then about an hour later Gina went back to get Carl and wheeled him out into the living room in a wheelchair. He was very sick. His skin was so yellow. Except for his beard he had hardly any hair. The fucking chemotherapy had really done a number on him. Up until then, Daria had been afraid of anyone with a beard. Beards made her cry. But when Carl reached for her, she put her arms out and went right to him. She rested her head on his shoulder. We all got the idea that it would be her first and last visit with her uncle Carl. Before we left, Carl said he was looking forward to coming to Chicago to sing with me on my new record. When Melinda and I got back in the car, we looked at each other, and both of us had tears in our eyes.

A few weeks later we were back in St. Charles, working on the record. It was our anniversary, so I took Melinda into Chicago for dinner at Morton's. We had a great night, really meaningful and happy after the sadness of seeing Carl slipping away, and we went back to the St. Charles house. As soon as we got home, Joe came rushing over. "I have some bad news," he said. We knew and we didn't know. "I am very sorry to tell you this," Joe said, "but Carl just died."

It really broke me up. Carl was a nice kid. He never got in trouble. He was the peacemaker in the family and certainly the peacemaker in the band. He was the most spiritual person I knew. One of the reasons I wanted him to sing certain songs, especially "God Only Knows," was that he could put such innocent and natural feeling into things. Singers can practice hitting notes. They can learn about styles by listening to jazz vocalists or singers from other countries. But just to go out there and sing a song in a simple way that makes everyone who hears it feel something deeply, that can't be practiced or even learned. You have to be born with it. Carl was born with it. And when Carl died, that thing he was born with died with him also. Hearing about his death was one of the roughest trips I had to go through. I didn't understand it at all. Carl was gone. He went somewhere, but I didn't know where.

∽

A few months after Carl died, Frank Sinatra died also. I never met him, but I felt so connected to him. He did lots of his great records for Capitol, just like we did. I always loved his voice, and during rough times I put him on when I was trying to sleep. I heard that B. B. King used to do the same thing, and it made sense; there was something so soothing about the way he could find the sad part of a song. My daughter Carnie even wanted to do an album of his songs with me. I felt strange about it, so I didn't do it. I'll never be Frank Sinatra.

Once I was backstage before a show and I was very nervous. I'm always nervous before a show. I never know how an audience is going to respond to it. Someone there at the show had known someone else who worked with Sinatra, who knew that Sinatra threw up before every concert. I loved hearing that, not because I liked to think of Sinatra sick but because I couldn't believe that someone as cool as he was had the same problems I had. I wrote a song for him once called "Still I Dream of It." He didn't say yes to the song, and that bothered me. It was a beautiful song about loneliness and hope:

> *Still I dream of it*
> *Of that happy day*
> *When I can say I've fallen in love*
> *And it haunts me so*
> *Like a dream that's*
> *Somehow linked to all the stars above*

The song ended up on an album named *Adult/Child,* which was filled with those kinds of songs. It was a Beach Boys album that never came out. I made it in 1977 during a period that was pretty interesting for the group, even though it was a hard period. *Adult/Child* had arrangements by Dick Reynolds, who worked with us on *The Beach Boys' Christmas Album* back in 1964, the same year he worked with Sinatra himself. I wanted to make a record with a similar feel as the records by classic vocalists like Sinatra, so I called in Dick Reynolds to help us out. Other guys in the group didn't like the idea. Mike couldn't believe it. When he heard the demos he just shook his head and stared at me. The record label wasn't sure about the album either. Often the record labels agreed with the other guys in the group. The album never came out, though I ended up putting the demo of "Still I Dream of It" on the soundtrack for the Don Was documentary we made in 1995.

Adult/Child was Dr. Landy's title. He meant that there were always two parts of a personality, always an adult who wants to be in charge and a child who wants to be cared for, always an adult who thinks he knows the rules and a child who is learning and testing the rules. I also thought about it in terms of family. I thought about my dad and me, and all the things he did that were good and bad, all the things that I can talk about easily and all the things I can't talk about at all.

In December 1963 the Beach Boys released "Little Saint Nick," our first Christmas record. A month after that, Frank Sinatra started working on an album called *America, I Hear You Singing*, which was the one Dick Reynolds helped arrange. It was an album of hopeful, patriotic songs done in duet with Bing Crosby; they recorded it in response to the Kennedy assassination, which had happened back in November. The day of the assassination, I was at home, playing around on the piano and relaxing. When the shooting happened, everyone knew instantly. It was all over the TV and on every kind of news. I called Mike and he asked me if I wanted to write a song about it. I said sure. It seemed like something we had to think about, and songs were the way I thought about things. We drove over to my office and in a half hour we had "The Warmth of the Sun." We didn't think of it as a big song. It was a personal response. But it got bigger over time because of the history linked to it.

౭⌀

I'm scared of lots of things, and I can say for sure that going on-stage after *Imagination* was one of the hardest things I've ever done. Playing live with the band wasn't something I liked very much, even in the old days. When I watch myself on *Ed Sullivan* or the *T.A.M.I. Show*, I can remember how uncomfortable it felt. Many of my worst memories are from being nervous up there, and many others are from the things I did to keep myself from being nervous up there.

Some of the drinking was because of that. Some of the drugs were because of that. Some of the voices in my head I heard just before I went onstage, and they didn't have anything good to say about me.

When Melinda told me I should think about doing some solo concerts for *Imagination*, I had all kinds of excuses. But every time I told her one, she had an answer. People only wanted to hear the old hits? No, they didn't—the album was getting some great reviews. I was too old? No, I wasn't—other rockers were still doing it even if they were older than me. I didn't have a band? This stopped her short for a little while. Then one night we saw a group called the Wondermints in Hollywood. They played lots of Beach Boys songs in their show, and I liked what they did with them. They kept the spirit of the originals. The main guy in the Wondermints, Darian Sahanaja, seemed to understand the way my songs were built. That night, I told someone to go ask them if they wanted to be my band. The Wondermints loved the idea. We added in some other Chicago musicians we worked with when we were recording *Imagination*—especially Scott Bennett, who played guitar, keyboards, and vibes, and Paul Von Mertens, who played sax, harmonica, and organ—and all of a sudden I had a band.

Playing with the new band was different than playing with the Beach Boys. Hearing my own backing band behind me, that was a trip. In the old days, I always felt like I was right in the middle of everything. With the new musicians, there was a little distance—not in a bad way, but they were behind me, helping me bring my songs to life. There wasn't the same kind of ego and the same kind of infighting because we weren't family in the same way. That made things a little less intimate, but maybe it also made them better. And then eventually we were family.

We did a few dates with other people, including Jimmy Buffett, shows where we came out and played some hits. Our first real show was in Ann Arbor, Michigan. It was March 9, 1999—I remember the date because it had so many nines. I was on the floor of the dressing room. I wasn't sure I could go out. All the nervous things were happening to me. My friend Ray Lawlor came backstage to see me. When he saw how I was feeling, he sat down in silence for a minute. Then he said my name. "Brian. You've already hit the home run. Now you just have to jog around the bases." I went out and kicked ass that night, and the audience loved it.

The next night in Chicago at the Rosemont Theatre, I didn't have to sit on the floor backstage anymore. I went out and looked straight into the crowd. Jerry Weiss, a friend of mine who later took care of everything on the road, was there. David Leaf was there. Melinda was always there. I made sure to find out exactly where they were because they gave me confidence. And that night I had it.

We toured around the Midwest for a little while: Michigan, Illinois, Wisconsin. After a few weeks we had a barbecue at the house in St. Charles. It was great—so many hamburgers and hot dogs. I went downstairs into the studio with some friends and started playing "Marcella." That's a song that always made me happy because it had some of the rock and roll energy of the Rolling Stones. It's an energy song. Then I did another medley of the oldest stuff I could think of at the moment; "Be My Baby" was in there, and also "Surfer Girl."

"Should we go back upstairs?" someone asked.

"Why?" someone else said. "Let's just stay down here. This is the life."

That made me think of "Busy Doin' Nothin'." It was a song from the late '60s that I wrote about just hanging out. I sang it mostly by myself, which didn't happen very much back then. Marilyn, my wife at the time, was on the song for a few seconds, but otherwise it was all me. It was a nice little song with a kind of bossa nova melody—sweet, light, with lots of nice places for my voice to go up into the corners of the song. I got through about half of the song there in the basement and then suddenly forgot the rest of it. "I can't remember," I said.

"Come on," someone said. Everyone must have thought I was joking. But I wasn't joking. I didn't remember the rest. I was tired.

"I'm done here," I said. I lifted my hands off the piano and went upstairs to take a shower. I brushed my teeth and hair. About a half hour later I went back downstairs in my bathrobe. I sat at the piano and it came back to me immediately. I called upstairs. "Hey," I said. "Come here." Some people came downstairs, and I played the whole song for them.

I wrote a number down
But I lost it
So I searched through my pocketbook
I couldn't find it
So I sat and concentrated on the number
And slowly it came to me
So I dialed it

It's a real pretty tune. It was a song about forgetting and remembering what I forgot and then remembered. That seemed funny at first, but then it seemed sad. Life is so much about losing. These days losing a phone number is no big deal. You can find it anywhere on your phone. But back then it was more of a worry. Maybe you wouldn't be able to call the girl or guy whose number it was. You thought for a second they might be gone forever. That's how I felt about "Busy Doin' Nothin'" when I lifted my hands from the piano and went upstairs. But it came back to me.

Some things never come back. When I was a kid we had a dog named Chico. He was a Chihuahua. We let him play baseball with us, and he started to get good at it. He ran away from home. We didn't know where he went. Then one day I was walking home from school with Dennis and we saw Chico lying in the gutter dead. We both broke down crying.

Thirty years later I was sitting on a couch trying to think of a song when Dr. Landy came into the room. "I have something for you," he said. He bent down and stood back up and there was a puppy on the floor. It was beige, and its eyes were happy but its tail wasn't wagging. Maybe it was a little afraid. I got down on the floor right next to the puppy and hugged it. I named the dog Buddy. A few months later Dr. Landy wanted me to sit at the piano and write a new song, but I couldn't. I just didn't have one in my head or my heart. Dr. Landy went into the room, grabbed Buddy, and said he was taking him out of the house. Gloria told him not to, but he did. I sat on the couch and couldn't stand back up. I couldn't even speak. All I could do was cry, and that's what I did.

There's another song on *Imagination* called "Cry":

> *A silly quarrel*
> *That's what we had*
> *Then I heard you cryin'*
> *You broke my heart*
> *Broke it in two*
> *How could I have left you alone*
> *Like that to cry*

The song was one of the ones I worked on with Joe Thomas. It was about a fight I had with Melinda. We were in our backyard, lying in the sun by the swimming pool, and we started arguing. I told her that I was going to leave—not just the house, but her, the whole thing. I wasn't really serious, but I wanted to see how much it bothered her. She started to cry, which almost never happened. I tried to make her feel better, but I still felt bad. Then I went right off and wrote a song. "Left you alone like that to cry" was a sad thing to sing. It was sad because of the idea of crying, and because of the idea of being left alone. I dedicated the record to Carl, who was gone. Dennis was gone. My dad was gone. My mom was gone. They were in me, still, to remember or to imagine. But I was the last Wilson.

CHAPTER 3

Foundation

Well, back in time with just a rhythm and rhyme
Gregorian chants were a real big thing
They took that chant and added harmony
It was a different sound
But had the same meaning
I know it took us a long while
To go and find us a rock style
I know that we can take it one more mile

—"That Same Song"

Many days I have the same routine. I wake up. I come downstairs to sit in my chair. I watch my family move around in the house. Some days I find my way back up to the piano. This house where I live now has a separate music room, though it's upstairs rather than downstairs like in Illinois. In the house where I lived just before this one, the piano was right out in the middle of the living room. This way is better. I have a little more privacy. Everyone else in the house can hear that I'm playing, but they aren't right there watching me. Sometimes after I figure out a melody, I'll bring it to Melinda. She'll tell me if she likes it, and she'll also tell me if she's not sure she likes it.

Those melodies I'm working with sometimes stick around for a while and become songs. Even if I have a title or some lyrics, I like to bring them to a collaborator to finish. But that first part of the process, the part where I'm at the piano just playing and listening to what I'm playing—that's the way I discover new songs. What is a song, exactly? It's something that starts as an idea and becomes more than that. It becomes physical and emotional and spiritual. It comes out into the world. It can soothe you when you're feeling at your worst. It can make you happy when you're sad.

But if you spend your life trying to find songs, you realize pretty quickly that you're not the first. People have been doing that as long as there have been people. And if there are periods in your life when you stop doing it—because something distracts you or makes you weak—you realize how important it is to jump right back into the game. Songs are out there all the time, but they can't be made without people. You have to do your job and help songs come into existence.

My experience making *Imagination* with Joe Thomas wasn't perfect. I wasn't sure about some of the things he did on that record. Sometimes when I listened to it, I heard more of him on it than I heard of me. That was strange because it was my name on the cover. So why wasn't I hearing myself in the music? I felt the way I had when I came in and the string overdubs were happening without me. I felt like my control was being taken from me.

But the album was a great experience in other ways. It got me making music again. It got me back on the road. And in the summer of 2000, I released a live album of the *Imagination* tour. I recorded it at the Roxy in West Hollywood with my new band. The Roxy was a great place with lots of history. Lou Adler opened it back in the '70s. I knew Lou from the old days. He managed Jan and Dean and produced *Tapestry* with Carole King, which is one of the great records of all time. The Roxy concert was an amazing experience all around. We played lots of old Beach Boys songs and even two new songs. One of the new songs was called "The First Time," a love song that was also about personal peace.

In the nighttime when it's dark and cold
I find peace of mind 'cause I have you to hold
When we're sound asleep
And we're breathing slow
Angels up above
And the devil below

Performing "The First Time" for the first time in concert was a real experience. This was during those early years when the Wondermints first came to be my band and I was getting used to being onstage again. During those years it was especially hard for me. Sometimes my mind would wander or I would hear voices and blow a cue. Going back onstage to play "The First Time," or really any song, was a learning experience. I had to learn everything all over again, from the ground up. Once during a show, right in the middle of "Caroline, No," I completely spaced out. I just forgot every single word. I started yelling into the mic. "Stop, stop, everybody stop!" I said. "Let's start at the top of the bridge." The crowd loved seeing me take control like that, and I saw a big smile on Darian's face. That gave me more confidence. Once in Japan we were doing "Barbara Ann" and I got so excited that I stood up from my keyboard, grabbed the mic, and walked around the stage singing my parts. During the instrumental break, I even flipped the mic behind my back and caught it with my other hand. All the guys in the band were laughing their asses off. When you feel better that way, you can do all of it better: play the old songs, bring in the new songs, connect with the band, connect with the crowd, connect with yourself.

Once we were playing a concert in Baltimore, by the harbor. We were in the middle of "Sloop John B," and when I looked out onto the stage, I saw Jerry Weiss in the audience with my daughter Daria on his shoulders. I kept on singing, but every time I looked out into the crowd, I saw Jerry with Daria. It was distracting the hell out of me. My mind was wandering anyway in those days, and I couldn't deal with seeing Daria out there without Melinda. I decided I had to do something about it. Right in the middle of a verse, I yelled into the mic really loud. "Jerry Weiss," I said. "Jerry Weiss. Bring my daughter back to her mother." I went right back to singing, but I was the only one. The rest of the band was laughing. Since then, almost every time Jerry walks into the room during a sound check, one of the guys in the band leans into the mic and imitates me: "Jerry Weiss . . . Jerry Weiss." Jeff Foskett started it, and now it's usually Nicky Wonder who does it, sometimes Probyn Gregory, too. I love it. It makes everyone laugh—like it did the first time onstage, like the mic flip during "Barbara Ann"—and that makes me feel like one of the guys.

Those early tours got me connected with the band, and also with everyone else. When you're on the road, moving from place to place, you see people in each city: fans, musicians, friends of friends. And when we played in Los Angeles, it was even more special. I remember we had a date at the Wiltern Theatre early in that tour. It was like a reunion. Almost everyone I knew was there. I was so happy to see my daughters Carnie and Wendy at the show. That meant so much to me. They mean so much to me. David Anderle was there—he worked with me and Van Dyke and helped set up Brother Records for us in the early '70s. And another David, my friend David Leaf, was also there helping me out, like he did on all tours in those days. David is originally from New York and is a huge New York Yankees fan, like me. After sound check, David and I watched the World Series with Ray Lawlor, who's also a Yankees fan. It was the first game. I forget who the Yankees were playing, but I know they won.

☙

I wrote "That Same Song" for an album called *15 Big Ones*, though it wasn't called that originally. This was back in the mid-'70s, and I had spent some time away from the Beach Boys. I was always either coming back into the group or drifting away from them. It was like a tide. I came back because it was my family. It was where I felt comfortable. But it was hard to be there when I wasn't able to get my ideas heard the way I wanted, and in those times the whole thing started to make less sense to me. Plus, there were drugs and there were problems with the way I was seeing things. There was destruction all around me.

Sometimes when I stepped away from the Beach Boys, I got into my own head more than I wanted to. Sometimes I managed to find another place to land. In the mid-'70s I started working more with a group of guys I knew. Bruce Johnston, who had replaced me in the Beach Boys when I stopped touring, had recently left the band, and he was thinking up a new project with Terry Melcher. They were collaborating with Gary Usher, who had written some of the early Beach Boys songs with me, and a guy named Curt Boettcher, who had come out from Wisconsin and made some nice records with a bunch of different bands. Dean Torrence, from Jan and Dean, was also there. All of the guys were trying to make new songs that were actually old songs. They loved the rock and roll we grew up with, and they wanted to make it new again with everything they had learned about making music in their other groups.

There were lots of names for that group. I was thinking about names all the time back then. A few years earlier I had worked on an album with Marilyn and her sister Diane. I made the record with a guy named David Sandler. We called that group Spring, but that ended up confusing people for some reason, and everywhere outside of the United States they were called American Spring, which seemed even more confusing. The Pendletones had become the Beach Boys when we weren't even looking, and that new name did well for us. It was easy to remember and put an idea in people's minds of what they were about to hear. The group with Bruce and

Terry and the rest called themselves the Legendary Masked Surfers, which was kind of a Lone Ranger name. A few songs came out with that name, but it didn't stick. They ended up calling themselves California Music, because all the guys had ideas about California music, and they were different from other people's ideas—different from the singer-songwriters like Jackson Browne, different from groups like Fleetwood Mac, different from people like Van Dyke. They had their own sense of rock and roll, of harmony and vibe and tempo.

California Music never really got off the ground. The group made some records according to the original idea. I actually produced a version of "Why Do Fools Fall in Love," the Frankie Lymon song, that included a little spoken-word snippet that was a nod to the Beatles' "Get Back." They did a version of "Jamaica Farewell," a calypso song that everyone knew from the Harry Belafonte album. Everyone had that record, the one with the red background where he was wearing a green shirt. It looked like one of his hands was coming right out of the cover photo. I helped out with some other songs, but I wasn't in the best shape. I felt unsure as a producer because I felt unsure as a person. But I tried.

During the time Terry and Bruce were doing California Music, they had a company called Equinox Records. I signed a contract with them, even though the Beach Boys were still with Reprise Records. No one was happy about my deal with Equinox, and everyone started to lean on me to go back to the Beach Boys. Marilyn did lots of leaning. She thought it was wrong of me to turn away from the group. She had seen lots of times when I'd drifted, but she thought that I was drifting too far, and that I didn't have a life preserver. The drugs and the problems in my mind were dragging me down. It was right around then that she brought in Dr. Landy for the first time, and I ended up going back to the Beach Boys. First time, same song.

It was a strange time to rejoin the Beach Boys. The group was on Reprise, but it had been a while since we had released a record. The last record was *Holland*, which the label didn't like. They weren't even going to release it until we added a song that could be a hit. The song we ended up adding was "Sail On Sailor," which I wrote with a record producer and singer named Ray Kennedy, and with Van Dyke. I don't mean that I wrote it with both of them. There were two separate times. I wrote it once around 1970 or 1971 with Ray and Danny Hutton, because I thought it would be a good song for Three Dog Night. But we didn't finish it. It got too complicated. Then a few years later, when Reprise didn't like *Holland*, Van Dyke came over and played me something he had, and I worked on that with him. All of it together became "Sail On Sailor." That went on *Holland* and became one of our biggest hits in the early '70s. But we hadn't given Reprise anything since *Holland*, and I wasn't sure where things were headed.

I was spending most of my time at the Bel Air house, with Marilyn and the kids. I remember once a young guy came up to the house. He had met Dennis at a show and Dennis gave him my number and address and told him to come see me. I didn't know that, but I knew that one day there was a ring at the doorbell and I opened up. "Hi!" I said.

The guy had a kind of surprised expression on his face. Maybe I didn't look the way he expected. My hair was longer than it was on the *Holland* album, my beard was bigger, and I was heavier. Most of the extra weight was in my gut, and that's where the guy was looking. "Hi, Brian," the guy said. "You don't know me, but I wanted to come and meet you. I got your address from your brother Dennis in New York."

"In New York? What was he doing there?"

"He was playing a Beach Boys concert."

"Oh," I said. "Come on in." We went to the music room. I asked him why he'd come to see me, and he said that he wanted to thank me for all the music I'd made. He said that the songs had helped him through some hard times. "You really want to see me?" I said. "Are you sure you don't want to see John Lennon or Harry Nilsson? I'm all washed up."

The guy laughed. He must have thought I was joking. But I wasn't joking. I didn't know where things were heading. I didn't want to think about it. As far as I was concerned, the California Saga was the best thing on the record we had just finished.

I stayed sitting at the piano and played the guy some songs I was working on: "Just an Imitation," "Spark in the Dark," "Shortenin' Bread," "I'm into Something Good," "Ding Dang." I must have played about a dozen songs. Then I got impatient. That happened all the time. I didn't like what I was doing and I wanted to do something else. "Hey," I said. "Let's go over to my friend Danny Hutton's house." We jumped in the guy's car.

First, I decided we needed to make a pit stop, so we went to the first liquor store we passed. I wanted something sweet for a buzz. There was a chocolate liqueur that I drank all the time in Holland called Vandermint, and I went through the place looking for it. It was up on a top shelf and I scored it. I was tall enough to reach. I opened the bottle right there in the store and took a few chugs. "Well," I said to the guy, "I guess we bought it." He started to laugh. "Hey," I said. "Do you have any money?" He stopped laughing and gave me a twenty-dollar bill.

At Danny Hutton's house in Laurel Canyon, there was a party going on. Danny always had a party going on back then. There were girls and drugs and everything. I went straight to his records, found the 45s, and started pulling them one by one. The Four Tops. "Nope," I said. Ray Stevens. "Nope." Rare Earth. "Nope." I didn't stop until I found the one I wanted, and then I held it up so everyone could see it. "I knew Danny would have this one," I said. It was "Be My Baby," sung by the Ronettes, written and produced by Phil Spector. I put it on the turntable.

The opening of that record, the thumping drums, sent me back a decade, to the fall of 1963. This was before the Kennedy assassination, before "The Warmth of the Sun." I was driving down the street listening to the radio and the DJ came on and announced a new song. It was "Be My Baby" and it just knocked me out. I think I said something out loud, even though I was the only one in the car. I said, "What in the heck?" and then I pulled over to the side of the road and listened to the rest of the record so I could hear the chorus again. I tried to figure out how all the instruments were working.

Before Spector, people recorded all the instruments separately. They got great piano, great guitar, and great bass. But he thought of the song as one giant instrument. It was huge. Size was so important to him, how big everything sounded. And he had the best drums I ever heard. The song was on the radio, which meant that it was coming to me from far away, but it was also right there with me in the car. It reminded me of the BB gun I had when I was young, which was the strangest thing. There was a bean field to the east of our house, and one day there was a guy sitting out there on a motorcycle. When I fired the BB gun, the guy just fell off his motorcycle. I thought maybe it was because I had hit him with the BB. It could have been a coincidence, but I thought about it in that way, that I had affected this guy in the bean field. That's how great music worked, too. You were out in a bean field and something hit you when you were least expecting it and knocked you off your motorcycle.

In Danny's house that day, when I put "Be My Baby" on the record player, I couldn't stop listening to the intro. Those drums were so huge the way that Phil Spector did them. I played the beginning ten times until everyone in the room told me to stop, and then I played it ten more times.

‿

In the meantime our old label, Capitol, had put out *Endless Summer*, a double album with all our early hits that was named after the famous surf movie. *Endless Summer*, the album, came out in 1974 and started selling like crazy, and that made Capitol put out a second set of hits, *Spirit of America*. Both of them had cool illustrated covers. *Endless Summer* had all our faces. *Spirit of America* had Mickey Mouse and a baseball glove and a girl lying down with the Playboy bunny logo on her underwear.

Al and Mike noticed how well the two Capitol albums were doing—there was no way not to notice. They figured it was a sign we should capitalize on people's love for our old music. Our record label, Brother Records, temporarily got the rights back to our old songs and put out a compilation of our own, *Good Vibrations*, on Reprise. That sold pretty well but not as well as the Capitol records. But Al and Mike weren't just interested in rereleases. They wanted to make more music like "I Get Around" or "The Warmth of the Sun." There were other ideas in the room, too. I rejoined the group with ideas similar to what the guys in California Music were doing. I wanted to do covers only of old songs, to make a record about the records that I loved. Dennis and Carl wanted to keep going forward and making new music like what we were making on *Holland*. They didn't want to go back to the '60s, or the '50s either.

We had long discussions about the best direction—endless discussions, you could say. And Dr. Landy was in lots of them. He was trying to get me into shape, but he thought that also meant getting the group into shape and putting himself in the middle of the way we talked to each other. He dragged us through some real marathon conversations. I remember one that lasted six hours, without a break. Everyone said what they thought, and also said they heard what everyone else was saying, and then said they thought it was important for everyone to be heard. Even though I was the only one officially with Dr. Landy, lots of the guys had gotten into similar things, gurus or meditation or special diets. Mike had been into it for years, since the late '60s, and it had been in his songs.

We talked so much that I decided we should call the album *Group Therapy*. That was the name of a band Ray Kennedy was in back in the '60s, and that might have been in the back of my mind, but mainly I thought of it because it summed up everything that was happening at the time. It summed up the arguments over creative direction, and the difficulty of me coming back to the group, and the arrival of Dr. Landy. But the band didn't go for it. I guess they thought it showed people too much of what we were going through. We renamed the album *15 Big Ones*, because we had been making music for fifteen years and there were fifteen songs on the record. I didn't like the cover for that album very much. It was an Olympic year so they made an Olympic cover, with five rings and the guys from the group inside them. It ended up looking like a game show, *Hollywood Squares* or something. I'm in the top middle ring, which is white on the album cover but black in the Olympics logo.

I loved the version of "That Same Song." Marilyn sang the high part on it because it was out of my range. She has a great voice. But those moments were rare. That album was a compromise. No one was really in control. You need control in life. You need self-control, and you need control over ideas. The reason for control is that it lets one idea happen instead of two or more ideas that don't happen. That's why you have a control room in a recording studio or a TV studio. But control isn't all good. It can make harmony, but it can also lead to hurt feelings from the people who aren't in control. That can happen with husbands and wives. That can happen with parents and children. That can happen with doctors and patients.

A lack of control leads to other problems. When *15 Big Ones* came out, the record company made a big deal that I was on it. They had a big campaign with a "Brian's Back!" slogan, and they had a TV special for us where we sang "That Same Song" with a gospel choir and did a comedy sketch with the Blues Brothers. Well, they weren't the Blues Brothers in that sketch. They were the guys from the Blues Brothers and they played cops who came and got me out of my room and made me go outside and surf. It was kind of a kick. Belushi and Aykroyd—funny guys.

But I was really thinking about the album, and how the ghost of that original album I wanted to make, the old rock and roll record, was there underneath everything else. And the parts of the record that were great in so many ways. Carl was out of sight on "Palisades Park." It's one of my top five Beach Boys vocals. He nailed it. I always heard one lyric, "the girl I sat beside was awful cute," as "the girl I sat beside was . . . aw, fuck you." It makes no sense in the song, but that's how I heard it. The great original was by Freddy Cannon, who also did "Tallahassee Lassie," but Carl knocked it completely out of the park. For "Just Once in My Life," he and I sang together and I played the synthesizers and piano. We had a great time singing. With that and "Chapel of Love," I had laryngitis. I wasn't using my normal voice. It was an assumed voice. I had to make it up to get through all the singing. For me, it's basically a laryngitis album.

It's also a Phil Spector album. Many of the songs on 15 Big Ones are songs he did first. As a producer, Phil did the originals of "Just Once in My Life" and "Chapel of Love." His version of that, with the Dixie Cups, was on top of the charts when the Beach Boys first charted in 1964. There was even a song of his that almost no one knew, "Talk to Me."

Phil Spector is one of the main reasons I wanted to make 15 Big Ones a record about old rock and roll, because he's one of the main reasons I wanted to make rock and roll. His records meant everything to me when I was learning how to become a producer. If albums are all about control, he was the ultimate in control. I knew about voices, or at least knew something about them, from pretty early on. I listened to harmony groups and figured out how all the voices came together. I worked with lots of other producers when I was young, and lots of them taught me things—tricks with vocals or instruments, how to double track or where to place a microphone—but I think I learned the most from listening to Phil Spector's records. I always say he's the one who taught me how to produce records.

Hearing "Be My Baby" in my car was the first lesson. A few days after that, I drove over to the studio in Ventura where Phil Spector was working. I went in to meet him. He knew about the Beach Boys because "Surfin' U.S.A." had been a big hit and everyone was talking about board shorts and huaraches. I told him that I had heard "Be My Baby" and it was fantastic. We talked about other songs. "Then He Kissed Me" was just a few months old. He told me he was just starting on a Christmas album, which was exciting for me to hear. But "Be My Baby" stayed so important to me.

Years later I went to see Phil Spector at United Western Recorders. It was in the mid-'90s, and he was producing Celine Dion for a big comeback record that never ended up happening. Phil sometimes had bowling parties, and he sometimes invited me. Melinda and I were going to go and then I crapped out. Phil never invited me again. And then years after that, I was playing at B. B. King's in New York and songwriter Ellie Greenwich came backstage to see me. I hugged her. "Every single day I wake up and thank you," I said. She looked confused. "You know," I said, "for writing 'Be My Baby' for me." That's how I felt—that it was just for me. There have been other songs that hit me almost as hard: "Rock Around the Clock," "Keep A-Knockin'," "You've Lost That Lovin' Feeling," "Hey Girl." But it's hard to re-create the feeling of first hearing "Be My Baby."

∽

When you think songs are just for you, you pay special attention to them, and then you grow from them. It's like a building going up. You have a foundation, and then you keep adding stories until you look down and you're so far from the ground that you don't know how you got up there. That's how it's always been for me.

When I was first interested in music, I took a class in high school with a guy named Fred Morgan. He was an interesting teacher. He taught us that music was a contrast, pale parts versus emotional parts, and that not all the instruments in a song had to go in the same direction. He failed me in the class because I didn't know how to write classical music, but he got me thinking about some of the different ways music can work. Later on I ran into him at a high school reunion. "You failed my class, but you scored big in music," he said. My own ideas were just beginning, but I knew I was on the right track when I heard myself playing the boogie-woogie Uncle Charlie taught me.

A little later I learned how to write manuscript music from a friend of my dad's named Dean Brownell. He taught me how to really notate: to get down quarter notes, half notes, eighth notes. Around that time my dad got me a tape recorder, a Capitol, and it did this thing called ping-pong where you could record many voices and mix them down to a single track. I tried to record a Four Freshmen song on that by having my mom, dad, Dennis, and Carl sing on the tape recorder with me. The song was called "It's a Blue World": "It's a blue world without you / It's a through world for me." We all sang together and it was beautiful.

After the Freshmen, I heard bits and pieces of melody in my head, but I couldn't focus on anything concrete. It was like watching goldfish swim around. They dart one way and you see a little flash of orange, but you don't really know whether they're coming or going. But then one afternoon I was in my car and I thought of a piece that grew into a longer piece. It started out with me humming a Disney song, "When You Wish Upon a Star," which Dion and the Belmonts sang. Their record was red like the Harry Belafonte album with "Jamaica Farewell." I started humming that, but it changed in my head. It combined with other songs I knew, like the Four Freshmen's "Little Girl Blue," and eventually it didn't sound like anything I had heard before. It sounded like maybe it was my own. I wrote part of it in my head in my car, and then I finished it when I got back to the house. That song ended up being "Surfer Girl." It was a slow ballad. The harmonies I heard in it were sort of like the harmonies I heard from the Four Freshmen, but they were only a foundation. I built something on top of that foundation, and it was sort of my own house. We recorded it at Hite Morgan's, but that version never got released. I mean, much later it did, on a big box set, but it wasn't released on a real record.

The one that everyone knows was recorded later. Still, even then, I had done it. I had written a song and the group had recorded it.

It's been more than fifty years now, and I wonder all the time about what let me think I could write something of my own, that I could build something on top of the foundation I got from other singers and groups. What made me think I could have my own songs? There must have been something deep inside me, another kind of foundation. Part of it came from my dad, who also loved music and who also wrote songs. Part of it came from all the people around me who loved music and wrote songs. Al wrote songs. Mike hummed things he heard and tried to make them into something. But there was something deep down in there that wasn't in other people.

In lots of interviews people have asked me what I would have been if I'd been born in a different time. I think I would have been a classical composer. But not like Mozart, Beethoven, or Tchaikovsky. I would have been like Bach, using counterpoint, layering things. Of all the composers, he's the one who makes the most sense to me. *Switched-On Bach*, the Walter Carlos record, was one of the most electrifying albums I ever heard. When I first heard it, which was right around the time we were finishing *Friends*, it turned me on so much that I can't even explain it. It was so intricate and so clear at the same time.

I didn't grow up in a time of classical music, though. I grew up in a time of pop music. And "Surfer Girl" was the first real song I wrote. It didn't come out for a while, though. In fact, it didn't come out until our third album. It had just come out when I met Phil Spector. I don't remember if he mentioned it. It seems like the kind of thing I should remember but I don't. I just know that hearing "Be My Baby" on the car radio made me feel so alive. And what it did to my brain and the sounds that were in there was like a rebirth. It was a leap forward.

～

Those early years were all leaps forward.

When we put out "Surfin'" as our first single on Candix, I didn't know where things were headed. We were all running around in the street thrilled to hear it, but maybe it wouldn't be any more than that. Maybe we would be older and working in different jobs and call each other on the phone and remember that time when it came on the radio and we ran around in the street. People in rock and roll have long careers now, but the whole thing was pretty new back then. Would it last a year? Would it last two years? I remember my dad talking about our hits and saying it was hard to imagine it going much past that.

But it went a little past one song, at least. "Surfin'" was moving along and people were asking us for a second song. I had written "Surfer Girl," but it wasn't time for that yet. It was a ballad. Mike and I had another fast song. We had written "Surfin' Safari" and we went in and recorded it for Hite Morgan. At that point, because "Surfin'" was a hit, we knew we needed to sign to a bigger label. We looked for one. My dad looked with us. He brought us around to everyone. We sat in so many offices and heard Dad explain our kind of music to guys his age. They usually nodded slowly. Sometimes there were younger guys in the room who nodded more quickly. But when we left it wasn't with a good feeling. We were rejected by labels like Dot and Liberty. Decca, who turned down the Beatles, turned us down also.

Eventually we met with a guy named Nick Venet from Capitol Records. Nick was a little older than me, but he had been around for a while. He had started off in jazz, working with people like Chet Baker and Stan Getz, and then came to Capitol, where he signed the Lettermen. They had a hit with "The Way You Look Tonight." Nick understood harmonies and he understood song and he liked our sound. My dad arranged for him to take us onto the label. People say that my dad was pushy, and he sure was. But he had a sense of how songs got put together and how to fight to have songs heard. There are so many things that I wish wouldn't have happened with my dad, but without him, nothing would have happened. That's the thing about a foundation. You have to have it to build up from it.

Capitol liked "Surfin' Safari" as our second song. But they said we needed to rerecord it. Whenever we made new songs, I would write and arrange them and Nick and my dad would produce them. Nick was the most pleasant guy, and I learned so much from him.

We started to work with other people, too. A friend of ours named David Marks, who used to come over to the house to sing, joined the band playing rhythm guitar, and another friend of ours named Gary Usher started working with us writing new songs. Gary's uncle lived near us in Hawthorne and got to talking with my dad about music. Someone said that we had a band, and someone else said that Gary was a good musician and that he could also write lyrics. That was great for me, because I liked having someone who could take the things I was thinking and turn them into the right kinds of words.

Gary also had some production knowledge, even though he was only a few years older. He taught me how to open up my voice by putting track on top of track. The first Beach Boys song we tried that with was "Surfin' U.S.A." I went to Mike and told him what Gary told me, that you could sing on top of your own singing. We also did some songs where Gary was out in front, though they didn't get released. One was called "One Way Road to Love." We sang backup on that and we didn't really mesh with Gary's vocals—he had a kind of early-rock hiccupping thing going, a Buddy Holly sound. Another one was called "My Only Alibi." We hung back on that with the backing vocals, and that made it better. Phil Spector taught me to put in everything, but other people taught me that sometimes what you didn't include was as important as what you did include.

> Why do you expect more than my love, dear
> Why can't you accept it as it is
> I can only love you just so much, dear
> Don't you know that's all that I can give?
> Human
> I'm only human

At some point along the way I ended up producing a song. What that meant was that I was the one telling people what to do, and that the song had my name on it. As a producer, I also said that I thought we needed to do the song at Western Recorders, which was a place Gary liked, instead of at Capitol's own studio. I was proud of making decisions but also scared. If you made decisions, if you had control, then that meant you were responsible for what happened. That first song I produced was "Surfer Girl." I had sung it so many times in my own head, and the group had sung it at Hite Morgan's. But at Western it was different. The melody was sweet and had a little rise and fall like waves. The band back then was just the family—the extended family, with Carl playing guitar and Dennis drumming and me playing bass and David Marks also playing guitar. Some producers maybe went into the studio without ideas, but I was too nervous for that. I had everything worked out in my head before. It was the only way I could imagine getting from one place to the next. But to keep everyone moving forward I also tried to joke a little bit. I would say, "Take two" and then before anyone played a note say, "Take three."

"Surfer Girl" was a song about love, or at least a song that wondered about love.

> *Little surfer, little one*
> *Made my heart come all undone*
> *Do you love me, do you surfer girl*
> *Surfer girl, my little surfer girl*

The guy in the song sounds like he hasn't even talked to the surfer girl. He just watches her and thinks about her. That was me. I was kind of shy, and whenever I started talking to a girl she would end up talking to Dennis or Mike instead. They were slicker and more aggressive, and I sort of got moved off to the side to wonder if the girl ever liked me or was interested at all. I felt a little lonely at times, but I also knew that it made for good songs. Loneliness was something that everyone felt but that people were afraid to talk about. That was something I learned from the Four Freshmen. They always had an ache in their songs—not just in their voices but about the things they were singing.

The big early song everyone wants to point to as being about loneliness is "In My Room." People say it's about how I pulled back from the world. The funny thing is that it was a song Gary wrote with me and we all sang on it—me and Dennis and Carl and Mike and Al. Two people wrote a song about loneliness, and five people sang it. We worked out the harmonies over and over again until they had a certain sound. I didn't think of it as sad, really. I wanted it to be beautiful. I think that came through. When Gary and I first wrote it, we were in Hawthorne playing outside. We were probably throwing a baseball back and forth and pretending we were the Yankees. Then we went home and thought of the idea for the song. It came together quick, maybe an hour to get the basics. My parents were coming in and out while we were working. My mom loved it. She told Gary that it was beautiful. Even my dad liked it. He was a tough critic, but he told Gary he did a good job.

⌐

Time jumps from the fall of 1961, when we heard "Surfin'" on the radio, to the summer of 1963, when we heard "Surfer Girl." It jumps from 1958, when I was in my bedroom with my brothers teaching them "Ivory Tower," to 1965, when we were all over the radio.

Time jumps and sometimes time lands. It really landed in 1964. That seemed like more than one year. We played more than a hundred shows, all over the world, and recorded all or parts of four albums. We had our first number one hit with "I Get Around" in May, over "My Boy Lollipop." The flip side of "I Get Around" might be one of the best songs I ever wrote, "Don't Worry Baby." I wrote it with Phil Spector in mind. I thought it could be the follow-up to "Be My Baby" for Ronnie Spector, but Phil Spector didn't go for it. That year, it didn't matter. It was Beatlemania and it was Motownmania, but it was also us-mania. We were one of the biggest things going. And then we were one of the biggest things gone: the year ended with my freak-out on the plane to Houston. That shook everything down to its foundation. It turned out what we were building the whole year went up too fast, and it toppled.

But all year, we built. We started 1964 with *Shut Down Volume 2*, an album that we started recording on New Year's Day. The name was a little strange—maybe a little more than strange. We hadn't recorded a *Shut Down Volume 1*. We had a song called "Shut Down" that had been on our album *Little Deuce Coupe*, and when Capitol released a compilation of hit songs in 1963, they included that song and even named the record after it. It was enough of a hit that people thought it made sense to name our next album *Shut Down Volume 2*. Did it make sense? We had a title song on there, but it wasn't really anything like "Shut Down." It was an instrumental that Carl wrote. Carl also sang his first lead on "Pom, Pom Play Girl."

When we were making "Surfin'" or "Surfer Girl," we still played like we were a real band. We had my piano and bass and Carl and David Marks on guitar and Dennis drumming. But for *Shut Down Volume 2*, we had started to be a real thing, both in California and in the country, and that meant that when we went into the studio to record, we got to play with older studio musicians. The ones we used were the best in LA. You could play them a song once and they would play it right back to you, and add in their own ideas along with yours. Later on, people called them the Wrecking Crew, but at the time I don't think people called them that. But they called them all the time. They worked with Phil Spector, which was one of the reasons I knew about them, and they worked with Jan and Dean on "Surf City." That was a song I wrote, or started writing but didn't finish, and Jan and Dean finished it up. It was a huge hit for them, the first surf song to go to number one.

It was a little weird that another group had a number one with my song. My dad wasn't happy about it at all, but I didn't mind. I thought it was cool that there was a sound starting to happen, a sound that had started with "Surfin'." It was like a little family of songs. It was melodies I was making and lyrics that other people were adding and sounds that arrangers and players were making. The guys who would later be called the Wrecking Crew were on "Surf City." Hal Blaine drummed, and so did Earl Palmer. Billy Strange, who arranged the record, liked to have two drummers, and so did Jan. It made it bigger, closer to the huge sound that Phil Spector was getting.

I especially didn't mind Jan and Dean having a number one hit with "Surf City" because it taught record companies that it made sense to spend money on groups like us. It's another kind of foundation, a business foundation: when you see that there are lots of people going to a store to buy things, you add another floor to the store. At that time there were actually two families of songs that were close cousins: surf songs and hot-rod songs. Surf songs were about going to the ocean and getting sun and catching waves and looking at girls. Hot-rod songs were about getting in the car with your buddies and driving around with the top down and getting burgers and looking at girls. Our car songs were written with Gary Usher and sometimes with a guy named Roger Christian, who wrote "Little Deuce Coupe," "Shut Down," and "Car Crazy Cutie":

> Well, my steady little doll is a real live beauty
> And everybody knows she's a car crazy cutie
> She's hip to everything, man, from customs to rails
> And axle grease imbedded 'neath her fingernails
> Wo yeah (Run a-run a doo ron ron)
> Wo oh oh oh (Wo run a-run a doo ron ron)
> Oh oh oh now cutie (Wo run a-run a doo ron ron)
> Oh oh oh oh oh oh oh oh (Wo run a-run a doo ron ron)

That was on the *Little Deuce Coupe* album, too. Those are the songs that got people to think we were into car culture, and I guess we were, through them.

Even though "Shut Down" and the Capitol compilation album were part of the hot-rod thing, most of the songs on our *Shut Down Volume 2* album weren't. "Fun, Fun, Fun" was, and it was a big hit. But other songs were love songs, like "The Warmth of the Sun" or "Keep an Eye on Summer." Thirty-five years after we did *Shut Down Volume 2*, I rerecorded "Keep an Eye on Summer" for *Imagination*. Remaking a song is strange, especially when it's a song you did when you were young. You try to remember the things about it that made you happy the first time so you can get some of those feelings into your singing. Otherwise it's just new technology and new musicians doing the same song. Another thing about a remake is that you're aiming at a target. The second "Keep an Eye on Summer," even if it had different ideas from Joe Thomas or me, was still trying to get parts of the original. The original was the bull's-eye.

It was completely different when we took songs in for the first time. When we showed up at the studio with a song I had written, there wasn't any bull's-eye yet. We were firing arrow after arrow. There wasn't any foundation yet. We were pouring concrete. When I try to think of an example of how that worked, I think about the crazy year of 1964, and I think about one of the most important songs from that crazy year, "When I Grow Up (To Be a Man)." We did that song in early August, and it was out by the end of the month. That's how fast everything went back then. The building was going up overnight.

We did that song at Western, too, in room three, which was the best. We did almost forty takes over six days. Can you believe that, forty takes? You can hear me counting each one out. Sometimes we got as far as a few bass notes from Al Jardine before it fell apart. Sometimes we got through my first piano part. We didn't even get to the vocals for a while, but when we did, those gave me fits, too. I wanted it to sound like an update of the Four Freshmen, but my voice sounded too thin. People tell me you can find those tapes sometimes circulating around, with names like "When I Grow Up (To Be a Man) (2nd vocal overdub take 14)." It's exhausting to look at, and to think of how far we went in search of the perfect thing. We didn't know we were making history. But that's what we were making.

Sometimes, even when I worked as hard as I could, I didn't line up with the rest of the band. Sometime during that crazy year, I wrote a song with Russ Titelman called "Guess I'm Dumb." It took a while to get it right because I was trying something more adult. I was trying to score a Burt Bacharach vibe. I think we did twenty-three takes of that one. When I was finished, no one from the band wanted to sing it. The message was okay, but maybe it was just the idea of being dumb. Glen Campbell had been singing my parts in concerts so I gave it to him.

> *The way I act don't seem like me*
> *I'm not on top like I used to be*
> *I'll give in when I know I should be strong*
> *I still give in even though I know it's wrong*
> *I guess I'm dumb but I don't care*

It's a sad song, and also one that was easy to think about when I was in charge of the band. Later on, when I didn't run the band as much, it was difficult for me to listen to. The Beach Boys never recorded it, but Glen played it in concert for most of his career.

࿇

There are so many songs from that period they seem like one big song. We're singing that same song. All year long I picked things up and tried to make them into songs. Usually I didn't even have time to really look at what I was picking up. In summer 1964 we put out *All Summer Long*. There is a real maturing of our sound on that record. There's a start-stop cadence on "I Get Around" with a driving bass. Nobody had done a record like that before. There's a great instrumental break on the title song, all these subtle shifts that then feed back into a really stellar group harmony. In "Little Honda" I used a fuzz-tone bass. Carl thought it sounded like shit, but I knew it would be great. Our last real surf-type song, "Girls on the Beach," is on that record. Dennis does a nice job on the bridge, and our harmonies are just out of sight. That whole album is a turning point for me and for the band—or maybe it makes more sense to say it's a turning point for how I understood how to write for the band.

After that we rolled right into our Christmas album, and after that I got on the plane to go to Houston. Houston and everything that came after it was a change, definitely, because after that I started to use the studio differently. I tried to take the things I had learned from Phil Spector and use more instruments whenever I could. I doubled up on basses and tripled up on keyboards. That made everything sound bigger and deeper. I was able to do more ballads and give them their own feel. *The Beach Boys Today!*, which came out in early 1965, was made both before and after Houston. It was the first time I could do songs like "Please Let Me Wonder" that had all this space in them. I was also smoking a little bit of pot then, and that changed the way I heard arrangements.

Chuck Britz was our engineer on those records. He liked the way I worked, to have ideas coming in and then add more ideas, and put everything in place right away. He wasn't the kind of person to linger in the studio and wait for inspiration. I remember him telling Mike that he needed to stay focused. "You can't screw around because I gotta go in a half hour," he'd say. And he meant it, too. If Mike didn't listen, Chuck would just split.

But that was also the beginning of control issues. Capitol didn't get the hits they wanted from *The Beach Boys Today!* The songs were great. Everyone thought so. "Do You Wanna Dance?" and "Dance, Dance, Dance" were successful. But they weren't successful the way Capitol imagined. They imagined a situation where the tower of

With my grandfather in California in the mid-1940s.
(BriMel Archives)

Outside the Hawthorne house with Dennis and Carl, 1953.
(BriMel Archives)

I couldn't hit the curve—Hawthorne in the 1950s.
(BriMel Archives)

More ball with Dennis and Carl—Hawthorne in the 1950s.
(BriMel Archives)

Being true to
my school in 1959.
(BriMel Archives)

A school concert from very early in the band's career. *(BriMel Archives)*

B+

My Philosophy

Being the first time I have taken a close look at my philosophy, I find it hard to reveal my beliefs about living. I will try to give my general impression of life.

The first thing that I find about myself is that I am constantly trying to improve myself. I try to keep as healthy as possible and have good morals. I don't want to settle with a mediocre life, but make a name for myself in my life's work, which I hope will be music. The satisfaction of a <u>place</u> in the world seems well worth a sincere effort to me.

I think that the type of character that a person develops comes largely with the background of family living. A family should live co-ordinately and happily together. The type of disposition, the taste, and ambition a person possesses is reflected by his family relations. I am fortunate to have parents who are interested in the way I develop my character, and how I act. Not all people grow up with brothers or sisters; however, it is a good way to learn how to get along with others, and to understand people. Maybe the most important aspect of family living is generosity or the ability to share willingly. I don't like greedy people.

I feel that a lot of people

My Philosophy—a paper I wrote in high school. (*BriMel Archives*) make the mistake of getting married before they have learned about life and before they have fully matured. I don't plan to get married until I have had an education and some money in the bank. I think that a person can get married with more confidence if he is prepared. I have often wondered what the girl I marry will be like. I want someone who will love me (of course), and who will reason with me and understand my way of living. Right now the thought of having kids sounds like a large responsibility, but I know I will have at least two kids. I want my kids to be healthy and good-natured. I will try to raise them in such a way that they will have confidence and the desire to make a good living.

I go to church every Christmas and Easter but I have certain beliefs. I think that a person can live with more confidence if he has a religion in which he faithfully believes in. When life gets rough most people go to God one time in their life. This is an optimistic way of thinking. Most people who believe in a God are happy. I think that a person should be able to choose his own religion regardless of his parents beliefs.

a slightly unfinished sound!

An early live gig; my dad's lurking in the background. *(BriMel Archives)*

Cutting the
Surfin' Safari album,
with David Marks, in 1962.
(Courtesy Capitol Records)

Rehearsal at the
Hollywood Bowl
in 1963.
(BriMel Archives)

I started out onstage; this is the Beach Boys live in 1964. *(BriMel Archives)*

In 1964 we went everywhere, including Paris.
(Courtesy Capitol Records)

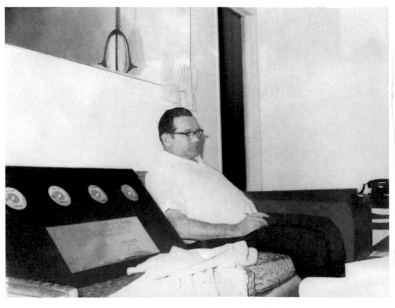

The great Murry Wilson. *(BriMel Archives)*

hits would just keep going higher and higher. After *The Beach Boys Today!*, they put pressure on us to bring them big sales. If it's what they wanted, it's what I wanted to give them. The next record, *Summer Days (And Summer Nights!!)*, was probably our best rock and roll album. It had "Help Me, Rhonda," a song Al sang lead on that was a remake of a song from *The Beach Boys Today!* It went to number one. That was one of the hits that Capitol wanted. There was another big hit on that album, but I don't remember what it was at the moment. Oh, I remember: "California Girls." I was just joking. How could I forget "California Girls"? It's one of my favorite songs of anything we ever did. It's our anthem song. If you ask people to name one Beach Boys song, that's probably the one they'll name.

The idea of "California Girls" is that there's this guy who thinks about girls all the time, so much that he starts to imagine all kinds. But there's only one kind he really wants, and that's the kind that's right there at home. The music started off like those old cowboy movies, when the hero's riding slowly into town, *bum-ba-dee-dah*. I was playing that at the piano after an acid trip. I played it until I almost couldn't hear what I was playing, and then I saw the melody hovering over the piano part.

When we got into the studio with Chuck, he said that he wanted Carl's twelve-string guitar in the intro to sound more direct. I didn't know what that meant. "Can he play it in the booth?" Chuck said. I had never thought about that before, but it seemed like a good idea. Carl was standing next to me in the booth and all the other musicians were out in the studio. I conducted it like an orchestra. It's not often that you get a perfect song, but that was one of them. It was so perfect that when David Lee Roth did it twenty years later—and reached the same spot on the charts, number three—he used Carl to sing backup on it to keep the vibe. I love that version. My favorite part is where he ad-libs, "I dig the girls."

When we released "California Girls" as a single, we put another great song on the B-side, "Let Him Run Wild." When I came off the road after I freaked out on the flight to Houston, I spent lots of time in my apartment, thinking about the perfect songs for the group. We had done so many surfing songs and so many hot-rod songs by that point, and I wanted to branch out. I wanted to write songs about relationships. I was growing in my normal life and I wanted to grow up musically. I thought about how love worked sometimes but went bad other times. "Let Him Run Wild" was about a girl who was dating a guy who didn't stay close to her. The guy singing wants the girl to let her boyfriend run around and eventually leave her so he can come in and get her. He wants a bad thing to happen so that it'll turn into a good thing.

We recorded that song with the Wrecking Crew again, just like on *Shut Down Volume 2*. Leon Russell played piano for us. Carol Kaye played bass. Those are two pretty great ways to replace yourself on instruments. The only thing wrong with it was me. I never liked my lead on it. It's a crapped-out lead. It's an abortion of a lead. Sometimes I think about going back and fixing it. I could, but I haven't. But I can hear everyone else and how great they're doing; I can hear Carl, Dennis, Mike, Al, and Bruce. I can pick out Carl especially. The whole thing goes by in a little more than two minutes, and even with the screechiness, there's one part I can never get past without remembering how great it felt to make songs with the band. It's the pair of lines that lead into the final chorus:

> *And now that you don't need him*
> *Well, he can have his freedom*

Some songs come and go. Other songs last. "Let Him Run Wild" was one of those songs that lasted. I ended up rerecording it for *Imagination*.

But those weren't the only songs on the record I liked. I liked "Salt Lake City" and "Amusement Parks U.S.A." as much as anything we ever did. I really got off on them. When I listened to them again in later years, they brought back memories. I remember going to Salt Lake City on tour, and on a day off we went to the lake itself. It was amazing. It was so salty that you didn't have to paddle. You could just lie on the top of the water and float. Also, in town there was a bar called the Lagoon with more pretty girls than you could ever imagine. We put that in the song. My dad was with us on that tour and he wouldn't let us drink beer. It was like we were Mormons ourselves. Except that Dennis and Mike didn't listen. They went off on their own. I mostly kept to myself or stayed at the hotel and talked to girls down in the lobby. One girl stayed and talked to me for a long time and a few weeks later sent me a letter. Marilyn read it and didn't like it at all. The girl had ideas about how things might go with us that weren't what a wife would want to see. It made things harder at home for a little while there.

ℰℴ

We weren't working in a vacuum. The year was busy for us, but it was busy all around us. Rock and roll was taking over, and it was taking over fast.

One of the most important parts of the takeover was the Beatles. During *Summer Days (And Summer Nights!!)*, I wrote a song called "Girl Don't Tell Me." It was one of the first songs that Carl sang lead on, and one of the only songs we did from that time where we didn't sing in back of him. It was almost like a different sound. That's because I had written it with John Lennon in mind. I even thought about giving it to the Beatles. People said it sounded like "Ticket to Ride," but I didn't mean for it to sound like any one song of theirs. It just had that feel. People talk about a rivalry between the Beach Boys and the Beatles, but that's not the right word. There were messages that got sent back and forth across the ocean. They would do something and I would hear it and then I would want to do something just as good. When they played on *Ed Sullivan* in February of 1964, the world went crazy. Seven months later, we were on *Ed Sullivan*, too. And they were putting out records almost as fast as we were—*The Beatles' Second Album* and *A*

Hard Day's Night right after the Sullivan show, and later *Beatles for Sale* and *Beatles VI* and *Help!*

But the one that really got me was *Rubber Soul*, which came out at the end of 1965. *Rubber Soul* is probably the greatest record ever. Maybe the Phil Spector Christmas record is right up there with it, and it's hard to say that the Who's *Tommy* isn't one of the best, too. But *Rubber Soul* came out in December of 1965 and sent me right to the piano bench. It's a whole album of Beatles folk songs, a whole album where everything flows together and everything works. I remember being blown away by "You Won't See Me" and "I'm Looking Through You" and "Girl." It wasn't just the lyrics and the melodies but the production and their harmonies. They had such unique harmonies, you know? In "You Won't See Me," Paul sings low and George and John sing high. There's an organ drone in there, a note that's held down for the last third of the song or so. Those were touches they were trying, almost art music. What was so great about the Beatles was you could hear their ideas so clearly in their music. They didn't pose like some other bands, and they didn't try to stuff too much meaning in their songs. They might be singing a song about loneliness or a song about anger or a song about feeling down. They were great poets about simple things, but that also made it easier to hear the song. And they never did anything clumsy. It was like perfect pitch but for entire songs. Everything landed on its feet.

I met Paul McCartney later in the '60s, in a studio. I was almost always in a studio back then. He came by when we were at Columbia Square working on vocal overdubs, and we had a little chat about music. Everyone knows now that "God Only Knows" was Paul's favorite song—and not only his favorite Beach Boys song, but one of his favorite songs period. It's the kind of thing people write in liner notes and say on talk shows. When people read it, they kind of look at that sentence and keep going. But think about how much it mattered to me when I first heard it there on Sunset Boulevard. I was the person who wrote "God Only Knows," and here was another person—the person who wrote "Yesterday" and "And I Love Her" and so many other songs—saying it was his favorite. It really blew my mind. He wasn't the only Beatle who felt that way. John Lennon called me after *Pet Sounds*—phoned me up, I think the British say—to tell me how much he loved the record.

But Paul and I stayed in touch. Another time not too long after that he came to my house and told me about the new music he was working on. "There's one song I want you to hear," he said. "I think it's a nice melody." He put the tape on and it was "She's Leaving Home." My wife, Marilyn, was there, too, and she just started crying. Listening to Paul play a new song let me see my own songs more clearly. It was hard for me to think about the effect that my music had on other people, but it was easy to see when it was another songwriter.

More than thirty years later, I was opening for Paul Simon, which I didn't like. It was okay to share a bill with him, but we were playing to older crowds, and that meant the first act, which was me, played when the sun was still up and the crowd was still filing in. It was hard to have a good relationship with the people in the audience under those conditions. At the Greek Theatre in Los Angeles, I started the show when it was less than half full. We opened with "The Little Girl I Once Knew," then played "Dance, Dance, Dance," then "In My Room," and then a cover of the Barenaked Ladies' song "Brian Wilson." That was the strangest song we played back then. I didn't know about it until the guys in the band brought it to rehearsal. It was a song about a guy who is trying to write a song and can't and he compares himself to me when I was under the treatment of Dr. Landy. In the song, the guy has a dream that he gets up to 300 pounds and then starts floating until the ground is so far away that he can't see it anymore. I never had that dream, but I was cool with playing the song if we did a good job. We went through some more hits: "California Girls," "I Get Around," "Wouldn't It Be Nice." After "Add Some Music to Your Day," we started in on "God Only Knows." Right at that moment, the side door opened and Paul McCartney walked in. Everyone saw him. The theater erupted with applause and everyone stood up cheering for him. I saw Carnie in the audience put her hand to her mouth in shock. It was an "oh my God" moment. I waved from the piano. But waving wasn't enough. We were going into the final verse and I changed the lyrics on the fly to "God only knows what I'd be without Paul." After the set Pablo came backstage. That's what I call Paul sometimes, Pablo. I was happy to see him. He said that when he was coming up to the Greek in the limo, he rolled down the window so he could hear the music. "I wanted to hear those Brian sounds," he said. He had a question about the intro to "You Still Believe in Me." There was a keyboard in the dressing room, so I just played it for him. We did harmonies. It was incredible, Paul McCartney and I harmonizing on the intro to "You Still Believe in Me." Can you believe that?

The other Beatle that got to me was George Harrison. He was so spiritual. He had a way of making things simple: "Give me life / Give me love / Give me peace on earth." I remember that during the early years of the Beatles, it was hard to think of him as a separate songwriter. But after "Here Comes the Sun," I started to pay attention to his songs as their own kind of thing. Maybe every group needed someone like that, a deeply soulful presence who wasn't exactly at the middle of the band. We had Carl. I never met George, but many years later I did a show for him. In 2015 his widow Olivia called and asked me to play at George Fest in Hollywood. "Hell yes," I said. We played "My Sweet Lord," but I would have done any of George's songs. He wrote beautiful ones.

The Beatles may have been at the top of the heap, but the Rolling Stones weren't far behind. They had so many great riff records. They always got me with whatever they had coming out: "Satisfaction," "Get Off of My Cloud." My favorite Rolling Stones song was from a little later, "My Obsession," from *Between the Buttons*. I was invited to the studio when they were mixing it down. The Stones were in and out that day. I didn't meet all of them at any one time.

But I was blown away by that song. It has that opening that's close to "Get Off of My Cloud," Charlie Watts drumming, and then that awesome combination of organ and piano in the left track. Later on they come back but with backing vocals, too, a string of *ooh babys* that are sort of like the *woo-woos* they would do later on in "Sympathy for the Devil." And the *ooh babys* are almost R-rated; it's really a record about a girl's body.

What's great about "My Obsession" is that it isn't just a riff record. Because Keith Richards came up with such awesome riffs, people forget to look deeper in; if they do, they'll find these complex production tricks and moments of sophistication and beauty. In a song like "Sad Day," which isn't a record that most people know, there's a great little piano part by Jack Nitzsche, who was a Phil Spector–like producer on his own. He wrote "The Lonely Surfer," which had one of the earliest examples of that guitar sound in spaghetti westerns. The Stones took all those influences. They could. Their own personality as a band was so strong. That's sort of how the Beach Boys worked. Whatever we brought in ended up being ours.

Over the years I have written some songs that are tributes to the Stones. There's "Add Some Music to Your Day." You can hear their guitar in there, especially at the beginning, and that driving vocal part where we sing, "add some, add some, add some music." Our voices are likes the Stones' guitars, and the arrangement is, too. Listen real close. I tried for their vibe. And I mentioned them in the lyrics, too: "There's blues, folk, and country, and rock like a rollin' stone." But our Stonesiest song ever was probably "Marcella," which is on *Carl and the Passions—So Tough.* "Marcella" isn't deep like some other songs. It's not "Sail On Sailor" or "'Til I Die." It's about a girl who worked at this massage parlor I used to go to. It's a lust song, plain and simple, like "My Obsession." Just before and after the two-minute mark, you can hear the Stones, or at least my version of them. I did most of that session, but then I went upstairs for a while because I was tired. When I was up there, they added the "hey, yeah, Marcella" part, which Al Jardine sings. My favorite lyric there is one of my favorite Beach Boys lyrics in general. Carl sang it:

> *One arm over my shoulder*
> *Sandals dance at my feet*
> *Eyes that knock you right over*
> *Ooo Marcella's so sweet*

Complicated ideas and simple ideas—so much of rock and roll is both of those. People thought rock and roll was party music at first. They liked hearing about the simple things, about partying and girls and teenage life, and that's what rock and roll showed them. There were always complicated things in my life, but I kept them in or put them off to the side. But then things around me started changing, and things in me started changing. The flight to Houston and the time I spent alone writing without the band after that was a big change, but it wasn't the only change. Everything started shifting. Maybe some of it was because of smoking pot and relaxing. When I wasn't quite so nervous I wasn't quite so afraid of things being complicated. Maybe some of it was learning more about songwriting and producing and how I could put more musical ideas into the songs I was making. "California Girls" was a huge pop hit, but it had another piece of music at the beginning that was nothing like a pop song. And even though *Summer Days (And Summer Nights!!)* was further toward the pop side of things, there was a little symphony on there called "Summer Means New Love." That was me on grand piano, and a whole string section. There were times I thought I was building on the foundation and times I thought I was tearing down what we had built and starting a whole new foundation.

⌒

What did that new foundation look like? It looked like it sounded. It was complicated, with many parts that stuck out in all directions, but if you looked at it from the right angle, you didn't see anything sticking out at all. You just saw that it was beautiful.

I started building that foundation after the plane flight to Houston. I did it with *Beach Boys Today!*, which was a step forward, and *Summer Days (And Summer Nights!!)*, which was another step. I did it with *Pet Sounds*, which was a great experience, and with *SMiLE*, which was such a bad experience in some ways that it has sometimes made it hard to talk about the great experience of *Pet Sounds.* That doesn't mean I won't talk about it. It just means that it's a situation like the situation with my dad. I need to think a little more carefully about how to talk about it. The one case where it's easy to talk about the new foundation I was building is "Good Vibrations." There's been lots written about how that song happened. People say that the record label and the band thought I was going too far into art music and that I needed to come back to hits. That's probably true. But that's not how the song got made.

How it got made was that I was high after smoking pot and sitting at the piano, relaxed, playing. Mike came through with the lyrics for me on this one. He heard me playing and singing the "Good, good, good vibrations" part. That excited him and he went from room to room talking out the idea of good vibrations—what it meant, that it was connected to the peace and love happening in San Francisco and everywhere else. When I started the song, I was thinking of it differently. I was thinking of how people sense instinctively if something is good news or bad news—sometimes when the telephone rings, you just know—and I was thinking of how my mom used to say that dogs could read a situation or a person immediately. I already had some lyrics—some that I wrote, some that Tony Asher wrote—but I was not happy with them. But as soon as Mike started rolling, I knew that there was something bigger in the lyric idea. It grew from there. Mike finally wrote the lyrics on his way to the studio in his car. It was the night we were cutting the lead vocals, and what he wrote fit perfectly.

There are so many moving pieces inside that song, so many musicians and ideas. Don Randi is on it, playing amazing keyboards as usual, though Larry Knechtel plays the organ parts. Carl plays one of the bass parts. There's the theremin sound, like the one I heard at my uncle Wendell's, though putting the theremin on the song was actually Carl's idea. He wanted it. Maybe he remembered Uncle Wendell's, too. So I called up the musicians union and they said they had a guy named Paul Tanner who played an electro-theremin, which isn't the kind that makes half steps or notes. It just goes *wooooo*. That's the one we used, obviously—*wooooo*. That's the most famous part of the song.

But there are so many other things, too. There's some Stephen Foster, in the "Gotta keep those lovin' good vibrations happenin' with her" part. I wouldn't say he was an influence, exactly, but one of his melodies drifted into there. There's the rhythm in the chorus, with those cellos playing triplets, kind of a nod to Phil Spector's trip. He did something similar on "Da Doo Ron Ron" with pianos. There's the lead vocal, which was supposed to be Dennis but ended up being Carl, except for the high notes on the verses, which I did. Dennis had a sore throat. "Good Vibrations" was like a musical autobiography of everything I had heard up until that time.

The most amazing thing was how many places it went, not just musically but actually. I wrote it all at the piano but then picked different studios to record different parts. The verses were done at Gold Star. The backup for the chorus was done at Western. And then there's a section in the middle, the "Ah, my, my, what elation," that was done at Sunset Sound. That's another reason I say that it was a musical autobiography, the way we passed back through all those other studios we used when we were young. This is your life. These are the sounds you made. Here they are, all in one song. Assembling the whole song was really something. I didn't know what I was in for. I didn't know until I got into it, and then I got so far into it that I got lost in it. There are more than eighty hours of tape if you add up all the parts and all the takes. And I didn't even play on the tracks. I sang. I directed. I wrote. I produced. The whole thing took about seven months, and the cost was gigantic, more than fifty thousand dollars. At the time, a Cadillac DeVille cost around five thousand.

But it worked. I knew we had it the night we cut the vocal at RCA Victor. The guys and I looked at each other and we just knew: number one song. When I finished the final mix, everyone was stunned. "I just can't believe this record," Carl said. Or maybe it was Mike. It was both of them. It was all of them. They all said it. I couldn't believe it either. My engineer was blown away. It was one of the greatest moments of my life. It's hard to say that one song is the top floor of the building you're trying to build. "California Girls" is near the top. "Caroline, No" is near the top. "The Warmth of the Sun" is near the top. They might be as high as anything else. But nothing's higher than "Good Vibrations." It gives people so much happiness and probably also will.

Todd Rundgren did a version of it about ten years after we made it where he tried to re-create the song exactly, all the instruments and all the voices, and he did a great job. He came real close. For years, because I wasn't touring, I couldn't play it live. That was a loss. That was something missing. In 1999 when I started going back onstage with the Wondermints, one of the most fun things was to play "Good Vibrations." We liked to stretch it out. At the Roxy, we made it last for more than six minutes. Any minute playing "Good Vibrations" is a minute that I feel spiritually whole. I hope that any minute hearing it is the same.

CHAPTER 4

Home

You take my hand
And you understand
When I get in a bad mood
You're so good to me
And I love it, love it
—"You're So Good to Me"

In the '80s I went down to the Martin Cadillac dealership at Pico and Bundy to get a car. Dr. Landy came with me, and two other guys came along also. If you asked him who they were, he would say they worked for me. But that wasn't true. They worked for him. They were supposed to take care of me, but mostly they just watched me and reported back to him. So we all got in a car and drove over to the dealership to pick out another car.

I didn't know so much about cars. I knew what a 409 was because of the song Gary wrote with us, and I was hip to everything from customs to rails because of "Car Crazy Cutie," but I couldn't tell you exactly what a power shift in second was. Dennis knew more. He worked on cars when we were younger and raced them when we were older. He always had great sports cars like Stingrays.

I had a few Corvettes also, but I can't remember what years they were. As I got older, I kind of switched over to sedans. Still, I knew what kinds of sedans I liked, and there was one I liked right near the front of the showroom, a brown Seville. I was standing next to it, touching the hood, when someone came up behind me. I thought it was one of Dr. Landy's guys, or maybe even Dr. Landy himself, but then I heard a woman's voice.

"What do you think?" she asked.

"It's nice," I said.

I turned to see the face that went with the voice. The saleslady was pretty, with long blond hair. She was wearing a skirt and my eyes went right to her legs. "Hi," I said.

"Hi." Her voice was nice and bright. It was the voice of someone who was interested in whether I wanted to buy a car, but it also sounded like maybe it was the voice of someone who was interested in me. "Melinda," she added, holding out her hand.

"I'm Brian," I said. Sometimes when I introduced myself people nodded quickly to show me they already knew who I was. That made me feel strange. Sometimes they pretended they didn't know, which made me feel even stranger. Melinda just looked straight at me when I was introducing myself, stayed calm, didn't do one thing or the other, and that made me feel normal.

We talked for a little while about the car. I didn't know exactly what to say. I was interested in buying the car, but I was just as interested in making the conversation with her last longer. I think I asked something about the seats and how comfortable they were even though I already knew the answer.

As we were talking, she kept looking over at Dr. Landy. She was looking at the other guys, too, who came along with us. She didn't say anything about them, but the way she looked at them made me feel like I wanted to talk to her. On the way upstairs, I started telling her about Dennis. He had died a few years before. "He was my brother," I said. I think she knew who Dennis was because when girls knew about the Beach Boys, Dennis was usually the one they knew. We talked some more upstairs, and then Dr. Landy came by and told me it was time to go. I couldn't leave without doing anything. I wrote a note on a card and left it on her desk. I put the only words on it that I could think of to describe how I was feeling: "Frightened, scared, lonely."

Maybe a week later I went back to pick up the car. Dr. Landy wasn't with me that time, just the bodyguards watching me. Melinda and I didn't talk much. But I talked about her to Dr. Landy, and about a week after that he called and asked her if she would be interested in going to a concert with me. He really meant "with us," but she said yes.

We went to see the Moody Blues at the Universal Amphitheatre. The Moody Blues had been around almost as long as the Beach Boys and they were still going strong, which was great. They had just put out the song "Your Wildest Dream," which was a big hit, and they were playing a bunch of shows in LA. I remembered playing at the Universal in 1983. Dennis wasn't with us. He had been put out of the band for a while. He was drinking more and more. I remember some shows that spring where he looked gray and baggy. He wasn't completely there, or maybe he wanted to be anywhere else. That was a time when people were put out of the band all the time. The year before that, the guys had put me out of the band for a while. I was drinking more and more. There were plenty of shows when I wasn't completely there. Around the time of that Beach Boys show at the Universal Amphitheatre, Dr. Landy came back. The guys in the group thought that it was the only way to keep me from disappearing completely. That show in 1983 was strange. We missed Dennis. We missed his drumming. We missed his vibe. I missed my brother.

The Moody Blues playing at the Universal was the same band that had been around since the '60s, but also different. Justin Hayward was there, and Graeme Edge and Ray Thomas and John Lodge, but some people were missing and some people were new. The Beach Boys had to do that all the time. When I came off the road after the airplane flight to Houston in 1964, the guys plugged in Glen and then Bruce. When Dennis hurt his hand in the early '70s and couldn't play, Carl plugged in Ricky Fataar and Blondie Chaplin. We had a kind of agreement about situations like that. Whoever was left agreed that the person who was missing wasn't really missing, or that the person who was there in place of that person was trying their best to be a replacement. The Moody Blues were doing that at the Universal, just like the Beach Boys did hundreds of times, but it made me think of our Universal show and how hard it was to pretend that Dennis wasn't missing. That night we were there back in 1983, we played a cover of John Lennon's "Imagine," because just a few years before he had been killed. John was missing and he wasn't coming back. That made a hopeful song sad. We also played "Heaven," a song from a solo album Carl released in 1981, just a few months after John Lennon died. It's a beautiful, soulful pop song.

> *It's like I'm sailing on the ocean*
> *Every time I see your eyes*
> *You could be the wind that keeps me floating*
> *I could be in heaven for all I know*
> *Heaven's a place for me to go*
> *No one ever could have told me how*
> *No one ever could have told me how*
> *Heaven could be here on earth*

Carl wrote most of the songs on his album with Myrna Smith, who had been in the Sweet Inspirations, backing up Elvis Presley. Elvis was missing, too. He wasn't coming back. I met him once in a studio. He was down the hall. I heard that he liked karate and I did some moves, but he didn't seem impressed. About a month after our show at the Universal, Dennis died. He was in and out of hospitals for drinking. He didn't want to stop drinking, or maybe he wanted to but couldn't. He was at Marina del Rey, drinking all day, and then he went swimming because he got the idea that he wanted to find some things he had thrown into the water a year before. He drowned, and he wasn't even forty. He was missing. He wasn't coming back.

I didn't speak about any of those things to Melinda when we were seeing the Moody Blues show. We went backstage and I said hi to the guys, which let us get away from Dr. Landy for a minute. After the show we went to dinner at the Polo Lounge. Dr. Landy didn't come, but he sent all the bodyguards. When the bill came, it was more than two hundred dollars. "Wow!" I said. Melinda told me later that it didn't seem like very much for the number of people with us, but it seemed like a big number to me. That's how disconnected I was from financial reality. Two hundred dollars!

We went on a second date to a movie and then on a third date to a Johnny Mathis concert. Before the Johnny Mathis concert, I told Gloria that I had a date. She was so happy for me. "That's great," she said. But she asked lots of questions, too. Did I like Melinda? Did she like me? Was she pretty? Had she ever been married before? How did she feel about Dr. Landy? I answered whatever questions I could, but lots of them I couldn't answer and I just stayed quiet. Gloria eventually stopped asking questions and just told me that if Melinda liked me, then Gloria would like Melinda.

For a while we were seeing each other as much as we could. Melinda lived in Santa Monica and there was this place we'd go for bagels and whitefish. I liked taking our bagels to a table and then sitting and talking. Her voice was just as nice as it was at the car dealership. Plus it was fun to be with a woman again, just sitting there. I hadn't had a girlfriend of any kind in a long time. I told her things that I needed to tell someone. I told her I was having a hard time with Dr. Landy. She told me he had been into the dealership a few weeks before I had, and he had been loud and demanding. He made it seem like he was so important, but he was also so sloppy, walking around in sweatpants. "That's him," I said.

She laughed for a second, and then she didn't laugh. She told me he had tried to make sure she didn't get any business from him, that he'd come back to the dealership and said he was going to buy his car through a phone service. What he didn't know was that she also worked for the phone service, so she got the sale anyway. She also told me he watched me too much and too closely. I told her he had me on lots of medications and there were times I wasn't even sure what the next pill was because of all the pills before it. She said I needed to be careful, or that someone needed to be careful for me.

I also told her about the voices that would come into my head and threaten to hurt me or kill me. It was such a relief to be able to talk to someone about them, and she seemed to know exactly what to say. She said the thing I have already mentioned, that I had been hearing them for twenty-five years and I had never been killed. I nodded when she said that. She was right. When the voices came back, I thought about what she said, and that helped me to think about them differently.

Other times Melinda and I went to the horse track, either to Hollywood Park or Santa Anita. I think one of the bodyguards liked betting on horses. They would give me a little bit of money to play on races, and once I even won three hundred dollars. This is all bunched together. It wasn't just one time at the bagel place in Santa Monica or a few times at the horse track. In real life it was weeks, and it was months, and it was starting to be years.

Melinda became so important to me. I thought about her whenever I thought about anything. Things didn't seem real to me unless I told them to her. When she wasn't around, I didn't know what to do. What I did mostly was sit in the house and try to live through the hard parts of my life. I remember once Melinda came to pick me up and I was talking to Dr. Landy on the phone. It was tilted so she could hear how loud he was yelling at me, and later she said I had a look on my face like I was trapped. That's a good way to put it.

We had more bagel conversations and more dates in the evening, and she came to my place more or I went to her place more. Dr. Landy didn't like the idea of Melinda. He said she was calling the house too much. He said she was a distraction. Around that time, Dr. Landy decided he wanted me to focus on making music. He wanted to make music with me. He had this idea that he and I were a team, both personally and professionally. He even started a company with me called Brains and Genius, which was a joke about our names. "We're partners," he said, but his idea of the word was completely different from mine. My idea of the word was someone like Melinda, who listened to me when I talked and said things back to me that seemed they were designed to get me feeling stronger. Dr. Landy didn't like listening to me, and even though he had gotten me stronger back in 1976, by that time in the '80s he was only making me more afraid.

Partners. What it meant to him was that we needed to make an album. He was obsessed with us making an album. Or maybe that's not quite true. He was obsessed with me making an album when he told me to. "You have to work," he said. That made sense. I needed to work. Work kept me calm. Work let me push aside some of my bad ideas of the world and put good ideas in their place. I remembered working on other things. I remembered being pleasantly high at the piano, banging out some chords and trying to sing Tony Asher's lyrics and Mike coming by and singing the beginning of what would end up being "Good Vibrations." That was a great memory. I remembered driving from my house to the office on the day that Kennedy died and writing "The Warmth of the Sun." That was a memory that fit into my other memories about how work kept me calm.

But Dr. Landy's idea of work was different. It had no calm in it, and it had no kindness in it. It had no love in it. His idea was locking me in the music room and screaming in my face and telling me to make songs even when I was exhausted and filled with pills that were making me more exhausted. When I missed Melinda, he would scream louder. To distract me from her, he started bringing other girls around to spend time with me. I didn't like it. They didn't dress nicely, didn't dress in a way that made me happy. I didn't let myself spend a night with any of them. But the pills kept coming in bunches. They made me so tired. Sometimes when Melinda would come to take me out I would get into her car and just lie down in the front seat with my head in her lap. I was so tired. I didn't have any energy and I didn't know where to find it.

I'm not sure how I got through it all and made the record. I remember too many days sitting in the music room not sure how I was going to get to the next note or the next word. I did it, though. In 1988 I released an album. It was my first official solo album, even though *Pet Sounds* came together like a solo record and there were later songs like "Busy Doin' Nothin'" that were basically just me. The record was called *Brian Wilson* and the cover was a picture of me. It came out on Sire, which was part of Warner Brothers. Andy Paley was a big part of how that record happened. Before the record, I put out a single I wrote with Gary Usher, "Let's Go to Heaven in My Car." It was on the soundtrack to one of the Police Academy movies. It didn't do well. Soon after that I did an event at the Rock and Roll Hall of Fame honoring Jerry Leiber and Mike Stoller. I sang "On Broadway" completely solo. Andy liked my performance and so did Seymour Stein, who was Andy's boss at Sire Records. Andy talked to Seymour and they signed me.

I liked that record even though I didn't like the circumstances of making it. It had some really great songs on it. One of them, "Walkin' the Line," was written with Gary. I had started working with him again and remembered an old bass line that I never could figure out how to use. Music is like that sometimes, a drawer with pieces of things in it. There are days when you go in the drawer and it all looks like junk, and then there are other days when you go in the drawer and you find the exact right thing you need. I went into the drawer and found the bass line, and then Gary and I made a song around it. It was a happy song, but it was also a worried song in a way: you are walking the line because you're afraid to fall off the line. Another song, "Melt Away," was also about worry, but it was about how to get rid of worry.

> *I wonder why nothin' ever seems to go my way*
> *But every time I see you*
> *I get that same old feelin'*
> *And my blues just melt away, melt away*

The world can get you down, but there are people who lift that burden off your shoulders. Melinda was one of those people for me. She made my blues just melt away. My friend, the writer David Leaf, told me that when Andy Paley played the song for him, he knew it would be his favorite song on the record. There was a song on there called "Let It Shine" that Jeff Lynne wrote with me, and a song called "There's So Many" that had beautiful harmonies, more than a dozen voices on there in layers. The record ended with a big multipart song named "Rio Grande." The idea for that came from Lenny Waronker, who was president of Warner Brothers, the big label that owned Sire. Lenny thought that any album I made should have that kind of song, with lots of sections and lots of shifts between them, like *SMiLE*. I wasn't sure about it at first. It wasn't the kind of song I was thinking about. But it happened.

The song that has lasted the longest from that record is "Love and Mercy." It ended up being the name of the movie about me, and it also ended up being a message I carried with me all the time. Like lots of other songs, it grew out of a song I was playing at the piano. I was sitting there with a bottle of champagne, kind of buzzed, thinking of a song by Bacharach and David, "What the World Needs Now Is Love." I don't know if I took musical cues from it or message cues, but I wanted to write a song about what the world needed. It needed love and mercy. My world at that time needed love and mercy. I wrote the whole thing in about forty-five minutes, and I knew right away it was a special song, a very spiritual song. It kept me going through the time that Dr. Landy was trying to keep me away from friends, away from health, away from Melinda.

I remember once I asked Melinda out on a date. Dr. Landy let me do it that time. He sent us out on a sailboat. The captain of the boat was his son. It was like the first visit to the car dealership but worse. The only thing I could hope for was that the noise of the wind would cover up what we were saying and we could get some privacy that way. Melinda kept asking me if I was okay. I couldn't say yes because that was a lie, but I couldn't tell her the truth either. The whole situation was just so strange: out in the middle of the ocean, away from it all, but still right in the middle of it. At one point the boat got close to the shore, maybe a hundred yards. I had an idea. "Can you swim?" I asked her.

"Of course," she said.

"Let's jump," I said. "From here we can swim to my house." At that time Dr. Landy had me swimming up at Pepperdine for an hour a day. It was part of the whole regimen: run, swim, eat chicken and rice instead of steak and potatoes. I felt like I could do it. How far away could land be? We splashed down, almost at the same time. We made it to the house and we had about three hours to ourselves before anyone came to check on us. It was the most romantic three hours I had had in a long time. I told her that Dr. Landy made me say "I love you" to myself three times a day. I asked her if it was okay to say it to her, and she just smiled and said, "I'd like that very much."

A little while after that, Melinda came by the house. I didn't talk to her inside. I went outside to meet her. Dr. Landy wasn't there but the bodyguards were. We were talking about music or a restaurant and I just burst out with how I was feeling. "I'm living in a hellhole," I said. "I can't stand it any longer."

She looked straight at me. "Do you really want me to help you out of this?" Later she would tell me that she was already helping, that she had started talking to Carl's lawyers and trying to explain the situation to them. It was probably hard for people to believe at first. "I'll help you, Brian," she told me. "Just say the word."

"Yes," I said. "I can't stand it anymore."

I went to go back inside, but I guess even outside wasn't safe enough. One of the bodyguards had heard me talking to Melinda, and he told Dr. Landy. After that, Dr. Landy was angry. "That's it for Melinda," he said. He took her number away from me, and because of the pills there were times I couldn't remember it well enough to call her. Other times I remembered but the phone calls were short because I thought someone was listening in. "Melinda?" I would say, and she would say, "Yes," and I would say, "Gotta go" and hang up. A few times I saw her while I was doing my jogging on the Pacific Coast Highway, but even that was a problem because Dr. Landy timed my runs and if I took too long he would know. I could stop and talk for a minute or so but nothing more than that.

Without Melinda, the days got worse again. I don't even re-member them as separate things. I gained back some of the weight I had lost. There were hours on end spent in bed. I didn't always remember to clean myself up. Old friends were fuzzy pictures; once I was at lunch with Ray Lawlor and I asked him who he was. "I think I know your face," I said. But I was lying. I didn't know his face.

At the house there was more screaming about making music. Since the first solo record had been a success, Dr. Landy wanted me to go right back and make another record. We started one that was going to be called *Brian* and then was going to be called *Sweet Insanity*. The title wasn't exactly the best. It was supposed to be a comment about the way that mental illness could turn into some-thing beautiful, but I wasn't sure I wanted a title like that. I had spent a lifetime proving that point, but why did we have to say it straight out like that? Plus the way Gene was trying to force me to make the record wasn't a good scene. He kept on me all the time. He asked questions about every part. It was the strangest and worst way to make a record, with so much pressure and so much interference. People like Andy Paley who were my friends and really wanted me to make music came around during that time or visited studio sessions, but I could tell they didn't like what they were seeing. But some of them liked some of what they were hearing. There was one song, "Water Builds Up," that started with keyboard chords almost like "Good Vibrations," but it had the opposite message. It was all about bad vibrations and what happened when I got too anxious or frustrated.

So many times I've had that helpless feeling
And no kind of booze or medicine helped at all
I'm drowning in too many contradictions
I'm about to lose all my self-control
Water builds up
Water boils over
Gettin' too hot
The pot's starting to whistle
Running over the edge
Steaming up my aching head
The water getting higher
There's a dam bursting in my soul

Sweet Insanity never came out. The record label wasn't sure about it, and then the master tapes disappeared. But tapes that go missing aren't the same as people who go missing. Even though the tapes were gone, they started popping up on cassettes, and then people started making CDs of them. For an album that never existed, lots of people have heard it.

It was a jumbled time. Everyone around me grew more and more sure that Gene was hurting me worse than before. Melinda wasn't around, but she was still talking to Carl's lawyers. Eventually they went to a judge and argued that the way Gene tried to take control of my money and my songs was wrong. The final straw was when he had me change my will so he would get most of my money when I was gone. Somehow Melinda scored a copy of the will from Gloria and got it to Carl's lawyers. It was robbery. The judge ordered him to stay away. Gloria took care of the house for me, and I was slowly getting a clearer head. One of the main things that helped was walking. It made my head a little clearer. I walked all the time from the house down the Pacific Coast Highway. It was where I used to run into Melinda. But I didn't run into her anymore.

One day I wasn't out walking, not on the PCH. I was at my studio on Pico, trying to make music. I decided that I needed to sneak some cigarettes, and I went across the street to a liquor store. On the way back, I stepped off the curb and almost got hit by a car. It was Melinda. Can you believe that? She actually almost killed me! She pulled over and said hi and then as we talked she said we should get together. "Sure," I said. "Do you think it was fate that you almost killed me?" We laughed like hell about that.

It was obvious that she was as happy to see me as I was to see her. I couldn't wait to ask her out, but she said she was splitting town for three weeks. I was sad, but she gave me her number again and told me to call when she was back. For three weeks I was looking at my watch every half hour or so. When the time came to call, I called, and the very next day she came to the house and took me down to Hollywood Boulevard. It was beautiful to look at, all the souvenirs and the way the street was a little run-down. We went to Musso and Frank, and I think I had a steak. I didn't remember being there since the '60s, but I might have been.

Melinda took me to another lunch and then to a dinner, and we drove around listening to K-Earth 101 and pretty soon we started kissing and expressing love to each other again. We were back together for real. That time blends together, but it blends together in good ways, like the conversations at the bagel place in Santa Monica, not in bad ways, like the weeks and months with Gene. I had a partner again for real: not Brains and Genius but Brian and Melinda. Around that time I started seeing new doctors at UCLA, three guys including Steve Marmer, and they worked hard to undo the damage Dr. Landy had done. They got to the questions of my medication mostly, and explained how important it was to have the right balance. Without it, I couldn't even really take a step into the world. But they explained it in a way that didn't make me feel like I was dependent on it either. I was independent on it. When you are dealing with a mental illness and you're not afraid to call it that, then you do what you can to make sure you get it under control. That's the three things I mentioned earlier: the right doctor, the right medicines, and the right people around you. For the first time I could ever remember, that was starting to happen.

Melinda was basically living with me then, and had been for about a year. She still had her own place, and she would have to drive home after work to feed her dogs. Then she would come over. Eventually the animals started coming with her. Once we were at my place and there was a wildfire. They announced it on the news but then we saw it in real life, coming toward us. It was a hazy orange. We split our house quick. We had to take all the animals with us, and we went over to Thousand Oaks. Nothing happened to the house, luckily, and we came back. It felt like home there with Melinda. I didn't think about getting married so much. But Gloria was always asking me about it. She told me I needed someone to take care of me. I told her she was doing that, and the conservator, and the doctor, and she shook her head. "No," she said. "A wife."

Then one night Melinda and I were having dinner at Lawry's the Prime Rib on La Cienega. "Why don't we talk about marriage?" she said.

I didn't think it worked that way. I thought that was for the guy to ask the girl. But it didn't seem like a bad idea either. "Well, why not?" I said. I didn't say anything else. She kept looking at me. She was probably worried that I was bothered by her question, or that I didn't want to do it, but none of that was true. I was just thinking.

We got back in the car and drove home. It wasn't the car she had sold me, not anymore. I got rid of that one and bought a yellow

Corvette. I think there was a white Corvette in there somewhere, too. Corvettes were cooler cars than Cadillacs, even though I liked the smooth ride the Cadillac gave you. We drove home. When I was with Dr. Landy all those years, I was in a house but I had no home. That night in bed, I decided to ask the question back to Melinda. "Would you marry me?" I said. She said yes immediately. She was so happy. We called a bunch of people right there in the middle of the night: her parents, my mom. Now there was a home again, for the first time since my first marriage. I had a home with my parents back in Hawthorne, but that was so far away.

❧

My first car, a light burgundy Mercury, was my mom's car, but after that it became mine. I called it my Merc. I drove it first on a permit, but when I went to get my license, I failed the first driving test. For my whole life people said I wasn't a good driver because I was always distracted, but I was good enough to pay attention. I just didn't like thinking only about the driving.

My dad worked with me on driving. He was great and patient, which was a surprise considering how he usually was. He told me where to put my hands and how to move my foot down on the pedal. I thought for a minute that it was like playing an instrument, because it worked by feel. You couldn't be too hard or too fast or the car wouldn't do what you wanted. But it was different from playing an instrument because in music it was a good idea sometimes to get different or unique sounds. In driving you didn't want to do anything too unique. It took me a couple days to get the knack of it with my dad's help, and a couple weeks later I went back and passed the test. It may not seem like very much time, but to a teenager it was like waiting forever.

A year after that I got a Ford Fairlane—not a new one but a '57. In Hawthorne it was a great car. But guys from other neighborhoods had better cars. They came in with them from Inglewood or Morningside. They might be driving Fords that were only one or two years old, with something custom on them. Our cars were ten years old and in great shape, but with nothing fancy. If it went bad, you just took it to the junkyard and bought another car. The '57 Ford, I loved. That was the car I was driving when we first heard "Surfin'" on the radio. After that the station had a thing called Pick of the Week, where they played a few songs and then people would call in and vote. We won and my family was so happy. There was a tunnel near the neighborhood that ran under a corner of the airport. I drove the Ford fast in there. No one believed me. I told people I could and they said I couldn't. I revved it as much as I could. I think I had it in low gear, though.

We were in the car all the time. My buddies and I would go to Skippy's, a hamburger stand. Other times it was the Foster's Freeze, an ice cream place near school. I loved the shakes and cones there, mostly the cones. My favorite flavor was strawberry. I didn't like chocolate. On the weekends we would drive to a place called Crestline. It was a little city in the mountains near Lake Arrowhead. Once on the way there, a car was following us pretty close. We didn't know the people in it, but it was on our tail up these mountain roads. On one straightaway something ran in front of the car; I hit the brakes hard for a second and this car behind us ran right off the road. I pulled off to the side to see if they were okay. They were, and we kept going up to Crestline. It shook me the hell up, though. Someone really could have gotten hurt.

Crestline was where we had our times as teenagers. We would play horseshoes and maybe go to a store and wait until an older guy came by and then ask him to buy us a six-pack of beer. That was the first time I got drunk, up there on a weekend. I wasn't completely into it. I wasn't one of those kids who dove right in and drank a whole six-pack every time he could. I was just looking to score a few beers and a little buzz. We had our times and slept them off, and then we got back in the car and headed home.

Cars took you places. They took you away from home and then they brought you home. So did girls. The first girl I ever went with, at least any way I can count, was Mary Lou Manriquez. We walked together back and forth from school, and I made jokes about weird trees along the road or weird dogs in people's yards or else I told her about things I had seen on *Time for Beany*. When I was eleven, I gave her a ring. It wasn't anything fancy. It was a ring I found on the ground, but it was nice and shiny and I wanted her to have it. We walked together for another month, and then one afternoon without warning she gave the ring right back to me. "Don't hurt me," I said and ran home and cried.

After Mary Lou I was even shier around girls. I liked to look at them, but I wasn't brave enough to start a conversation. Sometimes they started talking to me or a louder kid would introduce us or pull me into a group. Once that happened they liked me fine. They told me secrets and I was a pretty good listener. In high school, when it became more important to be noticed in that way, I hung out with younger girls. I was friends with fourteen-year-olds when I was seventeen. I was friends with freshmen when I was a junior or a senior. That way I could make sure they would look up to me. We had proms and we had backward dances and I went to them, but I was never what anyone would call a convincing dancer. The way I showed interest when I really liked a girl was by writing something. For one pretty girl named Renee Osler, I wrote a poem called "Lavender." It was just words in a notebook, but then Hite Morgan's wife, Dorinda, helped me finish it as a song. We even cut a demo of it, but it never turned into an actual record.

My first real date was with a girl named Carol Mountain. In my junior year in high school, I absolutely was out of my mind for Carol. She was beautiful: her hair, her eyes, her voice, her legs, everything. She knew that I had feelings for her. She was dating a kid named Gordon Marin, and when they split up Gordon asked me to take her to a party he was throwing. I guess he wanted to keep tabs on her or maybe make her jealous by showing off his new girl. Carol and I went to that party and became friendly enough that we started to spend more time together. I was over at her house more than she was over at mine. Her parents liked having me over because I was a polite kid. I could do rude pranks with other kids, but with people's parents I was polite, and if I ever made a joke, it would be a joke that parents understood also. I guess I was a little old-fashioned in that way.

I was old-fashioned in other ways, too. In my senior year of high school, I wrote a paper called "My Philosophy" where I talked about how I saw the world. "Being the first time I have taken a close look at my philosophy," I wrote, "I find it hard to reveal my beliefs about living. I will try to give my general impression of life." The beginning of the paper was about how I always wanted to get better: "The first thing that I find about myself is that I am constantly trying to improve myself." I also had an idea of what kind of job I wanted: "I don't want to settle with a mediocre life, but make a name for myself in my life's work, which I hope will be music. The satisfaction of a place in the world seems well worth a sincere effort to me." I talked about how my parents helped to develop my character, and then there was a long paragraph where I discussed my ideas about romance. "I have often wondered what the girl I marry will be like," I wrote. "I want someone who will love me (of course), and who will reason with me and understand my way of living." Those were all big parts of my life, and all things I thought were important to deal with honestly. But I was still so young. I couldn't even see past high school.

Right after high school graduation, I asked Carol out on a real date, and she said yes. We went to get some food and walked around. The whole time I was silent, almost shaking. I could barely even talk. I had so much to say that I had nothing to say. That's how my brain worked back then, and how it sometimes still works. There are a million thoughts, but unless there are other voices and instruments to bring them all out, I end up with just a few words or no words at all. Carol was nice, but I could tell there was something keeping us apart. That was the only time I went out with her.

Ten years later, after the Beach Boys were famous, I was back in Hawthorne and someone told me that Carol was home, too. "Oh," I said, trying to sound cool. "Carol Mountain? I remember her, I think." She was over at her mother's house, the house where she grew up, and I went over and talked to her there. We had a great time trading stories about high school. That brought back lots of memories, memories of my own youth and her youth, and before I left I put my hand on her leg. It wasn't completely innocent—it was still a great leg—but it was mostly innocent. Later that year I was on the road with the band, staying at a hotel somewhere, and I got a note from the front desk that there was a message waiting for me. It was a message from her husband. "If you ever touch my wife again, I'll blow your head off!" it said. That never happened.

Then there was Judy Bowles. I met her at a Little League game. Her younger brothers were playing and maybe I had a cousin playing, too. Someone introduced us and I flipped for her because she was so pretty. I asked her if I could come to her house and see her there, and soon after that we started going together. That was the most fun I had with a girl up to that point. She liked sitting close to me, and there was nothing like the feeling of having her there. We sat in my car and played this game where we would name cars, not for their models but for their looks and personalities. We would say that one car seemed like an Oscar, or a Bill, or a Jimmy. It was so fun being with Judy, sitting in the car, naming things. And it wasn't just with her either. I got along with her whole family. Judy had a brother, Jimmy, who was a surfer. He was always talking about the points and the spots where the great surfers wanted to go. I knew that I wanted to do a Chuck Berry–type song about surfing, and whenever Jimmy talked about surfing I liked the names of the places. I asked him for a list and used the places he gave me to make up the lyrics of "Surfin' U.S.A.": Santa Cruz and Trestle, Narrabeen, Doheny Way.

Judy and I dated for about a year, but other people started to come between us. They were people on my side. Once, Mike was dancing with her at the Rendezvous Ballroom in Balboa and I said, "Hey, that's my girl you're dancing with." He split and Judy apologized. A little while later, she started digging Dennis. I don't remember how I found out. But that really hurt. It was heartbreak of all kinds. It was hard for me to feel real love after that, to trust that things with a girl were going to go along without going wrong. I got more into my music and myself and my own thoughts and backed away from other people for a little while.

And then soon my music brought me to other people. In the early '60s the Beach Boys met a group called the Honeys. They were a singing group that started off a little later than we did. There were three sisters in the group—Diane, Marilyn, and Barbara Rovell—and they sometimes sang with their cousin, Ginger Blake. We met them at a nightclub called Pandora's Box in Hollywood. It was early for us, after "Surfin' Safari" and "409" but before "Surfin' U.S.A." I think maybe I had just written and recorded "County Fair." Gary Usher knew Ginger and he told her about us, and Ginger told her cousins and we all ended up at Pandora's Box. We were performing and after the show people came up to say hello. There were always some girls in the group. That time, the Honeys were in the group. They were cute girls and we had a connection through Gary and they asked us to come and sit with them. The girls were great. I was a little nervous, and I spilled hot chocolate on Marilyn's blouse. Later that night we went backstage and my dad started yelling at us about some mistakes he noticed in the show. He didn't usually yell in front of girls, and I think he half turned to them and half apologized and explained that he just wanted us to be better. The girls took it in stride. They were different from other girls we met after shows. It wasn't like they were fans who wanted to look at us and wanted us to look at them. It was like they were in the same business and wanted to work together.

That turned out to be true. Soon after we met the Rovells, I brought them into the studio and recorded some songs for them, like "Shoot the Curl" and "Pray for Surf." I liked the idea of having a girl version of the Beach Boys. They did the backup cheerleader voices on "Be True to Your School." We did songs like "Marie" and "Rabbit's Foot" that didn't get released until they were collected for compilations much later. I was in the studio all the time, and I even wrote them a song called "Surfin' Down the Swanee River," which was a surf remake of the Stephen Foster song. His melodies were so clean, so American. I had hummed them my whole life, and it made sense to bring them into new music.

> All the guys are sad and lonely
> Because we like to roam
> We're surfin' down that Swanee River
> Searching for a surfer home

When we started spending time with the Rovell sisters, I fell in love with all of them a little bit. I liked Barbara because I always gravitated toward younger sisters—I was shy and it was easier for me to talk to her than to the others. I liked Diane because Diane liked me. Marilyn liked Carl at first, and I was still with Judy off and on, but then once Marilyn and I were out walking and we started kissing and soon enough we were dating.

I wanted to get married early. Everything was early. I was only twenty-two and Marilyn was only sixteen. But even though we were kids, I didn't think about it that way. I thought of myself as someone who was growing up. I was making records. I was doing things that my dad had done and things that he had just wanted to do. I was the oldest in my family. And the next natural thing was to be a man. It was something that was drummed into my head anyway whenever I was scared: "Don't be a baby . . . be a man." Marriage was one way to do that. I sang about it in a song, "I'm So

Young," that was originally done by the Students. It was written by a guy named Prez Tyus Jr., but it was something I wish I could have written. Actually, it's a song I could have written.

Marilyn and I went to her parents and sat down with them on couches. I loved her parents. They were wonderful people. If I was over there and I was hungry, her mom would invite me into the kitchen for food. Her father talked with me about the band and what I wanted to do with it, and he was never mean or short with me. He had daughters in the same business, and he didn't take any of it lightly. There's one story people told me that I didn't see myself: Once Dennis was over there and he was boasting about how much money we were making, and he took a dollar bill out of his wallet and ripped it up in front of Marilyn's dad. Her dad made a pained face. It hurt him to think that someone could be so stupid with money. Dennis was just a kid and he was just acting out, but Marilyn's dad didn't like to see wastefulness. He was a good man.

Marilyn and I went to her parents and told them we wanted to have a sit-down. When everyone was sitting we explained that we wanted to get married. I don't know if I was bracing for someone to stand up and yell at me or for her mother to burst into tears, but none of that happened. They were in favor. For a few months we lived with her parents, and then we went to an apartment of our own, on Hollywood Boulevard. Near there, on Sunset and Vine, I had my own office. What was more grown-up than that?

At first Marilyn and I were like any young couple. We went to movies and went out to eat and drove around. But we weren't like any other young couple because it was 1964. It was the year of everything. We got married in December, and then a few days after that I got on the plane for Houston. Sometimes I think about that year and I wonder how it could have all ended in a breakdown, and other times I think about that year and I wonder if there was any other way it could have gone. There was just so much happening.

We went on our honeymoon at the beginning of 1965. I was sitting around, looking at the water or closing my eyes out on the beach, and a whole song came to me. It was "Girl Don't Tell Me." I didn't have any way to get it down. I didn't have a pen. I didn't have a guitar. I didn't have a piano. But I just heard the whole thing up there, from start to finish, and I remembered it well enough to go later and write down the lyrics on a piece of paper. It was a real trip to write a song that way. I thought it would keep happening like that. It never did again.

Marriage was tough, and I was young and not very good at it. I spent too much time with other girls. I tried to make it up to Marilyn by writing more songs for her. I wrote "All Summer Long," where I made a joke about that first meeting at Pandora's Box and spilling hot chocolate on her. I changed things around a little. I changed the hot chocolate to Coke because it fit the lyrics better, and I changed it so that she spilled it on herself because that seemed funnier.

Another song I wrote about the situation was "Don't Hurt My Little Sister," which is one of my favorites from *Beach Boys Today!* It was written in 1964 or so, and I gave it to Phil Spector to use with the Ronettes, and I watched him produce his track for that. It was amazing. Phil said things to his musicians that I learned to say to mine. If he said, "The guitar isn't coming through right," I would go back to Western and say, "Hey, guys, wait a second, I need more guitar." He didn't end up using the song the way I wrote it. He changed the title and the lyrics and turned it into a Blossoms song called "Things Are Changing." Our version was more about me and the Rovells. I wrote it from the perspective of one of them telling me not to treat another one of them badly.

> *You know she digs you and thinks you're a real groovy guy*
> *But yet I'm not sure that I feel the same*
> *Well, we both know that you've been making her cry*
> *I hope you don't think it's some kind of game*

I might have thought it was some kind of game. I was so young. That's not an excuse. I was unsure of myself. I didn't understand why I was getting any of the rewards I was getting, or the fame, or the attention. I just wanted someone close to me who I could trust. I wanted a feeling of home to balance the feeling that everything was starting to be a stage or a store.

In the '80s, before Dr. Landy came back, everything was a stage or a store. Everything was a way to sell things I had already made or to stand up in front of people and feel uncomfortable. I couldn't deal well with any of it. When I went onstage with the Beach Boys, I would just smoke cigarettes or sit on the edge of the stage and laugh. One of the other things I did back then was think about "Don't Hurt My Little Sister" all the time. Maybe it's because it was a song about protection and I felt scared that no one was protecting me. Between songs I would break into the bass line from "Don't Hurt My Little Sister." It didn't matter what the songs were before and after. We'd finish "In My Room" and you'd hear the bass playing that riff. Then we'd go back, play "Sloop John B," and when that faded out you'd hear the bass from "Don't Hurt My Little Sister" again. I was just playing that riff over and over. I needed to come back to it. I needed it to come back to me.

◦◦

I wasn't in love often. I thought about girls, but if they didn't think about me, how was that love? Other people were in love. When friends would tell me that they were seeing a new girl, I would ask them if they really were in love. That was important to me. It seemed like a real thing. Were they in love? Did something happen inside them that made them feel closer to that other person and closer to themselves? It's why I wrote so many love songs, because it's a real thing.

When I think about writing songs about love, I think about the ones I wrote for Marilyn and also about the ones I wrote for Melinda. I think about the ones I wrote for girls along the way, either in my own life or in other people's lives. But one of the songs I think about isn't about any specific person. It's about love in general. It's on *Sunflower*, which came out in 1970, and it's a song called "This Whole World." That song came from deep down in me, from the feeling I had that the whole world should be about love. When I wrote that song I wanted to capture that idea. I produced that record. I taught Carl the lead and the other guys the background vocal, especially the meditation part at the end: "Om dot dit it." I cut it at home. It was a house in Bel Air, where I was living at the time, that felt comfortable enough that it started to feel like a home. That song worked so well. The background singing is an amazing kind of trip, and Carl hits that last note amazingly. He's great on "Darlin'" and he's great on "God Only Knows." But "This Whole World" is another one of my favorite Carl leads. And there's one lyric that gets me every single time:

> When girls get mad at boys and go
> Many times they're just putting on a show
> But when they leave, you wait alone

For years I didn't understand that, but when I met Melinda, I understood again.

When I said yes to Melinda and we decided to get married, we made a new home. We moved from where I was living to a house on Ferrari Street. It had a great jukebox, loaded up as nicely as the one my dad had in Hawthorne when I was a kid. When Melinda came into my life, lots of pets came with her, too. She had two dogs and three cats and a bird. One thing about the dogs is that we always had more than one. I watched how they acted around each other. They had their own partnerships. That was something I needed, and I never knew how much I needed it until I didn't have it. I needed it in my life and I needed it in my music.

Melinda and I got married at a chapel in Palos Verdes. I picked as the date February 6, because it was Marilyn's birthday. That way,

I figured, I would never forget the date. Melinda agreed. Between the time we picked the date and the actual wedding, we went up to Sundance, the film festival in Utah, for the premiere of the Don Was documentary. Then we came back and got married. There were about one hundred fifty people at the wedding. There were only supposed to be about a hundred, but people kept coming, which was a little surprising for a Monday night in February. My brother Carl was my best man. Afterward, we went to the Hotel Bel-Air for music and food and danced and had a good time.

When Melinda and I were first married, we fought often. We were already used to each other, but there was still a difference between dating and actually being married. It was hard to figure out how to bring her into my life, even though she was already there. At first I didn't like the fighting. I didn't understand it. Maybe I was afraid that she wouldn't listen to me, the way that people hadn't listened to me in the band. But she didn't do that. She didn't back down and she didn't try to take over. She stayed in there and tried to explain what she meant. She was patient, but she kept pushing toward her point. We fought all the time until I realized that maybe it wasn't even fighting. Maybe it was that she was trying to show me she cared enough to tell me the truth. That was a new feeling for me—I wasn't being told what I wanted to hear while I was worked behind my back. I wasn't being bullied or betrayed. I was being talked to by a partner. And so was she. It's like we had each other's back. That had never happened to me before, not like that. I'd never trusted someone else enough to share my true feelings without worrying they might leave.

Cigarettes are a good example. I was smoking all the time back then. Dr. Landy wouldn't let me smoke when he was around, and by the time he left I really missed it. I missed it so much that I started again. I smoked when I was at the piano. I smoked when I was watching TV. Smoking is what made me run into Melinda again out on Pico. But Melinda didn't like the cigarettes at all.

"They smell terrible," she said. "Not to mention that you have trouble with your weight. Add those two together and it's no good." Or she'd start her argument with my weight and then go to the way the cigarettes smelled. She put the patch on me and that did it. I haven't smoked since.

Now I really hate the smell of cigarettes. I can smell them a mile away. The smell sticks to your clothes and follows you around. I remember one night at Royal Festival Hall in London, on one of the tours, we were getting on an elevator and someone got on who smelled like a whole pack of cigarettes, or maybe even a whole cigarette store. "Who the hell has been smoking?" I yelled. The guy jumped off before the elevator door closed. I guess he was embarrassed, you know?

Melinda also pushed me to exercise, to keep walking, to do stretches and other things so that my bad back wouldn't flare up as often. There have been periods with her when I was healthier and periods when I was less healthy, but the main thing that happened is I learned how to think about it in a different way. It worked better for me than the Radiant Radish had, the health food store I ran in 1969.

Melinda was also good with my mother. We would go visit her when she was older. She died just before Carl died. Before that we would go visit her. We would bring the kids over to her house when they were little. There was a grand piano in the place and I would sit down and play it while Melinda talked to my mother. When I got up it was time to go.

Maybe most importantly, Melinda helped give me my solo career. I had made those records with Dr. Landy, but that was almost impossible. He was yelling at me all the time. He humiliated me. He used music as a weapon against me. Melinda didn't do that. She was patient, but she kept talking about it whenever she had a chance, and slowly I started to see how much I needed my songs near me. And it wasn't just about the records. She helped me get my mind ready for concerts and tours. Without her, I might have still been the last surviving Wilson, but I wouldn't have been completely alive.

I have sometimes come back from tours and gone right into the house and told her to sit down with me. Then I tell her how happy it makes me to be out onstage now. I don't always say the other part, which is that it wouldn't have happened if she hadn't been there for me. Listening to her was one of the best decisions I ever made.

CHAPTER 5

Fathers and Sons

I'd listen to my radio
But he took it and he's using it in his own room
(Now it's gone)
I wish I could do some homework
But I got suspended from school
(Blew my cool)
I'm bugged at my ol' man
And he doesn't even know where it's at
    —"I'm Bugged at My Ol' Man"

We were going to a Four Freshmen show. What a dream. It wasn't the original Four Freshmen. It was the Four Freshmen the way they were in the twenty-first century: not young men anymore, not even older men performing the hits of their youth, but new members singing those great old songs. Bob Flanigan, one of the original members and the guy who really taught me to sing falsetto, was overseeing the whole operation, and the new Freshmen he hired were guys in their thirties and forties. I was in a car with Ray Lawlor and Jeff Foskett, and we were driving down to Newport Beach to see them sing.

When we got to the show, we sat down outside in folding chairs arranged around round tables. "I'll have a margarita," I said, "and double the alcohol." Jeff looked at me funny. When the waiter left, Ray got up to go to the bathroom. I wondered if he was really going to the bathroom. When I ordered drinks, sometimes my friends would follow the waiter and try to fix the drink so it didn't have any booze in it, or if I ordered a beer they would try to get the restaurant to bring me an O'Doul's instead. But Ray didn't go for the waiter, and I got my real drink. There was no need for anyone to worry anyway. I wasn't in the mood to gulp it down and go for another one. I just sipped at it.

The Four Freshmen came out and started singing their hits. They did "Graduation Day" and "It's a Blue World." Midway through the first half of the show, one of the Freshmen held his hand up across his eyebrows like he was trying to find land from a ship. "I hear we have a special guy in the audience tonight," he said. "We've made some good records, but he's not a bad record producer himself." Then he said my name and the whole audience applauded. I waved—not at the Freshman who had called my name or at anyone in particular, but at everyone.

I first heard the Freshmen on the radio in the late '50s in Hawthorne. They were young voices back then, when I was even younger. When I paid close attention to their songs, they fell apart a little. I don't mean that they broke down, only that when I really gave it my all, I could hear all the different voices that made up the one sound of the group. To hear them all, I had to go close to my radio and put my left ear almost right up against the speaker. It was my only good ear. When I made sense of all the parts and layers, I gave them to Dennis and Carl and Mike and whoever else was around.

"Graduation Day" is one of the songs I remember best. It was about leaving school and being sad to go, but always having happy memories of the place. For that one, a neighbor kid named John came and sang with us. It was a song I always loved and kept with me. When I got an honorary doctorate in music in 2003 from Northeastern University in Boston, I used that song again. The degree ceremony was early in the morning, and we were playing a show in Boston that night. The other honorary degrees went to Christine Todd Whitman, the former governor of New Jersey, and the astrophysicist Neil deGrasse Tyson. I see him all the time on TV. I knew that the honorary doctors were supposed to give speeches, but speaking has never been my strong suit. During the event, Christine Todd Whitman spoke. Neil deGrasse Tyson spoke. They were both great—very inspirational. When it was my turn, I called out four guys from my band—Jeff Foskett, Nicky Wonder, Probyn Gregory, and Gary Griffin—and we did a five-part harmony version of "Graduation Day." We got a huge ovation. Then I leaned into the mic and said, "Congratulations and drive home safely."

It wasn't until we got in the car that I spoke again. "Goddamn, guys," I said. "Did you hear those harmonics?" I hope the kids at Northeastern got something from them. There's so much to get. If you can hit them right, you have everything you need in the world, just for a moment. It's a trip to not just remember that song but to remember all the acts that did a version of it: the Rover Boys, the Lennon Sisters, Bobby Pickett. They're all from another time. Later, the Beach Boys sang a version of it as the B-side to "Be True to Your School." In Newport Beach, when the Four Freshmen sang, "Sit there and count your fingers," I almost stood up out of my chair. That was the beginning to "Little Girl Blue," which is one of their best songs. Rodgers and Hart wrote it and almost every singer sang it: Ella Fitzgerald, Sarah Vaughan, Nina Simone, Janis Joplin. Frank Sinatra sang it on *Songs for Young Lovers*, one of his best albums. But the way the Four Freshmen did it meant the most to me. There was just something magical about those voices working together, making a song that went straight to the heart of everyone listening. It's one of the things that helped me write "Surfer Girl." When my dad heard "Surfer Girl," he told me to write more songs like it. It wasn't that he didn't think it was good enough. It was the opposite. He thought it was good enough, and he thought I needed to do more. So in a way, the Four Freshmen were responsible for it all.

I went backstage at intermission to say hello to the Four Freshmen. I told them how I first heard them on a demonstration record at a department store. It wasn't those Four Freshmen, of course, but I liked pretending. It was a kind of time machine. I was in my sixties, and I was seeing the singers I loved when I was in my teens, but they were the same age they were back then. One of the singers—I think it was Bob Ferreira, who sang bass—came up to me. "Will you sing with us?" he asked.

I froze. "Uh," I said. I wasn't ready to go onstage. I wasn't as nervous about it as I once was, but I needed to prepare. I had a ritual.

He noticed the look on my face. "No, no," he said. "Just back here in the dressing room."

"Oh, right," I said. "I knew that."

He laughed. My entire body relaxed. We did "Their Hearts Were Full of Spring." It was an amazing feeling. It's a beautifully sad love story about a boy and a girl who become husband and wife. Even death can't put an end to their love:

> *Then one day they died*
> *And their graves were side by side*
> *On a hill where robins sing*
> *And they say violets*
> *Grow there the whole year round*
> *For their hearts were full of spring*

The Beach Boys recorded that song, too. We did it on *Little Deuce Coupe*, though Mike changed the lyrics so they were about James Dean and how he died in a car crash. We renamed it "A Young Man Is Gone." It was a cautionary tale on a hot-rod album.

I told everyone about "A Young Man Is Gone" in the car on the way back from Newport Beach, and then went through everything

I remembered about James Dean. He was trying to get to Salinas for a car race, and he decided to drive up from LA to put some miles on his new Porsche. Near Paso Robles, a Ford Tudor made a bad turn and got trapped in the middle of the intersection. James Dean smashed into the side of the Ford, broke his neck, and died. It was a terrible story, but it was part of American history.

Dean died in 1955, which was the same year I got my hands on *Four Freshmen and 5 Trombones,* the first album I ever bought. It had two beautiful Gershwin songs on it, "Somebody Loves Me" and "Love Is Here to Stay." I remember the cover so well. The bells of the trombones were pointed outward and it made the cover look like Olympic rings, except that there were two on the top and three on the bottom. The Freshmen were shrunken down tiny and standing on one of the trombones' slide. It was like a better version of *15 Big Ones.* That Four Freshmen album was on Capitol Records, just like we were later.

I was so jazzed from seeing the Four Freshmen and thinking about how things started and ended and connected in between that at one point I turned to everyone in the car and said, "That was the best day I had in my life." I had to say it out loud because I meant it so much.

⟿

That Four Freshmen concert in Newport Beach made me happy, but the more I thought about it, the more I felt sad, too, because thinking about my childhood in Hawthorne made me think about my dad. Thinking about my dad was the big can of worms. I started young and I got older, but he stayed one of the most important people in my life, in good ways and bad. He could be generous and guide me toward great things, but he could also be brutal and belittle me and sometimes even make me regret that I was alive. I learned all those things when I was too young to understand them. Maybe they are the kinds of things that you're never supposed to understand.

I had seen the Four Freshmen with my dad, too, when I was young. One day I was coming downstairs and my dad was getting his coat and his hat. "Come with me," he said, but he didn't say where we were going until we were in the car driving away from the house. "It's a Four Freshmen concert," he said. I was real nervous. I didn't know what it would be like to see them singing live. Would they make the same music I knew from the radio? Would it be different? Would it be disappointing?

The concert was great. It was like the concert when I was older, except that I was different. I didn't know what to listen for yet, but I was more amazed by what I was seeing. Afterward, my dad got us backstage. I don't know how. I don't think he knew anyone special. He just asked where the stage door was and then acted like we were supposed to be there. He walked right up to the Four Freshmen and introduced himself. "Hi," he said. "I'm Murry Wilson. This is my son, Brian. He loves your music." He didn't push me forward or anything. He just kind of stepped to the side and swept his arm over my head to show me to the Freshmen. They were so gracious. They thanked us for liking them and coming out to see their show. I couldn't talk. I was locked into a kind of smile.

I said that the Four Freshmen show in Newport Beach was like a time machine. It wasn't really a time machine. If it was, I would have gone back to the earlier Four Freshmen show and thought less about how I felt and tried to notice more about how my dad felt. It must have been a big meeting for him, too. My dad had a company that sold lathes, but he also loved music. Just like I sang with my brothers, he sang with my mother. He played piano and she played organ. When he was on the piano he was always in a good mood. That's why we loved watching them sing and play together.

My father didn't only play other people's songs. He also wrote songs of his own. My dad didn't do it until he already had kids and a job. He was in his thirties by then, and he liked the kind of music that was popular around Los Angeles: big band music that grown-ups listened to when they went out to nightclubs. He imagined his songs finding their way into the hands of bandleaders like Tommy Dorsey or Stan Kenton. They were good songs, too. There was one that went, "When a bee loses his queen bee / His days are numbered / It's true." One of his melodies was so beautiful, for a song called "His Little Darling and You." Sometimes in school I would think about it and get tears in my eyes. People ask what made it a good song. He did. My dad did.

Most of his songs were love songs, but he wrote faster songs also. He had one called "Two-Step Side-Step" that was a dance song:

> Two-step side-step
> Two-step side-step
> Throw my girl away
> At the dance last Saturday night

He loved that song. He wanted the world to hear it. He worked all the channels that any songwriter would. He called people on the phone and sent letters in the mail and talked to people at parties. At one point someone got his song through to Lawrence Welk, and word came back that they were going to play it on the show. When he announced it to the family, I burst into tears. I was so touched that his work had paid off. It was something he wanted so much, and it was happening. We all sat down and watched the show. It was in the middle of dinner and we stopped eating and went to the television in the living room.

Lawrence Welk came on. I could hardly breathe. I was ten years old and I knew I was about to hear my dad's name on the television. "We're going to have a band now play a song by Murry Wilson," Lawrence Welk said. "It's called 'Two-Step Side-Step.'" My dad was beaming. He smoked a pipe and usually wore his glasses, partly because when he was younger he had worked at Goodyear and there was an accident and he lost his left eye. He had a glass one. He was also losing his hair from pretty early on. Because of all that he always looked older, like a dad, but for a second he looked younger. "How 'bout that?" he said. He couldn't stop smiling. "The great Murry Wilson." The song ended, but it wasn't the end of the song. A man named Johnnie Lee Wills did a country version of it a few years later, and then a woman named Bonnie Lou did a rockabilly version. This was in the 1950s, long before there was any Beach Boys or even Pendletones, and we already had a songwriter in the house.

∽

The great Murry Wilson. Lots of things have been written about my dad and the way he treated me and my brothers. Lots of them are true. Some of them are dirty lies. But even the things that are true aren't always what they seem. I have said how hard it is for me to talk about my dad, and that's partly because I want to get it right. He's not here to explain himself. He's been gone for decades. My mom's gone, too. Carl's gone and Dennis is gone. I'm the only one from that Hawthorne house left in the world. And because of that, I want to try to do the best to explain my dad. Explaining doesn't just mean telling stories or remembering things he did and said. Explaining also means understanding. I have to try to understand him.

My dad's love for music was a gift he gave to all of us Wilson kids, but there were other gifts, too. My dad got me lots of things. He got me clothes. He got me cars. He got me presents every single Christmas. My dad also took things away, by being rough and demanding. He asked for so much from you and kept asking when you thought you had given him everything you could. He sold lathes and drills that he imported from England, and he used to take us to work with him on the weekends to clean the machinery. His company was called ABLE, which stood for Always Better Lasting Equipment. I didn't like being dragged to ABLE to work on the weekend. I wanted to go play football or baseball or hang out at the house, but most Saturdays my dad would stand up after breakfast in a way that made me see where I was headed for the day. That began when I was just barely a teenager, when he started his company, and went on for years. It taught me two things at once, which was to understand how to do hard work and also to like time to myself to sit around and be busy doing nothing. Lots of things about my dad are like that, two things at once, two opposite things.

When I was barely a teenager, I was afraid of my dad. He yelled at me all the time and it made me nervous. He was not only a tough guy but also rough. He was rough with all of us, me and my brothers—he grabbed us by the arms and shoved us and hit us with hands that were sometimes open and sometimes even closed. When I went to school I would think everyone was my dad. It was a little trick I played to keep myself in line. Then one afternoon I went home and cried and decided that I wasn't going to be afraid of my dad anymore. I didn't tell anyone else. I'm not even sure I said anything to Dennis or Carl, about being afraid or not being afraid. That's not how things went back then in Hawthorne. Everyone thought it was better to keep those kinds of things inside.

My dad was violent. He was cruel. What makes people that way? Maybe he was rough because he had a rough life. When my dad came to California from Kansas with his dad, my granddad, they were real poor, to the point that they had to live on a beach in a tent. That was in San Diego. My mom might have told me that. I didn't hear it from my dad. He thought it was better to keep those kinds of things inside, too. Buddy, my dad's dad, was a hard guy to get to know, especially when I was a kid, but as I have gotten older I see that he had some of the same personality I have, and some of the same hard time with it. He loved music and he was good at it. He sometimes drank too much. He had trouble with his moods. One thing that makes us different is the way we deal with anger. I always kept it inside, or if I did let it out I kicked a can or punched a wall. I was usually lucky enough not to get the stud. But Buddy wasn't always very nice to my dad. There was a story that once my dad did something that made his dad angry, and Buddy swung a lead pipe at the side of my dad's head. His ear was hanging off. They rushed him to the doctor and eventually it was okay again.

I wasn't there for that, obviously. It happened long before I was born. But things repeat, and they repeat in strange ways. When I was out playing in my neighborhood, between my house and another, a kid hit me in the head with a lead pipe. His name was Seymour, I think, either his first or his last. The feeling was just shock at first, but the next day I realized that I couldn't hear as well out of my right ear. I told my mom and she took me to the doctor, who examined me and said that the eighth nerve in my head was severed. I say that my right ear's completely deaf, though doctors are more specific. Some say 98 percent and some say 95 percent.

The ear affected me deeply for the rest of my life. When I was a kid, whenever my mom would talk to me I would turn the left side of my head toward her. It was like I was tuning a radio station. It also affected the way I spoke. I couldn't hear myself out of the right side, so I started to push the speaking over to the other side of my mouth. It made me look lopsided, like I was coming from the dentist with one side numbed out from novocaine. In old films of the Beach Boys performing, there are some cases where the crooked mouth is very pronounced. I've seen film of Munich in 1964 where it almost looks like I had a stroke. Over the years I have learned to give people instructions when they first come speak to me: move to the left side or, if you have to be on the right, lean around.

But the ear helps to create the music, too. When I make music I make mono music. I can only hear out of one side, which means that it's already mixed down. That one ear is doing all the work. Maybe limits help you to focus, in a way. Beethoven was deaf, of course. Bill Haley was blind in one eye. Maybe that's not the same thing. I know I have learned to work with my ears the way they are, and I think I hear fully with whatever partial hearing I have. I don't go around collecting things that people say about me, but there is one I like. It's from Bob Dylan, and it's one of the nicest compliments, and one of the funniest. "That ear—I mean, Jesus," he said, "he's got to will that to the Smithsonian." I might.

And things repeat. When Daria and Delanie were little girls, a few years after we adopted them, they started telling Melinda that they wanted a baby brother. She came to me and asked me about it. "That would be cool, to have a boy," I said. We found a baby who was supposed to go to another family but their arrangement had fallen through. The day we were supposed to go the hospital, they called and said that the baby had failed his hearing test and would probably be deaf in one ear. On the way there, I told Melinda how strange it was for something like that to happen again. As it turned out, the baby could hear fine. He had water in his ear when he was tested. We named him Dylan. When we got him home, I held him for the first time and sang "Mr. Tambourine Man" to him. The name felt just right.

⁓

The way my dad treated me was tough, and it made me tougher. I don't know if I needed to be tougher, but that's what happened. He made me work and he made me pay attention and he made me have good manners, but he had a funny way of doing it. Some people hear about what he did and call him a monster, and I guess that you could say that. He was scarier than anything in *The Beach Girls and the Monster*. But the way I grew up shaped me in many ways, not all good and not all bad. I don't like making the discussion all about how terrible my dad was, even if that's true. The way he brought me up made me more focused on getting certain things done. It wasn't only that he had me work at his shop every weekend. It was that he encouraged me to get other jobs also. His idea was that if you weren't working, you were lazy. My first real job was at a lumberyard. My job was to move around stacks of wood. I told the manager of the yard that my name was Lupe, or Loopy. I wasn't thinking of Spanish names or English names necessarily. I was just thinking of a fake name, something funny. One afternoon I was working, but not quickly enough. "Hey, Loopy," the boss yelled, "get your ass in gear and move that stack in the corner to the door."

"My name's not Loopy," I said. "It's Brian."

"Well, Brian, Loopy, whatever the hell your name is, move that stack in the corner to the door."

I didn't last long there. Later I worked at a jewelry store, sweeping up after it closed, and for a few winters I got hired at a Christmas tree lot. I was big enough to move the trees for people and I liked it more than lumber. Lots of the motivation to do that came from my dad. He thought that the world was there so you could work hard at things.

When I was young, friends of mine loved my dad. He was nice to them. He would try to arm wrestle them. And they would have never heard me say a bad word about him. I was scared, to start with, and I was trying to be as nice as I could so my dad wouldn't get mad at me. I was always asking him questions to try to make him happier. If I mowed the lawn, I'd say, "Do you like that I mowed the lawn?" I was so happy if he said yes. Or I would wash his car and ask him if he liked the job I did washing it. But that wasn't always safe either. Sometimes he wouldn't like the job I did mowing or washing, and then I'd wish I had never asked the question in the first place. My dad had lots of mood shifts. He was a Cancer, born in July. Cancers have lots of mood shifts. I couldn't tell when they were coming, though, and even if I could, I'm not sure I knew what to do with most of the moods. He showed love through music, but the rest of the time there was mostly quiet that exploded into anger.

Maybe the worst thing about my dad was how he dealt with my fear. He couldn't deal with it. Whenever I got afraid, he would yell at me or slap me or call me a pussy. Lots of the grabbing and the shoving started because something made me nervous and I didn't know what to do. He couldn't stand to see me that way, and he did everything wrong to get me feeling differently. But then there were kinder moments. When we went to the Long Beach Pike roller coaster, I didn't want to go on it. He told me not to be afraid, and though his voice wasn't nice, it wasn't mean either. It was straight as an arrow. I got on with him, and the damn thing went up so high. "Take a deep breath, Brian," he said. "It'll be okay." I liked being told that things were okay, even though I didn't always believe it.

I'm not saying that the way he treated me was okay. I'm just saying that along with telling stories that show how bad it was, I want to tell other stories, too. The great Murry Wilson.

Once when I was a teenager, my dad and I were sitting in the kitchen. My next-door neighbor, Michael, came by. "Hey, Brian!" he said.

I put up a hand. "Michael!"

"Say that again," my dad said. I did. And he slapped me hard across the face and said, "Don't ever yell again at anybody." I was crying, not just because it hurt so much but because it was so surprising. It happened again and again and again. At some point it wasn't surprising. When he didn't put his hands on us, he tried to scare us in other ways. He would take out his glass eye and make us look into the space where the eye used to be.

When someone scares you so often, gentleness is its own kind of shock. Once in high school I was doing my homework and I couldn't understand some part of it. I got mad and read it again, but I still didn't understand. Finally I threw the book as hard as I could against the kitchen wall. My dad came in and stared at the book on the floor. "What are you doing?" he said. "Did you throw that book?"

I was sure that he was going to come after me. "I did it," I said. "I just couldn't figure out that question." He didn't get the usual mad look on his face. He cooled down and talked to me about how it was important not to get too frustrated in school.

Sometimes I provoked my dad. Once I took a shit on a plate and brought it to my dad. "Here's your lunch," I said. He was sitting down with his pipe in his mouth. He didn't even stand up. "Get in the bathroom," he said. Then he came in there and whipped the hell out of me. That one I may have deserved, but I was bringing the plate to him because of the times I didn't deserve.

There were hundreds of those times, at least. And it didn't just happen to me. When I was seventeen, our cat had a litter of kittens. I think there were seven or eight of them in a box out in the garage. Dennis came out to see them. He bent down over them and decided that he wanted one of them. "I'm going to pick up this one," he said. All of a sudden my dad was there in the garage. It's like he just appeared behind Dennis. "Get your hands off of that kitten," he said.

"Shut up," Dennis said. He was the only one who ever said those kinds of things to my dad.

My dad stepped toward Dennis. "I'm going to knock your block off if you don't put that kitten down," he said.

Dennis didn't put the kitten down. Instead, he took a swing at my dad. He tried to knock his block off. The two of them got into a fistfight, right there over the kitten box, and our next-door neighbor heard the noise and came over to the garage and broke it up. We ended up giving away most of the kittens.

Another time Dennis was reading a girlie magazine and my mother caught him. "Your dad's not going to like this," she said.

Dennis didn't even look up at her. "Get outta here," he said.

When my dad came in he marched over to Dennis and took the magazine and ripped it in half. "That's it," he said. "No more magazine."

Dennis didn't say anything about the magazine, but he wasn't exactly silent about it. A little after that he left the refrigerator door open. My mom saw it and came for him. "Dennis," she said. "Shut the door. You're letting the cold out." When she got to the word *out*, she slipped on a grape someone had dropped on the floor and flipped right onto her ass. Dennis started laughing so hard that we all started laughing. My mom didn't think it was anywhere near as funny.

In a situation like the one in our house, kids have to decide how to deal with things. Do they show anger? Do they hide it? Do they talk? Do they escape? Carl was a pretty quiet person. He was always pretty gentle. Dennis went the other direction. He fought all the time: against my dad, against my mom, against whoever. He was fighting for a kind of fairness and justice some of the time, but other times he was just fighting. The day we were writing "Surfin' Safari," Dennis wanted to arm wrestle. I went to the table and set up and he sat across from me. I did the best I could, but he kicked my ass in record time. Mike was watching and he wanted a shot at Dennis. Dennis kicked his ass, too. Carl tried after that and he couldn't stand a chance.

Dennis's life is a whole book by itself. It wouldn't be a happy book all the time. He loved the outdoors and he loved cars and always had beautiful girls around him, and he could really sing when he wanted to, though he didn't always want to. I remember that in 1980 I was living in Pacific Palisades, in a house called Green Tree, and Dennis would come over. I was into drug stuff at the time, cocaine and whatever else, but he was even more into it. He brought coke and alcohol. I tried to party with him, but it was hard to keep up and felt like a terrible time.

After Dennis died, people used to ask me all the time what I thought about his solo record, *Pacific Ocean Blue*. I have said that I never heard it, that I won't listen to it, that it's too many sad memories and too much for me. That's sort of true, but not really. I know the music on it. I was around for much of the time in the mid-'70s when Dennis was cutting the record. I loved what he was doing. My favorite song that he ever made was on it. I don't know for sure what he ended up calling it, but there was a part that went "No more lonely nights / I'll never make the headlines." Is it called "You and I"? I love that cut. But I haven't ever put the record on and listened through it the way I have with other records, or the way that other people have with that record. If I want to know what Dennis's soul sounded like, I can just remember the songs—"What's Wrong," "Dreamer," "Farewell My Friend," "End of the Show." They tell the whole story of how sad and beautiful his life was, how the beauty tried to grow but the sadness kept it in the dark.

Kids who get hit don't just turn into one thing. They turn into all kinds of things. Dennis turned into one thing and Carl turned into another thing and I turned into a third thing. We had something in common, of course. We had my dad. And that meant that we all had to deal with it, though we all had our own ways of dealing with it. I kept lots of what I felt inside, but sometimes it came out. It came out on *Summer Days (And Summer Nights!!),* in a song I wrote called "I'm Bugged at My Ol' Man." It's a song that critics writing about the record didn't like very much. I remember Carl reading me one review where the writer said the song wasn't complicated enough. But I wasn't trying to be complicated. I was trying to say that my dad was bugging me. My brothers sang along with me, but I sang lead. On the back of the record, where we listed who sang and played on all the songs, the vocals for "I'm Bugged at My Ol' Man" were credited to "Too embarrassed." That's how direct it was.

As I get older and older, I am more and more like my mother. I don't think I am like my dad. In my twenties I was like my dad. I was tough in the studio, but then I slowly got off of it. Now I am more like my mom. I am more loving than I used to be.

～

The story of my dad is the big can of worms because it's connected to everything else. He wasn't only the great Murry Wilson, songwriter for Lawrence Welk and Bonnie Lou. He was also the main force behind the early years of the band. He brought us from the garage to the Pendletones to the Beach Boys. We were just kids. We were his kids. In a way I was ambitious. I loved singing and then a little later I loved writing songs. But we might not have gone forward the way we did without my dad. When we started out, he produced all our records. He was tough. He used to come into re-cording sessions and yell. He would say, "Surge!" for more guitar. "Punch that guitar!" he would say, or "Put life in that guitar!" He was the one who kept things sharp and demanded more energy.

I think of the things he said always with exclamation points. Even if he wasn't yelling, his tone was like that. He wanted us to work all the time, and nothing we did was every really good enough. He would set up our amps and scream at us to do more. I was a hard worker, but Mike and Dennis could be goofy. We were all kids and there's no reason to blame them, but they didn't always want to work hard.

But we grew up. We thought we grew up more than we actually did, but it was happening at some speed. I was learning things from my dad, and I was also learning things from everybody else. I started to understand songs better than him. I could see where the things he was saying in the studio made sense, but also I could see where other things made no sense. You didn't always have to punch up that guitar. Sometimes you could get a bigger sound with other instruments, or you could add a harmony in an unexpected place, or you could work with silence before you worked with noise. When we got to "Surfin' U.S.A.," I went to talk to him. I told him that we didn't need him to produce our records anymore. "You think you can do it?" he said. "You can't." He wasn't mean about it, even. He just thought I couldn't do it.

I went off with the band and we cut "Surfin' U.S.A." with Nick Venet. Without my dad there, Nick and I talked about how to make it sound brighter and bigger. We thickened up the harmonies. It made sense to me to do a wall of voices. It was partly something I heard on Phil Spector's records and partly something I heard in my own head, in my one ear, where all the sounds flattened down to one layer. When we were done with the song, I brought it back to my dad. I wasn't sure what would happen. Maybe he would be proud of me. Maybe he would take a swing at me. Maybe he would say nothing and just stare at me angrily until I left the room. But what happened surprised me. He listened, tapping his fingers, and then he looked up. "Good record!" he said.

Once I knew I had made a good record, I knew that I could make more. When we were doing "I Get Around" in early 1964, my dad came down to the studio. He wanted us to turn up the guitar and turn up the bass. Surge! I didn't want him there. I knew how things should sound. We argued about it, and that time I reached my limit. "Get out of here!" I said. I shoved him and he went sprawling backward. He didn't fall down, but he lost his balance. He didn't come back at me with fists or even angry words. He just left. I didn't see him for a while after that. The other guys and I talked it over and decided that he couldn't manage or produce us anymore. It wasn't just about the sound of the records. They weren't always happy with him on the business side either. We were playing these frat parties for maybe a hundred dollars. My dad said that we needed experience, but Dennis and Carl thought he was selling us short.

All of us got together and wrote him a letter. It wasn't easy at all, but I kept reminding myself that there was no other way for things to go. Anything else would have been backward, and you can't go backward because you might get stuck there. We handed the letter to him at the next recording session. Even after all these years, I don't remember what song we were recording. I was so nervous. "What is this?" he said. He looked surprised. His pipe was still in his mouth.

"Read it," I said, but we told him what it said anyway. He wasn't cut off from the Beach Boys completely—he was still in charge of our publishing company, Sea of Tunes—but he was relieved of management duties. That was right around the same time I freaked out on the plane to Houston and decided I was going to stay in the garden apartment and think of more songs. That was right around the time I got married to Marilyn. That was right around the time we recorded four records. That was right around the year of everything.

When I came off the road, my dad argued with me about it. He told me that I was being weak and letting things get to me. The only way I could convince him was to talk about the group's success. I told him that if I stopped touring, it wasn't going to hurt the Beach Boys, and that it might even help. "I just want to write some more songs for those guys," I said. That stopped him. "Okay," he agreed. "That's a good decision."

One of the first songs I wrote in the garden apartment was "Help Me, Ronda," later remade as "Help Me, Rhonda." I wrote the bass line before I wrote the song. Once I had that bass line I kept it in my head and started fooling around with it on the piano. I thought I'd try C-sharp. So I started playing around with my left hand in C-sharp. Then I wrote the chorus and then I did the melody. There's always some mystery when I try to remember how I wrote back then. My God, how the fuck could I have written all those songs? I couldn't do that nowadays if I tried to. Even if I get the feeling that I want to, I don't get the same inspiration. Back then it was a little bit of mystery and a little bit of magic.

My dad came by the studio with my mom while we were recording the song. At that point, the two of them were having some trouble in their marriage. It wasn't a big surprise. My mom saw the way my dad acted, and she was a loving person. She loved him, but she loved her kids also. Still, they came down to the studio together. Thinking about that day is like thinking about the Four Freshmen concert. I remember how I felt but I have no idea how my dad felt. It was probably embarrassing for him to see how we were doing without him. He talked constantly while we were recording. He tried to convince me that we still needed him to guide us. "The Beach Boys are going downhill," he said. "You have to sing harder," he said, "like you care." "I'm a genius, too, Brian," he said. Brains and Genius.

The tape of the session still exists. You can hear it all. When I hear how I answered him, it's a little amazing to me. I wasn't happy. I had to take off my headphones and talk to him. "We would like to perform in an atmosphere of calmness, Dad," I said. I said something else also, over and over again: "Times are changing." It was never easy to have him around, but it wasn't easy to be without him either.

Once we were coming back from San Diego. I was driving and my dad was on me the whole time. "Slow down," he said. "Slow down." It really freaked me out. It was making me nervous to drive, and it was worse with him on me all the time. Another time he came to the studio to tell us about a band he was managing called the Sunrays. The lead singer was a friend of Carl's, a guy named Rick. My dad brought their record in for me to hear. It was called "I Live for the Sun." The chorus was originally "Run, run, run, run" but the song was rewritten and it got changed to "Sun, sun, sun, sun." That made it make sense with the title and made it more of a surf song. But it was also so weird for my dad to be bringing in a song he was working on with all those *suns* in it when he had all those sons who weren't working with him anymore.

A few months after we fired my dad, he sent me a long letter. This was in May of 1965. It was eight pages, typed on the Sea of Tunes stationery. He wasn't the kind of person to communicate like that, but when he did it, he really did it. It was a letter that summed up everything about him. He talked lots about the code of honor in our family: "First, I tried to teach all of you never to be greedy or dishonest with anyone and be generous with each other. Second, if anyone ever approached any of my children with pills, bennies or dope of any kind, to run away from them, not just walk away. Thirdly, you were all told that if anything ever happened to me that I hoped you would take care of your mother."

The letter went on. He wanted me to know how important we were to him and how important it was for us to know that and give him credit. It even had an explanation for the hitting and the beating: "I can remember giving all three of my sons love in many forms and actually, when I was strict from time to time, it was because I felt it was my duty as a father to give you the security a punishment gives. As boys grow into the adolescent time of their life, their brain tells them when they have done something wrong, and, believe it or not, children are sometimes disappointed when they are not punished because their brain tells them right from wrong."

He talked a little bit about his troubles with my mother and how they were falling out of love. She didn't go against his authority, he said, but she had a "look of resentment." He thought that she had given all her love to her sons and taken it away from him because of how she was raised. I don't know. Maybe it was true. But he was very sad about it. "Maybe now you can begin to understand that the last seven years has been almost a living hell for me and although I have wanted to give up completely on two separate occasions, something told me to hang on and keep trying because I felt my sons were worth it." I don't know how I could have understood that in any way when I was twenty-three years old.

Most of the letter was about our business as a band, and how we were doing it all wrong. My dad said that rock and roll wouldn't last. He was sure of it. "The way things are shaping up now, The Beach Boys cannot go on and on because cycles of music change as well as fads, like The Beatles, Presleys, etc." But the reason wasn't just that music changed. It was because I had changed. He told me that I had broken contracts with Sea of Tunes by giving songs to other groups, but mostly he criticized me for believing in myself. It was a group with all the Wilsons, he said, but I was making it all about me. "The fact that my sons' singing your beautiful ballads and very catchy novelty songs can sustain you in this business over a longer period, and because you <u>know</u> this, you have used this extraordinary harmony talent and your great song writing ability as a tool towards your own ends. I mean specifically that when you found out that The Beach Boy image and success was on its way you began to listen to phonies who said that The Beach Boys needed you and that you didn't need them (meaning your own brothers) . . . the fact that I was included as your guiding factor and manager didn't mean much to you either, and if you don't think this hurts to know that your son would abandon not only his brothers but his father as well, then you are completely mistaken." The real punch came right after that. He always ended everything with an explanation point: "I cannot believe that such a beautiful young boy, who was kind, loving, received good grades in school and had so many versatile talents, could become so obsessed to prove that he was better than his father."

My dad's letter has become famous all on its own. I was talking to a guy once after a Beach Boys concert, and between the rest of the stuff that always happens—people bringing up rare pressings and asking me for autographs—we got on the matter of the letter. "It's an extraordinary document," the guy said. He had a faraway look in his eyes. I know what he meant. My father wasn't even fifty at the time. He had put so much of his life into our group, which was his group, too. He was at a crossroads in his life where he didn't know if the things he had built were making any sense. A few years later he put out a record called *The Many Moods of Murry Wilson.* It had four of his own songs and arrangements of some Beach Boys songs, including "The Warmth of the Sun." But the letter was the place where he put the most of himself, for better and for worse. It was kind of his *SMiLE,* though I doubt he was smiling at all when he wrote it.

◡ᴑ

That letter hung over my head—or maybe in my head—for years. It was with me when I was doing *Pet Sounds,* when I failed to do *SMiLE.* It was with me when we did a bunch of albums in a row, knocked them out pretty quick and pretty basic, and where the other guys in the group came forward to contribute more songs. That was happening all over rock and roll. In the Beatles, George started to write more. In Creedence Clearwater Revival, John Fogerty let everyone else in the band write songs. With us, it was a chance to get back to being a rock and roll band. I still got plenty of songs on records and plenty of ideas. For *Wild Honey,* I tuned my piano slightly out, more like a twelve-string guitar, to get a more mellow sound. I got the idea to slightly detune from my piano tuner, and I loved what it did to the sound of the record. That album had such good energy, especially on the title song where Carl gave us another great vocal. That whole record had so much soul. We put a theremin on that one for old time's sake. Mike got the album title from some actual wild honey that was out on the kitchen table. Eating healthy was good for our music. *Wild Honey* was one of the records that I made a point of going back and listening to after a while. It was after more than forty years. It kind of swept me away.

On the records after that, *Friends* and *20/20,* the other guys were doing more writing, sometimes with me, sometimes on their own. I wrote lots with Al, especially on *Friends,* where we did "Wake the World," "Be Here in the Mornin'," and "Passing By." Mike, who had met the Maharishi in 1967 and then gone to Rishikesh to study with him at the same time as the Beatles and Donovan, started writing about those kinds of things in songs like "Anna Lee, the Healer" and "Transcendental Meditation." In general, it seemed like we were turning a corner into something more adult. We weren't kids anymore. We didn't have a dad around to tell us we were kids. There were marriages and kids and mind expansion.

In the summer of 1968, we released "Do It Again." I was playing around with Mike, playing some chords, and slowed it down a little bit and started to get a melody. He started writing lyrics and we got the thing done. It was probably the best slow rock song we ever did. I had this idea for the intro where our engineer, Steve Desper— the great Steve Desper—rigged up a kind of defibrillator thing to the drums so that each hit vibrated at like a thousand beats per second. There's never been an intro like it. It's mixed back in the mix of the main body of the song. It was a strange song, or was about something strange. At that time, we were already nostalgic. I felt like we were already so far past surf music that we could turn and look back at it. We put "Do It Again" on *20/20*, which was named that because it was our twentieth record, if you counted greatest hits, but it was also because of hindsight. I made a joke about it on one of the inside photos, where I hid behind an eye examination chart. The cover photo for that record is really nice and colorful. The Boys are all standing up except for Al.

"Time to Get Alone" was one of my favorite songs from that record. It was like a grown-up version of "Wouldn't It Be Nice," where the guy who's singing doesn't have to imagine what it's like to be alone with a girl. He can just invite her to go with him:

> *And now we know it's*
> *Time to get alone*
> *To get alone*
> *And just be together*
> *We'll only be together*

I wrote that song for my friend Danny Hutton's band, which was called Redwood at the time. We laid down tracks and everything. Danny had this piano he played through a busted speaker and it came out sounding like a stretched-out guitar. But then Mike decided he didn't like the idea that I was writing for Danny. I was in the studio working and he came by with Carl and Dennis and started asking questions about "Time to Get Alone." It wasn't just one question. It was a bunch of questions, one after the other, as a way of telling me he thought it was wrong of me to go outside the group. Mike did all the talking; Dennis and Carl just stood there with their heads down. They couldn't look me in the eye. Mike really put the screws on me. I had to take the song away from them, along with another song I had cut a track for called "Darlin'." Danny and Redwood went on to be Three Dog Night. They did fine without those two songs. They had more than twenty Top Forty singles and sold something like forty million records. And Carl did a great job singing "Time to Get Alone" when we released it on *20/20*. He even got a producer credit. I don't know if Mike was proud or ashamed of what he had done in taking the song back from Redwood, but he reminded me of how my dad had acted a few years before with "Surf City."

And the real Murry Wilson didn't go away completely. He was my dad, after all. He was the dad of all of us. We were making records without him, but we were carrying on in the same tradition. He came back in 1968 to sing on "Be Here in the Mornin'," on the *Friends* album. He gave us some of the lower notes. And then in 1969 he and I wrote a song together. He was watching Joey Bishop's television show, and just as Joey Bishop was going to a commercial, he said, "We're going to break away for a minute." That put an idea in my dad's head. He wanted to write a song called "Break Away." He came over to my house on Bellagio and we knocked it out in a half hour. He called himself Reggie Dunbar on that record for some reason. We put it out as a single. I thought it came out great, but it didn't do very well. The B-side was a song that Dennis wrote with Gregg Jakobson called "Celebrate the News." It was a song about being optimistic because things were looking up after a long time down.

> *Hello*
> *My luck was so bad*
> *I thought I used up all the luck I had*
> *Every time I thought I'd get it on*
> *Someone put me on*
> *There's been a change*
> *Beautiful and strange*
> *My life's gone through a change*
> *Somehow I know (somehow I know)*
> *Bad luck's in the past*
> *All good things here at last*
> *So now we'll grow*

As it turned out, things weren't looking up. Soon after "Break Away" and "Celebrate the News" came out, we had a break with Capitol. We had been with them almost from the start, right after Candix. The Four Freshmen had been with them. Frank Sinatra had been with them. The label had been our home. But at the end of the '60s, it was just a house. And it was a house that wasn't standing up straight. They weren't paying us the way we thought was fair. There was lots of money that seemed to disappear between the time people spent it on records and the time it came to pay us. In the spring of 1969, right after *20/20* came out, we sued Capitol for unpaid royalties. That messed up contract negotiations. In June, when our contract with them ended, they deleted our back catalog, which meant that we weren't earning any more money on it. It got ugly for a little while there.

In November, my dad sold Sea of Tunes. He got $700,000 for it, which seemed to him like lots of money. Plus, he believed we were washed up. "Break Away" hadn't done well. The Capitol situation was a wreck. The other guys couldn't believe it. No one could believe it. He had taken the only thing that we knew would last, our songs, and sold it off like he was running a garage sale. I was scared of my dad lots of the time and angry at him lots of the time, but that was one of the only times that I was just disappointed. He made the wrong business decision for the wrong reasons, and he created a bad situation that would last for years.

✑

When we went looking for a label, we ended up following Frank Sinatra, sort of. He had been with Capitol until 1960, but he wanted more control of his music. He tried to buy Verve records but ended up starting his own label, Reprise, with Warner Brothers. That's where we ended up, Reprise. We set up our own label, Brother Records, inside the big label—they were Warner Brothers and we were the Wilson brothers, so it made sense in both directions. David

Anderle helped run it. He was one of the only guys back then who understood the trip we were on and the right direction for us to go. We brought on other artists we trusted and knew had the same vision, like Danny Hutton. And we got down to making our own music. The first record we made for Warner was *Sunflower*, the record with the cover photo taken at Hidden Valley. We worked with Steve Desper, a genius engineer. He's the one who put all that organ high up in the mix and really helped give that record its sound. On "Add Some Music to Your Day," Mike sang a great lead vocal. We recorded in my house in Bel Air, the Bellagio house, in the den. The room was meant to be.

Sunflower was an important record for us because it was the first for Warner, and also because of Jack Rieley. Jack was a radio DJ and record man I met right after *Sunflower*. I liked him and he understood where the band was going, so we hired him as our manager. Jack did a lot of good for the Beach Boys, helped to get us moving that year when we were kind of stuck. He was a really great lyricist; he worked on the lyrics for songs like "Long Promised Road," "Marcella," and "You Need a Mess of Help to Stand Alone." And Jack had a great narrating voice. A little later, on *Holland*, we used him to do the narration on *Mount Vernon and Fairway (A Fairy Tale)*.

Jack had lots of ideas to add to our ideas. When I first met him, we were talking about "Surf's Up," a song I had started that I couldn't finish producing. He encouraged me to make a whole record around it. Jack also came up with a kind of new direction for the band. He thought that the Beach Boys shouldn't be so cut off from the world. I knew what he meant. The mid-'60s were all about exploring inside yourself, figuring out peace and love and then bringing that to society. That's what I was trying to do with songs like "Good Vibrations." But in the late '60s and early '70s, lots of bands started to write songs that were more political, songs about Vietnam or Nixon or Kent State. Mike wrote a song called "Student Demonstration Time," which was a remake of Leiber and

Stoller's "Riot in Cell Block No. 9" with new lyrics about all the college kids who were trying to make a difference. It was kind of the same idea as "Surfin' U.S.A."—take a rock and roll song we loved, put in some lyrics about a new scene, and make a new song.

But mostly we decided to be political in different ways. Our concerns were more about the earth and what people were doing to it. The cover image for *Surf's Up* was an illustration based on a famous American Indian sculpture called *End of the Trail. Surf's Up* was a warning that there was a kind of crisis. If people didn't treat the earth with love and respect, we might be near the end. Al and Mike wrote "Don't Go Near the Water," which was a kind of anti-surf message. It told people that if they couldn't treat the ocean with respect, they shouldn't use it for recreation. The big new song that I wrote for *Surf's Up* was also about the environment. It was called "A Day in the Life of a Tree," and that's basically what it was: a tree thinking out loud (or thinking silently but singing out loud) about all the bad things that were happening to it. In the back of my mind, I might have been thinking of the tree in Rosemary Clooney's "Tenderly." Jack Rieley and I talked about the idea of the song and then he wrote lyrics:

> *Feel the wind burn through my skin*
> *The pain, the air is killing me*
> *For years my limbs stretched to the sky*
> *A nest for birds to sit and sing*
>
> *But now my branches suffer*
> *And my leaves don't bear the glow*
> *They did so long ago*
>
> *One day I was full of life*
> *My sap was rich and I was strong*
> *From seed to tree I grew so tall*
> *Through wind and rain I could not fall*

But now my branches suffer
And my leaves don't offer
Poetry to men of song

Trees like me weren't meant to live
If all this world can give
Pollution and slow death

Oh Lord, I lay me down
No life's left to be found
There's nothing left for me

I wasn't sure who was going to sing the lead vocal on that one. I tried to do it, but it wasn't working out. I didn't sound right. I thought Jack would be perfect for it. He understood the lyrics perfectly because he had written them. Plus, I wanted the lead to sound like a dying tree, and if that's what you're going for, Jack Rieley's your man. But he had never sung on a Beach Boys record before, and there was no good way to ask him. So I came up with a plan where we told Jack I'd be putting the lead vocal in while he listened in the studio. I tried once. I tried again. Then I got angry and frustrated. I came out of the booth and told him I didn't understand the way the song could work. "I'm confused," I said. "I don't know what this means anymore."

"You know," he said, "you're just tired."

"I'm not tired," I said. "I'm tapped out on this song. I need you to give me a guide vocal."

Jack came in and did a few takes, and then I came out and thanked him for singing lead on it. He didn't understand at first. Carl and I had to explain to him what we did. "A Day in the Life of a Tree" is a big song because it's about how people treat the earth, but it's also a small song because it's about how one living thing can feel stripped down and wrong for the world. In a way it's not so different from "I Just Wasn't Made for These Times."

I wasn't always tired then. For those records in the early '70s, I was really up, with lots of energy. Part of the reason was that I was eating better. In 1969 I opened up a health food store in West Hollywood called the Radiant Radish. A *Rolling Stone* reporter came to write about it. I was at the store alone in my bathrobe. While we were doing the interview, a guy came by and wanted a bottle of B-12 vitamins. "I can't give it to you without a script," I said. I was joking, I think, but I wasn't really much of a businessman in that way. The store closed about a year later, but I learned how to use a cash register.

And the store stayed open as an idea. One of the songs I did during that period that didn't make it onto a record was called "H.E.L.P. Is on the Way." It was all about the store. I wasn't close to my high weight, but I was getting kind of soft.

> *Stark naked in front of my mirror*
> *A pudgy person somehow did appear*
> *Seems lately all I've eaten, sugar and fat*
> *It's getting obvious that's not where it's at*
> *A big pot and triple chin*
> *Oh, what condition my condition was in*
> *Laughing at myself at what a crying shame*
> *Whatever happened to my Greek godly frame*
> *Cyclamates, juicy steaks, sweet things too*
> *Aren't always good as they seem*
> *Doughy lumps, stomach pumps, enemas too*
> *That's what you get when you eat that way*

At the end was a commercial for the store.

> *Radiant Radish is gonna be on Fairfax and 3rd . . .*
> *Ooh, get yourself in for a snack*
> *Yeah, but stop by the Radiant Radish*

Years later, I drove by a little grocery store near my house called the Glen Market. There were two cars parked outside so it looked like it was doing good business. I went home and told Melinda that we should buy it. She didn't think it was a good idea. She asked me who would run it. "You could," I said. She looked at me like it was an even worse idea. "But there were two cars outside," I said.

When the time came for a new Beach Boys record, I was working with Marilyn and her sister Diane on their American Spring record. That was a cool project because I got to work on songs that we all loved that came from other songwriters but were meant mostly for girls to sing. They did versions of Carole King's "Now That Everything's Been Said," the Shirelles' "Mama Said," and the Carpenters' "Superstar." I didn't do the whole record or anything close, but it was recorded at my home studio so I was around lots of the time. Steve Desper, our engineer from *Sunflower*, did whatever I didn't do.

Because of that, Carl mostly was in charge of the next Beach Boys record, and he did a great job with it. Being in charge of the Beach Boys that year wasn't easy. Dennis had hurt his hand when he punched through some glass at his house, and Bruce Johnston wasn't getting along with Jack Rieley. Carl brought in some other guys from a South African band called the Flame: a drummer named Ricky Fataar and a guitarist named Blondie Chaplin. I wrote a few songs for the record, which ended up being called *Carl and the Passions—So Tough*. I wrote "Marcella" for that album, which is one of my favorites, and also "You Need a Mess of Help to Stand Alone." That one I did with Jack Rieley. It was a love song from a man to a woman but also a song about how even though I was doing stuff away from the group I also wasn't completely ever on my own.

> *I need the warmth of your smile*
> *To heat my frostbitten sorrow*
> *I need your hand on my shoulder*

> *To lead todays to tomorrows*
> *I need your strength to lock me to the track*
> *I need your trust to bust the things I lack*

And then I stopped, or at least slowed way down. I was having problems. I still had energy, but everything was starting to feel hollow. There wasn't less health food, but there was more drinking and drugs to go along with it. Jack took us to Holland to record, but that didn't solve things. *Holland* came out in January of 1973, and then in June I was home downstairs when I heard the phone ring. I heard Marilyn talking softly. She came into the room to find me. "Your dad died today, Brian," she said. "I'm so sorry." I started crying and we drove out to Whittier, where he lived at the end. I had a rough time with it for a while after that. It fucked me up big time. I didn't go to his funeral. I went to New York with Diane, my sister-in-law. I wasn't staying away out of anger or anything. It was just too many things all at once, and I was not in the mood to go to my dad's funeral. But during the time of the funeral, the actual hours of it, I thought only about him. There were times that my dad was nothing but mean to me. I walked around afraid that I'd get cracked across the face. My dad brought out the belt like lots of dads brought out the belt, but my dad didn't have any patience and when he brought out the belt, he used it. I don't always blame him, but sometimes he went too far.

But I also thought about what a gifted guy he was and how much he meant to the group and to me. He was more than just talented. He was gifted. Sometimes it frustrated him. He could joke around. He could make people laugh. He was nice to my friends. But when you got in close to him, you saw all the parts of him that weren't filled up with anything but doubt and anger. I think of the very last sentence of his letter: "Please try to understand that all I tried to do was make you all honest men, and instead of hating me for it, I ask that you all try to search your own hearts once in a while and try to be better." If you pull that sentence away from the rest of it, everything makes perfect sense.

After my dad died, I used to go to Jimmy Guercio's place, Caribou Ranch, in Colorado. He had a bunch of little bungalows there and a recording studio. I went there a few times—sometimes with my brothers, sometimes with the rest of the band—and cut a few things, including a song called "Just an Imitation," which was a really beautiful ballad and kind of a tribute to my dad. We didn't use any of the Caribou sessions for the album, though. I didn't know what kind of album to do. I didn't know the right direction. My dad was gone, and it wasn't just my dad. It was everyone's dad. He had been there since the start and had managed us and pushed us so hard in good and bad ways. Even when we had pushed him away, he was still close. He was fired as our manager, but he couldn't break away for a minute.

And then he was gone. He was the first one to go. I shared my sadness with my brothers mostly. It was easier sharing it with them than with my mom. I spent a few hours with her every now and then, but that was hard, too. I felt uncomfortable calling her all the time, and then when I didn't call I felt guilty as hell. I know she loved me. I know that she would have told me so. I just felt like I knew too much about what everyone had done, and what had undone everyone. I just think that things were so strange then.

CHAPTER 6

Echoes and Voices

They say I got brains
But they ain't doing me no good
I wish they could
Each time things start to happen again
I think I got something good goin' for myself
But what goes wrong

   —"I Just Wasn't Made for These Times"

My sixtieth birthday was normal most of the day, which was the best present I could have asked for. It was rainy, which was a surprise for Los Angeles, but otherwise it was an ordinary warm summer day. In the afternoon, Melinda reminded me that she was taking me to dinner. "I know," I said, even though I had forgotten. We got in the car and drove to the Mulholland Grill in Bel Air. While I was going into the restaurant, I saw a guy who looked like my friend Danny Hutton. Then I saw the rest of them—Van Dyke Parks; the guys in my band; Melinda's mom, Rose; Tony Asher; David and Eva Leaf; Jerry and Lois Weiss; Ray Lawlor; Steve Desper—and I realized that it was a party for me. "I told you I didn't want a big party," I said to Melinda, because I had, and everyone laughed.

It was a really great time. I didn't think there would be so many people, and I didn't realize that each of the people would bring up so many memories. When I looked at Steve, I heard an echo of "Add Some Music to Your Day" from *Sunflower*, and that got me thinking about that record, and that cover photo. When I looked at Van Dyke, I heard an echo of "Surf's Up," and that got me thinking about *SMiLE* and how it would have been such an amazing record, and how I still hoped that it could come out. Some of the echoes I was hearing were on delay, like they were coming in from far away. Other echoes were closer. When I looked at Melinda, I heard an echo of "You Still Believe in Me," which had come out on *Pet Sounds*. It was a love song from a guy to a girl, thanking her for not giving up on him.

I know perfectly well
I'm not where I should be
I've been very aware
You've been patient with me
Every time we break up
You bring back your love to me
And after all I've done to you
How can it be
I try hard to be more
What you want me to be
But I can't help how I act
When you're not here with me
I try hard to be strong
But sometimes I fail myself
And after all I've promised you
So faithfully

When I originally wrote the song with Tony, it wasn't about Melinda. It would be another twenty years before I sat in the car at the dealership on Pico and Bundy. But I wasn't hearing an echo of that original version. I was hearing an echo of the newer version that had just come out on *Brian Wilson Presents Pet Sounds Live*, a concert performance of the entire record that I did with Darian and the band at Royal Festival Hall in London at the beginning of the year. I had to sing songs that were originally sung by Mike, like "That's Not Me" and "Here Today." I had to sing "God Only Knows," and God knows I couldn't do as good a job as Carl had.

But I also had to sing songs that I had been singing my whole life, and that wasn't necessarily easier. When you have hits and you have to perform them again and again over the years, it's a strange process. You have to give the audience a version that they recognize, but you also have to give yourself a version that makes sense. Singing a song I made when I was twenty-five and believing in what it meant when I was almost sixty wasn't easy. Melinda made it easier. She made all the love songs easier. But it was still weird to hear the original spirit of those songs across the years and then make them work in front of a crowd. I was a little nervous—more than a little nervous—but we did it. Hooray for us, and hooray for the audience. One review said that the harmonies were even better than the ones on the original album. I appreciated the compliment. I tried hard to make them work.

The year of my sixtieth birthday, I also went to a half-century celebration for someone else. And not just anyone: it was Queen Elizabeth II's Golden Jubilee, which was an extended celebration of her fifty years on the throne. I was one of two American artists chosen to represent the United States at the queen's Golden Jubilee. Tony Bennett was the other. It was such an honor. There was a huge concert scheduled for London just a few months after we did *Pet Sounds* at the Royal Festival Hall. We flew over about a week before to rehearse and stayed at a hotel on the Thames, right across the bridge from Westminster Abbey. London always has a really cool vibe, but this time was even more special because of the buzz over the Jubilee.

In our rehearsal hall, other rock stars would drop by to pitch in. My band and I would play "California Girls," and then Eric Clapton would come out and sing a duet with me on "The Warmth of the Sun." He said it was his favorite song, which was as amazing as hearing that "God Only Knows" was Paul McCartney's favorite song. When Eric sang with me that time, he added a little inflection to the vocal that I now use myself whenever we do the song. And in the harmony-stack fade, he played a guitar part that was so great it's indescribable. I will never forget the look on Paul Von Mertens's face as he was watching Eric. It was like he was stoned! We also sang "God Only Knows" with the Corrs and "Good Vibrations" with everyone.

One of the nights in London, Melinda and I went out to dinner with Jerry and Lois Weiss at this steak place called Christopher's. It was so good that we went back there three or four nights in a row. The first night, we exited the place onto streets so crowded with the celebration that it was hard to believe. You couldn't get a cab—and even if you could, it couldn't have moved a foot down the street. So the four of us took the London Underground. We got off by Westminster and walked across the bridge to the hotel. I tried to think about the last time I rode on a subway. Maybe it was New York City in 1964. Public places are always strange. Sometimes people recognize me and I get a little paranoid. No one did on the Tube, but the next day I was having lunch in a pub and a woman at the next table kept staring at me. I wondered if she recognized me from the Underground. Finally she came over. "Excuse me, sir," she said, "but do you know you look exactly like the American musician Brian Wilson?" "I know," I said. I didn't want to tell her it was me. It seemed too egotistical.

The day of the concert, Paul McCartney was running through a rehearsal of "All You Need Is Love," which was scheduled as the night's closing song. Almost everyone was onstage, and Paul turned it into a group song. He had Joe Cocker doing one verse, Rod Stewart doing another, Eric contributing guitar. I stood in the back just singing the "love, love, love" background part when Pablo stopped the take. "Hey," he said, "we've got something here.

Brian, you come up front and sing that part." They moved my mic up front and I ended up on the front line along with Joe, Rod, Eric, and Paul. It was a hell of a band! It worked great in the show. The place went wild. I heard there were over a million people watching it live in the streets on huge screens. What a trip. What a great song to close on. What a great celebration for the queen.

At my sixtieth, we didn't close on that. But there was a closing song. Someone brought out a cake from the kitchen, and everyone sang "Happy Birthday." Those harmonies were pretty good also, and the cake was great.

I tried to eat the cake slowly. People say I'm the fastest eater in the world, but I don't know about that. I haven't seen who is the champion. But I am a fast eater. That's one of the reasons I have always had trouble with weight. Also, I love sweets. My daughter Carnie cooks. She's a great cook. She makes pudding. She makes fish. Once on Father's Day she called and asked me what I wanted. I really wanted cheesecake, but I told her she couldn't make it because of my diet. I asked her to make macaroni and cheese instead. But for that same celebration Wendy brought an apple pie. I wasn't supposed to eat sugar, but I kept asking her for the pie. They didn't want me to get it, so I started to pretend it was like Christmas or a birthday. I started singing, "Happy Father's Day to me." Just like at Mulholland Grill, I figured that was a good way to get the apple pie.

But all that cake and pie adds up. Sometimes when I go to the doctor and get weighed in, the numbers stop me in my tracks. When the Father's Day party ended, I did what I did when I got back from Mulholland Grill. I walked. As I have gotten older, walking has saved my life. I have always used it to lose weight but also to get out and think. There's a kind of spirituality in making music but also in moving under your own power through the world. When I was in high school there was a song by Jimmy Charles called "A Million to One." I remember hearing that in the car when I was driving with my friend Keith. We went to the beach and ran along the shore for almost an hour. I can't run so much anymore now that I'm older, but I try to walk whenever I can. When I'm home I go to one specific park, a little triangular place off Bel Air. There's a path around the edge that's five-eighths of a mile. When I was doing my best I might be able to go around it seven or eight times. Now it's less than that, but I still try. It's both meditation and health. The vendors there know me. I sometimes stop and talk to them. If I'm getting a bottle of water, they'll ask me if I'm thirsty or they'll say, "How you doing, buddy?" Someone told me once that Frank Sinatra used to go to the same park.

If I'm not at home, I still try to walk. There are parks and beaches everywhere. In Maui once I came up a path and someone else was coming the other way. It was Magic Johnson. "Hi, Brian," he said. I waved, saying, "Hey, Magic." I kept walking. I had season tickets to the Lakers back then, so I knew I would see him again.

⌒

When I came off the road at the end of 1964, I was sure I wouldn't play any more shows. In fact, Hawaii was one of the rare places I went onstage with the band after that. We went there in 1967. A promoter had scheduled a pair of shows there that we were going to film, maybe for a live album. I didn't want to travel. I hadn't traveled since Houston. But the guys kept asking me to go and finally I said I would, but only if they would let me bring my Baldwin organ. I loved the sounds it got. That meant that Carl would have to play bass. Bruce didn't want to take the trip. It was funny, in a way. He had gone out on the road instead of me, and now I was going out on the road instead of him.

We did two shows in Hawaii like we were supposed to, but the record label didn't think we sounded right. When we got back, we went up to Wally Heider Studios in San Francisco and tried to remake the whole live record in the studio, like with *Beach Boys' Party!* That didn't work, and we ended up scrapping the album.

Off the road in '64, I was happier in the studio. I was a little worried that I was letting the guys down or that I couldn't live up to our reputation. I decided the only way to prove my decision wasn't a mistake was to write the best songs and make the best music.

It wasn't easy at first. I was trying to get peace and quiet so I could think of new songs, but there were so many voices. Some of them were the voices of the band, trying to figure out what I was doing. My dad's voice was in there, telling me I was weak. And then there were all the other voices, the ones that tell me that I'm worthless, that I should give up, that they'll kill me.

I have heard those voices for a long time, maybe fifty years now. They first came to me when I was twenty-two, after I took LSD. LSD was something that people told me made your mind larger, and that sounded interesting to me. I was interested in exploring ways of getting expanded. The first time I took it, I had to go hide in a bedroom, and I thought mostly about my parents and whether I should be afraid of them. I also started to play what became "California Girls" on the piano, that sound of the cowboy riding into town. I played it and played it until I heard other things inside of it. But about a week after that, the first voices started to pop up. They'd sound like a real person's voice, a person different from me who I couldn't control, but inside my own head. I didn't know what to do with them.

I stopped with the acid for about a year but then took it again when I was twenty-three. I'm not sure why I went back to it. Just young and stupid, I guess. Doctors have told me that the voices didn't come from the acid, that they would have happened anyway, but I'm not sure. I didn't have them before. When I was fourteen or fifteen I had anxiety spells. I would try to talk and fall into a stammer or stutter. I got locked up for a few seconds, frozen in place. That phase lasted about six months and it went away.

The voices are different from that. They are frightening. There have been times when they came every day and other times when they left me alone. When I'm working on a record in the studio, they're less likely to be there. Lots of the music I've made has been my way of trying to get rid of those voices. Other strategies didn't really work. Alcohol didn't work, and drugs didn't work, and sleeping didn't work, and never sleeping didn't work. All those things worked for a little while, but they never worked long. Those are the voices that people call mental illness. What does that mean exactly? It's part of my brain that doesn't change, so what has to change is the way I deal with it. The voices won't disappear, so I have to make sure that I don't disappear because of them.

What made it worse, at least early on, was that the voices in my head that were trying to do away with me were in a crowded space. They were in there with other voices that were trying to make something beautiful. Voices were the problem but also the answer. The answer was in harmony. That's what I worked on after I came off the road in 1964. There was a period when I tried to make music that captured all those voices. One of the first songs we recorded then was "Do You Wanna Dance?," a cover of an old Bobby Freeman song. Dennis sang lead vocals on it, and he did a great job—just straight-ahead rock and roll, with guitars and saxophones churning underneath. Then, around thirty seconds into the song, we got to the chorus and the whole thing just exploded. Al came in. Mike came in. Carl came in. I came in. We're singing high. We're singing low. We're weaving around each other and through each other.

Because that's a dance song, people don't think of it as a spiritual thing, but it is, because it's harmony. Our harmonies were always a very spiritual sound, a very beautiful sound. You start with one voice and go a third up and a third up to an octave. All of it is serving this one main melody, and it's really wonderful. It makes you feel so good, and that's one of the main jobs of music. Any music that gets to your soul like that is soul music. And it helps to remind you that voices are beautiful instead of dark things that echo in your head. What's strange with harmonies is that I can hear them very much when I'm in the studio but not very much outside. When I walk into the studio, music happens and the voices stop happening. It's a kind of magic. I don't know what kind. But it happens for me mostly in the studio.

Recently I was watching the news, like I do every day. It's news at four, then *Wheel of Fortune,* then *Jeopardy!* One of the stories on the news was about how anxiety and creativity are linked. There was some big study at a university, and the doctors who did the study said that anxiety and creativity are sort of the same thing: both of them are about dealing less with what's in front of you and more with what's in your head. Listening to what's in your head, especially when you're a person with anxiety, leads to negative emotions. But they're also a form of imagination. If you can worry about problems when there aren't problems around, then you can also think of stories or songs when there aren't stories or songs around. You can make things go from not existing to existing.

I thought about that news report after I turned off the TV. So what if my brain gets worried before I go out onstage, wondering if the audience will like me? Maybe that's because it's the same brain that thinks of new melodies. So what if my brain gets worried before it gets on an airplane? Maybe that's because it's the same brain that can put instruments and voices together. When we were getting ready to go to London to do the concert that became the *Pet Sounds Live* album, I was nervous. I don't like planes. But these days, being on the plane isn't the worst part. The worst part is thinking about them before I get on them. I didn't sleep the whole night before we were flying. Jerry Weiss, who takes care of everything for me when we're on the road, asked me what I think about when a plane is taking off. I think, "Don't blow up . . . don't blow up . . . don't blow up." I hear myself saying it inside my head, and in a weird way I'm happy to hear it. I need to hear that voice, not to silence the other voices but to try to make some kind of harmony with them. Learning to let all those voices work together is what let me make records like "Do You Wanna Dance?" or "Help Me, Ronda."

Or *Pet Sounds*. I thought about *Pet Sounds* at my birthday party at Mulholland Grill, because I was thinking about "You Still Believe in Me" when I was looking at Melinda, and also because the live record had just come out. But the truth is that I think about it often. It's one of the records people ask about the most.

It's hard to say exactly when the sound of *Pet Sounds* started. It was something that was coming for a while. Maybe it started when I first heard "Be My Baby" on the radio and I began to understand how you could make emotions through sound. Maybe it started when I began to understand more about soul singers like Dionne Warwick and Aretha Franklin and how they could make you feel amazing things with small vocal gestures. Maybe it started on the second side of *The Beach Boys Today!* when I started to make softer and slower songs that weren't exactly love ballads but instead were snapshots of how I was feeling as I grew up. It was probably all those things put together. But it started to change what I was doing.

The first song on that album is "Please Let Me Wonder," which I cut at ten o'clock at night at Western. I was starting to sing more about what people were thinking and dreaming about when they were in love, and how sometimes it was about what they didn't have more than what they had. "Kiss Me, Baby" was one of the last songs we recorded in 1964, though we did the vocals early the next year. It's about romance, but really it's about a fight and maybe even a breakup; the romance is just imagined. "She Knows Me Too Well" had a great whiny falsetto sound, much better than "Let Him Run Wild." I would call myself a versatile singer. I can sing sweet with emotion, but I can also do other kinds of vocals. It's a cool message, too, one of those lyrics about a guy who is insecure and is able to say so in the song:

> *I get so jealous of the other guy*
> *And then I'm not happy 'til I make her break down and cry*
> *When I look at other girls it must kill her inside*
> *But it'd be another story if she looked at the guys*

But she knows me
She knows me too well
Knows me so well
That she can tell
I really love her
She knows me too well

And "In the Back of My Mind" grew out of a song that already existed; the seed of the melody was the Skyliners' "Since I Don't Have You," a beautiful ballad from the late '50s. That must have been echoing in my head somewhere, and I wrote a new song about a guy who wasn't able to be honest about everything that scared him.

I'm blessed with everything
A world to which a man can cling
So happy times when I break out in tears
In the back of my mind I still have my fears

That was one of the most honest lines I ever wrote: "In the back of my mind I still have my fears." I've never been afraid to admit fear. But I didn't sing that line. I had Dennis do it because he never really had a chance to sing very much. I thought his vocal was great.

The quieter and sadder songs on the record were good, but the fast songs were great, too. "Dance, Dance, Dance" was fantastic. We cut that in Memphis, and when we got back to LA we did it again in a second version that I preferred. Carl wrote the guitar intro for that one. The record ended with "Bull Session with the 'Big Daddy.'" People say it's a spoken-word track, but it's not really a track at all. It's tape from an interview we did with Earl Leaf, a famous photographer who wasn't related to my friend David Leaf. We put it on the end of the album to show the way we were in the studio when we weren't making music. We ordered burgers with

French fries and pickles. Al wasn't there but Marilyn was. The part I remember best from that is when Earl asks about a show we did in Paris. The guys were talking about whether they played well or not, and whether they made any mistakes. "I still haven't made a mistake in my whole career," I said, and Dennis said, "Brian, we keep waiting for you to make a mistake." Back then I was young and I said things out of confidence, but I was right to say it. I was strict with the guys if they got their harmonies wrong. I was searching for a sound that I wanted to get, and I knew how to get it. I tried never to be mean about it, but I also didn't want to relax too much and let that sound get away.

If the sound of *Pet Sounds* didn't start on *The Beach Boys Today!*, maybe it was on *Summer Days (And Summer Nights!!)*. Even though that record had big hits like "California Girls," they were hits that were pushing us further in the direction I wanted to go. The song had an orchestral lead-in, and the main beat sounded like a cowboy and his horse walking into town but was borrowed from Bach. It was an opening, and I went through it. The other big hit was "Help Me, Rhonda," which was a remake of "Help Me, Ronda" that we did faster and with slightly different lyrics. It was also just a better feel. The whole year after the flight to Houston, I kept thinking about what kinds of songs I should be making, and whether there were any limits to how a pop song could sound. I couldn't really think of any limits.

I knew I had to explore that sound more. I had to go further in that direction, bring more orchestration and different kinds of arrangements into our music. One of the first songs we tried after that was "The Little Girl I Once Knew." It was like a sequel to "California Girls." The first two notes of the intro are Chinese tones. I sang harmony with Carl on that record. It was one of our best, but it didn't sell at all. And when records didn't sell at all, record companies started to put pressure on us. They wanted more music fast. I didn't have more music fast. I was exploring. That wasn't good enough for Capitol. The holidays were coming up, and they requested an album they could sell at the holidays. Maybe "requested" is the wrong way to say it. They expected one. I wasn't ready with any new material yet, so we put out an album called *Beach Boys' Party!* It was recorded to sound like it was live, but we cut it in the studio and sang mostly covers: we did the Rivingtons' "Papa-Oom-Mow-Mow," the Everly Brothers' "Devoted to You," and Bob Dylan's "The Times They Are A-Changin'."

There was one big hit from that record that everyone knows, an old doo-wop song by the Regents called "Barbara Ann." It was pretty simple, and we tore through it. Dean Torrence sang with us. It almost got to number one on the charts. Lots of people know that song because of what happened later, in the '70s, when the ayatollah in Iran took American hostages and people started to make parodies of "Barbara Ann" called "Bomb Iran." But in 1965 it wasn't that kind of party. The whole record was just for fun, a way of getting a new Beach Boys record into stores. I got to sing "There's No Other (Like My Baby)," a Phil Spector song he did with the Crystals. And then we did two Beatles songs, "Tell Me Why" and "I Should Have Known Better." Just after we released the party record, the Beatles put out *Rubber Soul.* It came just at the right time. I was right in the middle of the next big thing.

The next big thing, at least at first, was an old song. It was a Bahamian folk ballad called "The John B. Sails." Al recommended the song. He was a folk guy from way back, and he always loved the Kingston Trio's recording of the song. He kept saying that we should do our own version of it. I wasn't sure because I didn't know that much about folk music, but Al kept saying he knew it could work as a Beach Boys song. To show me, he sat and played it on the piano. When he did that, then I heard how I could make the song work, and I got excited. I worked for a day and then called Al to come back and listen to what I cut. He loved it. It wasn't just that, though. Sometimes you love something because it's familiar.

Sometimes you love it because it reminds you of something else you loved. That's what I would have expected. But I watched him while he was listening to it, and I could tell from the way he looked that he loved it in a different way. He loved it the way you love something new, like a girl you have just talked to for the first time. I knew that we were going in a new direction. The song deserved its own title. The original folk song was called "The John B. Sails," and the Kingston Trio version was called "The Wreck of the John B." We changed the title again, to "Sloop John B," which was the same name as a version Dick Dale had done. We weren't completely past our surf roots.

When we recorded it, we went to Western with Chuck Britz, and I tried to match the arrangement I had in my head with all the studio players, who were the same people as usual, Hal Blaine and Carol Kaye and Billy Strange playing a twelve-string and the rest. We double tracked the bass. We had a glockenspiel. We had flutes, more than one. I don't remember exactly how many takes we had to go through to get it right, but I know it was more than ten, because that's where I lost count. When we put it out as a single, I held my breath a little bit. It was the first song in a while that I knew was going into uncharted territory, but I didn't want that to mean it would miss the chart. It didn't. It was the fastest-selling single we had ever put out. It sold a half million copies in its first two weeks, went to number three in the United States, and did even better around the world. It went to number one on three different continents: Europe (Austria, Germany, the Netherlands, Norway, Sweden, and Switzerland), Africa (South Africa), and Asia (New Zealand).

The song's success meant that I could keep going and keep exploring. It meant that the other voices that doubted me—in the group and at the record label and inside my own head—quieted down for a little bit. I was writing songs as fast as I could. Some of them came easy. Some came hard. I was doing the lyrics with Tony Asher, who I was introduced to by a guy named Loren Schwartz.

Loren was the same guy who introduced me to marijuana and LSD, which gave me some ideas, and also to Tony Asher, who gave me more. Tony was working in advertising and he was interested in music, and I just went on my gut instinct that Tony would be a great lyricist. It was complete vibe and instinct. I liked the way he talked. The rest of the band was in and out of Los Angeles; they went to tour Japan in January, the Midwest in February and March, Texas in April. When they came home between tour stops, they put down their vocal tracks. It was a new way of working, and it was better in some ways but worse in others.

One of the first songs I did in that new style was "Wouldn't It Be Nice." Tony and I talked about the feel we wanted. We started with the idea that it was a song about childhood, about hoping that things would turn out a certain way. There's nothing like being a kid before you see that life is going to force you to deal with certain things. That was the spark of it, though Tony's lyrics pulled it more into things that teenagers would worry about. It's as much a song about sex as "My Obsession," though it's completely different, because it talks mostly about the emotions behind it. What would it feel like when you didn't have to ask parents for permission to be with a girl? What would it feel like when you could listen to your own inner voice without hearing all these voices of authority?

> *Wouldn't it be nice if we were older*
> *Then we wouldn't have to wait so long*
> *And wouldn't it be nice to live together*
> *In the kind of world where we belong*
> *You know its gonna make it that much better*
> *When we can say good night and stay together*

The instrumental tracks for "Wouldn't It Be Nice" were done pretty easily, because I made them with the Wrecking Crew when the rest of the band was out on the road. When I say that they were done easily, I don't mean that they were done quickly. I lost track of how many takes we did at twenty. But we got there, and we had a song that sounded perfect. It was a totally new bag of sound for us—or anybody else, for that matter. On the intro I had Barney Kessel playing this really great guitar he had, a one-of-a-kind twelve-string mando-guitar built by Gibson. It sounded like nothing else. He played right into the board. And I had two accordion players who made this amazing vibrational tone when I buried them in echo. We didn't add vocals until March, when the guys were back from a quick tour in Oregon. To me, it was complicated because I was trying to teach the band a new way to sing on a new kind of song and they were doing the thing they knew best, which was to sing the old way better than anyone.

There's a story that I helped Dennis get over his shyness at the microphone, and that's partly true. It's hard for some people to give it their all while they're standing at a studio microphone. It's an artificial place to be, but you're trying to get real emotions. Some people put their hands over their mouths, cup them there, to give them a little more privacy. I suggested that to Dennis, and it worked great for him. I sang lead, Mike sang the bridge, and he has been credited with the part at the end, the "Good night, my baby / Sleep tight, my baby." That part is great. It's really the whole idea of the song pushed into two little lines: the guy is finally with his girl, or maybe he's imagining being with her and sending her wishes. I kind of knew that would be the first song on the record.

Because the guys were in and out of town, because I had so much time to go down to the studio and try take after take, the musical canvas for that record just got bigger and bigger. For "You Still Believe in Me," I used a harpsichord, just decided to try it out to see if it would work. On "Don't Talk (Put Your Head on My Shoulder)," I used a string quartet. I wrote out the parts in a manuscript and then I conducted. On "I Just Wasn't Made for These Times," I wanted it to sound eerie, and that ended up with a situation where I introduced a new instrument to rock and roll: the theremin. Lots of the songs had Don Randi on them—he's an amazing keyboard player, one of my favorites of all time. And then there were percussion effects that were mostly trial and error, like one song where someone beat out a rhythm on an empty water jug, or another time when we had a bongo but played it with a stick instead of by hand. The musical experimentation got held in place by the lyrics, which were sort of about the same kinds of things as "Caroline, No": how teenagers and other young people felt out of place, how the world wasn't always a good fit, how love was supposed to save you but ended up sometimes deserting you when you needed it the most.

The title track was an instrumental I wrote that I thought might be a spy movie theme. I loved *Thunderball*, which had come out the year before, and I loved listening to composers like Henry Mancini, who did these cool themes for shows like *Peter Gunn*, and Les Baxter, who did all these big productions that sounded sort of like Phil Spector productions. The instrumental was going to be called "Run James Run," and I made it without the rest of the band, just me and some session guys. Roy Caton played the trumpet. We had Jerry Cole and Billy Strange on guitar, and we fed them through a Leslie speaker. Richie Frost played percussion on two empty Coca-Cola cans. We talked about sending it over to the James Bond movie people but put it on the album instead. It wasn't the only Coke thing we used on the record. "Let's Go Away for Awhile," the other instrumental, had a guitar where we strapped a Coke bottle to the strings so it sounded like a Hawaiian steel guitar. It was supposed to have words, but I liked it the way it was so we left it alone.

The guys didn't always get what was happening. We were living such different lives. They were out moving around, getting to new places. I was in one place, at home. Someone played me a song once by Frank Black. He was in the Pixies, a band I don't know very well, and then he had some solo albums. On one of them he did a cover of "I Know There's an Answer" where he put the original lyrics back in, when the title was "Hang On to Your Ego." I wrote that after taking acid, about taking acid. People took it to get away from themselves, but that wasn't the right way to take it. It was supposed to make you go deeper into yourself. I wanted to remind people that they could survive everything best if they remembered who they were. Mike didn't like that title. He didn't like the idea of it. He kept telling me that he wasn't going to sing a song about drugs. Eventually I decided that maybe he was right, partly because of what the song itself was saying. I had to remember who we were. We were the Beach Boys. It also reminded me of what my dad said in his letter to me. I changed the title and the lyrics.

There are so many songs on that record that I love, but there are a few that I love even more. "God Only Knows" gets named as people's favorite Beach Boys song regularly. Some people pick it as their favorite song of all time by any artist in the rock era. Some people pick it as their favorite song of all time, period. So I could say that I really worked forever on it, that I spent a year imagining how the melody would work and another year on the lyrics. But the facts are that Tony and I sat down at a piano and wrote it in forty-five minutes. I guess we had some concepts in mind before we started, mostly in pairs of rhymes we wanted to use. If you're writing about faith and you're writing about emotion and you're writing about being afraid of losing connection, it's easy to imagine what they would be: love/above, leave/believe. But we were also trying to go big with the song. It opened with the line "I may not always love you," which was a strange way to start a love song. True, but strange. It made it so there was something at stake.

Also, it was a little daring to mention God in the chorus or the title of a song, at least at the time. There were really old-fashioned songs that did it. When Tony has given interviews, he has mentioned Kate Smith singing "God Bless America." But this was a different God. This wasn't any public God or American God. This was something more private, whatever force helps a person control their hopes and doubts. That made people nervous. It made Marilyn nervous. It made me nervous. But it also made me calm, because it let me get to a new world of thought and emotion. The lyrics were perfect from the first word to the last. You cannot write a better lyric than that.

The song went so smoothly in the writing, and then we migrated it into the studio. We had a big orchestra lined up for that one. I think there were more than fifteen musicians, which was lots for a pop song at that time. But we needed to get the details right. The devil is in the details, but the details are in God. Does that make sense? It makes as much sense as having a cello and a flute and a clarinet and a viola and an electric bass and an upright bass and a baritone sax and an accordion and a harpsichord. Tony played the sleigh bells. I was especially proud of the French horn part. I knew how I wanted it to sound and I hummed it to a guy named Alan Robinson. He was a great player who had been under contract at Twentieth Century Fox, and he had played on a bunch of movie soundtracks, including *High Noon*. I wanted him to do it glissando, which means sliding down the notes instead of skipping from one note to the next and leaving out the in-betweens. We went in and just kicked ass. If you look at the studio logs, it shows almost two dozen takes, but it didn't feel that way at all. "God Only Knows" felt easy. It came out like melted butter.

When it came to the vocal, I had planned to do it myself, but I thought about other songs I had sung where I wasn't able to do everything I wanted with the lyric. Mainly, I thought about how I would sing it as a lyric. I'd know where the meter was and where the rhyme was. But if I gave it to Carl, he could sing it just as a set of words that meant something. It would take away some of the self-consciousness. That was the advice I gave him: "Sing straight" I think I said. I didn't mean that he needed to hit the words on the nose, only that the words were already there. The meaning was already there. Just do the words as they're written. He did it, and he did a beautiful job with it. The first version had lots of other harmony vocalists on it, too, because that's what we were doing around the time of *Pet Sounds*. It was me singing lower than Carl, and Bruce Johnston singing higher, and also Marilyn and her sister Diane, and

Mike and Al, and Terry Melcher. I think I even spotted a guy who worked in the studio hanging around the edges hoping to get in. When I listened back to it, the layering was wrong. The song was so simple at its heart. It had just one voice. It's an "I" song more than a "we" song. It had loneliness. It's an anxious song, maybe, but also one that's sort of at peace, because the character singing it—Carl, but Carl with the words of the song—can't control it one way or another.

I'm proud of lots of my songs, but "God Only Knows" is one of the ones I'm most proud of because there's a real message in it. And then there's the way we ended it, with a round. I liked all those old songs that used rounds, like "Row, Row, Row Your Boat" (which I did a version of with Marilyn and her sisters in 1965) and "Frère Jacques" (which we used pieces of in "Surf's Up"). I liked rounds because they made it seem like a song was something eternal. At the end of "God Only Knows," that's the feeling, that it could go on forever, that it is going on forever.

I love the whole *Pet Sounds* record. I got a full vision out of it in the studio. After that, I said to myself that I had completed the greatest album I will ever produce. I knew it. I thought it was one of the greatest albums ever done. It was a spiritual record. When I was making it, I looked around at the musicians and the singers and I could see their halos. That feeling stayed on the finished album. I wanted to grow musically, to expand our horizons and do something that people would love, and I did it. Lennon and McCartney were blown away. Marilyn was blown away. Carl was blown away.

Other people didn't say as much about it, like Dennis and Mike. There was a feeling in the band at that point that maybe we were going too far away from hit records. "Sloop John B" was a hit and that was on the record, but it was different than the rest. The record company wasn't sure either. They thought it was going in the wrong direction. But mostly everyone who wasn't sure about it when it was released came around to it over time, even if they didn't always admit it. And I did it all on four tracks, mostly. Bob Dylan said something nice about that: "The records I used to listen to and still love, you can't make a record that sounds that way. Brian Wilson, he made all his records with four tracks, but you couldn't make his records if you had a hundred tracks today." I don't know about that. There's lots you can do with more tracks. But I know that four worked for me.

⁓

"God Only Knows" might be the best song on that record, but my favorite might be "Caroline, No." I did it all by myself. I wrote the music. I sang the vocal. I even wrote the title, in a way. Tony was telling me about a new song he was working on. He wanted to call it "Carol, I Know," and he said it on my right side, and I heard "Caroline, No." He started to correct me but then he stopped. Caroline was a more beautiful name to sing than Carol. Chuck Berry had already done most of what anyone could do with Carol. Also, Caroline rhymed with Marilyn, and when I thought about the song and what it meant, I thought about Marilyn. We had been married for about a year and a half by then, but it seemed like so much longer. So much had happened. Maybe ten years of things had happened in less than two. I hadn't lost my love for her, but I saw how love could be lost, and that scared me. Tony had experiences of his own that were the same or similar, and the song came together around those kinds of things. It was released as a Brian Wilson solo single two months before *Pet Sounds*.

> *Where did your long hair go?*
> *Where is the girl I used to know?*
> *How could you lose that happy glow?*
> *Oh, Caroline, no*
> *Who took that look away?*
> *I remember how you used to say*
> *You'd never change, but that's not true*
> *Oh, Caroline, you*
> *Break my heart*

I want to go and cry
It's so sad to watch a sweet thing die
Oh, Caroline, why
Could I ever find in you again
Things that made me love you so much then?
Could we ever bring 'em back once they have gone?
Oh, Caroline, no

Even though "Caroline, No" was a sad song, it was fun in the studio. It's kind of a Glenn Miller thing in the chords. It has that vibe. And I learned more about using certain arrangements or instruments to create the right emotions in whoever is listening. In that opening section, the one with tambourine, someone did percussion on a water jug, which had a lonely feeling. We had harpsichord and we had flute. When we were all done my dad made a suggestion that we ended up using, which was to speed everything up a half step so the vocals were even higher and more lonesome. At the end of the song there are some sound effects, a train and dogs barking. We were trying to think of the loneliest sounds. The dogs were my dogs, Louie and Banana. I recorded them at home and then we added them into the song. Louie was a Weimaraner. Banana was a beagle. Louie was my absolute favorite pet ever and Banana was my second favorite. People say the title of the record came partly from that, because Louie and Banana were making pet sounds when they barked. Some people say it's about Phil Spector and that's why it uses his initials. And other people say I named it that because the music is so personal. All of that is true and mixed together. The only thing that's not true is that the album was named after the cover photo. We already knew what we were calling the record when we went down to the San Diego Zoo for the photo shoot.

Lots of other songs on *Pet Sounds* have sadness in them. They are all beautiful, but they are about how the world can be a hard place emotionally. "Wouldn't It Be Nice" is a song about someone who doesn't have something he wants. "God Only Knows" is as much a worried song as it is a peaceful song. "Here Today" sounds like it's a love song, but the very next line shows that it's a lost-love song: "Love is here today / And it's gone tomorrow / It's here and gone so fast." And "Caroline, No" is about a girl changing over time, or changing in the mind of the guy who loved her. In the song, she does change for real, at least partly. Her hair gets shorter. But most of the change is in how the guy sees her. She doesn't seem as happy to him, and when she doesn't seem as happy, then she doesn't make him as happy. It was a cycle that kept going.

∽

I met Van Dyke Parks because someone played him an early version of "Sloop John B," and that's how we ended up working together. I think it might have been David Crosby who introduced us. At that time I had decided I was going to make a record even more amazing than *Pet Sounds*, and I asked Van Dyke to write lyrics with me. That led to the idea of *SMiLE*. *SMiLE* was a completely American record, in its music and in its ideas. We were right in the middle of an amazing time of music, but so many of the bands were British bands. The Beatles were doing great stuff, and the Rolling Stones and the Who and the Kinks, and underneath that there were dozens of other bands. The Zombies—man, they made some great records, too. Van Dyke and I wanted to do something just as good but for American music. He had a funny quote about that that was also about me.

> Everybody else was getting their snout in the British trough. Everybody wanted to sing "bettah," affecting these transatlantic accents and trying to sound like the Beatles. I was with a man who couldn't do that. He just didn't have that option. He was the last man standing. And the only way we were going to get through that crisis was by embracing what they call "grow where you're planted."

I didn't know about snouts or growing where I was planted. I thought about what we were doing in the *SMiLE* songs as a kind of travel line. You know when they show people in movies traveling on a bus or an airplane by showing a red line stretching across a map? *SMiLE* was a line like that, but through time also. It started at Plymouth Rock and went all the way across to Hawaii, and it stopped along the way at important places in America like Chicago and New Orleans. There was a song that used a piece of "The Old Master Painter," a Beasley Smith and Haven Gillespie song that Frank Sinatra had recorded, next to a piece of "You Are My Sunshine," a great song that was the state song of Louisiana because the guy who wrote it, Jimmie Davis, became governor. There was a song that used "Gee" by the Crows, one of the first rock and roll songs. But it wasn't just about taking pieces of musical history. There were songs about being healthy, about being healthy for yourself and for nature. "Vega-Tables," later reworked as "Vegetables" for *Smiley Smile,* is the one that people know about because we used the sound of Paul McCartney chewing celery as percussion. "Child Is Father of the Man" was about mental health and knowing yourself so you could do the right things in the world. And then there were two huge songs at the corners of the project, "Heroes and Villains" and "Good Vibrations."

That's the album we started, a way of collecting poetry and sounds and myths and making a perfect thing from them. I was trying to create a spiritual vibe and love for the listener. It was partly about forgetting the ego, which is the reason all the letters are capitalized except for the lowercase *i.* I was trying to put my arms around everything that music could do, which was everything. "Heroes and Villains" is probably the best song in the whole project, and one of the best songs we ever made. There's such a genius in Van Dyke's lyrics, especially "Heroes and villains / Just see what you've done." It has such perfect rhythm in the words. It pushes itself forward. That's my favorite song from that set most of the time, but there are other great ones, too. Once someone told me that someone they had met said that "Surf's Up" was important and really great. "Oh," I said. "Who?" My head was turned when they said the name so I didn't really hear. "Say it again," I said and turned my head the right way. The person who thought it was great was Leonard Bernstein. Can you even imagine?

That album came during the sandbox time. The sandbox is sort of a famous thing. I wanted to have a different way of writing, so I brought a sandbox into the living room and set it up around the piano. In a way it didn't seem like that big a deal. It was an environment that helped bring in ideas. One of the first songs Van Dyke and I made there was "Wonderful," which almost felt like a classical piece with lyrics put over the top. I was completely locked in and focused. I knew exactly how the vocals should sound, the way they're laid over each other like blankets on a bed. "Cabinessence" was another sandbox song, and another America song. Van Dyke wanted to write something about the railroads and how they brought people out to the prairie so they could start farms, homes on the range. And I had an idea for a big whirlwind of voices, just every voice you could imagine. Maybe they were the voices of people from the past. There's banjo in there to make it sound like the America of the past. I tried to think about what it was like to go out into a completely unsettled place. And "Surf's Up" is so beautiful. It really is a rhapsody, with all the key changes and tempo shifts. At times it seems like it's just wandering, but it's wandering in an amazing way. Van Dyke's lyrics in that song are great, too:

> *Hung velvet overtaken me*
> *Dim chandelier awaken me*
> *To a song dissolved in the dawn*

People say they're too complicated or they don't mean anything, but that's the thing about poetry. It's ideas, and it makes you have ideas when you listen to it. For those kinds of lyrics, I never asked Van Dyke what they meant. I sang their meaning the way it seemed to me.

Sometimes we started working on songs and they didn't get very far past instrumentals with no lyrics or at most a few fragments of lyrics. "Look" was like that. "Child Is Father to the Man" was like that. It was based on something written by Karl Menninger, a psychiatrist who had interesting theories about mental health and mental illness, and how people develop, and when doctors should try to help and when they should keep their distance. He was one of the founders of the Menninger Clinic in Kansas. Someone, maybe Van Dyke, also told me there was a similar idea in a poem by Wordsworth.

Poets and writers sometimes gave me great ideas. One of my favorite books was *The Four Loves* by C. S. Lewis. It was a great way of looking at all the different ways people express love: romantic love, friendship, charity, and sex. All of them are so important. They're all things I have used in my life. Charity is especially interesting as an idea because it's so simple. You share what you have with people who need it, and maybe when you need something, someone will share with you. What could be more pure than that? If I see a bum on the street, I will give him whatever cash I have on me, though I always tell him not to spend it on booze. If a guy asks me for a quarter, I'll give him a twenty. My daughter Daria says she remembers going to McDonald's with me once and I gave a homeless guy a hundred dollars. I don't remember that, but it's possible. I also play charity shows whenever I can. I should write a song about that, you know? I haven't managed to do it yet. But I did write a song, "Child Is Father to the Man," about the Menninger book. That was something.

We were trying so many things. You can say looking back that it was too many, but that wasn't my concern at the time. I just wanted to reach for the highest heights, and sometimes it was too far over everyone's head, including my own. There was a song called "The Elements: Fire" that started as a piece about Mrs. O'Leary's cow, who supposedly kicked over a lantern and started the Great Chicago Fire back in the 1870s. History was funny that way. The idea that one little accident could wipe out a whole city was fascinating. For the recording session, I asked people to come into the studio wearing fire hats. I had a bucket with burning wood so the studio would smell like smoke. What I really wanted to do was record the pops and creaks of the wood while it was burning. But as it turned out, that song never made it. A few days after the recording session, a building near the studio burned down. Two days after that, another building burned. I don't know if there were more fires or if I was suddenly just noticing them, but it made me uncomfortable. I put the masters away. There are stories that I even tried to burn the tapes, but either that's not true or I don't remember it. I don't think I would have done that. I did sometimes have superstitious habits. During "Time to Get Alone" a few years later, I started worrying that the pollution in LA was messing with my lungs, so I arranged for an oxygen tank to be brought to the studio. But burning things would have been going too far.

The way that "The Elements: Fire" came apart, that's how the whole thing came apart. There was a line at the end of "Cabinessence" that Van Dyke wrote: "Over and over / The crow cries, uncover the cornfield / Over and over / The thresher and plover, the wheatfield." Mike sang it over and over, like it said. But he had no idea what it meant, and he didn't think that Van Dyke could explain it either. I didn't know what it meant, but I knew that it meant something. Maybe it was just me, but I often found it hard to explain anything to Mike, and I wasn't sure who should be explaining anything to anyone anyway.

And then there was the whole thing with Carl and his draft status. He didn't want to go to Vietnam so he didn't report to the draft board. They said he was a draft dodger, and the problem got worse and worse when he refused to do the things they asked of him. He wouldn't do community service or anything. He had money so he could hire a lawyer, and they fought it out over the years. But it was more trouble at a time when I was trying to bring all the pieces of *SMiLE* together. It was like putting together a jigsaw puzzle on a wall instead of a tabletop. It kept falling.

I couldn't tell you the exact day I stepped away. It was almost fifty years ago. But at some point I knew *SMiLE* was done—or rather, that I was done with *SMiLE*. It was too much pressure from all sides: from Capitol, from my brothers, from Mike, from my dad, but most of all from myself. We were late in our delivery to Capitol. "Heroes and Villains" was supposed to be the follow-up single to "Good Vibrations." The label wanted it by Christmas, but it wasn't ready. Nothing was ready. Van Dyke had already split the scene, and there were still holes in the lyrics of other tracks. No one could do them like Van Dyke, which meant that no one could do them at all. I tried but they were too sophisticated. I couldn't come close. And with no lyrics, we had no way to do our vocals. The rest of it was just chaos. I didn't know which fragment went with "Cabinessence" or "Do You Like Worms?" I didn't know how to finish "Surf's Up." It was all over the place. It was too rhapsodic.

And the voices were everywhere. I heard Phil Spector's voice, talking to me about whether I could do something as complicated as his records. I heard my dad's voice: "What's the matter, buddy? No guts? Too scared to finish it? Can't do it, can you? I told you that this so-called masterpiece of yours was going nowhere." And I heard the other voices, the ones that wanted to do me harm. *We're coming for you, Brian.* I heard them more and more. The band needed to move forward, to grow. But I couldn't do it. I couldn't do it the way I wanted to, and then I couldn't do it at all. I just chucked it.

SMiLE eventually had a happy ending. But it was a long eventually. For years it wasn't happy at all. When I couldn't finish it, I went into a period where the bad things seemed to happen more and more. There were more fights with the rest of the band and more drugs and more voices in my head. When I think of that period, I think more about *Pet Sounds* than about *SMiLE*, and I think about "Caroline, No," which was sort of about Marilyn, but, as time went on, sort of also about me. It was a song that was a story about how you can lose yourself and worry that you will never get yourself back. I know Tony didn't write it that way, but sometimes I needed it to be that way to help explain things.

Years turned into other years that were the same year. When the band left Capitol for Reprise, when we went to Holland, when my dad died, when I went off to try to do the group California Music—those years, that year, got worse and worse. It got darker and darker, with more voices, more drinking, and more drugs.

The drugs started like they started for lots of people: sort of innocent, not very intense, because they were around, because they were part of what it meant to be a creative person in the '60s. I first started smoking pot in late 1964. It was great that first time. I had a glass of water and I couldn't believe it. The water tasted so good, you know? And it made me less nervous, which was always my biggest problem. The first song I wrote when I was smoking was "Please Let Me Wonder." I got stoned on pot, went to the piano, and I wrote that song in a half hour. Lots of the songs from that period worked that way: "She Knows Me Too Well," "Let Him Run Wild." Pot locked me in with my piano, and that gave me more ideas about what it could do. I also heard how instruments sounded when you put them together. If you put the piano and guitar together, it was almost another instrument. The bass and drums were a third thing, not just two things that were going at the same time. I got freed up to think outside of what pop songs were.

Other drugs had different effects. Acid was something else, like I said, because it put voices in my head. That was a bad drug. I'm sorry I did it. I liked Seconals, downers—they were a relax pill. Cocaine came along in the late '60s, maybe 1969. When I wrote "Sail On Sailor," there was coke around. I also cowrote, with Al and Mike, "He Come Down," which sounded like it was about the end of a drug trip but was really more of a gospel thing. That was for *Carl and the Passions—So Tough*. I love that tune. Mike's lead is so soulful. Spirituality was the other side of drugs back then, or maybe it was its own kind of drug, in a way. So many people who didn't like to be in the world the way it was looked for other ways to deal with it. Mike got deep into meditation. He took me to meet the Maharishi, who was a great spiritual master. His speaking voice was very gentle and kind of high-pitched. I started meditating, and it worked great for about a year. It really calmed me down. Then it stopped working. At some point I was so nervous that I couldn't even relax enough to meditate. That sent me back to drugs.

The drugs weren't something that I liked for themselves. They were ways of dealing with the fact that my head wasn't right. But they didn't solve a thing. With the drugs, in fact, came every other kind of problem. Bad days turned into bad months and then bad years. The music stopped almost completely. Or the music went on without me. During bad years, I hid in my apartment or my house, wherever I happened to be living at the time. I was out of the light, and mostly the light was out of me. Sometimes I had to go to hospitals for a little while, to relax and think—or to relax and not think. It was hard at those hospitals. They were unfamiliar places. The lighting was different than what I was used to, and the sounds were different and I had a hard time sleeping. I stayed up most nights. One of the times I went, in the late '60s, I was there in bed, trying to get to sleep, and I heard a noise at the door. I turned and there was a guy there with a huge hard-on. I looked away from it, up to the guy's face, and it looked just like Tonto! I mean the actual Tonto from the TV *Lone Ranger* show, Jay Silverheels. I wasn't sure that it was him. He had everything but his horse, Scout. "Are you Tonto?" I said. The guy didn't say anything. He just stared at me. Then he turned and left the doorway.

◡๐

The thing about being in a hospital is that you're stuck in the same room. You see the same door. If you're at home working, you see the same few doors: the doors of your house, the doors of the studio. If you're at home not working, you see even fewer doors. You see your bedroom door and maybe the door to your music room. Eventually you only see your bedroom door, and then it's like another kind of hospital. You have only four walls and whatever you say echoes off them. It's an echo chamber, but the sounds in it aren't music. They're more like the bad voices.

In the '70s I was home all the time. But what I did when I was home wasn't necessarily what you were supposed to do when you were home. A father is supposed to come home and ask his kids about their day. Most of the time I didn't come home. I was already home. And when I went out and came home, I didn't ask anyone about their day. I was taking speed or doing coke or coming through the door drunk with a cigarette in my hand. I would hug the kids. How did I not get them with the cigarette?

We lived in a house on Bellagio with so much glass. We had a dining room table that got covered with glass. We had stained glass in one of the rooms, a big pattern with a butterfly or a bee. There's a piece of it on the cover of *Wild Honey*. We had these big refrigerators that were all glass. Glass was transparent, so I could see what was happening on the other side of it. It was clear when my head was not. Once I painted the house purple, but Marilyn didn't like it and I had to put it back to its regular color, a kind of cream.

During those years, between making albums, many strange things happened. Sometimes they probably seemed funny to other people. I remember one warm day when I went outside wearing only pants. It didn't seem like I needed more clothes. Carnie was coming home from school on the bus. I was waiting for her. When I saw the bus, I stepped out in front of it, waving my arms. The driver opened the door. Kids were making noise and he quieted them. "Do you have a cigarette?" I said.

In that house, we had a top-of-the-line stereo with big speakers. I tried to play all the music that was coming out of California. I played the Carpenters. I played the Eagles. I played Fleetwood Mac. I played the Beatles, too, and the Stones, and ELO. I made sure to play "Be My Baby" every single day. The stereo was one of my instruments.

The clock was not. The day had certain times for things, but they weren't necessarily my times. Meals happened without me. Kids went to school and came back and I might still be in a bathrobe up in the bedroom or downstairs sitting at the piano, still in the bathrobe.

We had visitors. Paul McCartney would come over with Linda and Mary and Stella. Paul was dressed cool then, too. He was in all white leather with these red shoes. The kids went outside to play, and Paul and I sat down at the piano and we sang together. I think we sang "My Bonnie Lies Over the Ocean." Sonny and Cher would come over and bring Chastity. John Phillips from the Mamas and the Papas was around, too. We played basketball. Elton John hung out with us sometimes. When Carnie was six, she invited him to her birthday party. He couldn't come but he sent her back a note with a teddy bear. And once Shaun Cassidy dropped by. The girls really liked that. They screamed and screamed and screamed. Now and again I got out into the world. I ran into Michael Jackson briefly at a party—very nice guy, very pleasant. I met Stevie Wonder a few times, but it was hard for me to get a feel for the kind of guy he was.

We had more visitors. Rich Sloan, my old buddy from Hawthorne, came by. Once we went to Westwood for lunch and I asked him to buy me some cigarettes. I smoked two of them as fast as I could before we got back to the house.

There was so much glass in the house, but the walls between the rooms weren't glass. You couldn't see through them, which was good. There were so many bedrooms in the house. I wasn't a good husband. Sometimes there were other girls around.

I wasn't much of a father, but I could be a good father at times. The backyard had a pool and there was an upper level with a pond. We had koi in there. Wendy fell in. Marilyn saw and started yelling and I ran. I didn't usually run, but I ran that time. I got my hand down in there and got her with one arm and rescued her.

I spanked the kids sometimes. I found cigarettes once in Carnie's room, maybe a bottle of something. I spanked her and then I was really upset over what I had done. I was crying so hard. But I made them laugh, too. I remember taking them to Farrell's Ice Cream. Someone ordered the Zoo, which had thirty scoops and weighed something like six pounds. On the menu it said that it served between one and fifteen. I'm sure it was a joke, but I decided to take it seriously for a second. I decided that it served one. I asked them for the serving spoon from the kitchen and tried to eat the whole thing.

Those years are blurred from drinking and drugs, and they're blurred because of how fast they went by. Once I came home and before I was even inside the door I threw up. Once I started sneaking drinks again with medicine and I fell and hit my head. That scared me. I stopped for a little while. I let my hair grow longer so it covered up the bump and the scrape. A little while later I went back to short hair. I cut it myself. I mean I started to cut it myself, but it was uneven and I went from one side to the other, making it shorter and shorter. I got a haircut that was right down to the head. People said I looked like a soldier. Where did my long hair go? How did I lose that happy glow? It was so sad to watch a sweet thing die.

✧

Even at the worst of it, I tried to get to my kids with music. I tried to create a link with them. I taught them songs on the piano. I taught them "California Girls" and "Sloop John B." They would ask me how many songs I wrote. I didn't know. I said hundreds. If they asked me to make up a new one, I would, though it would be about a dog or cigarettes or the weather.

I went outside wearing just pants, and usually inside I didn't have a shirt either. That was not a good time. I was 270 pounds. I didn't always remember to shower. I stayed in bed or roamed the halls of the house like a ghost. The only place I could settle down and feel like I wasn't coming apart was at the piano.

I loved Marilyn but it wasn't working at all. She had been with me since the beginning. It was so important to have her because she was one of the only people who helped me get through anything with my father or my brothers or the band or the voices or the drugs. But things were whirling around me. It was all happening a thousand miles an hour and I was afraid to even step off. You can't step off of something going that fast.

Carnie was singing at her grade school graduation. I had my short soldier hair then. She was in a play about a circus, and in her part she worked with a magician and sang a song. I couldn't believe how she sang. It was beautiful, and I knew singing. That was a nice feeling. That made me proud.

Another time Marilyn and I went to Disneyland. I love Disneyland. It's one of my favorite places. We watched the fireworks. We came home and brought candy for the kids. They were scared because there was an earthquake, just a little one. We sat in our bed and ate candy.

∽

Things got worse. I was at home or out in the driveway without a shirt. I was deep inside drinking and drugs and almost never with the group. The voices were still coming, and I was having a harder time doing things that would quiet them down. Then Dr. Landy came for the first time, and for a little while I got better. I was back with the group starting right around the Bicentennial, and we were making the kinds of records I wanted. One of the best of those was *Love You*, in 1977. I was able to use the studio again the way I used it with *Pet Sounds*, and I wrote some songs that were about how I felt in my thirties, the same way that *Pet Sounds* was about how I felt in my twenties. I wanted to make a record to help everyone around me feel better. We picked up an old song called "Good Time" that Al and I did back around the time of *Sunflower*. "Good Time" was just what it said it was, a light song about spending time with girlfriends:

My girlfriend Betty, she's always ready
To help me in any way
She'll do my cookin'
She's always lookin'
For ways she can make my day
And when I'm lookin' at her
The sound of pitter-patter
On rainy days like today
Could get you feelin' warmer
And you know what-a that can lead to
Maybe it won't last but what do we care
My baby and I just want a good time
Might go up in smoke now but what do we care
My baby and I just want a good time

"Good Time" was originally on the album Marilyn did with her sister, in the group we called Spring, but with all the names of girlfriends changed to boyfriends: Betty was Eddie instead, and then later there was a girl named Penny that we had to change to a guy named O'Ryan. "Ding Dang" was another song brought in from an older session. It's one of my favorite songs ever, even though it's less than a minute long. It makes the whole album for me. I wrote that with Roger McGuinn. I was at his house, talking to him, and I said we should write a song together. We started with a simple line: "I love a girl, I love her so madly / I treat her so fine but she treats me so badly." Later on I wrote the "Ding Dang" part. The keyboard riff has been stuck in my head for years. I love it so much. When a riff is that great, there's a bigger song that stretches out on both sides of the song on the record. The "Ding Dang" on the album is only like a snapshot of a larger idea.

Lots of that record is great party music: "Mona," "Honkin' Down the Highway." There's a beautiful ballad called "The Night Was So Young." We sang great harmonies on that. "Johnny Carson," which Mike sang with Carl, was a very intimate tune. I tried to depict the mood of watching *The Tonight Show*, and also how hard it was to be an entertainer year after year.

> *When guests are boring he fills up the slack*
> *Johnny Carson*
> *The network makes him break his back*
> *Johnny Carson*
> *Ed McMahon comes on and says, "Here's Johnny"*
> *Every night at eleven thirty he's so funny*
> *Don't you think he's such a natural guy*
> *The way he's kept it up could make you cry*

People thought it was a strange way to use music, to write a song like that, but I was using everything I had learned. That album has lots of sounds. I love the way the vocals leapfrog each other during the "Don't you think he's such a natural guy" line. Marilyn and I did a duet on "Let's Put Our Hearts Together," which was a really sweet song about marriage. One thing on that album was the synthesizer bass lines. I did all the bass lines for the record with an ARP and a Moog synthesizer. A song like "I'll Bet He's Nice," which is about a guy telling a girl that he doesn't want to hear about her new guy and how great he is, could have easily been on *The Beach Boys Today!* but it would have sounded completely different. The way it is on *Love You*, it's an amazing machine bass sound that just pulls the whole song into it. It's like an undertow. Those were some of the best bass lines I ever wrote.

I also love the cover of that record. It was really colorful. The overall mood was trying to celebrate good things even if they were surrounded by problems. I tried to carry that mood into the shows we did for that record. It was fun to go out behind a record that I really believed in, but it was tense. Sometimes I was hoarse. Sometimes the other guys were—Dennis came out for an encore in Philadelphia to sing "You Are So Beautiful," which people know mostly from the Joe Cocker version but don't know that Dennis helped write. And sometimes there were backstage blowups. Mike was getting on my nerves at that time. He always had a slightly different idea about who we needed to be as a band. He wanted to be at the center, and he had the energy to do it. Sometime during that tour, I socked him. He didn't like what I was wearing. It was a blue-and-silver pleated cape, like an Elvis thing. Mike told me I looked silly and I just started slugging him. I was really hitting. Stan Love, Mike's brother, and a guy named Rocky Pamplin, who went with us on the road as bodyguards, pulled me off him. Mike didn't hit me back. If he did, he would have knocked me unconscious. Instead, I remember a strange feeling of waiting for something that never happened. Lots of that tour was that feeling.

It wasn't just the band. On "Good Time" there was a lyric that could have been about the band or also could have been about my marriage to Marilyn: "Maybe it won't last but what do we care / My baby and I just want a good time." Well, I was only partly right. It didn't last, and I did care. When I was in the mental hospital in San Diego, I called Marilyn and asked for a divorce. She said yes. I didn't know what else to do. Things were either whirling even faster or they were just stopped still in the air around me. There was more of my life to live. I had to meet Melinda. I had to get back in the studio and onstage. But I didn't know any of that yet. I was floating on the sea for a while there.

In 1978 I went back to a mental hospital in San Diego. Some people said mental facility. It wasn't the first time. I had been to one back in the late '60s. I don't remember much about the time in San Diego. It was the same time as my divorce from Marilyn. One of the nurses there was a girl name Carolyn, a black woman, and when I got discharged I asked her if she would come work for me and take care of me. We ended up going together for a few years. I was living first in a rented house on Sunset and then in Pacific Palisades. My head wasn't on straight at all and I would sometimes say stupid things to her. Once I got impatient and said, "Get your black ass in there and make me lunch." I apologized immediately but I didn't feel right about it. She split pretty soon and it was mostly because of me. I'm sorry about it even today. Carolyn, no.

I didn't feel right about her or myself or anything. Dr. Landy was gone and things got worse, and then he came back and things got better for a little while. Then they got worse again. He took the Green Tree house where I'd been living and had me rent another house on Latigo Shore Drive in Malibu. In that house, he had me on lots of medications. I wasn't sure I needed all of them, but some of the ones I was taking prevented me from saying anything about the other ones. I used to lie in bed and make noises to calm myself down. Someone came in and asked me what was wrong. Maybe it was Gloria. Was she there by that time? Whoever it was didn't get an answer. She went to open the curtains and I told her not to. I had it in my head that someone was coming to kill me. I heard noises coming. She listened with me and said it was just the ocean. But it didn't sound like the ocean to me. Sometimes the noises and the voices made me angry and I started punching the wall. I punched it hard enough to bleed. I got a stud.

Daytime was better. The drapes were usually closed, but I could sense the light and I knew that it was there. I heard voices during the daytime, too, but they were gentler. Gloria came and sat with me. I'm sure it was Gloria. I tried to tell her what the voices were saying. They were telling me bad things about myself. Sometimes they told me to do things I knew I shouldn't do. Sometimes she would say that she heard voices, too. The voices she said she heard were telling me that I needed to rest. I don't know if she really heard them. But I was tired and I couldn't tell if there was light behind the drapes and I listened to her voices. I know Gloria was there because once Dr. Landy was trying to get my attention by grabbing my chin and squeezing. Gloria told him that it wasn't right to do that, and then Dr. Landy said that he was going to call immigration. I told him not to do that.

At the worst of it, I didn't have any energy. I forgot to brush my teeth. Sometimes I couldn't make it to the bathroom at all. It's nothing I remember very well. It was like being drunk all the time but worse. It was just like being in dark clouds.

So many things happened, but I can't easily put them in order. Once I was in the Malibu emergency room getting a weigh-in and this guy walked up to me. He had curly hair and was on the short side. "Are you Brian Wilson?" he asked.

"Yeah," I said.

"Hi," he said. "I'm Bob Dylan." He was there because he had broken his thumb. We talked a little bit about nothing. I was a big fan of his lyrics, of course. "Like a Rolling Stone" was one of the best songs, you know? And "Mr. Tambourine Man" and "It's All Over Now, Baby Blue" and so many more. What a songwriter! I invited him over to my house for lunch the next day.

That was a longer conversation. We just talked and talked about music. We talked about old songs we remembered, songs before rock and roll. We talked about ideas we had. Nice guy. He added vocals to a song I was working on around that time called "The Spirit of Rock and Roll."

But that was a rare bright spot. Most of the time that house in Latigo Shore was bad. It was bad for eating. It was bad for sleeping. It was bad for thinking. And it was bad for playing music. Once I was in the Jacuzzi relaxing and Dr. Landy came storming right at me. "Get your clothes on," he said. He led me by the back of the neck down to the music room in the basement. We were in there for five or six hours. He kept asking me to make songs. But I didn't have any songs in me. I didn't have any voices in me, good or bad. There was no echo, only emptiness. Dr. Landy had no patience for the emptiness he had helped to make. He screamed at me. When my dad used to scream at me, the words were sharp. When Dr. Landy screamed, the words were flat. They didn't sound like anything. I was numb to them. He bent down and put his face right next to mine, but I hardly heard a thing. He threw papers and threw pens and finally he left. Another day he put a sheet with music notation on the piano and asked me to play it. The music was simple. I could have played it. But I was so tired that I just wanted to go to bed. Dr. Landy wouldn't let me go. "Do it," he said. He screamed again, again without an exclamation point.

The worst part of all of was that I ended up disappointed in myself. Maybe I could have written a song. Maybe I should have played the music. In my life before Dr. Landy, in my life before the drugs that brought Dr. Landy, I knew how to deal with disappointments. When I was young, Phil Spector called me in to watch him produce a song for his Christmas record. We had met after I heard "Be My Baby" on the radio and drove over to tell him how much it meant to me. The Christmas song was "Santa Claus Is Coming to Town." He was using so many session musicians, an entire orchestra almost. Hal Blaine was there, and Leon Russell and Tommy Tedesco—all the guys who later played with the Beach Boys. Phil Spector asked me if I wanted to play piano. I couldn't believe it. That was exactly what I wanted. "Just one thing," he said. "Play it hard." I played it as hard as I could. I really leaned on the keys.

Fifteen minutes later, Phil Spector came back into the studio. I was so excited. I stood up when I saw him coming. "Brian," he said. "I don't think I'm going to need you on this one." I was disappointed, but I was cool about it. That was the business. You didn't cry over spilled milk. And we ended up cutting our own version of the song the next year, on our own Christmas record. I didn't play piano on that one either. It was Gene DiNovi, a great jazz pianist who played with almost everyone, from Dizzy Gillespie to Anita O'Day to Artie Shaw.

                          *

Not being able to play piano on "Santa Claus Is Coming to Town" was bad news and a disappointment, but it didn't depress me. But other times I would be in the middle of a perfectly good day, with no bad news for miles around, and I would get depressed. I would go to bed and wouldn't get out for days. Sometimes it was simple depression, and sometimes it was other things, too—the voices in my head, or the sense that the world wasn't spinning right. It felt like a big cloud moved over me after I junked *SMiLE*.

Even when we moved past it, I wasn't okay with things. The idea of the record kept weighing me down. I could feel it on me whenever I started to get too far into hope and possibility. I would write a really cool tune, start the recording process, call the guys in, then suddenly lose interest and walk away from whatever I was doing. I started making up excuses like I didn't feel good or I had a sore throat, anything I could come up with to avoid confronting my own work. I was afraid of failing, afraid my dad was right, afraid I couldn't live up to the example that Phil Spector set for me. It was the depression creeping up on me that would eventually go over me completely, take away my spirit, and paralyze me for so many years.

I was in bed in the early '70s. We recorded at my house, but for most of the morning I'd stay in bed. Then I would come down-stairs and one of the guys from the band or an engineer would pull their head up and squint at me. "What's the matter with you?" they would say. I wouldn't know exactly. "I just feel down," I'd say. I would work for a while and then go back upstairs. It was just a matter of steps. Back upstairs I would try to hear what they were doing, and sometimes someone would call up to me and say they needed me again. That's how "Marcella" worked. I was mostly done with the production and I ran out of gas, so I left. A while later I heard them calling up to me. They wanted my voice. I went down and finished up the song. Once or twice I asked the guys to forgive me when I couldn't be there, though I wasn't sure why I was asking for forgiveness for something I wasn't doing on purpose. Depression was something that went over me like a kind of tide. I can hear it in some of the music I made back then. Mike started saying that even the happy songs sounded sad.

Later on my mom told me that when my dad was upset about something—like when we fired him as the manager of the band— he got depressed and stayed in his bed for days. That wasn't something I knew at the time. It's strange to think about it, because maybe everything gets handed down through the blood. My dad drank, maybe because his dad did. That was what people did back then. They tried to make life better so it wouldn't get worse. How they tried were just guesses, and sometimes they were wrong guesses. They were stabs in the dark.

I was listening to the radio once and they were interviewing some jazz producer. He was talking about how Miles Davis once watched a movie that he had been asked to write a soundtrack for. It had a plot twist. One of the characters wasn't who she was supposed to be, or maybe someone was dreaming and woke up in the middle. Anyway, he had a specific thing that he said about the movie afterward: "It's got a wrinkle in it, don't it?" I never saw the movie he was talking about. I don't know that much about jazz. I don't even know that much about Miles Davis. But what he said is true about life and every part of it. It's got a wrinkle in it, don't it?

꙰

When we put *SMiLE* away, Capitol was still on us for a next record. The record that came out of it, *Smiley Smile*, was a different kind of thing completely. The story has been told so often about me completely bailing out from the Beach Boys after I junked *SMiLE* and just cutting out to my room, but no way is that true at all. It's total bullshit. *Smiley Smile* is the first and best piece of evidence. My instinct told me it was time to get the other guys involved in some of the production work. I leaned on Carl for most of it. He had been working with me in the booth here and there, especially during the *Beach Boys' Party!* sessions, so it felt like he had it in the pocket.

For starters, we pared down some of the tracks I did for *SMiLE* and recut them ourselves, without the Wrecking Crew guys. We used only a few pieces: the backing track from "Heroes and Villains" came along with us, and also the end of "Vega-Tables." We took "Good Vibrations," which was already a huge hit and needed an album to be on. But other than that, it was all new. We went back into the home studio in Bel Air and cut the album in a month and a half, June and July 1967. The studio wasn't quite ready yet. I had set it up to make demos. So to get certain effects, we had to do so many different things. We recorded vocals in the swimming pool. We recorded them in the shower. We got incredible effects with nothing fancy at all. We did them ourselves, without the Wrecking Crew guys. That was amazing. I would like to do that again, something kind of modest, without really rambunctious instrumental tracks.

The instruments on that record were a little softer. Carl called that record a bunt instead of a grand slam. But it had some incredible things on it. "Little Pad" is really cool. "Fall Breaks and Back to Winter," too. And the sound is as interesting as the songs. I had a white Baldwin organ that was just fantastic. I don't know where that is. It might be in storage. But that's the kind of thing I would like to try again, to go for those low organ notes. They did great things to "Heroes and Villains," kept it warm. I used the other guys to make the record more than any time since *Beach Boys' Party!*, especially Carl. For the first time, an album came out with the credit "Produced by the Beach Boys."

Smiley Smile bombed. It was such a different sound for us—for anybody, really. The public wasn't ready for it. Next was the *Wild Honey* album. That was a quick one, maybe the quickest. We were going to do that Hawaii live album but it didn't pan out, and right after *Smiley Smile* we went back to the studio. I got inspired and wrote a whole batch of songs in an R&B style, collaborated with Mike on the lyrics, and started recording in my house. The band played all the instruments ourselves. We started in late September and had the record done by mid-November and out by mid-December. I thought it sounded great, another total departure. *Wild Honey* did much better than *Smiley Smile* and got us back on the radio—we scored two Top Twenty singles, "Wild Honey" and "Darlin'," with Carl wailing on lead vocals—and we were on to another record.

Through that whole time, the real *SMiLE* stayed on the shelf as we moved on to *Friends* and *20/20*. It was a high shelf also—too high to reach. I never talked about it to people. I knew that people discussed it, because it was kind of a legend, but they rarely brought it up with me. Then, after *Imagination*, I was at that Christmas party at Scott Bennett's and I sat down at the piano and started to play "Heroes and Villains." I don't know why I did it, exactly. It wasn't to show it off or bring it back up. I just heard something that was an echo of it and it got me thinking. Someone told me it sounded great and I went further into it. That was the beginning of starting to play those songs again.

About a year later there was a tribute show at Radio City Music Hall. People could pick any songs they wanted. Paul Simon did "Surfer Girl." Billy Joel did "Don't Worry, Baby." Elton John did "God Only Knows." I sang "Wouldn't It Be Nice" with Elton and "Heroes and Villains" on my own. Wilson Phillips—my daughters Carnie and Wendy and John Phillips's daughter, Chynna Phillips—sang "You Still Believe in Me," and it blew my fucking mind. It was a real trip hearing all the different singers. I liked seeing how people changed a little part of an arrangement, or re-created songs that we built in the studio. Vince Gill, Jimmy Webb, and David Crosby did such a beautiful version of "Surf's Up." It was a great night and really amazing to hear so many people who wrote such great songs on their own playing my songs.

During rehearsals, I dozed off on a couch in the back of the green room. The Harlem Boys Choir was singing "Our Prayer," which I had set aside when I stopped work on *SMiLE*. A version of it was on the *20/20* album, at the end, with "Cabinessence," another song from the project. I was half-awake in the green room listening to the choir, and I flashed back to the original sessions. It pulled me up into the harmonies. I was listening harder now, up on my elbow. When it was over, I ran out to the stage. "Hey, guys," I said. "I wrote that!" From the darkness there was applause.

After that I started thinking more about *SMiLE*, not just "Heroes and Villains" but the whole thing. There were so many great songs and pieces on there, and they had come out wrong. I don't mean that they weren't recorded well. I was okay with the version of "Our Prayer" that the other guys put together for *20/20*. What I mean is that they were supposed to come out as one whole thing. The original album was a big idea about America and myth. Forty more years of America had passed and finally I could see my way across all the music we were trying to make back then. The more I thought about it, the more it seemed like a living thing again instead of something in a museum.

After the live *Pet Sounds* record, I put out an album called *Gettin' in Over My Head*. It was a mix between a compilation and a spring cleaning, even though it came out in summer. I still had some of the songs I had done with Andy Paley, and I still thought they were great. I wanted them to see the light of day. I had made some more songs with Steve Kalinich, who was great, and I had leftovers from working with Joe Thomas. I had the idea to send the songs around and see if I could get some other singers to perform them with me.

I could. Lots of people wanted to do it. We went into the studio to record. They were other rock singers around my age, and it was a blast to produce them. I didn't go easy on them either. Elton John did a song called "How Could We Still Be Dancin'," which is one of my favorites of all my solo stuff. I told him to get out there and play the piano like Billy Joel. Eric Clapton did one called "City Blues" with me in London. I wasn't happy with the first takes, so I went in to tell him. "Hey, man," I said, "if that's the best you can do, I guess we'll just use it." Eric killed it on the very next take. And Paul McCartney sang a song with me at Western called "A Friend Like You." Sometimes he was flat on his vocals and I had to say so.

The most important singer I brought in on that record was for a song called "Soul Searchin'." It was a song I had written with

Andy Paley, and the singer was Carl. It was his last vocal. He had recorded it with me years before, and I had never found the right spot for it. *Gettin' in Over My Head* was the right spot.

Four of the songs came from *Sweet Insanity*, though I didn't re-use "Water Builds Up." I did use "Let's Stick Together," which was "The Waltz" and had new lyrics written with Van Dyke Parks. Van Dyke had come back into the picture because I was thinking about *SMiLE* all the time. And because I was thinking about it all the time, I was also talking about it all the time. It was in many conversations with the band, and one day Darian asked me if I would ever remake it. It was a brave idea and a crazy idea. There were lots of memories in there that were hard for me. The memories of the music were great, but the memories of everything around it weren't. And even the music was a question instead of an answer. I sometimes heard songs on the radio that were great songs but simple songs, and I wondered about the people who made them. Was it easier to do songs like that? Was it healthier? They could just do them and then go on to other things. Melinda listened to the tracks and told me, "Brian, this is so brilliant—you have to finish it." But I still wasn't sure.

Darian took the lead. He loaded all the fragments of old songs onto his computer. We started to listen to them together. We started to think about how they could be whole again. He was my leader. But I was his leader. We were each other's leaders. He would tell me that something should be one way, and I would agree, and then a few minutes later I would have another idea.

I hadn't listened to all the tracks since I made them the first time. Some of it I remembered perfectly, but other parts were a real surprise. It was very emotional because I took a lot of drugs during the making of *SMiLE*, and I wasn't always at my best mentally. I had depression. I had fear. I wasn't sleeping well. The second time through I remembered sleeping so badly and worrying so much.

Darian didn't stop there. He found original lyric sheets for a song called "Do You Like Worms?" that we couldn't completely decipher, so I called Van Dyke Parks, who had been there for the original songs. The very next day he came by and helped make sense of all the lyrics. It was a real trip to listen to those old bits and pieces a third time, not just with Darian but with Darian and Van Dyke. I asked Van Dyke if he had ever thought about writing the rest of the lyrics. He had. Slowly, with the band, with Van Dyke's help, we started to rebuild *SMiLE*. We didn't use all the pieces. But we used lots of them. The thing I remember best was going through the third movement, from the California Saga into Hawaii. I was so proud about that. It brought back so many memories.

And it wasn't just the lyrics. We dug up old sounds and old ideas also and put them back into the old puzzle to make something new. There was a song called "She's Goin' Bald" on the *Smiley Smile* album in 1967. Originally, it was different. Originally, it was called "He Gives Speeches." It was a strange little piece, lots of voices. To do that in 1967, we used something called an Eltro Information Rate Changer, which changed pitch without speeding up or slowing down the tape. The Eltro was one of those toys we used as a tool. About a year after we tried the Eltro, it was the voice of HAL in *2001: A Space Odyssey.* When we were doing *SMiLE* again in 2004, people who heard it thought abut HAL, not the original record.

It reminded me of something that Ray Davies said once about using Indian music in his music, and the Beatles. He did it first, but then more people knew about the Beatles, so he went from being two years ahead of them to being two years behind them. Sometimes that's a more comfortable way to do it. It might feel like people don't remember all the ideas you had or that you were first, but it takes the pressure off. Making *SMiLE* again was like rebuilding a sand castle or raising the *Titanic*. Everyone remembers how it used to look. But everyone also understands that it's never going to be exactly the same as it was before. It can't be. That's not how time works. But it meant something new to people. One of the guys in my band, Probyn Gregory, had been a fan of the idea of the album forever. In the early '80s, he took out an ad in the newspaper asking Capitol to release some version of it. Twenty years later he played on it. Can you believe it?

Lots of my life has been a struggle with understanding how much my music meant to people. It took a long time for me to get it. Sometimes people needed to tell me. Other times I heard it in the music. That happened when I was finishing *SMiLE*. I started to hear again all the different things we were putting in there, all the different parts of American music. We were trying to reach everyone, and finally we did. People say *SMiLE* is one of the greatest albums ever made. I'm not sure about that. I am proud of it, but I also think it's a little overstated, overdone. I think it's too much music—not too complicated but too rhapsodic, with too many different sections. Still, finishing it was a huge relief. It was a weight lifted.

At the studio, Mark Linett, our engineer, walked over and handed me a box. "What's this?" I asked. "That's *SMiLE*," he said. I held it right next to my heart.

When the album came out, I sat with Van Dyke and asked him how the hell we did it in the first place. He didn't really answer. He had a little grin on his face. The CD was on a little table between us. I got goose bumps.

‿

SMiLE was hard in the studio—it was hard in the '60s and it was hard forty years later, though not as hard. It was easier onstage. By the time I finally finished the album I understood more about what I was supposed to do for audiences. I understood that I was supposed to make them happy. And so I got on airplanes even though I was tired and worried. I chewed on yellow Ricolas for my throat and drank some tea to try to slow my mind down. I pumped myself up as time got close and then circled up with the band. And then I went out and tried to give the album to the audience. All my fears disappeared whenever I was onstage. That's why I think that the only real answer is in music. Some answers are in my own songs, and some answers are in other people's songs. One of the songs that never fails is "Let It Be." I sing it to myself all the time. Whenever it comes on the radio, it lifts me. Whenever I have mental problems, it saves me, big time. It's like a Valium to me.

The other songs that lift me are my daughters' songs. That's for different reasons. That proves to me I made something that will last forever. Whatever talent I have, whatever I got from my dad or from wherever, I passed it on to Wendy and Carnie. They got some singing talent from me and some from Marilyn. I knew that Carnie could sing as far back as when I saw her in grade school in the circus play. It made me so proud. But I didn't know that both of them would end up singing for real. They had a singing act. Carnie and Wendy worked together along with John Phillips's daughter. They were big stars for a while. Their album sold ten million copies! I loved seeing how good they were as singers, but also it scared me. Not because of them but because of what else was out there. I told them to look out for the sharks. But I am happy they went into music. It reminds me all the time of what Marilyn and I gave them.

Later I called Carnie and asked her to record a song with me. It was called "Fantasy Is Reality/Bells of Madness." It was for a Rob Wasserman album. When we made the song, I watched Carnie as she sang. I was looking at my daughter and thinking about when she was little; about her sister when she was little; about how I was young then, too; about the cover of *Sunflower*; about feeling my mom's hands as she lowered me into the crib. People are beautiful. Life can be, too.

In the studio that day with Carnie, I was so happy that I told her to give me the telephone. I called a random number. Some guy answered. "Hello," I said. "Did you order a pizza?" The guy said no. "Well, screw you then," I said. We must have laughed for a half hour.

My kids have always brought out the kid in me. But I never really got over the guilt that I was a lousy father to Carnie and Wendy. I remember I took Wendy to lunch once in Malibu. I wanted to tell her I was sorry. I wanted to make sure she knew I loved her. I had things that took me away. Some of them were things I wanted to be doing. Some of them were things that happened to me. But I wished I had been there more. I didn't say everything I wanted to say, but I said some of it.

I hope I can be a good father to my younger kids. I have made the effort to stay involved with all of them. Sometimes I take the girls to the beauty parlor to get their nails done, or I take all of them out for ice cream. I have played concerts for Daria and Delanie's school, and once Jeff Foskett and I worked with Daria's school choir when they were performing my songs in a competition. That made me a cool dad, I think, or at least made me as cool as the other dads who put in time for their kids. When Daria was six, I arranged with Michael Jackson to have her birthday party at his Neverland Ranch. Her whole class went. What a far-out trip! I couldn't believe how excited she was.

Delanie is at school in Boston now, so it's a little quieter around the house during the school year. The two youngest kids, Dash and Dakota Rose, go with me for pizza and to watch Dylan's basketball games. And Daria drives now, so she can be in charge of the younger kids and bring them to me and Melinda. They meet us at the deli for lunch or at a great Mexican place on Ventura called Casa Vega. I love the flan there. And sometimes we go to the movies, load up on snacks, and enjoy the show. I hope the kids think I'm a good hang. One thing I love to do with my kids now is a thing I also liked to do with Carnie and Wendy, and that's play piano and sing. Their favorite song is the one I didn't write, "Barbara Ann." That's okay; the singing is the gift.

And the kids are the gift, because they keep the family going. When Wendy had her first baby, I got real excited and ran around the hospital saying, "Leo Wilson's here!" I knew it wasn't really his name. He had her husband's last name. But I liked the sound of it.

❧

There are lots of turning points in life. That year of *SMiLE* was a big one for me. In some ways it was one of the worst years of my life, and in other ways it turned into one of the best. It had ways in which it was the worst because I finally had to confront *SMiLE* head on, which meant thinking through all the ways that it almost sunk me, all the things I had hoped for it and couldn't handle. But I finally got it behind me. We toured the show all around the world in 2004 and 2005. I played it live around a hundred times. Can you believe that? And the record was a huge success, more than a million copies. It wasn't just a way of avoiding failure anymore. It was a success. It wasn't just that I put the bad vibes behind me. I put good ones in front of me. The end of that *SMiLE* tour was the start of a creative explosion, the first real time like that since the *Love You* album.

I remember when it started. I had been bringing a small Yamaha synthesizer on the road for the bus and the hotel room so I would have something to play whenever I got the urge. And I was getting the urge all the time toward the end of that tour. I was hearing music in my head again, and it was coming in louder and clearer than the voices. The music began pouring out of me, at all hours of the day and night. I was playing not only on the tour bus but in the hotel and in my music room at home. I wrote so many songs, had so many ideas, and a good portion of it was done on the road. I had the idea to do a children's album at one point, and I wrote a song called "Life's a Merry Go Round" that came to me all in a rush, complete with an arrangement—Hammond B-3, ukulele, bells, tuba, accordion. I couldn't believe what I was hearing. I was hearing me again, you know?

When we went to Carnegie Hall, I couldn't believe it. Brian Wilson in Carnegie Hall! I wondered what my dad would have thought. Would he be proud? We were staying at the RIHGA Royal in New York City, and I got to thinking about how the hell I got all the way from junking *SMiLE* in 1967 to playing it live at Carnegie Hall in 2004. It was a great feeling but also overwhelming. Melinda was right there with me, and every time the fear started to wash over me, she told me I had to keep going. Nobody ever did that to me in that way, with that mix of firmness and confidence and love. I came up with a title to explain Melinda, "Nobody Ever Did Me Like You Do." In a few hours I had the whole tune in the can—chords, melody, lyrics. It was a really sweet ballad with a really cool chord progression.

And then in Australia, at our hotel, I was talking to Jerry Weiss in the lounge. He was telling me about this path that he walked on every day. It was at a park near his house. I got the idea of writing about a path, and I couldn't get it out of my head. The next morning when I woke up, I went to the Yamaha and started playing what was in my head: four ascending chords followed by three descending chords. I knew I had something. I called Jerry and had him bring a piece of paper, and I started talking through all the ideas that came with the chords. I had a title, "Walking Down the Path of Life." I had some lyrics. Once I knew I was hooked into something real, I worked on it before sound checks and at the hotel. Finally I finished the song. It was a spiritual thing, almost a personal gospel track:

> *Walking down the path of life*
> *Feel His presence day and night*
> *In me, with me all the time*
> *His love comes to me so sublime*
> *Warms me, heals me, wash my sins away*
> *Shows me how to live my life each day*
> *Every night, I will pray*
> *I'll be good every day*
> *Make me strong, show the way*
> *When I was a little child*
> *I learned that prayer was so worthwhile*
> *As I grow, I'm on my own*
> *But I will never be alone*

A bunch more songs poured out of me at that time, some of which I knew I had to put out as soon as I could, some of which I never released. We finished up the *SMiLE* 2004 tour in Auckland, New Zealand, and I remember getting back to the house in California and telling Melinda it was the best tour I had ever been on. I thanked her again for pushing me to do it. It was the best thing I could have done, no matter how much it scared me at the time.

Christmas 2004 was a good time. The holiday vibe around the house was great, and I was sure that nothing would get me down. But then I was watching the news on TV the day after Christmas and the announcer came on and said that there was a massive tsunami in Asia. A few hundred thousand people were killed or missing. My heart sank. So many people were hurting. And then it hit me more personally. For *SMiLE*, we toured and recorded with the Stockholm Strings and Horns, great players from Sweden. Markus Sundland, our cellist, went vacationing with his girlfriend, Sofi, in Phuket, Thailand. They were there when the tsunami hit. They were sitting by a pool, and when the wave hit they were swept away. Sofi got lucky and was taken up into a tree. She was there for three hours with both of her legs broken, but she lived. Markus was missing. We were all devastated. Melinda and I went on CNN with Larry King to publicize Markus being missing and to see if we could get some help in locating him. They found his body weeks later. We were all heartbroken. But even then I noticed a difference. I was sad, but I wasn't so down that I couldn't get back up. I was sad and able to use the things I was feeling to put emotions into my music. That was the way it was supposed to work.

The photo shoot for *Summer Days (And Summer Nights!!)* in 1965. *(Courtesy Capitol Records)*

Up on a motorcycle in the mid-1960s. *(Guy Webster)*

Animal magnetism: the *Pet Sounds* photo shoot in 1966.

(Courtesy Capitol Records)

Teaching the Boys their parts during the *Smile* sessions in 1966.

(Guy Webster)

A *Smile* photo shoot from 1966.
(Guy Webster)

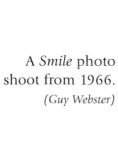

At the board in 1967.
(Courtesy Capitol Records)

A photo shoot for *Smile* in 1967. *(Guy Webster)*

In the pool at Laurel Way, 1967. *(Guy Webster)*

Beached boy: Getting ready for *15 Big Ones* in 1976. *(BriMel Archives)*

Back on tour in 1977. *(Brother Records Archives)*

Melinda and I getting married in 1995.
(BriMel Archives)

Getting the Kennedy Center Honors in 2008 was one of the thrills of my life.
(BriMel Archives)

Out on the town
with Melinda.
(BriMel Archives)

With Melinda
and the family
in 2009.
(BriMel Archives)

Zoo Sounds: With a giraffe, getting ready for *Pet Sounds* 50. *(Jerry Weiss)*

The *Pet Sounds* 50th tour, with the band and a giant giraffe, 2016. *(Jerry Weiss)*

CHAPTER 7

Sun

Catch a wave and you're sittin' on top of the world
—"Catch a Wave"

I never thought about topping *SMiLE*, not even after "Walking Down the Path of Life" got me pointed back in the right direction. It couldn't be topped. But I started to have some sense of the right direction. In the beginning of 2005, Clive Davis contacted me to see if I would be interested in making a Christmas album. It made sense, in a way. The first spark of the second version of *SMiLE* came at that Christmas party when I sat down at the piano and started to play "Heroes and Villains." And I loved Christmas albums. Phil Spector's *A Christmas Gift for You* was one of the best albums ever, even if my piano playing didn't make it onto "Santa Claus Is Coming to Town." And the Beach Boys' Christmas album, the one from 1964, was one of my favorite projects, in a way, because we got to work with Dick Reynolds. That Christmas album was a split. Side one was originals I wrote, some with Mike, about the holidays. We wrote "Little Saint Nick," which was a Christmas version of "Little Deuce Coupe." We wrote "The Man with All the Toys," which was a great song about Santa Claus that was like a postcard. It was just what someone would see if they happened to see Santa working in his workshop:

> *Someone found a lighted house*
> *Late one night*
> *And he saw through the window*
> *A sight*
> *A big man in a chair*
> *And little tiny men everywhere*

When I went back into the studio to do a new Christmas album in 2005, I rerecorded both of those songs. "The Man with All the Toys" felt different to sing now that I was older and bigger. I had some unfinished pieces of music that I gave to Bernie Taupin and Jimmy Webb to finish as holiday songs, and they did. Bernie took "Nobody Ever Did Me Like You Do," the ballad I wrote for Melinda in New York, and put on some new lyrics; the song ended up being "What I Really Want for Christmas," the title track. Bernie did a beautiful job, and it's a beautiful holiday song. Jimmy's song, "Christmasey," was great, too. There are certain guys who can write lyrics like that, and I don't know if there will be too many more of them. When you make something like the Christmas record, you can show the full range of what you know about production. Check out "On Christmas Day." Listen to the dynamics and the way it builds. It's got a great strong, slow-rock vibe. I did some traditional songs, too, though not "Santa Claus Is Coming to Town." I never did get to play piano on that song.

We recorded that album in April and then went back on the road for the summer. We were touring in Europe. We played a lot of great places, like the Glastonbury Festival. We went to Liverpool, where the Beatles were from, and sang their song "Tell Me Why" as a tribute to them—I hadn't sung it since 1965, when we did a version on the *Beach Boys' Party!* album. The next day we were flying from Liverpool to Ireland to play a few shows there. The airport in

Liverpool was called John Lennon Airport. Can you imagine that? The flight from Liverpool to Dublin was a real trip. The entire plane was full of fans coming to see us play in Ireland. I was talking to everyone on the airplane sitting near me. People were singing the whole way. Someone called the plane Wilson Air and that stuck. I decided to cook up something special for the Irish fans, and the next night, in Cork, I taught the band the vocals for "Walking Down the Path of Life." When we came out for the encore, instead of going to my keyboard at center stage, I went to Darian's on the side. It was just me and the band doing vocals, and me standing up and playing keyboard with no other instruments. It came out great. That was the only time I debuted a new song that way. It was a spiritual feeling.

On that summer tour we did two nights in Rome. On our day off we went to Vatican City. We were downstairs in the catacombs where all the popes were buried. The guide told us about each tomb and the pope who was inside it. While he was talking, I slipped away. I wanted to sneak off to the tomb of John Paul II, who had died just a few months before. He was a good man. I wanted to look at where he was buried and think about that. As I was walking back to the tour, at least a dozen people came up and thanked me for my music. They weren't all American. One couple was German. One woman was Japanese. There was an Australian family. They were from all over the world. I was still thinking about the pope and how everyone ends up the same eventually. All that's different is what we leave behind.

Those thoughts stayed in my head. That alone was a sign that it was a good year. I had been in so many periods of darkness and confusion when I couldn't hold on to my own thoughts. But toward the end of SMiLE my thoughts started to stay with me, and that continued on through 2005. I would go to sleep thinking about songs and wake up still thinking about them. They didn't disappear. They just got a little fuller.

My new ideas also helped me to think about old ideas. That came from SMiLE, too. I had been back in the old tapes with Darian and Van Dyke, and that meant that I had to go back in time and figure out why I made certain choices. After SMiLE, lots of other old songs started to pop up in my mind. At some point I had worked on a version of "Proud Mary." I love that song. I loved the original that John Fogerty did with Creedence Clearwater Revival, but I especially loved the version that Phil Spector did with Tina Turner. He took that cool rock and roll riff and just made it sound so big. I cut a version of it with Don Was where we had a big choir. It was a great version, but it never came out. I didn't even know where the tape of those sessions was anymore. Almost ten years later I woke up thinking about it. I cut another version at Scott Bennett's house. It was great. It had some pop. But I could hear that it wasn't perfect, that the mix didn't have enough left-hand synth bass on the second verse. I have to get Scott to remix that one of these days. It still bugs the hell out of me.

When I listened to that song or any other song, I started to hear those layers again. When a song came on the radio, I saw it in my mind as a whole thing, and then in pieces, and then I saw the pieces come together.

One day the song "That Lucky Old Sun" popped into my head. It was an old song about how hard it is to work and be a man but how easy it is to just be the sun and stay in the sky all day. The song was written by Beasley Smith and Haven Gillespie, the same people who wrote "The Old Master Painter," which we put a piece of on SMiLE. "That Lucky Old Sun" was a big hit for Frankie Laine in the late '40s, and everyone else sang it, too. Sinatra did it great. When I was little and his version came out, there was another version on the radio by Louis Armstrong. That was the version I liked the most. In California in 2005, I heard his version in my head. I thought I knew where the melody went and where the harmonies went. I thought I remembered that Gordon Jenkins produced it. Gordon Jenkins was a great arranger who worked with Sinatra, too. He did Where Are You?, which was one of Sinatra's great albums, in 1957, and that same year he did a Christmas album called A Jolly Christmas *from Frank Sinatra.* Sinatra didn't sing many of the same Christmas songs that I did on my albums.

I wanted to make sure that Gordon Jenkins did that version of "That Lucky Old Sun" for Louis Armstrong, so I went down to Tower Records to buy it. While I was there, I spent longer than usual looking through all the records. I looked at jazz and I looked at country and I looked at lots of rock and roll. I even bought a CD of the original *Pet Sounds.* No one could believe that I didn't already have one in my house. When I was driving home, I listened to it, which wasn't something I liked to do. Listening to *SMiLE* again was one thing, because that was a way of finishing it. Listening to *Pet Sounds* was more difficult. We had re-created it onstage, which I liked, but the original album was all memories. I had to skip "God Only Knows." It was too hard. It reminded me of Carl, and that reminded me of everything else.

After I got "That Lucky Old Sun," I reworked it completely. I used the lyrics but rearranged the chords. No one had ever done a version of the song like that. And then there was another burst of ideas. Or maybe it was that the burst at the end of *SMiLE* never went away. Ideas were coming almost faster than I could get to the piano. During that time I called Ray every morning to sing him little bits of pieces I was working on. I called him at five o'clock in the morning every day—he was back in New York, so it was eight o'clock his time. I never called so that he would hear the phone ring at 7:58 or 8:01. It was always eight. I was in bed still, but I needed feedback before I started working for the day. I would sing him a melody or tell him an idea for lyrics. I didn't want him to tell me that it was good if he didn't think so. But mostly he thought so. He would tell me that they were great. Or if he thought they were even better than great he would say that. He came up with a code so he could say it quicker: WCW, which meant World-Class Wilson. I was writing lots of WCW.

Right around that time, Dr. Landy died. He had lung cancer and got pneumonia and wasn't strong enough to fight it off. He had been living in Hawaii at the time. When I heard about it, I was shocked. There wasn't any good way to react. Parts of me were sad. Parts of me were guilty. Parts of me were relieved. Overall, it really knocked me back a step. But being knocked back a step in 2006 was different from being knocked back a step in other years. There were times in my life when it would have sent me to my chair or to my bed. But in 2006 I was working, and I just gathered up the news and kept moving into more work.

I don't think I really reacted, in some ways, and maybe I didn't even understand what it meant until years later when I read an interview with John Fogerty. John used to live down the street from me and Melinda; we would see him out jogging and sometimes at the deli. In the interview, John was talking about how he felt when Saul Zaentz died. Zaentz was the owner of Fantasy Records, and he took all of John's songs away from him after Creedence Clearwater Revival ended. They were tied up in so many lawsuits. John said that if you had asked him when he was younger how he would react when Saul Zaentz died, he would have said that he would go to the funeral and stand on the grave and dance up and down. But when it actually happened, he just looked at his wife and shrugged. Time passed. Things meant less or they meant different things.

That's sort of how I felt in a world without Landy. At first I mostly called people. I called my daughters and my friends. I called some people who had known me when I was with Dr. Landy. It was weird to give them the news about him. I was still around and he was gone, and I was the one who was strong enough to say so. And then I just sat in a room and thought. I thought about the first time I ever met Dr. Landy and how desperate I was back then to get control of my life, of any part of it. He helped me do that. But he went too far. He went too far in every direction.

People sometimes ask me if Dr. Landy was a father figure, if he did the kinds of things that my dad did. I don't think he was. Both of them liked to put themselves in charge of me and tell me what was best for me. But my dad loved me. He loved all of us. Helping us with the band benefitted him. He got profits. But he wasn't only interested in the profit. Dr. Landy seemed at some point like he was only interested in the profit, in getting his name on my songs and taking credit and taking money and getting his name on my legal papers. Landy might have helped me a little bit, might have helped so that I didn't sink lower and maybe even out of sight, but it was far outweighed by all the horrible things he did. Nine years of bullshit, remember. Also, I was partly my dad. I could sense things in me that were things in him. That didn't happen with Dr. Landy, not even when he died. I only thought about the things in me that were different from the things in him. When my dad died in 1973, it really knocked me down. When Dr. Landy died in 2006, I heard the news and sat and thought about it for a while, and then I got back to work.

⁓

The songs kept coming, in pieces and sometimes whole. I talked to Scott Bennett about them almost every day, and we were often at his house recording. On the way over, we used to listen to *Pet Sounds* in the car, especially "Don't Talk (Put Your Head on My Shoulder)." That was my Valium. I wasn't always up for listening to old songs, but that summer I really felt the connection. "That Lucky Old Sun" became a kind of beginning for the songs, and they moved out in all directions from there. I was excited about the new songs. I wanted to release them the way they were, but the band felt differently. Scott and Mark Linett and Jeff Foskett thought they needed to be rerecorded. Melinda agreed. Everyone agreed, really. They kept saying their opinion and eventually I decided they were right. I decided to turn them all into one album.

But when I laid out the songs, I didn't always see how they were related to each other. Some of them were about memory and how it repeated in you, how echoes either brought you back things you had heard earlier or let you hear things differently. Some of them were about California. One was about Mexico. A few were love songs. Sometimes it's okay to leave songs on their own. Sometimes you want to tie them together. That's the real meaning of an album, going way back—people collected songs in a kind of book. I wanted the songs to be their own book. The only person I thought could do that was Van Dyke. We were both still humming a little bit from SMiLE, and when we spoke about the new songs, I asked him to write some narration over theme music I was composing. I thought it would tie the whole project together.

The album came into focus that way. We started with "That Lucky Old Sun," the actual song, though not a full version of it. That became the title song. It was an album about suns moving across the sky all day, but also rising and setting. The whole thing would be like a day, and it would make you think of other days. That would let us make an album that was about memory and echoes. After "That Lucky Old Sun," the next song was "Morning Beat," which I wrote about a typical day of mine, and then I spoke a section of Van Dyke's narration that we called "Room with a View":

> *Just now I was thinkin' 'bout another perfect day*
> *Wishing it would come again your way*
> *Down below, a sparkled city scatters by the bay*
> *Tells you your suspicions are at play*
> *One by one, a carpet of star-spangled cities sleep*
> *Like so many dancing diamonds with a beat*
> *Each of them are home with walls of stories they could tell*
> *Meet the crack of dawn*
> *A freeway starts to roll*
> *An owl hoots it's last good-bye to a coyote on patrol*
> *Each day keeps me guessin'*
> *Will you take what I'm confessing?*
> *Will you find the heartbeat in LA?*

What was the heartbeat in LA? Partly it was old Beach Boys songs. Scott and I decided that it was okay to be nostalgic sometimes. I had been making music for almost fifty years. There must have been some songs or ideas that I could go back to and look at again. We wrote "Forever She'll Be My Surfer Girl" as a love song not to a girl but to the actual song. There's a line in the lyrics, "Sweet voices right from heaven / Radio seven," partly because "Surfer Girl" went to number seven in *Billboard* and partly because the BBC has Radio 2, and I liked the sound of Radio 7.

"Oxygen to the Brain" was an especially great song for me. It was about getting through challenges, no matter how difficult they seemed. When I sang it, I thought about all the times I refused to give up, all the times I had pain and doubt but decided instead to make music. That meant that I was thinking about every day. That's the thing about mental illness. It's a struggle every single day, so you have to invent ways of getting through it. You have to come out the other end with the right parts of you still in place. That's what that song was about, learning to do that:

> *Let yourself float*
> *Don't carry that weight*
> *Never destroy*
> *When you can create*
> *Ready steady*
> *California*
> *I'm fillin' up*
> *My lungs again*
> *And breathin' life*

Around that time Mike Love was over to my house for dinner. He and I were the only family left from the original band. Mike was a great front man. He always had so much energy. But seeing Mike was hard sometimes. He and I had been through so much that I didn't even like to think about it. We had been in court once in the '90s when he sued over royalties from the early songs. I lost that case during a trying time in my life. We were back in court in 2005 when he had a problem with a free CD that was given away by a newspaper in the UK. Mike had a funny way of looking at things. He was the one who wanted to try to arm wrestle Dennis the day we were doing "Surfin' Safari" even though it was obvious that Dennis was going to kick his ass. That was his choice, his thing.

What I thought about when I thought about Mike was something that happened before the lawsuits. It was the day the Beach Boys got into the Rock and Roll Hall of Fame. It was in 1988. I had finished the first solo record I made with Dr. Landy, which was going to come out later in the year. I made a short speech and talked about how much I loved "Be My Baby." I said I hoped that we would be back in twenty-seven years to get inducted again. It's funny, because that's how much time has gone by again. So much time has passed. After I spoke, Carl talked about missing Dennis. At that point it was only five years since Dennis drowned and all the sadness about it was still so recent. Finally Mike gave his speech. He talked about how harmony was both a musical idea and an idea about love. He said something about how Paul was suing Ringo and Yoko and couldn't be there, and that was a shame because it wasn't harmony. But then he started to talk about other bands. He said that we were still rocking better than them. He said he would like to see them do what we were doing. He called out lots of other people, like the Beatles and the Stones and Billy Joel. He said that Mick Jagger was "chickenshit to get onstage with the Beach Boys." Carl looked over at me during that speech and said, "We're fucked." I didn't really feel that way, but I didn't feel the way Mike felt either. I just felt embarrassed for us. Some people thought Mike was joking, but I didn't know him to joke in that way. Bob Dylan came on later and he joked for sure. He said, "I want to thank Mike Love for not mentioning me."

The day Mike came to dinner and I was working on *That Lucky Old Sun,* we went out to the car. I had written a song called "Mexican Girl," which is probably the best song ever written about a Mexican girl. I played it for Mike and asked him if he would want to work on the lyrics. "I could make it twenty-five percent better, but I don't want to," he said. "If we do anything, I want to start from scratch." There were times that would have made me sad or angry, but in the car it only made me laugh a little. Mike was Mike. You can't wallow in the mire.

The songs kept coming. I even recorded a tribute to my dad. I had always loved his song "His Little Darling and You." It was beautiful to me when I was a kid and stayed beautiful whenever I went back to it in my head. When I was doing *Lucky Old Sun,* I borrowed part of that melody, reworked it, and put it in a song called "Just Like Me and You." That ended up as a bonus track on a version of the album. But it was one of the ways I was proving I wasn't afraid of making new things that were also old things. I wasn't afraid of the past. That was the thing about the sun. It had to do the same thing every day and make it feel new. The sun was good at that. It was one of the reasons it was so lucky.

◡◠

The album reached back into the past in other ways, too. In 2006, during the time I was writing it, I was in New York. It was a sunny day and I was walking down Broadway with a group of friends. Ray Lawlor was there, and David Leaf and Jerry Weiss. David and I were in town promoting the DVD he made about the *SMiLE* record, *Beautiful Dreamer: Brian Wilson and the Story of SMiLE.* Someone suggested lunch at Baldoria, this great Italian restaurant, and someone else agreed, and we were on our way when we saw the Brill Building across the street. It was right around the corner from the restaurant. David stopped to look. It was like he was standing outside a church. "Can you believe it?" he said. "Everyone was here: Leiber and Stoller, Goffin and King, Mann and Weil."

I was hungry, but I needed to stand there for a while with him to soak up the vibe. I didn't say much, just tried to get the magic of the place. Eventually we remembered how hungry we were and headed to our lunch. I scored a margarita, with double the alcohol, but I didn't drain it. I just sipped a little to get calm and enjoy myself. We started talking about New York and songwriting and the city's past. Some of the guys were native New Yorkers and they told me about the first time they ever heard Dion or Frankie Lymon or the Del-Vikings, and I told them my version of the story, which happened in California.

After about twenty minutes, I noticed that Ray was staring across the room, looking at a table of two women. "Hey, Bri," he said, "isn't that woman with her back to us over there a dead ringer for Carole King?"

"She does look like Carole King," I said, "because it is Carole King." Everyone at the table laughed. They got my joke, that it would have been funny to see her right after walking by the Brill Building. I sipped more of my margarita until I had to go to the bathroom. "Gotta go take a piss," I said to all the guys, though none of them had asked.

I went to the men's room, opened the door, and the first person I saw was Barry Mann. Now I thought I was dreaming, maybe. Pass the Brill Building, walk to lunch, imagine you see Carole King, and then see Barry Mann? He cowrote so many great songs with his wife, Cynthia Weil. "Uptown" and "We Gotta Get out of This Place" and "I'm Gonna Be Strong." I said hi to Barry and took him to the table to meet the guys. I asked him if he wanted to sit with us. "I'd love to," he said, "but I'm sitting over there with Carole." There was a silence at the table, which I guess he thought meant he had to explain. "Carole King," he said. "And Cynthia."

"Cynthia Weil?" I said. I was still thinking of all the songs they wrote together. I don't know which one was in my head by that point. Maybe "He's Sure the Boy I Love" or "Walking in the Rain."

Barry laughed. "Walk over there with me."

I crossed the dining room with Barry. The two women were bent over their plates. "Look who I found in the men's room," Barry said.

Carole looked up and started to shriek with surprise. She got up and kissed me on the cheek. "What on earth are you doing here?" she said.

"Having some pasta with my friends."

"I cannot believe this," Cynthia said.

I went back to the guys in a great mood. "Can you believe running into Barry Mann in a goddamned men's room in New York?" I said. "I'll be goddamned. We're in the room with three of the greatest songwriters ever."

"Don't you mean four?" David said, which was nice, but I was still in disbelief. I told the other guys that we had to do something for them. One of my favorite songs that Barry and Cynthia ever wrote was "You've Lost That Lovin' Feeling." They wrote it with Phil Spector, and it was a huge hit for the Righteous Brothers in 1964, the year that everything happened. Right there at the table I worked out a little arrangement of "You've Lost That Lovin' Feeling," just the first verse, that had a part for me, a part for Ray, a part for David, and a part for Jerry. Then we went over and performed it for their table. We did well enough with the serenade that they couldn't stop smiling, and neither could we.

New York is the only place in the world where things like that happen. A few years later I was in town for a concert and Ray brought some pizzas to the gig. They were amazing. Sometimes good pizza just can't be beat. When I was getting ready to fly back home a few days later, I asked him if we could go to that exact pizza place. Ray told the driver and we went to the place, New Park Pizza in Howard Beach. When we walked in I went right to the counter and ordered a large pizza. The pizza came out of the oven, and I picked up the biggest slice and bit into it. It was hot, but it was great. "This is the best goddamn pizza I have ever had," I said, because it was. I flew back home, thinking about it the whole way.

A few days later I was still thinking about it. I called Ray. "Hey," I said. Remember that pizza we had?"

"I remember," he said.

"Can you FedEx me a pie?" He laughed but I didn't, and I guess that's how he knew I wasn't joking. So he went there and I guess they taught him how to pack it up and freeze it and it came the very next day.

ॐ

I picked one of Barry and Cynthia's songs that day in Baldoria, but Carole wrote a million great ones, too. One of my favorites was "I'm into Something Good." It also came from 1964. She wrote it and gave it to a girl named Earl-Jean, which is a strange name for a girl, though she did a great job with it. Some people knew her version, but most knew the version Herman's Hermits did later that year. They went to number one with it on the British charts in September, just a few weeks before we performed "I Get Around" on *The Ed Sullivan Show*. It really was the year that everything happened. "I'm into Something Good" is such a happy song. It's the kind of thing you can hum all day. I redid it a little bit back in the early '70s. I had ideas about how it might be arranged differently. In my head I heard slightly different backing vocals and piano parts, and this breakdown around the two-minute mark. It was the same song but not exactly the same. I played my version for some friends and even scheduled a recording session to cut it. About a half hour before we were supposed to record, I cancelled the session. I'm sure the musicians were mad, but I just thought that maybe I shouldn't do it. There was something about the arrangement that wasn't quite right, or maybe it was something about the room. Then I forgot all about it. Maybe thirty years later Ray was visiting me and he mentioned it. It all came right back to me. "In the key of A," I said. I went to the piano and played the beginning.

That was a time when I was remembering lots of songs. When we were doing *Lucky Old Sun* I decided to go back into the studio with it. I called Ray to come out. Why not? He was my memory on it. He couldn't come out right away. I think it was a Wednesday. But he said he could be in LA by Friday. Ray flew in, we went into the music room, and I started playing. The version I had was mostly just me on the keyboards and then singing the lead over the track.

When I listened back, it was missing something. "You know what?" I said to Ray. "It would be great on the track to have Carole King singing backup. Do you think we could make that happen?"

"Of course," Ray said. "Call her up."

I didn't think I could. It seemed like too much. So Ray did it. He called David Leaf, who gave him the number of Lorna Guess, Carole's manager, who was also married to Carole's guitar player, Rudy Guess. Then Ray called Lorna, and Lorna told Ray that Carole was working on a book and had just gotten to a part where she was talking about how she always wanted to work with me. Ray said that was great because I had an idea for a song. They worked it out and Carole flew in from Idaho. I guess Ray gave her directions to the house.

Ray kept saying that Carole was coming in a hybrid. I wasn't sure what that was. Finally this tiny green thing drove up and Ray went down to meet her. He brought her up, along with Lorna and Rudy. I couldn't stop myself from smiling. I was so happy to see Carole. I don't know if she thought it would be a normal studio. It wasn't. It was the music room again, with me and Scott Bennett and a computer. That was a great way for me to work. Scott was so fast and on top of things. But I wondered if Carole would mind. She didn't. "I'm ready," she said, and she started humming "I'm into Something Good." You couldn't help humming that song.

But I had another idea that I'd thought of between when I invited her and when she came. It's like I said, ideas were coming at me all the time then. "Wait," I said. "Listen to this." I had a song called "Good Kind of Love" that I wanted to use on *Lucky Old Sun*. It was another happy song about finding the right person in your life and how it helps you deal with things you might keep secret without that person. First, it talks about what the girl is feeling.

Imagine when she's sleeping
And all the dreams she's keeping
She keeps them in a jar
And not too far from her heart

Later on there's a part that sounds like it could have been from one of Carole's old songs, or mine: "Run to him, run to him, right to his arms." In fact, when I wrote it I was thinking about Carole, which is why I wanted her to sing it.

Carole didn't know the song, so I taught it to her. We went back and forth in the room. I sang a part and she sang a part. Bedroom singing, teaching people their parts. It was like what happened fifty years before in Hawthorne. Carole said she loved the song. She said it was better than "I'm into Something Good," which wasn't true. Then we started the recording. When she started on the verses, she came in a little bit wrong. "Carole," I said, "you are flatting, but I really like your dress." I wanted her to sing it right, but I also wanted to make her laugh. Near the end of the session, Carole was nervous that she was going to miss one of the high C notes, but she hit it perfectly, and when she did she went around the room slapping people's hands.

"Okay," I said. "We're done." I started to leave and turned around to say good-bye.

Carole stared at me. "What about 'I'm into Something Good'?" she said. "I came out from Idaho."

We did that for a while, too. It went so well. The two songs with Carole ended up on the special edition of the album with the song I wrote from my dad's song.

I loved working with Carole. She was a real pro. Back in the '90s, just after Dr. Landy left, in the years when Melinda and I would drive around and listen to the radio, there was a movie called *Grace of My Heart*. It was about a singer and songwriter like Carole, a fictional version, and it had a character in it who was a singer and songwriter like me, a fictional version. The movie showed how the Brill Building sound came together, and then the character like Carole went out to California, where she met the character like me and learned all about the music on the West Coast. California Music. There were things about the movie that I liked and things that didn't make sense to me, but one thing that it made me think about was how long we had been making records. We had been through so much, in our lives and in our music. When I was around Carole, or Barry Mann, we didn't even have to talk about it, really. We knew how much we all knew. I remember once I met Chuck Berry on an airplane. "Hey, how are you?" he said and then turned the other way.

When I was around younger singers, it was harder for me. I didn't know what they thought about what I had done, and I didn't know what they wanted me to think about what they had done. Sometimes they weren't even that young, but they were young to me. I was at the Ivor Novello Awards once and a young guy came up to me. "Brian, Brian," he said.

"Hey, man," I said, "can you score me a Diet Coke?"

It was Bono. I didn't know him that well.

Another time Don Henley came backstage and brought his copy of *Pet Sounds*. I think it was the original record he'd had since he was a kid. I knew the Eagles, of course. If the Beach Boys were California in the '60s, the Eagles and Fleetwood Mac were California in the '70s. Don Henley sat down next to me and started telling me everything about his history with Beach Boys music. He said that we inspired him so much when he was growing up, even though he was in Texas at the time and not in California. He told me that he listened to the harmonies of the group but also to the way we put songs together. Then he asked me to sign the record. I took a Sharpie from the table in the dressing room. There are always Sharpies around for signing things. I wrote on his record, "To Don: thanks for all the great songs. Brian Wilson." Don was so grateful. It was almost like he couldn't talk. He turned to leave. "Hey, Don," I said. "Wait a second." I took the record back, crossed out "great," and wrote "good." Some people would have been mad, but Don just looked at it and laughed. Another time Melinda and I were at the beach in Santa Monica and Don came up to say hello. "Hey, man," I said, "your hair's really been through some changes." Don laughed at that the same way he laughed at the album.

⁓

The songs I did with Carole ended up on the same special edition of *Lucky Old Sun* that had the song I remade from my dad's song. But every edition of the *Lucky Old Sun* album was special. It was just a great time when I was able to make music that was old and new at the same time. One afternoon we were working on "Midnight's Another Day." That was a song about feeling down and depressed, and how sometimes the only way to deal with those feelings is to wait them out until you feel good again. It was the kind of song that was easy to sing when I was feeling good again.

> *Lost in the dark*
> *No shades of gray*
> *Until I found*
> *Midnight's another day*
> *Swept away in a braying storm*
> *Chapters missing, pages torn*
> *Waited too long to feel the warmth*
> *I had to chase the sun*

The song was sounding strange to me. I liked the arrangement, but it was missing a certain sound. I could hear it in my head, but I couldn't hear it on the record. I kept slowing down the sessions and starting them and then finally I realized what it was: a small foot-pump organ. Scott and I hopped into the Mercedes and drove over to Studio Instrument Rentals, a place off Sunset owned by Jan Berry's brother Ken. The Berrys had a third brother, Bruce, who is mentioned in Neil Young's song "Tonight's the Night." I always liked Neil—talk about pleasant. When we got to SIR, it was full, but all the people working in the place knew me. They brought out a small organ and set it up right in the store for me to test out. I sat down and started pumping the thing with my feet, checking out how it sounded. It sounded great. "This works," I said to Ray.

"Great," he said. "Ready to go?"

"I want to try one more thing," I said. By now the entire warehouse staff and all the customers in the place were gathered around. I tried a version of "Surfer Girl" that was different from the original 1961 version. It was more like a version we did in 1967 in Hawaii. It was a slower and smoother version. When I played it at SIR, that was the version, and when I was done, everyone applauded. It was like a concert.

Ray and I took the organ and carried it down the street to the Mercedes, where we jammed it into the backseat. We went home, Ray split, and I worked more on "Midnight's Another Day." All the people who were around for that song—Melinda, Scott, and even Ray—couldn't believe it, all that effort just to get a few notes of a specific sound on a track. Ultimately Scott and I didn't use that little organ on the basic track. It didn't get the vibe I thought it would. But I had to try, you know?

For another song on that record, "Going Home," I had it in my mind that I needed Tommy Morgan, who had played with the Wrecking Crew and was one of the best harmonica players I had ever heard. I knew I wanted his sound. I hadn't worked with Tommy for years; I knew him back in the '60s and he had come to do some tracks with me and Andy Paley in the '90s. I didn't know how to reach him. I called up the musician's union and got Tommy's information and then called Tommy directly. "This is Brian

Wilson," I said when he answered. "I have a job for you. Bring all your stuff."

Tommy and all his stuff showed up on time, and he played a great part. Then he was done. But a few minutes later when I turned around, he was still there. "Hey," he said. "When are you going to cut the vocals?"

"As soon as you leave," I said.

"Well," he said, "actually, I'd like to stay because I've never seen the vocals cut. I always just did my parts and left. I want to see how you do it." Tommy stayed on the side and watched me sing.

The song itself was about my own life, about the ways I had let things unravel over the years and the ways I was picking up the threads.

> At twenty-five I turned out the light
> 'Cause I couldn't handle the glare in my tired eyes
> But now I'm back, drawing shades of kind blue skies
> It's good to travel
> But not for too long
> So now I'm home where I belong
> And that's the key
> To every song
> I'm going home

I loved the concert tour we did after that record. Taking the new songs out was so exciting. It was material I believed in—more than that, it was material that seemed like it was tapping into the same kind of vibe that had made the old songs special. In those shows, we closed the first half with "I Get Around" and in the intermission I went to hang out with the band. They were the same guys who had been playing with me for almost ten years at that point: Darian Sahanaja and Scott Bennett on keyboards; Jeff Foskett and Nicky Wonder on guitars; Mikey D'Amico on drums; Nelson Bragg on percussion; Probyn Gregory on guitar, horns, and theremin; Brett

Simons on bass (he had actually just joined up when Bob Lizik split for a few years); Taylor Mills on vocals; and Paul Von Mertens on saxophone and harmonica. I got comfortable back there with them. Some of them were studying like professors and some of them were acting like clowns. I knew that if I looked I would see a half-full beer bottle next to Mikey, or that Paul would be sitting a little apart, going through the second half of the show in his head, or that Scott would be bouncing around trying to keep the room's energy high. Just like every house isn't a home, every band isn't a family. But I had been in a band that was an actual family, and the band that played with me around 2006—most of them are still with me now—is the closest I've come since.

The new songs worked so well that I started to see old songs in new ways. We started those shows with some older Beach Boys stuff: "Do It Again," "The Little Girl I Once Knew," "Dance, Dance, Dance." We were also adding in "Salt Lake City," a song from *Summer Days (And Summer Nights!!)* that we had never played live before. In sound check, Paul was playing the sax break and all of a sudden I thought of something. "Stop," I said. "Stop everything." Everyone was confused. "Paul," I said, "when you get to the second four bars of the break, I want you to double up." We had our friends the Stockholm Strings and Horns with us on that tour, so we had a second sax on the stage. No one understood why I wanted it to go that way until they heard it, and then they understood completely. Dynamics! I don't know for sure that I wouldn't have heard those things a few years before, but I know that I was hearing them more clearly when we went out on the road after *Lucky Old Sun*. It was WCW more often than not.

CHAPTER 8

America

Hurry, hurry, hurry, hurry, folks
Step right up to the Beach Boy circus
The best little show in town
Hurry, hurry, hurry, it's only a dime, folks
One thin dime, just one tenth of a dollar
      —"Amusement Parks U.S.A."

Rock and roll was made in England and America, and you could say that the Beach Boys were made on both sides of the ocean, too. We learned from British bands, and we always played well in the UK and in Australia. Audiences there are more sensitive to artists. They have more love for American music than American audiences do. But we were only ever making American music, which is one of the reasons the end of 2007 was so exciting and rewarding.

One afternoon I came home from a walk in the park (my second walk of the day—I was feeling healthy and clear-headed) and I was watching the news when all of a sudden I heard Melinda scream. It wasn't a worried scream. It was a happy scream. She came into the room. "Brian," she said, "you just won the Kennedy Center award."

"What the hell?" I said. "What for?"

She told me that it was for my contribution to American music and my lifetime achievement in the field. We were invited to Washington to meet with President and Mrs. Bush. I couldn't believe it. I had watched the Kennedy Center Honors on TV before. I saw when Smokey Robinson was honored. He was such a great songwriter and singer, one of the people in the music world I respected the most. I couldn't believe that I was in Smokey's company. Melinda told me the other honorees, and they were incredible company, too: Diana Ross, Steve Martin, Martin Scorsese, and Leon Fleisher.

A few minutes later I remembered that it wasn't my first trip to the White House. Back in the early '80s, Reagan's interior secretary, James Watt, banned the Beach Boys from playing in the White House's official Independence Day celebration. He said that rock bands attracted the wrong element. All hell broke loose. People on all sides of the issue started expressing their opinion, louder and louder. Finally, Watt got called on the carpet by Nancy Reagan, who said that if we attracted the wrong element, then she was the wrong element because she was a huge fan of ours. That was a surprise to me, though I had heard the Reagans' daughter, Patti, liked our music. The next thing I knew, President Reagan was inviting us to play privately at the White House. I got to meet the president and the First Lady, and they were so complimentary about our music. I don't remember whether we met James Watt.

I found myself at the White House again in 2004. My band and I were on the *SMiLE* tour, and we were playing the Warner Theatre in Washington, DC. Melinda decided she wanted to take a White House tour. I don't know how she arranged it, but we all got into a car—me, Melinda, Daria, Delanie, Gloria, and Jerry—and we drove to the White House gates, where we were met by a guide. He was a nice young guy, and he took us through the whole place. It was incredible. We walked past the Situation Room. We went to the Press Room and I stood at the podium and did a fake Nixon voice. We went into the Rose Garden and saw the Bushes' dog, Barney. President Bush wasn't there during that time. He was in Texas. But

I talked to the guide about him. I asked what time he woke up, what time he ate breakfast, and what his favorite breakfast was. I don't remember the answers. We invited that guide and his family to our show that night.

I wish I had remembered what President Bush ate for breakfast because I could have made a joke about it when we went back to Washington, DC, for the Kennedy Center Honors. It was a few days of events, including a performance, a reception, and several meals. I was staying with the whole family—again, Melinda, Daria, Delanie, Dylan, and Gloria—in an incredible suite at the Mandarin Oriental hotel. All the other honorees were there also, and some other people from my band and my life. Jeff Foskett and his wife, Diana, were there. David Leaf and his wife, Eva, were there. Melinda's friend Susan was there. Ray Lawlor was there. It was a full group.

I was nervous when we got to the hotel and more and more nervous as the week went on. The night of the White House reception was the worst—I mean, it was the best, but I was the most nervous. I paced around the hotel corridors until it was time to get into my tux. I called Ray. "Come help me get dressed," I said. He helped with the tie and the buttons and the shirt. It's really complicated. I didn't feel completely dressed until Melinda hung the Kennedy Center Honors medal around my neck.

We still had about two hours until the ceremony, so Ray and I went down to the lounge in the lobby in our tuxes. It was an amazing elevator ride. The elevator stopped a few floors below us and in walked Diana Ross and her daughter. "Brian!" she yelled. "Oh my God!"

I yelled back, "Diana!" I don't think we had seen each other since the T.A.M.I. Show in 1964. That was forty years, which was hard to believe. We had both come a very long way from the Santa Monica Civic Auditorium.

Two more floors and another stop: this time it was Steve Martin and Martin Short. "Hi," I said.

"It's the two amigos," Ray said, and the two Martins laughed.

The last stop wasn't a Kennedy award-winner, but it was almost better: Cameron Diaz. I remember thinking that first she was in my song—she was in the lyrics of "South American," on *Imagination*—and then she was in my elevator.

Ray and I hung out at the lobby lounge drinking Diet Cokes. I talked a bit to Steve Martin. Then it was time to head for the White House. When the limo pulled up, I couldn't believe it. From Hawthorne to here. I might have even said it out loud. Some men in suits ushered us into a reception area where all the honorees and their families were standing. I don't think I ever felt so proud. President and Mrs. Bush came around and we were introduced. "I am honored to meet you, Mr. President," I said.

President Bush shook his head. "No, Brian," he said. "The honor is mine. I am honored to meet you." I couldn't believe it, you know? I remember how gracious the Bushes were to us. They were so nice. The president walked over to Gloria. "Mrs. Ramos," he said, "would you like me to sign anything for you?" You can't imagine a nicer guy. And Condoleezza Rice came up to Melinda and me to talk about music—she told us she was a classically trained pianist, but most importantly she was a California girl. She said she was probably going to go back to Stanford when she was done in the government. Then we all had pictures taken with the president and went to the Kennedy Center for the ceremony and performance.

The rest of the night was a blur, though I can pick out moments. Art Garfunkel gave a nice speech about me while a film was shown. The audience gave me a standing ovation. I was focusing all my energy on just keeping it together. It would have been so easy to be overwhelmed. Then people started performing. Lyle Lovett did a great take on "God Only Knows," and then Hootie and the Blowfish came out and sang "I Get Around." Then they segued into "California Girls" and I saw all these powerful Washington people act like any other crowd: they started dancing. First it was Senator

Ted Kennedy. He stood up. Then the distinguished gentleman next to him stood up. Pretty soon the whole place was rocking. I took a peek over at President and Mrs. Bush, and at Secretary Rice. They were up, too, singing along with every word. Music is bipartisan.

The last act in the tribute show was a boys choir group from England called Libera. They came out wearing white robes and sang "Love and Mercy." It just kept building and building. Everyone was crying. When they ended by dropping a bunch of beach balls from the ceiling, I could sense how powerful the night was for everyone, not just for me. I've had so many great nights in my life, but that was one of the greatest. At one point I scanned the crowd and saw Smokey Robinson on the aisle, half-turned toward me, clapping like hell and smiling.

⌘

The idea of America that was part of the Kennedy Center awards was always around the band. One of the Beach Boys' greatest hits records from the mid-'70s was called *Spirit of America*. People built their idea of America, especially California, from the things we talked about in our songs. We weren't the only artists like that, of course. In 2009 I was playing a benefit show at the Count Basie Theatre in Red Bank, New Jersey. The whole time we were playing our show, there was a guy sitting in a folding chair on the side of the stage. I sit on the side of the stage sometimes myself during sound check, so I was paying special attention to the guy. I couldn't tell who he was at first. I couldn't see very well from the stage. But he definitely was someone—everyone who walked past him shook his hand.

It turns out it was Bruce Springsteen. He was so quiet there on the side of the stage. It was almost like he was taking notes. At the end of that show, he came onstage and sat in with us; he played guitar on "Barbara Ann" and sang harmonies on "Love and Mercy." I remember turning and seeing him standing next to Taylor

Mills, our pretty blond backup singer, and thinking that all singers have moments when they are just guys (or girls) standing at microphones. It doesn't matter how famous they are. They still have to go to the microphone and sing. Bruce came by afterward and hung out for a little while. He had really nice things to say about the band and how perfectly it fit the music. He said that the songs were American masterworks. It was nice of him to say. He has written some himself.

After that, after the Kennedy Center, after *Lucky Old Sun*, Ray was in Los Angeles visiting me. He didn't bring any pizza that time. We went to the Beverly Glen Deli. That's where I like to go. I have been going there for at least fifteen years. They have a big diner menu with lots of choices and everything is good. We were eating dinner, and my mind was drifting a bit while Ray talked. I was thinking about movies—first, that movie *Educating Rita*, with Michael Caine and Julie Walters. He was brilliant in it, I thought. Then I was thinking about *On Golden Pond* and how strange it must have been for Jane Fonda to work with her dad, and then I was thinking about *An Officer and a Gentleman*, which had that great song "Up Where We Belong." Jack Nitzsche, who did "The Lonely Surfer," cowrote that song. Joe Cocker sang it. Something about thinking about Joe Cocker made me think about "You Are So Beautiful," and that made me think of an older song, "I Was So Young (You Were So Beautiful.)" It wasn't a song I knew that well, but I remembered hearing it. It was an early George Gershwin song. That made me think of something else. "Oh, no," I said.

"What?" Ray asked.

"I signed to do a Gershwin album," I said. It was a joke, but not completely a joke. I had remembered and then forgotten.

"What do you mean?" Ray said.

"You know, an album of George Gershwin songs that I would arrange and sing. They even agreed to let me finish some of his unfinished songs."

"That's great," Ray said. "That's awesome."

I told Ray that I had to go through all the great Gershwin songs and pick the ones I thought I could do well with my voice and my band. I had been talking about the songs with Paul Von Mertens, who was in my band and had ideas about which songs would be best for the project. And then I told Ray what I remembered. "The record company needs the first list of songs I might want to do by Tuesday." It was almost Tuesday.

We finished up eating and then Ray drove me home. I used to live down near Shaquille O'Neal. I never really hung out with him, but sometimes I would see him getting out of a car or getting into one. Paula Abdul and John Fogerty were near there also. But then we built a house farther up the hill. When we got inside, Ray went right to the computer and started calling out the names of Gershwin songs. "What about 'Summertime'?"

"Definitely," I said.

"What about 'It Ain't Necessarily So'?"

"I'm not sure about that one." It wasn't one of Ira's best lyrics. It had a dark vibe. But it was a song I liked singing.

"What about 'I Loves You, Porgy'?"

"Yeah, yeah," I said. "I have to include that. And it has to be sung a certain way. Are you writing this down?"

Ray turned and frowned at me. "You write it down, Brian. It's your album. It should be in your handwriting, don't you think?"

I got a piece of paper and started writing down all the songs that sounded good to me. Ray and I worked on the list until he had to leave that evening to fly back to New York.

The next morning I woke up early and went to look at the list again. But I couldn't find it. I called Ray in New York.

"Hello?" He sounded tired.

"Ray," I said, "do you have the list? I can't find it."

He sighed. "I'll retype it for you."

"And then what?"

"Then I'll fax it to you." He paused. "You do know how to use the fax machine, don't you?"

"Of course I know how to use the fax machine," I said.

About twenty minutes later, the machine started whirring and a piece of paper came through. I took it out and called Ray back.

"You got it?" he asked.

I said yes.

"So we're all set?"

"Well," I said, "I can't really read it. The letters are so small and I can't find my glasses. Can you send it back to me with bigger letters?"

Ray hung up while I was talking, but he sent me that second fax, too. The letters were the perfect size. I could read every title. And the best one, the one that I knew would start the album, was right at the top: "Rhapsody in Blue."

⌀

When I started the Gershwin album, Paul Von Mertens worked with me closely. He and I had already talked a little bit about the songs before Ray and I made the list, but we talked about them more and more. We talked about what they meant. We talked about which ones could be rearranged without taking too much away from the originals, and which ones should be done just like they were done originally. We listened to old versions by so many other singers. He helped me decide which songs would work best for my vocal range. Some of them went too high for my older voice, and I'm not even sure that I could have sung them when I was young. Paul, he's great, and he's a student of anything Gershwin. He arranged the strings and horns on the whole album. I made some adjustments to them, revamped what he wrote out, but he did most of it. He's very good. He's on top of it.

I had Paul Von Mertens. Gershwin had his own Paul. He had Paul Whiteman, a bandleader who played all around the West but came to New York in 1920 to work for Victor Records. He met Gershwin there, and the two attended a jazz show in 1923 with a Canadian singer. I think Gershwin played piano at the show. Paul

Whiteman went home from it and had an idea. His idea was to ask Gershwin to make a piece of music that represented America. Gershwin wasn't sure at first. He thought maybe the idea was too big, and that anything he made would collapse under the weight of it. I know how he felt. But then he read a newspaper article that said Vincent Lopez, another piano player and composer in New York, was about to do his own version, and Gershwin started to think that maybe he should do it. While he was taking a train from New York up to Boston, he let his mind roam around and think about the country and all the things it created even without composers, and how a composer might be able to organize all that energy into a piece of music. The piece came quickly after that, and Ira had the idea of calling it "Rhapsody in Blue."

"Rhapsody in Blue" was the first Gershwin piece I heard, or at least the first piece I heard that I knew was by him. I might have heard other songs sung by popular singers or jazz singers, but then one day I was at my grandmother's house and she played a copy of "Rhapsody in Blue," the Glenn Miller version that he did in 1943. I must have been two or three, which meant that the record was only about a year old. When she played it for me, I was blown away. I was transported somewhere else. I just smiled and listened and tried to take it all in. When it was over, my grandmother asked me how I liked it, and I couldn't answer. My mother asked me the same thing, and I still couldn't answer. I guess I was still trying to take it all in. Back then, that's what I did with music. My mother said that I could hum entire tunes when I was real small. After I heard "Rhapsody in Blue" that first time, I let it play through over and over again in my head until I could hum the entire tune. I liked the way it sounded, and I liked the way it had ideas in it, and I even liked the way he worked with his brother. If I had to pick a favorite section, I'd pick the middle, the prettiest part. The violins had amazing harmonies. He was doing amazing things with the way lines ended, with the way they put themselves down.

At the time, I hadn't studied Gershwin. I didn't know anything about how he was born Jacob but called George, the same way his brother was born Israel but called Ira. I didn't know anything about the Yiddish theater, or what his life was like on the Lower East Side in the early twentieth century, or how he didn't even start with the piano until he was ten. But I did hear his music, and that taught me one thing early on, which was that music is perfect. It's sound taken to a higher level. Some rock and roll groups and some rock and roll songs will be remembered. I hope that mine will be. But I am sure that Gershwin will be remembered. His music was very special. He was very advanced musically, ahead of his time. So maybe it's not just that he'll be remembered. Maybe it's that everyone else will catch up to him and start to hear things the way he heard them.

I wanted to show people his ideas when I made the record, but I also wanted to show people my ideas. In a way, the picks that Paul and I made were a kind of second *SMiLE*, another picture of America but with Gershwin's puzzle pieces instead of mine. That meant that I had to change things. I did "Rhapsody in Blue," but I changed it around a bit. The original key was too high. I put it in C, down a bit. I thought it sounded great that way. "I Loves You, Porgy" was a chance to try to capture the mood of a Negro spiritual. I left the lyric in the feminine; some people change the words, but that wouldn't seem fair to Ira, and I wanted to pay homage to him, too.

At times I went for a summer vibe, not only when it was obvious, in "Summertime," but also in "I Got Plenty o' Nuttin'." Other times it was finding the level of the song, like "Love Is Here to Stay." It was a real pleasure to sing those melodies. They are sweet and sensitive songs. I sang differently than I did with Beach Boys songs or my own. For "They Can't Take That Away from Me," I tried to make my voice convey the main idea, which is that you hold on to what you have tightly. It's also a shuffle beat, like "Little Deuce Coupe," so I could get right into it. And on "Someone to

Watch Over Me," we cut it with a harpsichord and ended up close to "Caroline, No" in feel. Going back to Gershwin and American music of that time, I had to pass through lots of the music I made, and that was a real interesting experience.

∽

When I think of an arrangement for a song, I don't get it down on paper right away. Other people take lots of notes. Paul McCartney did colorful drawings showing where all the instruments should go in the mix; some of them were published in the liner notes to one of his albums, and I thought they were amazing. I can't really draw, though I sometimes did little drawings for the singles. I drew a transistor radio once for the *Mount Vernon and Fairway* EP sleeve, and I also drew the sleeve for the "Love and Mercy" single. But I don't draw so much for my music. It's mostly mental with me.

I was sitting there at the board. We were doing the Gershwin songs. I was quiet. I didn't have anything to say really. I was looking straight at the board. Maybe ten minutes passed, though someone told me it was an hour. Someone else said, "We have to get going. What are you doing?"

"I'm working," I said. I was working out the arrangement in my head. I might lay down a vocal and peel it up. I might turn a track down so I could hear another track in isolation.

Fifteen minutes later I stood up from the board. Maybe it wasn't just fifteen minutes. I went over to the piano, though whenever I went over to the piano, it wasn't just to play the piano. It was to sing the melody line and demonstrate the harmonies and show all the parts of the songs. I wanted to make sure that everyone in the studio heard me and understood what I meant. I tried to be specific but not too technical. "I want to get a *chunk-a-chunk-a* melody," I'd say. Or I'd do the rhythms out loud: "I want you to play *boom, boom—boom boom.*"

I could be technical also. I was technical back when we did *Pet Sounds,* and I was technical sometimes on the Gershwin record, too. When we were recording "Summertime," I stopped the session on the talkback and told Todd Sucherman, who was drumming, "At the fourth bar of that transition thing, I want you to hit the snare hard three times—boom, boom, boom. Everyone else, drop out."

We went to Ocean Way Recording in Hollywood, which used to be United Western, for that one. I love that studio because of its design. I was cutting the vocal for "Someone to Watch Over Me." We went through the first take. "That's the take," I said.

Melinda and Mark Linett were there at the studio, and they turned to me with looks on their faces—and not supportive looks. "Why don't we try another one?" Melinda said.

"That's the one," I said. "I can hear it. I'm sure." They still didn't look convinced. I used Ray as a tiebreaker. "Ray, what do you think?"

"I think you've got a better one in you," he said.

I tried it again. I'm willing to try.

⟡

The two new songs were the most intense. The Gershwin estate let me work with fragments and turn them into songs. One of them was called "Will You Remember Me" and the other one was called "Say My Say." Scott Bennett wrote lyrics, I added some new melodies, and we turned them into two new songs, "The Like in I Love You" and "Nothing But Love." I especially liked the lyrics he did for "The Like in I Love You." It's a love song, but one that talks about how love is not just one great feeling but lots of little feelings that add up over time.

I see your picture coming through
The story's always you
It's more than harmony
When you sing with me
It's an entire symphony

The other great part of that song was when Scott wrote about the way that ideas happen in art. You have to be willing to look everywhere in your life.

The pain in painting
The muse in music

And the pain in music, too; even though the Gershwin songs could be light and sophisticated, they could also get to some of the scarier parts of life. Some days during the record I heard voices or I felt like I wasn't completely keeping things under control, and the music really helped me get centered again. Listening to Gershwin's melodies or even finishing some of them could be as satisfying as writing my own songs. I wondered what would happen if he could come back and hear it. What would he say? Hopefully he'd say that it was great. I hope I did right by him.

∽

Gershwin makes singers. In 2001, during the time of the tribute show to me at Radio City, I made some friends go uptown with me to a cabaret show. I didn't tell them who we were going to see. It was Rosemary Clooney. She did a record in the late '70s where she sang Gershwin songs. We didn't overlap much in our choices, except that we both did "Love Is Here to Stay" and "You Can't Take That Away from Me."

Tony Bennett was in the audience. I was in jeans and a flannel shirt. After the concert we went backstage. Rosemary looked up. "Oh my, it's Brian," she said. "When are you going to write a song for me?"

"I'll do it," I said. "I'll write a ballad."

She died not long after that. I didn't get to write a song for her. But in a way, all the songs are for her. When she did "Tenderly" back in 1956, she taught me how to sing. I'll never forget it.

∽

The Gershwin project did so well that the record label asked us to do a second album. The record label was Disney, and that led to the idea, which was to take songs from Disney movies and give them the same treatment as the Gershwin songs.

Disney was a big source of everything for me. I remember when Disneyland opened in Anaheim. I was thirteen years old. It was an amazing thing. I remember friends going there. It was like a whole other country inside America, but somehow even more American. I went with Carnie and Wendy when they were little, and I went with Daria and Delanie when they were little. I remember going with Daria and Delanie better. We were coming out of a candy store, and Daria had a big jawbreaker and Delanie had a huge lollipop. I asked them if I could share, and then I took a huge bite out of the jawbreaker and a huge bite out of the lollipop.

The Disney amusement park was a big deal, but the movies were an even bigger deal. The first wave of cartoons came out either before I was born or when I was a tiny baby: *Snow White* in 1937, *Pinocchio* in 1940, *Dumbo* in 1941. *Bambi* came out in August of 1942, when I was only two months old. I didn't see it then. But there was another round about ten years later—*Cinderella* in 1950, *Alice in Wonderland* in 1951, *Peter Pan* in 1953— when I was the perfect age, and then more classics in the '60s, like *Mary Poppins* and *The Jungle Book*. Those I remember catching on TV when my kids were little, which is also when I saw some of the movies from the '40s. One thing those movies did was give audiences great songs. It goes from the newer Randy Newman songs, which blow me away, all the way back to songs like "Baby Mine" from *Dumbo*. "Baby Mine" was beautiful. It has a beautiful melody and it's so much fun to sing. It's one of my favorite cuts on that record. Paul and I did selections and arrangements for that, too, the same way we had on the Gershwin. We tried to find songs that matched my voice or songs where I could match the emotion with a new arrangement.

Because there were so many great Disney songs and so many movies, we tried to go with only one song per movie. That made it kind of hard. There were so many amazing songs that the Sherman Brothers wrote for *Mary Poppins*, but we picked only "Stay Awake." That's my favorite song on the Disney album. I love the chords, and I think my lead vocal is one of the best of my entire solo career. From *The Jungle Book*, we did "The Bare Necessities," which was the only song the Sherman Brothers didn't write for that movie. "The bare necessities of life will come to you"—that really got to my soul. That was written by Terry Gilkyson, who also wrote "Memories Are Made of This," a great song that was recorded by Dino, Desi, and Billy—a group that Billy Hinsche was in with Dean Martin's son, Dean, and Desi Arnaz's son, Desi. I really liked those guys. Two of them were my brothers-in-law; Carl was married to Annie Hinsche first and then to Gina Martin after that. Billy and I wrote the group's last single, "Lady Love." That came out in 1970, right around the time Elton John released "Your Song." That was the only exception on the whole Disney record—not Dino, Desi, and Billy but Elton John. We did two of the songs he wrote with Tim Rice for *The Lion King*. We did "Can You Feel the Love Tonight," which was a big ballad we did a little smaller, still keeping the spiritual lyrics, and "I Just Can't Wait to Be King," which we did like an early rock and roll song, with a kind of shuffle beat. Those lyrics I didn't like as much. They embarrassed me. It was way too egotistical. I liked "Colors of the Wind" from *Pocahontas*. How can the wind have colors? It's a very pictorial lyric.

We closed the record with "When You Wish Upon a Star" from *Pinocchio*, which Dion and the Belmonts had covered back in 1960. I had been thinking about their version when I wrote my first song, "Surfer Girl," and when I thought about it again I realized how important the lyrics were to me. It was one of the songs that had always been with me, ever since I was a little kid. When I showed the track list around, some people wondered if "When You Wish Upon a Star" was my way of saying good-bye to recording, if I was ending things by going back to the beginning. I think they could probably have thought that about almost any final song on any record I could have made at that point. Lots of things seemed like ways of ending.

You'd think that by the time I got to sixty I would have learned everything about singing, but that turned out not to be true at all. I keep learning, and lots of that is about unlearning. Back in the '60s I was absolutely obsessed with my voice. I was really obsessed with how it sounded, especially the high parts. Now I don't sing as high anymore and I use it simply as an instrument to communicate love and good vibes. The Gershwin album was a huge help in that way because I was singing songs that so many great singers had done before me, and the Disney album was the same way. Those two albums have some of the best lead vocals I have ever done in my solo career.

The Disney record has one other place where it meets up with the other music I made. There was a song on *Surf's Up* called "Disney Girls (1957)." I didn't write it. Bruce Johnston did. It was one of the songs he did that became the most famous. It wasn't about any specific Disney girls like Annette or Darlene. It was about how certain parts of American culture were myths that kept people away from reality.

> *Oh, reality, it's not for me*
> *And it makes me laugh*
> *Oh, fantasy world and Disney girls*
> *I'm coming back*

It was a song about nostalgia, but not necessarily the good part of nostalgia. The guy in the song loves that he can think about Disney and Patti Page and Tootsie Rolls, but those things aren't really part of his life anymore. The guy is stuck in time and trying to go back to something that wasn't even real in the first place. I always thought it was a sad song, but a great song. The Disney album I made was different. It wasn't about the idea of Disney really. It was about all these great songs that happened to be from Disney movies. I could update the songs with new arrangements. I could combine old songs and new songs. No one was stuck in time.

_ᗒ_

The Disney album was also the final chapter in a run of albums that seemed very different but were all kind of the same thing. Those four albums—the live remake of SMiLE through Lucky Old Sun, the Gershwin album, and then the Disney album—were all ways of looking at America. SMiLE was about how America thought of itself, how it invented itself and what it thought about itself as it moved west. Lucky Old Sun was mainly about California, but it was really about all of America. Gershwin was writing mainly about New York, but he was really writing about all of America. And Disney was something that everyone had in common. The liner notes for the Disney record mentioned that. They said that the record was like a meeting between two people who created America's idea of California, me and Walt Disney. The cover art showed a surfing van driving toward a sunset, and the sunset had mouse ears like Mickey. It was a little strange.

The Gershwin and the Disney are the solo records I listen to most in the car. I don't know if it's because I don't like listening to songs I wrote or because I love the way I'm singing on those albums, but I like hearing them. I listen to the radio for other people's songs, too, and every once in a while one will pop up and catch me. Once I was driving with someone, maybe Carnie, and "Baby Come Back" by Player came on the radio. It's not a band that people remember very much, but I loved that song. That's how songs work with me. I don't go by a band's reputation or how many records they're selling. I listen for a kind of magic that gives energy to all the people listening. I heard that energy in Michael McDonald, "What a Fool Believes." I heard it in Diana Ross and in almost every Marvin Gaye song. I heard it in a song called "Pretty Little Angel Eyes," which was produced by Phil Spector and sung by a guy named Curtis Lee. That was all the way back in 1961. I don't even know if the guy made other records, but that record was a great one. He was a hell of a singer.

Those are all American singers or groups. I'm not saying that there's anything wrong with British singers and groups. I loved the Beatles. I loved the Stones. I loved the Who. If "London Calling" was on the radio, I wouldn't shut it off. But there's something special about American music that doesn't try to imitate British music, American music that just tries to be itself. It's like Van Dyke said about SMiLE. It's music that doesn't put its snout in the British trough.

CHAPTER 9

Time

After it's all been said
The music spinning in our head
Can't forget the feeling of
The magic of that summer love
Ooh, I wanna take you there
Do you wanna turn back the pages
Memories in photographs
The world is changed
And yet the game is still the same

—"Isn't It Time"

Over the years, I went to Australia as many times as I could. I went there with the Beach Boys in the '60s and I loved it, and I still love it now. The place has a great vibe. Sydney is a great town. The people are surfers, so they get our music. The cab drivers are really nice. I brought the live version of *Pet Sounds* there, and over the years I have tried to go back whenever I can. When I was in Australia with my band for the live *SMiLE* tour in 2004, I checked into the InterContinental hotel, which overlooks Sydney Harbor, the Victoria Bridge, and the Sydney Opera House, my favorite concert hall in the whole universe. There is a really good lounge on the thirty-second floor of the hotel where you can order this dish called Hokkien noodles; I think I had it at least twice a day there. The harbor area has such a cool vibe. You can walk from the InterContinental down around the opera house, and then along this nice path with a park on one side and the harbor on the other. There are native Australians just hanging out playing didgeridoos, this long tube instrument that has this really deep one-note sound that resonates like a bass harmonica. It's a great place to get your exercise in, and I walk it every day when we are in Sydney.

One day I went to walk with Jeff Foskett, who was by that time my assistant on the road as well as being my right-hand man on the stage. Out a little farther from the opera house, there was a memorial plaza with tiles for the war dead. I was checking out all the names, thinking about the battles and the soldiers. All of a sudden, under my feet, I saw a tile for a guy named Ray Lawlor. I told Ray about it, and when he got to Sydney I walked him out there and showed him. We talked about how strange it was that people with your same name were born, got old, and died. It was strange, but it was the most normal thing in the world. Time happened.

I've always known that about time, and I have always written about it. "When I Grow Up (To Be a Man)" was about that exactly. The Beach Boys recorded the song in the summer of 1964. I had just turned twenty-two. I was a single man about to be married. Our flight to Houston was still four months off. The band booked United Western Recorders for about a week and got the song done. There was lots of pressure on us because it was the next single after "I Get Around," which was our first big hit. It had been number one on July 4 weekend. It must have gotten played at every barbecue.

A month after that we headed back into the studio to make the follow-up. It was just the lean, mean main band—me and my brothers, along with Mike and Al. I had the instrumental track done, and then we started writing the lyrics. I did most of them and Mike did some, too. We were really trying hard to think about growing older. We were trying to imagine the things that would happen in the future, and whether we would recognize the people we became. When you stand in front of a mirror, you're changing. It's like a movie. But how fast are you changing? It goes back to another song.

> When I grow up to be a man
> Will I dig the same things that turn me on as a kid?
> Will I look back and say that I wish I hadn't done what I did?
> Will I joke around and still dig those sounds
> When I grow up to be a man?

It was a fun song to sing, and I think I did an okay job, though I think some of the same things about "When I Grow Up (To Be a Man)" that I do about "Let Him Run Wild." My voice goes up and up until it sounds like it's whining. It loses some of the sweetness it needs. During the song we started a countdown, or really a count-up. Between lines, the backing vocalists would call out ages, two at a time, starting with fourteen. They went up to the last chorus, and even past it—during the fadeout the backing vocals kept counting. They got all the way to thirty-one. I guess it was the oldest age we could think of then. Like I said, I was only twenty-two. That was so far in the future. Back then thirty was like some kind of magic number. You didn't trust anyone over it. You couldn't really imagine being it.

When I did turn thirty-one, it was 1973. I was heading deep into depression and my drugs. Sometimes it felt like everyone was right, that it was an age near the end of your life. But so many things hadn't even started. Dr. Landy hadn't come to treat me for the first time. I hadn't ended the marriage with Marilyn, or started the one with Melinda. I hadn't recorded "Johnny Carson" or "Love and Mercy" or *Lucky Old Sun*. I had heard "Rhapsody in Blue" but I couldn't have even imagined that someone would let me make my own version of it.

Now it's more than that many years past that. "When I Grow Up (To Be a Man)" keeps counting. I look younger than I did when I was younger, in some ways. In the '80s my chin was looking bad, like a turkey gobbler, and Dr. Landy didn't like that so I had a face-lift. I also got the bags under my eyes fixed. I kind of saw what he was doing, but then there were the facts. I wasn't young anymore. I couldn't get around the way I wanted to. I don't think I could've thrown a baseball twenty feet. I look in the mirror now and I think about all the things that have happened. Mainly, one thing happened. I grew up to be a man.

Do I look back and say that I wish I hadn't done some of the things I did? Of course. I wish I hadn't done drugs. It messed things up. I wish I had spent more time or a different kind of time with Carnie and Wendy. Do I dig the same things I did when I was a kid? I love the radio. I try to walk every day. One thing I find as I get older is that sometimes you can try new things by trying things so old that they become new again. A few years ago Melinda and the kids and I went to a place in Laguna Beach. You stay up on the cliffs, but you can walk down and get to the ocean. I was watching the kids play and I decided to go in the water myself. I hadn't been in the ocean for forty years. It was so great that I couldn't get out. It was early afternoon and then late afternoon and I still wanted to stay there. For forty years I kept away from the ocean, but then I went back in. "I can't believe I haven't done this in so long," I said.

ల

For almost twenty years I kept away from the band. The Beach Boys hadn't worked together, really, since the late '90s. We did that country record with Joe Thomas, *Stars and Stripes*, and then we kind of stopped. There were always reissues and repackaging of old albums, almost every year, and they got thicker and fancier. Usually there was a sun somewhere on the cover. Most of them were the same songs rearranged, though at the end of 2011 Capitol put out a set that was a much bigger deal: *The SMiLE Sessions*. It was a huge box with nine discs that collected everything I did in 1966 and 1967. It was amazing to see it all there in one place. I can't believe I did all that work. How did I? There was so much music, so many ideas, so many sections. No wonder I lost my way. When I think about the project, in whatever form, what gets me most is our vocals. They're so spiritual. I think they are the best vocals the Beach Boys ever sang, and definitely they're the most creative. To me, *The SMiLE Sessions* is a great box set, but I like the version we cut in 2004. That was when the album was finally finished. That was when the story was finally completed. That's when the weight was finally lifted. But the box set is great, too.

While all those records were coming out, I saw some of the guys some of the time. But we were getting older, and everyone was living life. Time kept happening. There was always a "Beach Boys" out on the road somewhere, but I didn't have anything to do with it in most of those years. Mike had the name. He got hold of it during the time I wasn't touring and he held on to it. In a way, that was okay with me, although I didn't know what it meant for there to be a Beach Boys without me or Dennis or Carl. I guess they were going around and singing songs that people loved, which was nice for the people who got to hear them. I was doing the same with my band.

One Thanksgiving I went up to Mike's house near Reno. We took a walk together. We talked about life and also about records. We could always talk about old records, ours and other people's. That always made us happy. Mike was telling me about songs that he still wanted to sing. "I want to do a version of 'Chapel Of Love,'" he said. It was the number one song before we got to number one with "I Get Around." We had done it on *15 Big Ones*. I sang that one. I guess Mike wanted to sing a version himself.

"Okay," I said. "We'll do it." But we never did it. Then in 2011, near the end of the year, someone called my office and said that 2012 was the fiftieth anniversary of the Beach Boys, if you counted the *Surfin' Safari* record as the beginning. If you counted the "Surfin'" song as the beginning, the fiftieth was 2011. And if you counted my teaching "Ivory Tower" to my brothers as the beginning, the fiftieth was 1998. But 2012 was a good enough year to call the fiftieth. People at record companies wanted to see if I would think about getting back together with Mike and Al and Bruce and put out a new album and tour around to celebrate.

At first I didn't like the idea. I thought it was too much trouble. The main problem with a reunion was always going to be whether or not I could handle Mike. I knew a fiftieth anniversary would be the same deal. Lots of the onstage energy of the band comes from Mike. He's the best at that. But Mike is also a stubborn guy. We spent too much time going to court. In the '90s he got angry about how Tony Asher and Van Dyke Parks were credited on early records, and he asked for some credit back. Now on *Wild Honey* he's credited on every song, even "Mama Says," even though that part comes from what Van Dyke wrote for "Vega-Tables" on *SMiLE*. And then in 2005 there was a lawsuit over the CD that came out in England. That one made me more mad and confused because I didn't understand it at all. It seemed to be about ego. That stuff was getting to me, and I hadn't even agreed to the tour yet. But then I talked to Melinda and I talked to some friends and I decided that there were more reasons to bury the hatchet than to take it out again.

The closer the tour got, the more I started thinking about old stories. In 1964 we were playing a show in Seattle and Mike was being his usual self, talking out to the crowd, getting everyone excited. There were lots of microphones set up onstage and he grabbed one with one hand and another with his other hand. He looked funny, stretched out like that between them, and he started making a weird noise to go along with it. We were laughing like crazy. After a minute or so, Al Jardine got concerned. "Hey," he said, "I think something might be wrong." Al went over and kicked one of the microphones out of Mike's hand. And Mike said, "My arms!" They were all purple. He had almost been electrocuted. Another time, in the middle of a concert, Dennis threw a spare drumstick at Mike and it hit him in the back. Mike covered up the microphone and said, "Dennis, meet me offstage." They went to the side and had a fistfight, right in the middle of the concert. Dennis won. Mike should have known that. But Mike didn't learn when he challenged Dennis to arm wrestling during "Surfin' Safari," and he didn't learn when he called Dennis offstage. After the fight, they came back and finished the show.

I couldn't remember everything. There was too much of everything to remember. But I liked the memories that came back to me. I liked thinking of them. They took my mind off other things, like my back. I had back pain on and off for years, but then it was on all the time, worse than ever. In the months before the tour, I was having real trouble getting around. I had to hunch over when I walked, and sometimes I felt numb spots in my hands. One evening Melinda and I were meeting Ray for dinner and I couldn't really climb out of the car.

"You okay?" Ray asked.

"They say it might be Parkinson's," I said.

Ray was shocked but not too shocked. He was quiet and walked behind me to look at how I was moving. When we were sitting down and eating, he didn't say anything for a while. "Look," he finally said. "If that's what it is, that's not the worst thing in the world. Nobody dies from Parkinson's. It's not like you're twenty years old. People usually die of something else while they still have Parkinson's."

I nodded but I wasn't really listening, mostly because the doctors hadn't really said that it might be Parkinson's. I was just testing out the idea. I wanted to hear someone tell me that things would be okay, like my dad did on the Long Beach Pike roller coaster. It turned out that it wasn't Parkinson's at all, which I knew. I was sort of testing my friend and testing out the worst possible news in my own head. The real news was better, but not much better. It was spinal stenosis, which Carl also had. It was terrible.

But it wasn't going to keep me from the tour. No way. Getting the Beach Boys back together was a big deal, organized by Joe Thomas and the entertainment lawyer John Branca. It was a big deal for me, but it was also a big deal logistically. There were papers to draw up. There were contracts to sign. There were promoters and lawyers and record labels that had to figure out what they would do when we were out there singing and playing our songs. As plans were coming together, I had to keep the news quiet. It was a big secret. When I was with friends who weren't in the band, I couldn't say anything. Instead we talked about the weather or about a great steak I might have tried at a restaurant.

One day a friend was visiting the house and just came right out and said something. "I heard you guys are doing a tour," he said.

I sighed. "I'm glad you know about it because I was running out of lies," I said.

After the preparing, the actual reunion was pretty straightforward. We met up at Capitol, all the guys, and recorded a version of "Do It Again." The song was already nostalgic when we recorded it in 1969, so it made sense to do "Do It Again" again. It wasn't just me and Mike and Al and Bruce. David Marks was there, too. He hadn't played rhythm guitar with us since the early '60s. The whole process of recording was a great feeling. You couldn't pretend that time hadn't happened. But the music brought everyone back. You couldn't sing an old melody and not go back there a little bit.

The reunion was also sad in some ways. Being back with the band made me miss my brothers. When we started, it was a family band, and I was the only part of the family left. We had never made a record without Carl, and we had only made a few without Dennis. I even missed my dad in some ways. I thought about the old songs and how he would stand there and tell us we were doing them wrong. Surge! At the time it wasn't something I liked at all, but over time you had more memories and less time to think about them.

Over a month or so we made a record, *That's Why God Made the Radio*. That was a kind of reunion all by itself. Joe Thomas came back and worked on it. It wasn't exactly the same as making a solo record. We had to find material that was right for everyone to sing. Joe and I still had a few songs we worked on around the time of *Imagination* that I didn't think were right for me to do as a solo artist. We got those and finished them. The title track was one of them. We had a piece of a song and Mike finished it up and turned it into "Spring Vacation." His new lyrics were great. They made the song at least 25 percent better. I wrote some songs like "The Private Life of Bill and Sue" and "Beaches in Mind." The album we ended up with was a good record, though it was different in spirit than any record we ever would have made before. That was partly because of the technology. We put the record together on Pro Tools, which is the modern way of doing things, instead of going into a studio with dozens of musicians.

I sometimes read in interviews that Mike wants to go into a room with me and write new material for the Beach Boys. But it's just not done that way anymore. That's a '70s idea. At this point, we go with the new way. I write lots in the studio. It's a real musical environment. That record started with "Strange World" and moved through other songs, like "From There to Back Again" and "Pacific Coast Highway." The last song on the album was "Summer's Gone." It was a beautiful melody. It was also one of those songs that people thought was a farewell, like "When You Wish Upon a Star." It was definitely nostalgic, but anything we made in 2012 would have been nostalgic. We were looking backward. That's how seasons went. When I sang it, I was thinking of Carl and Dennis and my dad, but it was like "Caroline, No" also, because I was thinking about younger versions of myself:

Summer's gone
Summer's gone away
Gone away
With yesterday

Old friends have gone
They've gone their separate ways
Our dreams hold on
For those who still have more to say

Summer's gone
Gone like yesterday
The nights grow cold
It's time to go
I'm thinking maybe I'll just stay

Another summer gone

Summer's gone
It's finally sinking in
One day begins
Another ends
I live them all and back again

Summer's gone
I'm gonna sit and watch the waves
We laugh, we cry
We live then die
And dream about our yesterday

Working as a group again wasn't only about thinking through the past and dreaming about the future. It was business, which meant that it included every other part of record making. We had a cumbersome photo shoot out by the beach where we all had to roll up our pants so they wouldn't get wet. I knew what they were going for, but I wish they wouldn't have gone for it. It was a fright. Then we took the show on the road. We premiered on the Grammy Awards, singing "Good Vibrations." I felt great about it. I wasn't even that nervous that time. I sounded good to myself in the hall.

We sang "The Star-Spangled Banner" and "Surfer Girl" at Dodger Stadium at the beginning of April. And then we were off, on the real tour: Tucson, Grand Prairie, New Orleans, Atlanta, Raleigh. The tour lasted almost five months. We did seventy-two concerts. It was almost one a year for my age. We did two nights in New York. We did two nights in Chicago. And that was just the United States. We went all over the world after that: to Spain and Italy and Sweden and Norway, and then to Japan and Singapore and Hong Kong. We went to Australia, of course. We had to go to Australia. And then we finished up in England, playing two of the most famous venues in London: one night at the Royal Albert Hall and one night at Wembley Arena. Between those shows Melinda and I threw a dinner for the whole band and crew at an Italian place in London. We wanted to celebrate the whole thing and all the great feelings. Mike and Bruce Johnston didn't come to that, which bummed me out.

Every night we played some new songs and some old songs. We did right by them. We also did right by Carl and Dennis by including old footage of them on video and singing along with it. Carl got to sing "God Only Knows," of course. Dennis got to sing "Forever," from *Sunflower*. It almost made me cry when I heard the song from the stage, the same way my dad's song "His Little Darling and You" made me cry back when I was in grade school. "Forever" was so beautiful. And even more than that, it was like a prediction. It was a song about going away from the people you love but keeping that love for them. Dennis wrote it more than ten years before he left, but it was almost like he knew what would happen. Singing that along with him was a real thrill.

If every word I said
Could make you laugh
I'd talk forever (together my love)
I ask the sky just what we had
It shone forever (together my love)

If the song I sing to you
Could fill your heart with joy
I'd sing forever (together my love my my my my)
Forever
I've been so happy loving you

Let the love I have for you
Live in your heart
And beat forever (together my love)
Forever
Forever
I've been so happy loving you

Baby just let me sing it, my baby
I wanna be singin', my baby

So I'm goin' away
But not forever
Na na na na
I gotta love you anyway

Forever

The tour wasn't always easy. I had to be Johnny-on-the-spot. I had to get every cue and pay attention to things I hadn't paid attention to in decades. And my back was getting worse and worse. Doctors gave me cortisone shots to ease the pain, and they worked a little bit. But easing it isn't the same as making it go away. I had trouble walking, though fans may not have really noticed; I was at the piano bench the whole time anyway.

But mostly I had the time of my life. Mostly I loved it. Everyone was together, singing songs we made when we were together, and that made me happy. That made me whole. I remember on one of the tour stops we had dinner. We were all there. Mike was there. If you closed your eyes you could almost forget the year. There were times that I wanted it to keep going forever, just like Dennis sang.

That tour ended in a weird way. We had played all the dates we were supposed to, but we were doing such a great job that offers started coming in to extend the tour. I would have done it, but Mike didn't want to do it. He went back to the way things were before, where he was touring with the Beach Boys name. He said he wanted to play smaller markets. And that was the end of the fiftieth reunion.

It took me a long time to come down from that tour. I came down hard. I was thinking about everything we had started again. I thought we were having the time of our lives. And then I started realizing that it was probably really over this time. Summer was probably gone. And that's sad. I would love to hear Mike sing some real rock and roll. It would be a big thrill. Maybe we'll do "Chapel of Love" again one day. But maybe not.

After that, Joe Thomas helped arrange a joint tour for me and Jeff Beck. Jeff is a virtuoso guitarist and has been for a half century; he was inspired by Cliff Gallup, the guitarist for Gene Vincent, but he took things so much further. Jeff has always been able to do amazing things. He puts so many notes into each bar. I love the complexity he brings to his music. But our tour was very difficult. It had a strange vibe from the start, and it never evened out. Jeff's guitar sound, for some reason, was annoying to me. There were too many times that set lists changed or energy shifted. I never got firm footing. We worked on a few tracks in the studio with Jeff, but they didn't get finished the way I wanted them to. They weren't up to standard. We didn't use them. As hard as that tour was, I got through it. I gave myself a nickname that helped me realize every hard part was just a corner to turn: Brian Willpower Wilson. It reminded me that the only way to go was forward. And I did get to play "Danny Boy" onstage with Jeff. What a beautiful song.

And then it was 2014, which was another fifty-year anniversary—not fifty years since the band started but fifty years since 1964, the year of everything. I thought about the way 1964 started, with so much promise. I thought about how much work we did: the albums, the shows, the interviews, the rehearsals. It seems like we fit ten years into that year. And then I thought about the way it ended, on that flight to Houston. It was always that cycle: always doubts, but always making sure that I got past those doubts. Any time in my life I thought the bad feelings or the harmful voices had gone away completely, they came back. But as Melinda taught me, any time they came back, they went away. I had to keep going, whether it was fifty years or fifty-two or more. I didn't know anything else to do. Brian Willpower Wilson.

☙

And then I bounced back from that period of exhaustion. I bounced back into the studio. I was working with Joe Thomas again after *That's Why God Made the Radio*. We decided that I would sing with younger singers, mostly women. I wrote new songs that sounded like old songs, and I put some young voices on them. Zooey Deschanel was good to work with. She had a real sweet voice. Kacey Musgraves moved right into the song she did, "Guess You Had to Be There." It took her only three takes. And she did something nice when she sang, a kind of gliding. That's a sound I always liked. You don't need to get down in the weeds of a song. Sometimes you let it move smoothly under you.

When I had fourteen songs, I decided that was an album. I called the record *No Pier Pressure*, partly because of the cover art, which was based on a picture of the Santa Monica Pier that my daughter

Daria took. It was also a little bit of a pun. I wanted to think about being free of the pressure to go back to the idea of the Beach Boys or people's ideas of rock and roll.

But I didn't just sing with young female singers. I also sang with some of the old guys. Al Jardine was on there. It was great to sing with him again. It brought me back to the good sound we used to have. Al's best-known vocals in the old days were "Then I Kissed Her" and "Help Me, Rhonda," but my favorite was the singing he did on *Holland*, on "The Beaks of Eagles." There's a lyric that's just beautiful: "In dawn's new light a man might venture." I sang a song called "Whatever Happened" with Al and his son Matt, and another one called "Sail Away" with Blondie Chaplin. Blondie had been with the band back around *Holland* and *Carl and the Passions—So Tough*, where he sang songs like "Here She Comes" and "Hold On Dear Brother." Al and Blondie sounded incredible on *No Pier Pressure*. Voices get older but they keep their spirit.

When it came time for the last song, I knew what I would call it. I called it "The Last Song." Like with "When You Wish Upon a Star" on the Disney record, like with "Summer's Gone" on *That's Why God Made the Radio*, I wasn't sure if it would really be the last song, but there was a greater chance each time I made a record. Lana Del Rey was supposed to sing it, and she started, but something happened and she wasn't able to come back and finish her vocals. The funny thing about "The Last Song" is that it wasn't really a song about things finishing up as it was about things continuing:

> *Don't let go*
> *There's still time for us so let's take it slow*
> *I wish that I could give you so much more*
> *Far away*
> *And maybe we'll be coming back someday*
> *Together in the end*
> *To sing with you again*

"The Last Song" ended with a sad line that was also true: "There's never enough time for the ones that you love." When I sang that, I thought about everyone. I thought about the ones who were gone and the ones who will be here when I am gone. I thought about Carl and Dennis. I thought about my mom and my dad. I thought about Wendy and Carnie and Marilyn. I thought about Melinda, Daria, Delanie, Dylan, Dash, and Dakota Rose. I thought of everyone, and I wondered if everyone ever thought of me.

ᴄᴏ

Friends came to the house to have dinner with me and Melinda: Jerry and Lois Weiss and Ray and some others. We ate early and then got ready to go. "We're leaving the house at six thirty," I said. And then I said it again, as a question: "Six thirty?"

Jerry was used to that from the road. He was used to me asking about the time over and over again. "Right," he said. "About fifteen minutes." But it was thirteen minutes.

We were going to see *Love and Mercy*, the movie about my life. It wasn't the first time someone had tried to make a movie like that. Dr. Landy had tried to get something started where William Hurt played me and Richard Dreyfuss played Dr. Landy. Then there was *Grace of My Heart*, which was really more a movie about Carole King's life, or someone like her. There was a character played by Matt Dillon who was someone like me. I wrote "Gettin' in Over My Head" for it and sent it to them, though they didn't end up using it. Then Don Was did the documentary about me, *I Just Wasn't Made for These Times*, and after we were done he told me that he thought there was more story there. He brought around a guy named Marvin Worth, a producer who had done a bunch of movies, including *Lenny*, the movie about Lenny Bruce that starred Dustin Hoffman.

Marvin decided that he wanted to do a movie of my life. We talked about it, and he had someone write a script, but then he passed away. The movie got shuffled around, moved from person to person, and eventually Marvin's wife took over and brought Rob Reiner to meet with us. Rob Reiner really wanted to make the movie, but he wasn't sure how to do it. It was like his *SMiLE*, almost; all the things that it could be started to overwhelm him. The movie went away for a while. No one was really thinking about it. In the meantime there was a TV movie called *The Beach Boys: An American Family* that Melinda didn't even let me see. She told me that it didn't show how I really was, or how I had ever really been. She said the movie made me seem unaware when, if anything, I was too aware, that it made me seem insensitive when, if anything, I was too sensitive. And since I was too sensitive, she said, there was no real reason to show it to me. That was what Melinda did then and what she always does. In the twenty years we've been married, she looks out for me and makes sure that certain things that might hurt me or ruin my mood don't get through. The actor John Stamos, who is a huge Beach Boys fan and was involved in that movie, even apologized to Melinda for how I ended up looking.

A few years after the TV movie aired, Warner Brothers got the feature film project to a guy named Bill Pohlad, who had produced movies like *Brokeback Mountain* and *Into the Wild*. Bill was really interested in getting the project moving again, though he wanted to have someone write a new script. Melinda and I were completely on board. We thought it was a chance to be honest about everything that had happened in my life. Bill hired a writer named Oren Moverman, and as Oren worked on the script, he and Bill started to talk about directors. Oren thought Bill would be the best director for it, even though he had never directed. "You should do it," Oren said. Bill said he couldn't imagine really doing it. One day Bill called and asked us what we thought about him directing. I was so happy. I knew he was the right guy for it. He just had the right ideas, and even though he loved the music I made, he wasn't such an obsessive fan that he was afraid to make the movie his own.

The movie was built as a two-track story. It was about two periods in my life, mostly: the time before and including *Pet Sounds* in the '60s, and the time with Dr. Landy in the '80s. Paul Dano played me when I was young. John Cusack played me when I was older. Elizabeth Banks played Melinda. Paul Giamatti played Dr. Landy. The movie went back and forth between those two periods and tried to show how lots of the other problems in my life, especially drugs and alcohol, were connected to mental illness. That was the story underneath everything. It was the story underneath the movie, like it's the story underneath this book, because it's the story underneath my life. I wanted to tell it as fully as possible.

As the movie went along, Bill wanted to involve me in the music, but I didn't want to get too much into it. Atticus Ross was doing the score, and he was weaving together pieces of old songs. But Bill kept asking. He said he wanted one love song for Melinda. I eventually did it to please him. The best way for me to approach it was to think of it as just another song, with a purpose and a deadline. I wrote one song called "Whatever Happened" that Bill wasn't sure about, and then another song called "One Kind of Love." That one Bill really liked, and he took it for the movie. When it came time for the final version, he had a hard time figuring out where to put it. I thought maybe it should play over the end credits, but he wanted "Wouldn't It Be Nice" for that spot and he wouldn't budge. It ended up going into a scene where Melinda and I were driving. It came out of the car radio.

So friends came for dinner. I don't remember what we ate that night. Then we all went to see the movie at a theater in Hollywood. My daughter Wendy was there, too. It wasn't the official Hollywood premiere—that was later, and all the actors came to that, along with my daughter Carnie. But it was the first time I saw the whole movie, and I was really proud.

The movie wasn't easy to watch. It was about the bad parts of my life as much as the good parts. The worst were the scenes with Dr. Landy, when he would yell at me. There were a couple of moments when some of what was onscreen was so intense that Melinda had to put her hand on my leg. But I watched the whole thing straight through. There were exciting scenes about creating *Pet Sounds* and also some softer scenes that showed how I was struggling with mental illness even back then. I liked one quiet scene especially, a scene where Paul Dano, playing the younger version of me, leaves the studio and goes to the parking lot to smoke a cigarette. Hal Blaine is out there, too, and he and I have a conversation about making things, and how it's not easy but it's worth it, and how talent has to be nurtured and protected. I liked that scene because it reminded me of one of the reasons I kept going all those years. I kept going to protect my love for music, and eventually I found people who could help protect me also.

Afterward the theater was quiet. Slowly people started talking. Wendy was saying that there was so much she didn't know about the Landy years. "I had no idea," she said.

Finally Melinda turned to me. "Are you okay with it?" she asked.

"I'm fine," I said. "Living it was so much worse."

The final scene in the movie showed me and Melinda holding hands, looking at the empty lot in Hawthorne where my house used to be. That was a way to finish the movie, but it wasn't how the real story ended. It ended with me marrying Melinda and being with her and being happy that I was with her. It ended with adopting kids and making more records. It ended with meeting friends at my house and agreeing to go see the movie. And then it ended with me walking out of the theater, still going, still there. I was proud of what the movie showed. It didn't try to pretend that I was a different kind of person, either better or worse. It didn't look away from mental illness, but it also didn't make me into a cartoon nut who went into his bedroom for years while his bandmates traveled around the world making music.

Having the real story out there was very appealing to me, because it did a job that was hard for me to do in conversations or interviews. I wasn't usually the kind of guy who would make a big deal about correcting a misunderstanding. If someone got the wrong idea about me, I might agree with the wrong story just to get out of the conversation. But the movie put it all out there. It was honest about everything I went through, and how I survived it. And for me, that was the other main point. Survival was the other main point. Finding ways to make it through was the point. If my life helped people get to the point where they could have that thought, too, that made the movie valuable.

When people started saying that the movie was good and might get some awards, I was excited that "One Kind of Love" might get awards, too. When it got a Golden Globe nomination, I was excited to see what would happen with the Oscars. What happened was disappointing. As it turned out, the song wasn't eligible for an Oscar nomination. The Academy had strict rules about what songs were eligible. Either a song had to be shown over the first end titles or it had to be in the body of the movie for at least forty seconds, in a way that moved the movie along from scene to scene. I was disappointed because without those rules the song seemed like it would be a shoo-in for a nomination. But we got to go to the Golden Globes, and that was really fun. We lost to "Writing's on the Wall," the song that Sam Smith did for the James Bond movie *Spectre*. That was funny in a way because fifty years before, the instrumental title song for *Pet Sounds* was originally written as a James Bond theme. It was called "Run James Run." That was the one where the percussion was Richie Frost playing on two empty Coca-Cola cans. There was no percussion like that on "Writing's on the Wall."

The most rewarding thing about the whole experience was to see what people took away from the movie, mainly the idea that mental illness should be handled in a humane and straightforward way. It's a struggle like any struggle. It's something I've had to carry around most of my life, and something that really kept me off balance until I learned how to get my head around it—and to have people around me who helped me do that. So many people wrote us or called to say that the movie helped them deal with similar problems in their own life, with family or friends.

One of the people who wrote was Michelle Obama. She helped set up a partnership between the movie and the Campaign to Change Direction, an organization that encourages people to see mental illness differently. I have met other presidents and First Ladies. I have played for queens. But I'm not sure that I have ever been prouder than when we made that arrangement with Campaign to Change Direction. I mean, I always knew that my music was inspirational. I could always look out into a crowd and see people dancing to "California Girls." But I didn't always feel the same way about my life. There were times that I worried about it, that I felt it was shameful, that I felt I couldn't be honest about the things I was thinking or the voices I was hearing. Making the movie was a challenge because it was an honest self-portrait, and when people responded to it the way they did, it made me proud of my life also. To be told that other people could learn from it and get stronger was even better.

CHAPTER 10

Today

So hard to answer future's riddle
When ahead is seeming so far behind
So hard to laugh a childlike giggle
When the tears start to torture my mind
So hard to shed the life of before
To let my soul automatically soar

But I hit hard at the battle that's confronting me, yeah
Knock down all the roadblocks a-stumbling me
Throw off all the shackles that are binding me down
　　　　　　—"Long Promised Road"

I didn't write "Long Promised Road." Carl did, with Jack Rieley, for
Surf's Up. It was the first song Carl really wrote for the band, and
I loved the message of it. We put it out as a single and "'Til I Die"
was on the B-side. The song was about the kinds of things that Carl
was feeling, and they were also the things that I felt all the time. It
was hard to feel happy and light when there were sad things in my
head. It was hard to feel free when I was tied down. But the only
choice was to try. When I woke up in 1971, or in 1975, or in 1995,
or in 2015, I had pressures on me. Did feeling those pressures make

me stronger? Did the times when I felt bound help me soar? I struggled through so many things and slowly, over time, found things that helped me. I found love. I found a support network. I found the right doctors and the right medications. But in my struggle, I had to pass through the wrong things. I made mistakes with people I loved, and people I loved made mistakes with me. I can't believe that some of them are gone. Carl is one of those who are gone, but his songs live on. And I keep going because of them and because of songs like theirs. I hit hard at the battle that's confronting me.

When I was watching *Love and Mercy* on the big screen, I thought about the small screen, too. I thought about Mike Douglas, the talk show host. I was on his show in the mid-'70s, right around the time of *15 Big Ones*. That was kind of a famous interview because he asked me about my meditation mantra, which was supposed to be a secret, and I told him it was "eye-neh-mah." At a different part of that interview, Mike Douglas was asking about how I kept going through all of it: through the drugs, through the lawsuits, through the bad feelings that came up between me and the people closest to me. I had an answer ready. "My name is Wilson," I said. "Maybe that's where I got the will." My career, off and on, had taken a beating. My body had taken a beating. My brains at times took a beating. But I tried to keep my spirit going. I was a survivor. I tried to survive every day. Lots of that came from my dad. People might say that he was one of the things I had to survive, but he also helped me figure out how to do it. He taught me how to be tough. He showed me a way to be the kind of person who has to forge ahead. Whenever I've been told to stop—by someone who thought they had power over me, by something that happened around me, by the voices I heard in my own head—I kept going.

I kept going, and I keep going. I have an idea for another album. It's an album about time and music. It would be all the songs that inspired me through the years, rearranged and sung the way they sound to me. It's in the early stages still, but I have started to pick out the artists. I want to do Buddy Holly. I want to do "A Beautiful

Morning" by the Rascals. I'm definitely going to do "Be My Baby," with all instruments doubled: two pianos, two guitars, two basses, plus horns and drums. Oh, and "Tenderly" by Rosemary Clooney. I can't leave that off. That's the song that taught me to sing.

And I like to think about people I might want to work with. I've worked with so many. I think about writing a song with Paul McCartney. I am not sure if he would really want to. I was thinking about Barry Gibb, too. I really admire the guy. He is like King Kong. He and I could probably work something up together. We met at the Rock and Roll Hall of Fame back in 1997. I presented them for their induction. They sang "To Love Somebody." Before the show Barry came down to meet me and he just sat in the room. I heard later that he was nervous. I was nervous, too.

Today or tomorrow or the next day I'll have some breakfast and take a walk and watch *Wheel of Fortune* and then check in on the score of the Yankees game. The season is just starting. I might go to my son Dylan's basketball game. I'll work on songs. There's one, "Loop de Loop (Flip Flop Flyin' in an Aeroplane)," that's about an airplane. I cut a demo for it back in the late '60s but I haven't finished it the way I want.

There are other, newer songs, too. I sometimes have ideas one by one. Sometimes they come in bunches. But I also spend time thinking about my old songs. In 2016 I'm thinking about *Pet Sounds*. My band and I are playing the whole record. We performed first in Australia, New Zealand, and Japan, and now we're in the United States. The biggest show will be at the Hollywood Bowl. It might not be the biggest crowd, but it's the most significant show. The Beach Boys played there almost yearly in the early '60s. We were there in 1963, in 1964. The band played there in the summer of 1966 on a big bill that also included the Lovin' Spoonful, Chad and Jeremy, Percy Sledge, Love, and the Byrds. I wasn't onstage then. I wasn't playing shows. I was at home, thinking about the songs I had just written. Those songs were *Pet Sounds*. That 1966 show happened about a month after we released the album.

This year's show will be a fiftieth birthday for both the show and the album. Fifty years. Some days it seems like just a few months ago I was back at Western, United, Gold Star, and Columbia, cutting the tracks. Other days it seems like it's an eternity away. Fifty years.

I can't remember so much about my own fiftieth birthday. It was around the time Dr. Landy was leaving. That was a new birth in a way. Maybe I should have started counting at zero all over again. I can remember the fiftieth birthday of the Beach Boys. That's a recent memory. And now the album that people think is our greatest is turning fifty also. My band is different now. Al Jardine tours with me, and we're still rocking, along with his son Matt, who sings all my high parts from the '60s. He does a great job. And Blondie Chaplin, who played with the Beach Boys back in the early '70s, is in our band also. He went from the Beach Boys to the Rolling Stones and stayed with them for ten years. Can you imagine that? Blondie brings a great energy to the band. He walks all over the stage with his guitar with a kind of Keith Richards vibe.

I love *Pet Sounds.* The melodies on that record are so beautiful. The arrangements and experiments are so cool. We did amazing things then, and they're still amazing when we return to them. Music has always been the light in dark times. It's my number one thing, and *Pet Sounds* is the number one record. The last word of the album is *no* but the album is a big yes. And that's what I want to keep working toward, whether it's with old music or new music, old collaborators or new ones. That's what I want to work toward with love and with mercy: the big yes.

And this big yes will happen right here at home. Melinda will be there with all the kids. Sometimes when we play in LA, we let my son Dylan help out delivering water backstage. They give him his own walkie-talkie and a code name, Wizard. The first time he did it, he was a little disappointed that he had to turn in his walkie-talkie at the end of the night. I am in my tour bus now, with Wizard and the rest of the family, and we're heading toward the

Hollywood Bowl from my house. Glenn, our bus driver, is taking everyone tonight. I am in the captain's chair in the front, thinking it all through. Melinda, Gloria, and the kids are on the couches. Everyone is talking. Everyone is happy. It's a family trip in every sense. When I first started touring with this band back in the winter of 1999, Daria was just an infant. Delanie, Dylan, Dash, and Dakota Rose weren't even born yet. Now they're all so big. They remind me of a song I once wrote, "Little Children": "Little children, they're marching along." They're not all grown up yet, but Daria and Delanie are getting there. Dylan, Dash, and Dakota Rose will join them soon. Time flies by.

We get off Mulholland Drive and make a right on Coldwater Canyon Drive. We go down the hill until we hit Sunset Boulevard and make a left. We pass the Whisky, where I played with the Boys a few nights in 1970, and the Roxy, where we cut my live album in 2000. Then we pass some of the studios where I spent so much of my life and created so much music. Ocean Way is back to its original name, United. It's on our right. If I look to my left, I can see the Capitol Tower, where we started out, where we rose to fame, where they told me they didn't think *Pet Sounds* was heading down the right path. But here we are, fifty years later, playing it live at the Bowl. I can see some planes overhead. They're coming from the Los Angeles airport, where I sat at the gate at Christmastime 1964 and waited to go to Houston. I didn't know what would happen to me on that flight. I didn't know where it would lead. And maybe those planes can see Hawthorne, where my house used to be, where my brothers and I, up in our bedroom, began to sing.

There's so much of the city going out in all directions, in time and in space. I would never live anywhere but here. It's my whole life. And then we're hanging a left—passing the huge Hollywood Bowl sign that says TONIGHT, BRIAN WILSON, PET SOUNDS 2016, SOLD OUT—and climbing up the hill to the backstage area.

The Bowl is still empty, but my head is starting to fill with thoughts of the show, you know? My routine starts. It starts with questions. What if the audience doesn't like the show? What if they don't like my music? Suppose the goddamn voices start coming at me while I am onstage? I go through this every time. But then I start thinking through who will be in the audience. It's almost everyone I know. It's Melinda and the kids. It's Gloria. It's Carnie and Wendy, too. It's Jean Sievers. It's all my friends. This is the biggest concert of the tour, and the guys and I are ready.

We do our preconcert circle up, and everyone says how much they love the music and how lucky they are to bring it to the audience. "We'll give a great show tonight," I say. "We have to. We'll kick ass out there." Then I'm backstage, asking myself questions, answering them again, imagining my way forward into the first notes of "Wouldn't It Be Nice" and that cannon of a drum beat, as big as anything Phil Spector ever recorded. There are so many people who are no longer here: friends, parents, brothers. I love them and I miss them. But I am here. I am here for them. I am here for myself. I am here today. I push myself up out of the chair and head for the stage.

Discography

Beach Boys

Surfin' Safari (1962)
Surfin' Safari
County Fair
Ten Little Indians
Chug-A-Lug
Little Girl (You're My Miss America)
409
Surfin'
Heads You Win, Tails I Lose
Summertime Blues
Cuckoo Clock
Moon Dawg
The Shift

Surfin' U.S.A. (1963)
Surfin' U.S.A.
Farmer's Daughter
Misirlou
Stoked
Lonely Sea

Shut Down
Noble Surfer
Honky Tonk
Lana
Surf Jam
Let's Go Trippin'
Finders Keepers

Surfer Girl (1963)
Surfer Girl
Catch a Wave
The Surfer Moon
South Bay Surfer
The Rocking Surfer
Little Deuce Coupe
In My Room
Hawaii
Surfer's Rule
Our Car Club
Your Summer Dream
Boogie Woodie

Little Deuce Coupe (1963)
Little Deuce Coupe
Ballad of Ole' Betsy
Be True to Your School
Car Crazy Cutie
Cherry, Cherry Coupe
409
Shut Down
Spirit of America
Our Car Club
No-Go Showboat
A Young Man Is Gone
Custom Machine

Shut Down Volume 2 (1964)

Fun, Fun, Fun
Don't Worry Baby
In the Parkin' Lot
"Cassius" Love vs. "Sonny" Wilson
The Warmth of the Sun
This Car of Mine
Why Do Fools Fall in Love
Pom, Pom Play Girl
Keep an Eye on Summer
Shut Down, Part II
Louie, Louie
Denny's Drums

All Summer Long (1964)

I Get Around
All Summer Long
Hushabye
Little Honda
We'll Run Away
Carl's Big Chance
Wendy
Do You Remember?
Girls on the Beach
Drive-In
Our Favorite Recording Sessions
Don't Back Down

Beach Boys Concert (1964)

Fun, Fun, Fun
The Little Old Lady from Pasadena
Little Deuce Coupe
Long, Tall Texan
In My Room
Monster Mash

Let's Go Trippin'
Papa-Oom-Mow-Mow
The Wanderer
Hawaii
Graduation Day
I Get Around
Johnny B. Goode

The Beach Boys' Christmas Album (1964)
Little Saint Nick
The Man with All the Toys
Santa's Beard
Merry Christmas, Baby
Christmas Day
Frosty the Snowman
We Three Kings of Orient Are
Blue Christmas
Santa Claus Is Comin' to Town
White Christmas
I'll Be Home for Christmas
Auld Lang Syne

The Beach Boys Today! (1965)
Do You Wanna Dance?
Good to My Baby
Don't Hurt My Little Sister
When I Grow Up (To Be a Man)
Help Me, Ronda
Dance, Dance, Dance
Please Let Me Wonder
I'm So Young
Kiss Me, Baby
She Knows Me Too Well
In The Back of My Mind
Bull Session with the "Big Daddy"

Summer Days (And Summer Nights!!) (1965)

The Girl from New York City
Amusement Parks U.S.A.
Then I Kissed Her
Salt Lake City
Girl Don't Tell Me
Help Me, Rhonda
California Girls
Let Him Run Wild
You're So Good to Me
Summer Means New Love
I'm Bugged at My Ol' Man
And Your Dream Comes True

Beach Boys' Party! (1965)

Hully Gully
I Should Have Known Better
Tell Me Why
Papa-Oom-Mow-Mow
Mountain of Love
You've Got to Hide Your Love Away
Devoted to You
Alley Oop
There's No Other (Like My Baby)
I Get Around / Little Deuce Coupe
The Times They Are A-Changin'
Barbara Ann

Pet Sounds (1966)

Wouldn't It Be Nice
You Still Believe in Me
That's Not Me
Don't Talk (Put Your Head on My Shoulder)
I'm Waiting for the Day
Let's Go Away for Awhile

Sloop John B
God Only Knows
I Know There's an Answer
Here Today
I Just Wasn't Made for These Times
Pet Sounds
Caroline, No

Smiley Smile (1967)

Heroes and Villains
Vegetables
Fall Breaks and Back to Winter
She's Goin' Bald
Little Pad
Good Vibrations
With Me Tonight
Wind Chimes
Gettin' Hungry
Wonderful
Whistle In

Wild Honey (1967)

Wild Honey
Aren't You Glad
I Was Made to Love Her
Country Air
A Thing or Two
Darlin'
I'd Love Just Once to See You
Here Comes the Night
Let the Wind Blow
How She Boogalooed It
Mama Says

Friends (1968)
Meant for You
Friends
Wake the World
Be Here in the Mornin'
When a Man Needs a Woman
Passing By
Anna Lee, the Healer
Little Bird
Be Still
Busy Doin' Nothin'
Diamond Head
Transcendental Meditation

20/20 (1969)
Do It Again
I Can Hear Music
Bluebirds over the Mountain
Be with Me
All I Want to Do
The Nearest Faraway Place
Cotton Fields
I Went to Sleep
Time to Get Alone
Never Learn Not to Love
Our Prayer
Cabinessence

Sunflower (1970)
Slip On Through
This Whole World
Add Some Music to Your Day
Got to Know the Woman

Deirdre
It's About Time
Tears in the Morning
All I Wanna Do
Forever
Our Sweet Love
At My Window
Cool, Cool Water

Surf's Up (1971)
Don't Go Near the Water
Long Promised Road
Take a Load Off Your Feet
Student Demonstration Time
Disney Girls (1957)
Feel Flows
Lookin' at Tomorrow (A Welfare Song)
A Day In the Life of a Tree
'Til I Die
Surf's Up

Carl and the Passions—So Tough (1972)
You Need a Mess of Help to Stand Alone
Here She Comes
He Come Down
Marcella
Hold On, Dear Brother
Make It Good
All This Is That
Cuddle Up

Holland (1973)
Sail On Sailor
Steamboat
California Saga: Big Sur

California Saga: The Beaks of Eagles
California Saga: California
The Trader
Leaving This Town
Only with You
Funky Pretty

Mount Vernon and Fairway EP (1973)
Mt. Vernon and Fairway—Theme
I'm the Pied Piper—Instrumental
Better Get Back in Bed
Magic Transistor Radio
I'm the Pied Piper
Radio King Dom

15 Big Ones (1976)
Rock and Roll Music
It's O.K.
Had to Phone Ya
Chapel of Love
Everyone's in Love with You
Talk to Me
That Same Song
T M Song
Palisades Park
Susie Cincinnati
A Casual Look
Blueberry Hill
Back Home
In the Still of the Night
Just Once in My Life

Love You (1977)
Let Us Go On This Way
Roller Skating Child

Mona
Johnny Carson
Good Time
Honkin' Down the Highway
Ding Dang
Solar System
The Night Was So Young
I'll Bet He's Nice
Let's Put Our Hearts Together
I Wanna Pick You Up
Airplane
Love Is a Woman

M.I.U. Album (1978)
She's Got Rhythm
Come Go with Me
Hey Little Tomboy
Kona Coast
Peggy Sue
Wontcha Come Out Tonight
Sweet Sunday Kinda Love
Belles of Paris
Pitter Patter
My Diane
Match Point of Our Love
Winds of Change

L.A. (Light Album) (1979)
Good Timin'
Lady Lynda
Full Sail
Angel Come Home
Love Surrounds Me
Sumahama

Here Comes the Night
Baby Blue
Goin' South
Shortenin' Bread

Keepin' the Summer Alive (1980)
Keepin' the Summer Alive
Oh Darlin'
Some of Your Love
Livin' with a Heartache
School Day (Ring! Ring! Goes the Bell)
Goin' On
Sunshine
When Girls Get Together
Santa Ana Winds
Endless Harmony

The Beach Boys (1985)
Getcha Back
It's Gettin' Late
Crack at Your Love
Maybe I Don't Know
She Believes In Love Again
California Calling
Passing Friend
I'm So Lonely
Where I Belong
I Do Love You
It's Just a Matter of Time

Still Cruisin' (1989)
Still Cruisin'
Somewhere Near Japan
Island Girl

In My Car
Kokomo
Wipe Out (with the Fat Boys)
Make It Big
I Get Around
Wouldn't It Be Nice
California Girls

The SMiLE Sessions (2011)
Our Prayer
Gee
Heroes and Villains
Do You Like Worms? (Roll Plymouth Rock)
I'm in Great Shape
Barnyard
My Only Sunshine (The Old Master Painter /
    You are My Sunshine)
Cabin Essence
Wonderful
Look (Song for Children)
Child Is Father of the Man
Surf's Up
I Wanna Be Around / Workshop
Vega-Tables
Holidays
Wind Chimes
The Elements: Fire (Mrs. O'Leary's Cow)
Love to Say Dada
Good Vibrations
You're Welcome
Heroes and Villains (Stereo Mix)
Heroes and Villains Sections (Stereo Mix)
Vega-Tables Demo

He Gives Speeches
Smile Backing Vocals Montage
Surf's Up 1967 (Solo Version)
Psycodelic Sounds: Brian Falls into a Piano
Our Prayer "Dialog" (9/19/66)
Heroes and Villains: Part 1
Heroes and Villains: Part 2
Heroes and Villains: Children Were Raised (1/27/67)
Heroes and Villains: Prelude to Fade (2/15/67)
My Only Sunshine (11/14/66)
Cabin Essence (10/3/66)
Surf's Up: 1st Movement (11/4/66)
Surf's Up: Piano Demo (12/15/66)
Vega-Tables: Fade (4/12/67)
The Elements: Fire session (11/28/66)
Cool, Cool Water (Version 2) (10/26–10/29/67)
Good Vibrations Session Highlights

That's Why God Made the Radio (2012)
Think About the Days
That's Why God Made the Radio
Isn't It Time
Spring Vacation
The Private Life of Bill and Sue
Shelter
Daybreak Over the Ocean
Beaches in Mind
Strange World
From There to Back Again
Pacific Coast Highway
Summer's Gone

Brian Wilson

Brian Wilson (1988)
Love and Mercy
Walkin' the Line
Melt Away
Baby Let Your Hair Grow Long
Little Children
One for the Boys
There's So Many
Night Time
Let It Shine
Meet Me in My Dreams Tonight
Rio Grande

I Just Wasn't Made for These Times (1995)
Meant for You
This Whole World
Caroline, No
Let the Wind Blow
Love and Mercy
Do It Again
The Warmth of the Sun
Wonderful
Still I Dream of It
Melt Away
'Til I Die

Imagination (1998)
Your Imagination
She Says That She Needs Me
South American
Where Has Love Been?
Dream Angel
Cry

Lay Down Burden
Let Him Run Wild
Sunshine
Happy Days

Live at the Roxy Theatre (2000)
Little Girl Intro
The Little Girl I Once Knew
This Whole World
Don't Worry Baby
Kiss Me Baby
Do It Again
California Girls
I Get Around
Back Home
In My Room
Surfer Girl
The First Time
This Isn't Love
Add Some Music to Your Day
Please Let Me Wonder
Brian Wilson
'Til I Die
Darlin'
Let's Go Away for Awhile
Pet Sounds
God Only Knows
Lay Down Burden
Be My Baby
Good Vibrations
Caroline, No
All Summer Long
Love and Mercy

Brian Wilson Presents Pet Sounds Live (2002)

Wouldn't It Be Nice
You Still Believe in Me
That's Not Me
Don't Talk (Put Your Head on My Shoulder)
I'm Waiting for the Day
Let's Go Away for Awhile
Sloop John B
God Only Knows
I Know There's an Answer
Here Today
I Just Wasn't Made for These Times
Pet Sounds
Caroline, No

Gettin' in Over My Head (2004)

How Could We Still Be Dancin' (with Elton John)
Soul Searchin' (with Carl Wilson)
You've Touched Me
Gettin' in Over My Head
City Blues (with Eric Clapton)
Desert Drive
A Friend Like You (with Paul McCartney)
Make a Wish
Rainbow Eyes
Saturday Morning in the City
Fairy Tale
Don't Let Her Know She's an Angel
The Waltz

Brian Wilson Presents SMiLE (2004)

Our Prayer / Gee
Heroes and Villains
Roll Plymouth Rock
Barnyard

Old Master Painter / You Are My Sunshine
Cabin Essence
Wonderful
Song for Children
Child Is Father to the Man
Surf's Up
I'm in Great Shape / I Wanna Be Around / Workshop
Vega-Tables
On a Holiday
Wind Chimes
Mrs. O'Leary's Cow
In Blue Hawaii
Good Vibrations

What I Really Want for Christmas (2005)

The Man with All the Toys
What I Really Want for Christmas
God Rest Ye Merry Gentlemen
O Holy Night
We Wish You a Merry Christmas
Hark the Herald Angels Sing
It Came Upon a Midnight Clear
The First Noel
Christmasey
Little Saint Nick
Deck the Halls
Auld Lang Syne
On Christmas Day
Joy to the World
Silent Night

That Lucky Old Sun (2008)

That Lucky Old Sun
Morning Beat
A Room with a View (narrative)

Good Kind of Love
Forever She'll Be My Surfer Girl
Venice Beach (narrative)
Live Let Live / That Lucky Old Sun (reprise)
Mexican Girl
Cinco de Mayo (narrative)
California Role / That Lucky Old Sun (reprise)
Between Pictures (narrative)
Oxygen to the Brain
Can't Wait Too Long
Midnight's Another Day
That Lucky Old Sun (Reprise)
Going Home
Southern California

Brian Wilson Reimagines Gershwin (2010)
Rhapsody in Blue / Intro
The Like in I Love You
Summertime
I Loves You, Porgy
I Got Plenty o' Nuttin'
It Ain't Necessarily So
'S Wonderful
They Can't Take That Away from Me
Love Is Here to Stay
I've Got a Crush on You
I Got Rhythm
Someone to Watch Over Me
Nothing But Love
Rhapsody in Blue / Reprise

In the Key of Disney (2011)
You've Got a Friend in Me
The Bare Necessities
Baby Mine

Kiss the Girl
Colors of the Wind
Can You Feel the Love Tonight
We Belong Together
I Just Can't Wait to be King
Stay Awake
Heigh-Ho / Whistle While You Work /
    Yo Ho (A Pirate's Life for Me)
When You Wish Upon a Star

No Pier Pressure (2015)
This Beautiful Day
Runaway Dancer
What Ever Happened
On the Island
Half Moon Bay
Our Special Love
The Right Time
Guess You Had to Be There
Don't Worry
Somewhere Quiet
I'm Feeling Sad
Tell Me Why
Sail Away
One Kind of Love
Saturday Night
The Last Song

Brian Wilson and Van Dyke Parks

Orange Crate Art (1995)
Orange Crate Art
Sail Away
My Hobo Heart
Wing of a Dove

Palm Tree and Moon
Summer in Monterey
San Francisco
Hold Back Time
My Jeanine
Movies Is Magic
This Town Goes Down at Sunset
Lullaby

Acknowledgments

In a long life and a career that's been almost as long, there are so many people to thank and to recognize. I want to start by apologizing in case there are any omissions. It's not my intention to exclude anyone. But memory serves imperfectly.

I'd like to thank, first, my family. That means so many things. Family means so many things to me, and it has shaped me over the years. There's my current family: my wife, Melinda, and my kids Daria, Delanie, Dylan, Dash, and Dakota. There's my first wife, Marilyn, and my daughters Wendy and Carnie. And there's the family I joined when I came into the world: my dad, Murry, and my mom, Audree—and their parents and siblings—and my brothers, Dennis and Carl. Families have been a source of love and sometimes of difficulty. They've been the place where I learned who I was and sometimes who I wasn't. You can't be anything without family, and you have to be so many things, both good and bad, with them.

∽

My brothers, of course, were the core of my second family—the Beach Boys. Dennis and Carl were in the Boys with me, and will be in it with me forever, even though they're no longer with us. My cousin Mike Love was there from the start. Al Jardine was there

305

almost as long, as was David Marks. The band has been a going concern in many different forms over the years, and there have been so many contributors at so many different levels, from on-stage singers to songwriting collaborators to studio musicians to engineers: Bruce Johnston, Gary Usher, Roger Christian, Blondie Chaplin, Glen Campbell, Tony Asher, Van Dyke Parks, Chuck Britz, Hal Blaine, Carol Kaye, Jack Rieley, Steve Desper, Terry Melcher, and so many more. I was in studios with them. I was on stages with them sometimes, and I was with them in spirit when I wasn't there in person. I was in hotel rooms and executive offices. Records got made (and sometimes unmade) in all those places. Some of those records became hits. Some included songs that are still played on the radio all the time. In some ways, those years in the Beach Boys are distant memories. In some ways, they're as close as yesterday.

After the Beach Boys, I had a band of my own, and I still have that band. Those musicians have sustained me for the last decade-plus, though some have come and gone. I couldn't have done it without them: Darian Sahanaja, Scott Bennett, Paul Von Mertens, Nicky Wonder, Nelson Bragg, Mikey D'Amico, Probyn Gregory, Jeff Foskett, Matt Jardine, Billy Hinsche, Brett Simons, Bob Lizik, Taylor Mills, Todd Sucherman, Jim Hines, and more. And those years have also brought me into contact with wonderful collaborators: Andy Paley, Joe Thomas, Don Was, Mark Linett, Wes Seidman. Jason Fine was a journalistic champion of my work since *Imagination*. It's strange when other people help you become more yourself. That's one of the amazing things about creative work.

Outside of the music world, I've had great friends like Danny Hutton, David Leaf, Jerry Weiss, and more. Their wives and families have stuck with me over the years, almost as much as my own. It's always amazing to look around me and see friendly faces. Ray Lawlor, one of those close friends, was with me through this book process, helping to keep me in the right headspace when it came to remembering the past. I also want to thank Melinda's family, the Ledbetters, for always being so good to me—I am grateful, Rose and Patrick.

I couldn't have made this career work without Jean Sievers, who oversees so many things for me, or my attorneys Lee Phillips, Larry Marks, and Eric Custer. I couldn't have made this book work without Ben Schafer, who provided a steady editing hand. Ben Greenman helped to bring thought into language.

Melinda and I are grateful to Bill Pohlad and his team for making the movie *Love and Mercy*. It wouldn't have happened without him—or Paul Dano and John Cusack, who played me at different ages, and Paul Giamatti and Elizabeth Banks, who also gave brilliant performances in the film. And the film's writers, Oren Moverman and Michael Lerner, told the story the right way.

That movie and this book tell a story that is sometimes dark and difficult. It was that way because of a group of people—one person in particular, and the group that followed him—who came into my life at a time when I was not capable of standing up for myself. I was worn down by medication and worn out by surveillance. I don't want to mention that person by name here in the acknowledgments. I mentioned him in the book. That was enough.

Lastly, I want to thank the world of musicians. Some were making music before me. Some were doing it at the same time. Some followed my lead. So many of them are inspirational, from George Gershwin to the Four Freshmen to Chuck Berry to Phil Spector to the Everly Brothers to the Beatles to the Rolling Stones and beyond. Doing what they do, doing what I do, is a spiritual act. It touches the human spirit right at the center.

Can you hear the music? I hear it all the time.

Credits

"Add Some Music to Your Day"
Words & Music by Brian Wilson and Mike Love
Copyright © 1970 Brother Publishing Company
Administered by Wixen Music Publishing, Inc.
All Rights Reserved. Used by Permission.

"Amusement Parks USA"
Words and Music by Brian Wilson and Mike Love
Copyright © 1965 Irving Music, Inc.
Copyright Renewed
All Rights Reserved. Used by Permission.
Reprinted by permission of Hal Leonard Corporation

"Busy Doin' Nothing"
Copyright © 1968 Irving Music, Inc.
Copyright Renewed
All Rights Reserved. Used by Permission.
Reprinted by permission of Hal Leonard Corporation

"Cabinessence"
Words and Music by Brian Wilson and Van Dyke
  Parks
Copyright © 1968 Irving Music, Inc.
Copyright Renewed
All Rights Reserved. Used by Permission.
Reprinted by permission of Hal Leonard Corporation

"Car Crazy Cutie"
Words and Music by Brian Wilson and Roger
  Christian
Copyright © 1963 IRVING MUSIC, INC. and
  UNIVERSAL MUSIC - CAREERS
Copyright Renewed
All Rights Reserved. Used by Permission.
Reprinted by permission of Hal Leonard Corporation

"Caroline, No"
Words and Music by Brian Wilson and Tony Asher
Copyright © 1966 Irving Music, Inc.
Copyright Renewed
All Rights Reserved. Used by Permission.
Reprinted by permission of Hal Leonard Corporation

"Catch a Wave"
Words and Music by Brian Wilson and Mike Love
Copyright © 1963 Irving Music, Inc.
Copyright Renewed
All Rights Reserved. Used by Permission.
Reprinted by permission of Hal Leonard Corporation

"Celebrate the News"
Words and Music by Dennis Wilson and Gregg
  Jakobson
Copyright © 1969 Brother Publishing Company
Administered by Wixen Music Publishing, Inc.
All Rights Reserved. Used by Permission.

"Cry"
Words and Music by Brian Wilson
Copyright ©1999 New Executive Music
All Rights Reserved. Used by Permission.

"A Day in the Life of a Tree"
Words and Music by Brian Wilson and Jack Rieley
Copyright © 1971 Brother Publishing Company
Administered by Wixen Music Publishing, Inc.
All Rights Reserved. Used by Permission.

"Ding Dang"
Words and Music by Brian Wilson & Roger
  McGuinn
Copyright © 1977 Brother Publishing Company
Administered by Wixen Music Publishing, Inc.
All Rights Reserved. Used by Permission.

"I'm Bugged at My Ol' Man"
Words and Music by Brian Wilson
Copyright © 1965 Irving Music, Inc.
Copyright Renewed
All Rights Reserved. Used by Permission.
Reprinted by permission of Hal Leonard Corporation

"In My Room"
Words and Music by Brian Wilson and Gary Usher
Copyright © 1964 Irving Music, Inc.
Copyright Renewed
All Rights Reserved. Used by Permission.
Reprinted by permission of Hal Leonard Corporation

"In the Back of My Mind"
Words and Music by Brian Wilson and Mike Love
Copyright © 1965 Irving Music, Inc.
Copyright Renewed
All Rights Reserved. Used by Permission.
Reprinted by permission of Hal Leonard Corporation

"Isn't It Time"
Words and Music by Brian Wilson, Joseph
   Thomas, Jim Peterik, Laurence Millas and
   Mike Love
Copyright © 2012 BriMel Music, Summer's Gone,
   BMG Rights Management (UK) Ltd. (Primary
   Wave), Jim Peterik Music, Larry Millas Music
   and Clairaudient Music Corporation
All Rights for Jim Peterik Music and Larry Millas
   Music Administered by Penny Farthing Music
   c/o The Bicycle Music Company
All Rights Reserved. Used by Permission.
Reprinted by permission of Hal Leonard Corporation

"It's a Blue World"
by Bob Wright and Chet Forest
Copyright © 1939 by Bourne Co.
Copyright Renewed
All Rights Reserved International Copyright Secured
ASCAP

"Ivory Tower"
Words and Music by Jack Fulton and Lois Steele
Copyright © 1956 Edwin H. Morris & Company,
A Division of MPL Music Publishing, Inc.
Copyright Renewed All Rights Reserved
Reprinted by permission of Hal Leonard Corporation

"Johnny Carson"
Words and Music by Brian Wilson
Copyright © 1977 Brother Publishing Company
Administered by Wixen Music Publishing, Inc.
All Rights Reserved. Used by Permission.

"The Last Song"
Words and Music by Brian Wilson and Joseph
   Thomas
Copyright © 2014 BriMel Music, Summer's Gone
   and BMG Rights Management (UK) Ltd
   (Primary Wave)

All Rights for Summer's Gone and BMG Rights
   Management (UK) Ltd. (Primary Wave)
   Administered by BMG Rights Management
   (US) LLC
All Rights Reserved. Used by Permission.
Reprinted by permission of Hal Leonard Corporation

"Let Him Run Wild"
Words and Music by Brian Wilson and Mike Love
Copyright © 1965 Irving Music, Inc.
Copyright Renewed
All Rights Reserved. Used by Permission.
Reprinted by permission of Hal Leonard Corporation

"The Like in I Love You"
Words and Music by George Gershwin, Ira Gersh-
   win Brian Wilson and Scott Bennett
Copyright © 2011 BriMel Music (BMI) Furvest
   Music Publishing (BMI) George Gershwin
   Music (ASCAP), Ira Gershwin Music (ASCAP)
   and WB Music Corp. (ASCAP)
All Rights Reserved. Used by Permission.

"Long Promised Road"
Words and Music by Carl Wilson and Jack Rieley
Copyright © 1972 Brother Publishing Company
Administered by Wixen Music Publishing, Inc.
All Rights Reserved. Used by Permission.

"The Man with All the Toys"
Words and Music by Brian Wilson and Mike Love
Copyright © 1964 Irving Music, Inc.
Copyright Renewed
All Rights Reserved. Used by Permission.
Reprinted by permission of Hal Leonard Corporation

"Marcella"
Words and Music by Brian Wilson and Jack Reiley
Copyright © 1972 Brother Publishing Company
Administered by Wixen Music Publishing, Inc.
All Rights Reserved. Used by Permission.

"Melt Away"
Words and Music by Brian Wilson
Copyright © 1988 Beach Bum Music
All Rights Reserved. Used by Permission

"Midnight's Another Day"
Words and Music by Brian Wilson and Scott
   Bennett
Copyright © 2011 BriMel Music (BMI), Furvest
   Music Publishing (BMI) and BMG Bumblebee
   (BMI)
BMG Bumblebee Administered by BMG Rights
   Management (US) LLC
All Rights Reserved. Used by Permission.
Reprinted by permission of Hal Leonard Corporation

"Morning Beat"
Words and Music by Brian Wilson and Scott
   Bennett

Copyright © 2008 BriMel Music (BMI), Furvest
Music Publishing (BMI) and BMG Bumblebee
(BMI)
All Rights for BMG Bumblebee Administered by
BMG Rights Management (US) LLC
All Rights Reserved. Used by Permission.
Reprinted by permission of Hal Leonard Corporation

"My Only Alibi"
Written by Brian Wilson and Gary Usher

"Nothing but Love"
Words and Music by George Gershwin, Ira Gersh-
win Brian Wilson and Scott Bennett
Copyright © 2011 BriMel Music (BMI) Furvest
Music Publishing(BMI) George Gershwin
Music (ASCAP), Ira Gershwin Music (ASCAP)
and WB Music Corp. (ASCAP)
All Rights Reserved. Used by Permission.

"Oxygen to the Brain"
Words and Music by Brian Wilson and Scott
Bennett
Copyright © 2011 BriMel Music (BMI), Furvest Music
Publishing (BMI) and BMG Bumblebee (BMI)
All Rights for BMG Bumblebee Administered by
BMG Rights Management (US) LLC
All Rights Reserved. Used by Permission.
Reprinted by permission of Hal Leonard Corporation

"Palisades Park"
Words and Music by Chuck Barris
Copyright ©1962 Claridge Music Company, a
Division of MPL Music Publishing, Inc.
Copyright Renewed All Rights Reserved
Reprinted by permission of Hal Leonard Corporation

"Palm Tree and Moon"
Words and Music by Van Dyke Parks
Copyright © 1995 Warner Tamerlane- Publishing
Corporation and You Call These Songs
All Rights for Warner Tamerlane- Publishing Cor-
poration and You Call These Songs Adminis-
tered By Warner Tamerlane Corporation

"She Knows Me Too Well"
Words and Music by Brian Wilson and Mike Love
Copyright © 1964 Irving Music, Inc.
Copyright Renewed
All Rights Reserved. Used by Permission.
Reprinted by permission of Hal Leonard Corporation

"South American"
Words and Music by Brian Wilson, Joseph
Thomas and Jimmy Buffett
Copyright © 1998 New Executive Music, On the
Fox Music and Coral Reefer Music
All Rights On the Fox Music Administered by
BMG Rights Management (US) LLC
All Rights Reserved. Used by Permission.
Reprinted by permission of Hal Leonard Corporation

"Still I Dream of It"
Words and Music by Brian Wilson
Copyright © 1976 Brother Publishing Company
Administered by Wixen Music Publishing, Inc.
All Rights Reserved. Used by Permission.

"Summer's Gone"
Words and Music by Brian Wilson, Joseph
Thomas and Jon Bon Jovi
Copyright © 2012 BriMel Music, Summer's Gone,
BMG Rights Management (UK) Ltd (Primary
Wave) and Bon Jovi Publishing
All Rights for Summer's Gone and BMG Rights
Management (UK) Ltd. (Primary Wave)
Administered by BMG Rights Management
(US) LLC
All Rights for Bon Jovi Published Administered
by Kobalt Songs Music Publishing
All Rights Reserved. Used by Permission.
Reprinted by permission of Hal Leonard Corporation

"Surfer Girl"
Words and Music by Brian Wilson
Copyright © 1962 (Renewed 1990) BMG Bum-
blebee
All Rights Administered by BMG Rights Manage-
ment (US) LLC
All Rights Reserved. Used by Permission.
Reprinted by permission of Hal Leonard Corporation

"Surfin' Down the Swanee"
Words and Music by Brian Wilson
Copyright © 1963 Irving Music, Inc.
Copyright Renewed
All Rights Reserved. Used by Permission.
Reprinted by permission of Hal Leonard Corporation

"Surfin'"
Words and Music by Brian Wilson and Mike Love
Copyright © 1961, 1962 by BMG Bumblebee
Copyright Renewed
All Rights Administered by BMG Rights Manage-
ment (US) LLC
International Copyright Secured All Rights
Reserved
Reprinted by permission of Hal Leonard Corporation

"Surf's Up"
Words and Music by Brian Wilson & Van Dyke
Parks
Copyright © 1971 Brother Publishing Com-
pany (BMI) Administered by Wixen Music
Publishing, Inc. and Crow Cries Music (BMI)
Administered by BMG Rights Management
(US) LLC
All Rights Reserved. Used by Permission.
Reprinted by permission of Hal Leonard Corporation

"That Same Song"
Words and Music by Brian Wilson and Mike Love
Copyright ©1976 Brother Publishing Company

There was no entrance fee allowed because of the Sunday observance laws at the time, which also meant there was no county or international cricket on that day, so instead a collection would be taken by passing a big blanket around the crowd. The counties got around it by letting in only those spectators who had first bought a programme or scorecard outside the ground. These games were essentially the forerunners of 40-over county cricket, which started in 1969. The counties, having seen how lucrative and popular these matches were, wanted some of it for themselves. When I spoke to Packer, this was what I thought he had in mind. Clearly he had bigger ambitions.

To put it in perspective, at that time there had never been a private promoter to challenge established cricket. So how could I realise the enormity of what he was proposing and its consequences? Perhaps I was naive but I never grasped his intentions.

He then began to pick my brains about the best players in the world and about the captaincy. I thought he meant captains outside the established Test teams, and that is why I recommended Raymond Illingworth. He had been the best captain I had played under and although he had lost the England job in 1973 he was still skipper of Leicestershire. More to the point, like me, he was not playing international cricket and would therefore be available. It was when Packer dismissed Illy's name that I put myself forward. Why not me? I was captain of Yorkshire and had always wanted to be captain of England, but it had not happened. If I had realised for a moment that it was his intention to sign up the best players in the world, I would not have stupidly embarrassed myself by putting my name up in front of guys like Clive Lloyd, Mushtaq Mohammad, Imran Khan and Tony Greig, who were already international captains.

Kerry asked me if I was commentating at the Centenary Test match, and I told him they had already got a full quota of commentators but I was going as an invited guest of the Australia Cricket Board, along with other former players. He asked if I would like to commentate and I said yes. He made two phone calls and informed me I would be offered a role. That is how powerful he was, and I just took it as a thank you for coaching his son or maybe the information I had just given him. I left the meeting having agreed he would send me a contract to play for him during the following winter.

Austin Robertson, a former Aussie Rules footballer who worked for Packer, came to see me during the Centenary Test in Melbourne and he showed me the official contract, which was huge. There were a lot of pages which involved selling your body and soul for 12 months over three years, with 11 clauses that gave Packer control over your cricket life.

I asked if I could take it away to show my solicitor in England, but he would not let me. He said that secrecy was the reason I could not have a copy, but added that he was coming to England soon to sign up players and to scout for suitable grounds where they could play matches in the future. I told him I could not sign the contract, as I knew enough about legal matters to understand that I already had a contract in existence to play for Yorkshire from 1 April until the end of September, so how could I sign for somebody else? I could just imagine what would happen if Yorkshire had taken me, their captain, to court.

When they later tried to discredit me, I was accused by Kerry Packer and Tony Greig of turning down the contract because I was not going to be the captain. That's nonsense because Packer told me at our meeting I was only the third player to be approached, so nobody could know who was going to sign up for him or what the team would be. I also did not turn it down because I didn't like Kerry Packer or because the money was not enough, because no sum was ever discussed. I never heard anything more from him about a possible role and did not even give it another thought.

We later learnt that a few days after the Centenary Test match, Tony Greig had gone to see Packer in Sydney. I can only guess that through his exposure to the Sydney business world, he must have realised it was an opportunity of a lifetime to talk to Packer, especially for a man like Tony who was always trying to work out how to maximise his earnings from cricket. He gathered straight away what the opportunity entailed and I believe he jumped at it. Maybe he was given a lot more information than me, or perhaps the fact I refused to sign led Packer to offer more incentives.

I don't believe he went into this meeting thinking he would throw away the England captaincy and help set up a rebel cricket tournament. He probably just wanted to earn a few quid, but in life opportunities do not always come at a time convenient to you. Tony was like a lot of cricketers, once you reach 30 you start to worry about the future and how you would pay the bills after retirement. Packer was offering some players a guaranteed £25,000 per year for three years, which was a huge amount at the time, so you can see why they would want to sign up.

To give you an idea of how much it was, when I rejoined the England team in July 1977 at Trent Bridge for the third Test against Australia, I was paid the princely sum of £400 for the week's work. If you played in all five Tests you would get £2,000. However, it wasn't guaranteed the selectors would choose you for every game and central contracts were a distant dream, so the money could easily be less than that. If you were selected for an England tour then you would get approximately £5,000. On top of that, my salary at Yorkshire was £3,000 to £4,000.

If you were a star player or captain of England, you could pick up odd bits and pieces to improve your income. However, if you wrote a newspaper column, it had to be shown to and approved by the Test and County Cricket Board (TCCB, the forerunner of the ECB). The articles were censored to prevent you from publishing any critical comments, which meant the newspapers were not going to pay very much money for copy that did not make headlines. The *Sun* newspaper paid me because my name carried some interest, but that was it.

Nowadays players earn a lot of money from sponsorship, but there were also strict rules in those days around bat advertising. The rules stated you could have only a bat maker's name on the back of your cricket bat, rather than a company or sponsor. It was a closed shop. Bat makers such as Gunn & Moore, Gray-Nicolls, Stuart Surridge, County Sports and Slazenger had us all by the balls. You got a couple of grand and some free kit – that was it.

As a result of my 100th first-class century at Headingley in the fourth Test, I became the first player to earn serious money from bat sponsorship. I negotiated a £9,000 per year guarantee, with a per centage of sales which meant I could earn up to £12,000 or £13,000 a year. It was an unheard-of sum of money. Nowadays Kevin Pietersen or MS Dhoni can earn hundreds of thousands of pounds from bat sponsorships alone.

If you added up all my cricket and bat sponsorship contracts, the money still did not equal what was on offer from Packer. And, as I later told the High Court, there was another vital difference: players did not have the security of contracts. As I mentioned earlier, at Yorkshire we had only a yearly agreement until I negotiated contracts in 1972. The club would write to me and say it was employing me for a year and then they specified the salary. I had no security as an England player either, as what money there was depended on my being selected to play.

The contrast was stark. In the summer of 1977, as the Packer story swirled around the game, the TCCB were shamed into giving us a pay rise. A businessman named David Evans and some of his friends offered to increase the England players' wages to £1,000 per match, meaning we were paid an extra £600 a Test if we did not sign with Packer. The money went to the TCCB who then passed it on to us, minus the tax.

It embarrassed the TCCB that someone else had to help pay our wages and the following year, partly out of the fear more players would defect to World Series Cricket, they did then pay us £1000 per match out of their own money. So, in a very small way, Packer did improve wages for Test match players that summer, but it was hardly a life-changing sum of money and we still had no guarantees that we would keep on receiving the money.

Just look at what happened to me the following year in 1978. I was a top player and still good enough to be picked at 37, but

I missed four Test matches (three against Pakistan and one against New Zealand) through injury after breaking my thumb fielding for England in a one-day international against Pakistan. I played just two Tests that summer, so instead of earning £6,000 I received only £2,000, even though I had been injured while playing for my country. You can see why cricketers were easy pickings for Packer. He found a group of men who were ready to sell out because they felt they had been underpaid for years.

Where money is involved, arguments soon follow and the controversy and backbiting started in May 1977 when the Packer story broke. It did not take long for me to be dragged into it and become a target. I first got wind of the storm brewing when Yorkshire played Sussex at Hove on Sunday 8 May. Sussex beat us by five wickets and Greigy won the match with 50 not out. As I was about to drive off, Tony suggested I join him for a drink in the pub. This was not something I would normally do, as pubs were not for me and so I declined.

Tony then advised me to have a look at the papers the following morning as the story was about to break that he had signed for Packer, along with a lot more players. I was amazed but it did not particularly bother me, as I still did not realise what it was all about or the enormous implications for cricket. How could I?

On my way back to Chesterfield for a Yorkshire match next day, I called in to see Greigy's wife, Donna, to thank her for being so kind to me when I had been in Sydney playing for Waverley the previous winter. Richard Lumb and Bill Athey were in my car and they also came into the house with me. This meeting would later take on importance to the Packer circus.

The next day all hell broke loose. The story about Packer and World Series Cricket was all over the papers, and every day after that Greigy was making statements, holding press conferences, going on television, trying to explain why he signed and why other players had signed up. He told the world how it would benefit cricket and cricketers, though how was never made clear. Packer was also making statements from Australia, explaining how he was basically pissed off that he had not been allowed to bid for television rights for Australian cricket.

A lot of normally gentle, good-natured, easygoing people were upset. They felt Tony had let English cricket down, the more so because as England captain he had become Packer's recruiting sergeant. He would have been better relinquishing the captaincy and then doing what he did. Alec Bedser said at the time: 'The secretive, clandestine manner in which the opposition to traditional cricket was set up with the English captain acting as a recruiting agent left a mixture of numbing sadness and anger.'

But secrecy had been paramount; Packer had insisted on it. If Tony had given up the England captaincy at the peak of his powers, as he was in 1977, the press would have sniffed out World Series Cricket, so he had to carry out this clandestine recruitment process that added to the poisonous atmosphere at the time.

Once the news was out, every day there was so much conjecture as to who had signed or who was going to be approached. There was talk of a conciliation meeting between Packer's people and the International Cricket Council (ICC), then called the International Cricket Conference. It started to become bitter and a lot of hurtful comments were made by both sides aimed at various individuals. Once it became public knowledge that Tony had been recruiting players to sign for Kerry Packer, the TCCB had no alternative but to take the England captaincy away from him. How can you be a senior manager for Tesco and yet be recruiting people for Sainsbury's? It was ludicrous.

Rumours were rife, because no one knew who had the correct information, and once Tony lost the England captaincy, he jumped in with all guns blazing having realised his whole life was now going to be with Packer and away from established cricket. He was like a salesman trying to convince everyone, or maybe just convince himself, he had done the right thing, and that this was going to be the salvation for cricketers.

Fact became fiction. The Packer team twisted everything to suit their side of things and there was a PR war raging. In my case, Tony told *Private Eye* that when I went to his house to see Donna, I had actually gone in alone and waited for him to come home. I had then pleaded with him to ring Packer on my behalf, as I had changed my mind and wanted to come on board. Tony went on to say in the article that he had done this, but Packer did not want to know. It was a pack of lies to discredit me. He was under so much pressure and criticism in trying to justify his own actions he got carried away and seemed to have no conscience.

The Packer saga was in full swing, and Dennis Amiss, Derek Underwood, Alan Knott and John Snow had all signed up. On 26 July 1977, the ICC issued a statement saying: 'No player who, after 1 October 1977, has played or has made himself available to play in a match previously disapproved by the conference shall be eligible to play in any Test.'

This was a warning to all players that if they signed for World Series Cricket they were going to be banned from established cricket. Both sides had tried in a meeting at Lord's on 23 June to resolve the issue and hammer out an agreement, without success. After the meeting Packer was angry, saying: 'I will take no steps at all to help anybody. From now on it is every man for himself and let the devil take the hindmost.'

Talk now started that anyone playing for Packer would also be banned from county cricket the following season. This is when Packer started legal action, as he believed that the restrictions suggested by the ICC and TCCB were unlawful. I was asked to be a witness in the High Court for the TCCB, a shock to say the least. They actually wanted me on their side for a change. I was not used to being considered one of the good guys. By then, news of my rejection of Packer had circulated worldwide and I was regarded as public enemy number one by him and Tony. As soon as it became clear I was to give evidence, Tony telephoned me to ask: 'How the hell have you got involved in this?' He then added: 'We'll have to work hard over the weekend to find some mud to throw at you.'

That Sunday we met at the Sports Fair in Birmingham, he had to appear for St Peter's and I for Slazenger. He repeated his remark about finding something to have a go at me with the next day in court. Presumably he had already forgotten the despicable story he had earlier circulated, accusing me of asking him to contact Packer to get me in on the team, when I had visited his home in Sussex. Surely had that been true, it would have been brought up in court. You can always remember the truth, but you forget what lies you have told.

The judge, on being apprised of Tony's remark that they

would have to find some mud to discredit me, decided that his words were only jocular and satisfied legal dignity with a warning.

At the High Court on Monday 17 September, I was cross-examined by Packer's lawyer for nearly four hours. They quizzed me on the contractual situation of county cricketers, the problems they faced in gaining employment in the winter and my view on whether Packer players should be able to represent England. I was clear on that point. 'If a man feels he can earn more money by going away and playing in another country in direct conflict or opposition with the already established cricketers, then it is fine for him to do that. He has to earn his living. But he can't come back to the same system that is pouring money in left, right and centre not just to keep a few cream players happy but to keep the whole game going. These players surely can't expect to go and earn a lot of money and then come back and play in the established game. It seems nonsense.'

Mr Justice Slade found against the ICC and the TCCB, ruling that their action amounted to an illegal restraint of trade. The High Court judgement did however leave a loophole. While he had made it impossible for the authorities to ban the 'rebels' from any form of the professional game, a good deal of power still remained in the hands of the Test selectors and county committees. They could dispense with the services of any individual on the basis of form or team spirit, which is so often a matter of opinion.

The Professional Cricketers' Association, formed in 1968, came out strongly against Packer almost immediately, voting that his recruits should be ousted from the County

Championship. They showed an impressive solidarity which persuaded me to join their ranks after I had ignored their existence for nine years, in the belief the PCA was little more than a talking shop. In the end, player power probably did more than anything else to preserve established cricket, a factor that came to prominence when I finally became captain of England in 1978.

Bearing in mind the way the fates have sometimes treated me, I should not really have been surprised to find myself captain and having to face the possibility of a strike by the England team over Packer players. Mike Brearley, the captain of the tour to Pakistan in the winter of 1977–78, broke his arm in a meaningless fixture at Lahore, so I stepped in to deputise in the third Test at Karachi on 18 January. In doing so I picked up a poisoned chalice.

Whatever the High Court's view, all concerned with the England party were under the impression that Packer players would not be selected during our three-match Test series, although the Pakistan authorities had lifted the ban on their five rebels and invited four of them – Mushtaq Mohammad, Majid Khan, Zaheer Abbas and Imran Khan – to join their squad. The fifth, Asif Iqbal, indicated that he would not be available and dropped out of the picture.

Initially, however, it appeared that this represented little more than a gesture by the Pakistani authorities, as our Test series clashed with the so-called Super Test fixtures Packer had arranged. It was reported that the five Pakistani stars had turned down an offer of around £270 per Test from their board. Majid spotlighted the dangers of the deteriorating situation when he admitted: 'I am always available for selection unless

I am under contract to someone else at the same time.' In other words, he was happy to let Packer dictate his programme, a point Mushtaq underlined when he pressed the Pakistani board to negotiate with the Australian.

People's suspicions increased when Mushtaq, Zaheer and Imran flew in to Karachi. Their arrival on the scene indicated the distinct probability that Pakistan were going to include them in their line-up for this final Test. The entire England party was against contact with the Packer trio and the degree of uncertainty in the Pakistan camp prompted Brearley, on his return to England, to voice our opposition. 'The lads were not scared of being beaten, but worried about the future and wanted to make it quite clear where they stand. They are unanimously opposed to Packer's players being considered for selection in ICC Tests.'

To a large extent, Brearley did no more than hint at the depth of feeling in the England camp, and his words emphasised his unease at any talk of a strike, but, putting it bluntly, England were not prepared to take the field against any Packer players and industrial action represented the most effective option. I had a mess to sort out.

Meanwhile, a good deal was going on behind the scenes. Cricket officials in Pakistan are wary of their public, who they worried might riot, cause trouble and virtually wreck the ground if their favourite personalities were not picked, and the would-be spectators on this occasion were certainly not interested in the complications of politics. Those running the game in Pakistan were under just as much pressure as the players, so we appreciated that nothing could be taken for granted. We had to plan our strategy in the knowledge that the Pakistan selectors could not afford to be seen to be backing down by not picking their players. They were trapped between the proverbial rock and a hard place.

Doug Insole, chairman of the TCCB, sent an urgent telegram from London to the Intercontinental Hotel, where we were staying, which read: 'Messrs Barrington and Boycott, please ring me any time after 0300 your time.' Ken Barrington was the tour manager but he didn't really know how to cope with such a dramatic turn of events. He was a fine, determined player and a good man on the cricket side, but in his managerial role Ken preferred to distance himself from this sort of turmoil.

Insole's concern centred on the legal position, as he thought Pakistan could sue the TCCB for a substantial sum if we did not play, so he stressed to me: 'It would be bad for England and it would be bad for you, as history will record that you were the captain and Barrington the manager. Those are the two names that will be remembered. Surely you don't want that to happen. You are a responsible, mature person and I implore you, as a personal favour, to persuade the players to play.'

How ironic that the man who dropped me for slow scoring ten years earlier, when England beat India and I scored 246 not out, was now coming to me for help. He had publicly humiliated me and given me the stigma of scoring slowly that has lasted to this day. Now he wanted a personal favour. I wouldn't have given it to him even if it had been within my power.

I admitted that I did not feel it was up to me to dictate to the rest of the squad, adding that no words of mine would have the desired effect as feelings were running very high. The news of the solidarity in the England camp clearly surprised Insole, so

I tried to make him appreciate the position from our point of view. 'Look at Bob Taylor,' I said. 'If he were being selfish after getting the chance to step into Knott's shoes, he would want to play and keep his nose clean. Then he'd have a good chance of keeping his place next year. I've got most to lose. I have just realised my life's ambition to be captain of England, so it is not in my best interests to rock the boat. At the moment my prospects of taking over from Brearley would be improved if I were to toe the official line, but I don't operate like that. I am trying to do what I honestly believe is best for cricket.'

Insole listened without really hearing what I was saying. He continued to plead the case for appeasement. 'I take your point,' he admitted. 'We are all aware of your sentiments at Lord's, but you need to show some leadership. You can carry the rest of the team with you.'

That made me angry, because Insole was implying that to prove my qualities as captain I had to make a resolute England dressing room follow me against their clearly expressed better judgement. To leave no room for any doubt, therefore, I put several players on the telephone to Insole in the course of the ongoing discussions. The resulting exchanges reflected our collective distress at the circumstances in which we were placed through no fault of our own. Chris Old had turned down Packer to play for England and couldn't stomach the thought of them returning. Ian Botham and Bob Taylor felt this was a chance to make a stand after the failure of the TCCB's court case.

The conversation went round and round in circles and, having reached stalemate, I advised Insole to send the Pakistan board a telegram to cover the TCCB, which he did. It read: 'The UK Cricket Council warns your board England players adamant will not play Test if additional players from Australia are selected. Team has been instructed to play, but Cricket Council cannot guarantee them complying. If such players selected, consequences at Pakistan board's own risk.'

The England squad also received their 'instructions' in the same way: 'Following the phone call with the England captain, should players decide against playing the Cricket Council confirms the instructions that the England cricket team should fulfil their obligations to play the final Test match with Pakistan and honour both the board's contractual obligations and also those of the England players to the TCCB, despite whatever selections made by the Pakistan board for their side.'

The England party agreed to stand firm, and it is worth noting that we received total support for our decision from the Pakistan squad. Obviously some of them were motivated by self-interest, because if three Packer men were recalled at the last minute then three of the original side would have to be dropped, but the captain, Wasim Bari, was in no danger of losing his place and he too backed our position.

Then the Pakistan board president Mohammad Hussain announced that Mushtaq, Zaheer and Imran would not play. He insisted that the selectors had not bowed to any pressure from outside, but I am convinced that had the England players not stuck out their necks so loyally and bravely the rebels would have been welcomed back into the fold.

Another powerful voice, probably the most powerful of all, belonged to General Zia Ul-Haq, Pakistan's martial law administrator. He watched play during the first morning and asked me to visit him to give my views on the Packer circus and outline our version of events in the tense build-up to the Test. I went for tea with the general, along with Wasim Bari, and sought his opinion. He told me he was against the Packer trio being part of the Pakistan team, an opinion which certainly had reached the ears of the selectors, who must have looked to him for guidance, particularly as the fear of civil unrest hung over their deliberations. He added that he had spoken to Mushtaq and Zaheer.

Mushtaq and Zaheer must have departed in some haste after that, and General Zia clearly understood things perfectly. Both Wasim and I took the opportunity to emphasise that we did not want Packer men to be included in the Pakistan squad to tour England in the summer of 1978.

As England travelled on to New Zealand, the players' hard line became cemented into a series of resolutions put forward for consideration by the PCA, which included not playing first-class cricket against any touring side that selected players contracted to professional cricket outside the control of the ICC and TCCB. It was also put forward that members of the association would not play with or against players contracted to professional cricket outside the control of the ICC and TCCB in first-class cricket, John Player League, Benson & Hedges Cup and Gillette Cup while their contracts precluded their availability for Test matches and their own countries' domestic competitions.

I deliberately did not put my name to any proposal, as I did not want World Series Cricket and Tony to have any more ammunition. However, on behalf of the squad, I did write to Doug Insole to confirm our position, which we all felt was justified. If the England players had followed the TCCB line and featured in that Karachi Test alongside the Packer trio, Test cricket would have had to accommodate the Packer circus and its players.

At the time of the Pakistan row, Tony Greig was miles away in Sydney and unable to restrain his frustration at the turn of events. Packer had released his Pakistan Test players as a PR exercise, and here was the England team putting a spanner in the works. Tony was so mad that in his weekly newspaper column he wrote 'The threatened strike is the work of Geoff Boycott and his cronies. I refuse to believe that Mike Brearley had anything to do with it. Boycott put the team up to this. Brearley insisted that I and the other Packer players should turn out for him and has always stood for compromise and no division.'

That may have been Brearley's stance in the summer, but once the ICC ban had come into effect in October even he could not have kept that same view. Tony was wrong if he imagined that Brearley could guarantee him, or any other Packer player, a welcome in the dressing room. There was now a ban in place regardless of who was captain, and Tony had not seemed to grasp that, or did not want to. Greig joined Doug Insole in mistakenly assuming I could control the England team and bend the players to my will.

Meanwhile, things were not going well in Australia. The Packer empire was not making the expected impact on the field at that time, crowds were poor, people were not turning up in great numbers to watch his players, and being charitable it may well have had Tony thinking: 'Have I made the right decision?' Because things were not going his way, Tony needed to hit out. As usual my name seemed the most likely to capture the headlines.

I suspect there was also a personal element to it all. Before the whole Packer episode, when Tony was captain of England for two years, he had tried to persuade me to play for him and I know it irked him that it never happened. Now I had not only turned Packer down, I had been a witness in the court case for the other side and here I was, captain of England. He could not hide his bitterness. He wrote: 'Boycott's ability to be where there were no fast bowlers was common knowledge in the game.'

This was a direct attack on me personally. He was saying I was afraid of fast bowling, citing as proof my absence from the 1974–75 tour to Australia, during which pace bowlers Dennis Lillee and Jeff Thomson destroyed England with their sustained hostility. His preposterous suggestion took no account of the facts. In early October 1974, when I made my decision to stay at home and not tour Australia that winter, hardly anyone had heard of Jeff Thomson, certainly not I or the rest of the England players. He had played one Test match, against Pakistan in Melbourne in December 1972, and finished with figures of none for 110 runs and as a consequence been dropped. He then spent 23 months in the wilderness and was a surprise choice for the first Test in Brisbane against England in November 1974.

Dennis Lillee had broken down with back trouble in the West Indies in February 1973 emerging from his last Test in Kingston, Jamaica, with none for 132. Nobody was sure if he was going to return to first-class cricket, never mind Test cricket, when the tour set off. So when he was selected for the first Test, he had also been off the scene for 21 months. It was only when England started collapsing against the ferocious fast bowling of Lillee and Thomson that my enemies started to say: 'Where's Boycott? England's best batsman should be here.'

But because I wasn't there and England were getting badly beaten, my critics started to fabricate malicious stories that I had made myself unavailable to tour Australia through the fear of top-notch fast bowling. Now, three years later, Greigy was repeating this myth in the hope of trying to hurt and discredit me. It was even more ridiculous this time, because only four months previously that summer I had just played with him in three Test matches in England against Australia, facing Jeff Thomson and Len Pascoe in full cry, and I managed to average 147 over five innings.

Two years later, when I was in my 40th year, I played five Test matches in England and four in the West Indies against the best fast bowling attack ever: Michael Holding, Andy Roberts, Joel Garner, Colin Croft and Malcolm Marshall, and I still averaged 40. Unfortunately, the more a lie is repeated the more it becomes fact and some people started to believe it, or hoped it was true. Even today this myth occasionally rears its head.

For Tony the end was nigh. He had been reappointed captain of Sussex for the 1978 summer, but this was in defiance of a private agreement between the counties to hold the future of the Packer men in abeyance. His personal attacks on me caused Sussex acute embarrassment. Lancashire and Nottinghamshire reacted most strongly, seeking to have Sussex expelled from the County Championship. They probably never expected to get backing for such an extreme step, however it did have the effect of Sussex sacking Greigy as their captain on 31 January 1978. As it transpired, he played only four more first-class matches in England and left the country to start a new life in Australia bitter at his treatment.

Was it worth all the fuss? When peace was finally brokered after two years of upheaval, did our wages improve at county or international level? No, did they hell. Tony had constantly tried to sell World Series Cricket to us all by insisting it would benefit every cricketer in the land, but that did not happen. Packer was the only one who won: he succeeded in the High Court case, and Channel 9 have shown Australian cricket for over 35 years. He got what he wanted and because of this there is a misconception that everything he said about helping all cricketers must have happened, and must be true.

There is no question that Packer won the battle, but that does not mean he improved the pay of all cricketers. The only cricketers he helped were the ones he signed up. The people who were to benefit were those who worked in and for World Series Cricket for two years, including players and umpires. Packer did nothing for the average county cricketer. The only pay rise we received was through those businessmen embarrassing the TCCB into upping our match fee.

What really did make the difference to wages? Television. Once the satellite television industry boomed in the 1990s, competition between the stations benefited the cricket authorities, who began to earn more for their TV rights. Sky, ESPN and other channels have created a market and it has rained money ever since.

To give you some idea of the scale of the change, in 1977, before Packer, the TCCB earned £1 million from radio and television rights from the BBC. The ECB's broadcasting contract with Sky from 2014 to 2017 is £337 million, an average of

£84 million per year. Television money started filtering down to the players, but it took another 20 years after Packer because it was not until 2006 that Sky finally owned the exclusive rights to England cricket and the millions started rolling in. Then along came the IPL in 2008 and that changed everything, making multi-millionaires of the top players.

In 1977 the TCCB were making only £200,000 per year from Cornhill in sponsorship. But if you have television, what comes after it? Sponsorship, marketing and perimeter board advertising at the grounds. In the 1980s, ground advertising started to become common for the first time. The non-Test match grounds received £13,000 and the Test grounds £100,000 per year. Most grounds still own that income stream today and the figures have increased by 500 per cent.

I saw this increased valuation with my own eyes. In 2000, I helped Kelvin MacKenzie and talkSPORT win the radio rights for England's winter tour to Pakistan. Kelvin told me he wanted live cricket rights and asked how we would go about it. I said you need to get to the right people and I had friends in Pakistan. It took me two phone calls to get to the head of Pakistan cricket, Salim Altaf – nicknamed Bobby. I had batted against him in Test matches at Lord's and Headingley in 1971 and told him the deal on offer. The BBC, not used to anyone else bidding, normally paid under £100,000 for the radio broadcast rights. I said that talkSPORT would give them a lot more, but we were not messing about or getting into a bidding war, so I gave them a couple of days and they came back and said fine. Nobody said a word, the BBC knew nothing about it. When they went for the rights, they found out they had already been sold and went doolally.

I did the same for the Sri Lanka tour that winter. This, in a small way, was how rights deals were starting to make money for cricket. When central contracts started in 2000, the PCA pushed for their members to receive a share and it was not long before they were taking home 11 per cent of the ECB's income. It is nonsense to put that all down to Packer. There is an argument to say he was the first one to put a value on cricket rights, but it took many years before that improved players' wages and by the time it did, Kerry Packer was dead.

So what does the game owe Packer now? Day/night cricket, and even then he pinched the idea off baseball in the United States and it worked only because in the warmer countries floodlit cricket is wonderful. His legacy? White balls, black sightscreens, coloured clothing and helmets. That is it. It was an awful lot of pain to endure for the birth of floodlight cricket, but unfortunately that does not fit the story for those who these days want to cast Tony as a hero and Packer as a saviour of the game.

And what about Tony? He had everything I ever dreamed of: he was captain of England, the pinnacle of English cricket, but he lost it all. Having led England on a highly successful tour of India where his leadership skills were praised by the players and media, he was absolutely on top of the mountain in his chosen sport and could have been England captain for years. His earning capacity, if not brilliant, was good and certainly better than any other cricketer at the time.

Why did he do it? It is a question that bothers me now and I still can't understand why he chose to jeopardise his job as England captain. Lots of theories were thrown around at the time, including the thought that Greig did not care about the

England captaincy because he was South African. In *The Times* John Woodcock wrote: 'What has to be remembered is that Greig is English not by birth or upbringing but only by adoption which is not the same thing as being English through and through.'

Answering that criticism, Tony always said: 'When I put on the Three Lions for England, I played and gave everything.' He would also mention his father fighting in the war and putting his life on the line for this country. Nobody questions his father's loyalty to England, or what he did while serving in the Royal Air Force during World War Two. Sandy Greig was a squadron leader by the age of 21 and flew 54 missions over Germany for Bomber Command, earning the Distinguished Service Order and Distinguished Flying Cross.

But Tony always missed the point: that was what his father did and not him. Just because his father fought heroically in the war, it should not have given Tony a free pass to play for England when he had not grown up here. After his father was shot down in the war, he went to South Africa to train pilots and met Tony's South African mother. Tony grew up in South Africa and went to Queens College, Queenstown and did not come to England until the summer of 1966, aged 19, when he had a trial at Sussex and then played in their second team. He came to England to use that passport of convenience inherited from his father because he knew the prospects were better here.

I have never agreed with cricketers moving to England and using this country as a ticket to international cricket. I have no problem with where people are born; babies have no choice because their parents could be working abroad. Men like Colin

Cowdrey, Andrew Strauss, Ted Dexter and Nasser Hussain were born overseas, but lived in England for most of their formative years. But there have been plenty of others for whom that was not the case.

My point here is not personal. Tony's sister Sally became a very good friend of mine and still is today, and she plays golf with my wife and me. When, in 1989, Tony's father had a heart operation which meant he could not fly back home to South Africa for many months, and Sally would ring up and say: 'Daddy's dying to talk cricket. Can I drop him off for a few hours?' She would deposit him in Woolley and he would stay all morning to while away the time.

I believe if you want to play for England at cricket, you should have attended school here and spent a long period of time in this country before you play for our national team. It is not how good you are, or how likeable you are, and it has nothing to do with race, colour or creed. I was brought up wanting to play for Yorkshire and England, and if my place had been blocked by somebody who spent 19 years in another country and suddenly took my place I would have been furious.

In 2012, the ECB recognised the problem and decided that England would go beyond the ICC regulations and impose a seven-year residency for English qualification, having decided the previous qualifying period of four years was too short. The ECB have taken the right step by making it seven years, but I would have gone further and made it ten.

Look at the recent England team. Jonathan Trott played for South Africa Under-19s but has played 49 Tests for England. How can that be right? I know he has a British father and an English wife, but that is irrelevant to me. If he thought he could have played international cricket for South Africa, would he have stayed there?

Kevin Pietersen is a similar case. I am guessing they come for the money and maybe a safer way of life, it's certainly not the climate. I love his batting and think he is a fantastic player, but he should be playing for South Africa. He made a clear-cut, ruthless decision to follow his career in England. He started out in South Africa and then moved to England because he thought he would get a county contract and his earnings capacity would be bigger. Eventually, he hoped it would lead to playing for England, which opens up many commercial opportunities these days.

I also don't agree with cricketers from Ireland playing for England. It is not personal. Eoin Morgan, for example, is a gifted one-day batsman blessed with a magical eye and wonderful hands. But the question is: are you British for convenience sake or are you really British?

This question continued to plague Tony for the rest of his life, especially when it was brought up in relation to the Packer affair. However, he brought a lot of the criticism on himself, as it was his choice to sign with Packer. Where he has been unfairly treated is that his cricket talent has been forgotten down the years, because people focus on Packer. It is a shame because he was an excellent player. As an all-rounder, he was more of a batsman who bowled and he was a terrific catcher, probably the best tall slip catcher I have ever seen.

His Test batting average was over 40, and his swing and seam bowling brought him 141 wickets at 32.20 which was pretty good. He was a clever cricketer, too. When he went to the West Indies in 1974, he could not get any swing or seam going in those conditions. He was walloped in the first two Tests, taking only three wickets for 166 runs. Then Raymond Illingworth, who was on the tour as a writer because they had given the captaincy to Mike Denness, suggested to Greigy: 'You have got big hands. Why don't you bowl more off-cutters, as they have got a lot of left-handers.' Roy Fredericks, Alvin Kallicharran, Garfield Sobers and Clive Lloyd were all left-handers who batted in the top six. Greigy took Raymond's advice and bowled off-cutters, taking six for 164 in the third Test on a good pitch in Barbados, and made 148 with the bat as well.

We then went to Trinidad for the final Test and he bowled them out twice with eight for 86 in the first innings and five for 70 in the second. Greigy had made it tough for them, by bowling with a high action, getting plenty of bounce and cutting the ball away from the left-handers. He was even awkward for right-handers, because in those days the Port of Spain pitch always turned. I made 99 and 112 and we won the game from nowhere.

After peace was brokered over the Packer affair, I had little contact with Tony for more than ten years, apart from in 1980 when he was working for Channel 9 in Australia and interviewed me as an England player after winning two man of the match awards against Australia. The next time I met up with him was on England's tour to the West Indies in 1990. Mark McCormack's company Trans World International (TWI) had bought the TV rights and sold them to the fledgling satellite company Sky. Tony was freelancing and fronted the whole show for TWI. I joined the commentary team of Tony Cozier, Michael Holding and Tony Lewis. Greigy had been commentating for nine years and I was the new boy.

We immediately gelled and received wonderful compliments when we were on air together. It was Tony who suggested to TWI that I should do the pitch reports, because he said that I read pitches better than anyone else. Ian Wooldridge wrote a smashing piece in the *Daily Mail* about how much he enjoyed us together and called it the Greigy and Fiery Show. We spent three months together and it was as if the whole Packer episode had never happened. We played golf together on days off, had dinners together and I loved it. It was a fun time.

Tony was also the person who got me to start wearing a hat. He'd started to wear one himself while working for Channel Nine TV in Australia, because he often had to stand out in the middle in the glaring sun while waiting for the producer to give the go-ahead to start his pitch reports. Sometimes there can be hiccups and you wait for ages to start.

That West Indies series was so successful for Sky that the next summer they bought the 40-over Sunday League competition in England, and signed up Tony and me to commentate, and he came over to organise and host the coverage. After that I worked with him on numerous occasions in India, Sri Lanka, Bangladesh, Sharjah and England. During our spells in commentary boxes around the world, I often teased him with the question: 'Who are you supporting today, Australia, South Africa or England?' Our colleagues in the commentary box invariably shouted: 'Whoever is winning.' He would just give that big smile and his infectious chuckle.

We never once mentioned the Packer period, I think we both felt it was too painful an issue and we did not want to resurrect it. We got on so well in later life that I don't think either of us wanted to spoil it. We were able to move on. As the years went by, I think he laid the Packer period to rest and made up with most people. I don't think he changed his view, and why should he? Packer had been very loyal and good to him.

However, it took the England authorities nearly 20 years to make him an honorary life member of MCC in 1998. This distinction is normally granted to all England captains after they retire. In Greigy's case, it had needed a period of cooling off and a change of regime at the top of English cricket. I don't believe it should have taken so long and I wrote to him at the time to say: 'Making you wait that long is wrong and unfair. Your record with England will stand any scrutiny from friends or enemies. It is an excellent one – something you can rightly be proud of.'

Tony Greig was no saint, but neither am I. He caused a lot of pain with his involvement in Packer cricket, but he could also be engaging, warm, and loved chatting about cricket over dinner with a glass of wine in his hand. We got on well as teammates, but for a decade our friendship was a victim of the Packer affair. We got over it, but that does not mean I should try to change history just because he was my friend.

CHAPTER 7

CLOUGHIE MY FRIEND

When I look back and think about all the people I have met during my life, there is one man who has left a lasting impression and, if circumstances had been different, could have had a huge impact on my cricket career: Brian Clough. I know he was a football man, the greatest manager of them all, but he loved his cricket too and we were very close friends for many years.

It always intrigues me when I hear successful people say they have never made mistakes during their lives, they must be joking or lying. As we get older, most of us learn from our experiences and become more mature and better people. At times in life we need someone to lean on, to offer advice and point out our mistakes; Brian did that for me when he could, but I just wish he had been around all the time.

Nowadays, the England cricket team have coaches for every

specific role. Every time I look, there is a new face, and I wonder what they can have been brought in to do. When I played we had no one to support us in the way that modern teams do. I had a bat, some gloves and some pads – that was it. There was nobody to manage or help us. When I was captain of Yorkshire, I was not even allowed to have Ted Lester, the team scorer, help me out. He travelled with us all the time and I wanted him as team manager, but it was blocked by the Yorkshire committee. This was a guy I revered, he played for eight years with great players like Len Hutton and a young Fred Trueman in his pomp, but the committee said no. Do it your bloody self was the message. It was penny-pinching and left me isolated, with so many other things to distract me from my main aim of leading the side to success. Brian would have seen that. He would have had the ability to spot I needed help.

I first met Brian when he was a centre forward playing for Sunderland and I was a young cricketer for Yorkshire. In those days, we used to play a lot in Scarborough during the high summer. Remember that back then working people very rarely went abroad for their holidays, instead many of them went to cricket festivals at places like Scarborough, Bridlington, Blackpool and Skegness. Games at those seaside venues were big occasions; the holidaymakers would go to the beach in the morning and, when the tide came in, the Scarborough cricket ground would fill up. Obviously there were die-hard fans there from the start of play who had just come over for the cricket, but mainly it was people having their only holiday of the year.

Cloughie would train in the morning with Sunderland and then travel down to Scarborough to watch the last two sessions of play. He would sit in the players' area, watching avidly. It was not a social outing for him; he would sit there and really watch and study the cricket. I can picture it now; it was one of those high summer days when I met him, sat in the Scarborough pavilion. I was introduced to him by Brian Close and in time Cloughie would become a lifelong friend. Years later, when Yorkshire played at Worksop near Nottingham, he would come to the ground, sit in a chair with a pint of beer and watch every ball with a couple of mates. He was not interested in going to the committee room, he just loved watching cricket and understood the nuances of the game.

When he retired from playing and became a football manager, I would travel to watch his teams at Derby County and Nottingham Forest, and he, in return, would come to see me bat. When I went to football matches at Derby or Forest, he would organise my director's box seat, a nice lunch before the match, sometimes in the same hotel as the players. After the match I would be invited into his office. Many a time I would be there chatting and the opposition manager would come in and have a drink before their team bus left. They usually came to pay their respects, because Forest had won and sometimes Brian's team had enjoyed a great result midweek in the European Cup.

As soon as Brian had finished work, he would say 'right let's go' and I would follow him in my car to his house in Derby. He always cooked dinner for me. I sat in the lounge talking to his wife, Barbara, and he would keep popping in from the kitchen where he would be cooking a steak. We would talk for a long time. I would want to talk football and he always wanted to talk cricket. If I wanted to take the mickey out of him, I would wait until I was talking to Barbara over dinner and would ask her: 'Who is your favourite player?'

She would reply Archie Gemmill and then go on to say: 'And I don't know why Brian sold him?' It was funny to get her started on the subject, but he would just sit back and roll his eyes because he knew what was coming.

I remember he had this rocking chair in his lounge at his house in Derby with the fire on the right-hand side and the television in the corner. Many team formations, transfers and European Cup campaigns were plotted in that rocking chair by the fire.

People thought he used to shoot from the hip, was full of himself and that's why he was called Ol' Big Head. They were wrong. He studied people and that was his great strength. When he made his outrageous comments, he usually did it for a reason, mostly to protect his players. He once said to me: 'They are paid to play, and in the end I do not have to go out and score a goal.' He was very clever as he took the pressure off them by making himself the focal point.

One of his innovations was that he realised very early on that the football season was a long slog, and the players and manager would see each other virtually every day for ten months. So he introduced breaks or holidays for the players and staff when he would send the team off to Spain, but he did not go with them. He stayed away because he thought they had seen enough of each other. Then sometimes unannounced he would disappear; the players would be expecting him at training but they would not see him all week, as he had gone on holiday and it kept everyone on their toes. There is a need to keep the players and manager fresh in sport, something cricketers are fully aware of after months on tour together.

The club would sometimes block some of his more ambitious holiday plans. In 1972, there was a Boxing Day match at Derby against Manchester United which County won 3–1, and afterwards there was a party for the players and their wives and he invited me along. He said he wanted to take some time off to 'watch Muhammad Ali fight, Frank Sinatra sing and Geoffrey play cricket'.

He did manage to fly to America in 1973–74 to see Ali fight Joe Frazier, but I'm not sure he saw Sinatra sing. He was planning to end the trip by flying to the West Indies to watch me play for England while we were on tour in the Caribbean, but he never made it that far, as he had to come back to work in the end.

I remember when I was going through my three-year break from playing for England, Brian would ask me if the then chairman of selectors, Alec Bedser, had been in touch. I explained Alec would phone me up once a summer, but Brian would keep pushing: 'Has he been to see you in person?' He could not understand why he had not travelled to see me. He said: 'If I were the chairman, I would come to your house and stay there and talk to you until I got you to agree to play for England. You are the best batsman, England are better with you playing. That would be my job: to get you batting for England at your best.' When you say it like that, the art of player management seems so simple, whatever the sport.

Would it have worked if Alec had come to see me? I don't know. Alec was a lovely man, but he did not have the Cloughie type of personality to carry it off, even if the idea had entered his head in the first place. Alec thought it wasn't his job to try to persuade or encourage any player to play for England. He probably felt once he had made his one obligatory phone call a year then that was all that was required of him and his selection committee. You could not say he was wrong, but he did not have the imagination to think differently.

Brian's gift was to understand people. There are lots of stories about him, but the best one for giving an insight into how he understood people was when Nottingham Forest played Liverpool in the first round of the European Cup in 1978.

Forest were the champions of England and Liverpool the European Cup holders. Forest won the first leg at the City Ground 2–0, but Brian sensed his players were terrified of playing Liverpool at Anfield in the second leg. On the way to the match, Brian could feel the tension so he stopped the bus at the next pub, brought on some beers and told the lads to have a drink, and those that smoked to get their cigarettes out and have a fag. They then had a sing-song on the way to the match, which was the biggest game of their careers at that point. When they arrived, they were not afraid of anything. To have the intuition to sense they were too tense to play, and then the courage to rectify that by letting them have a drink, knowing that if they lost he would be crucified by the press, was brave as well as inspired. I know times have changed, but can you imagine any manager doing that these days? No chance.

Forest drew the second leg 0–0, went through to the next round and eventually won the European Cup that season, beating Malmo 1–0 in the final, with Trevor Francis scoring the winning goal. They repeated the feat the following year, but if Brian had not shown that stroke of genius on the bus to Anfield many months before, then they might have lost that game and history would have been different.

I once had a more personal glimpse of his man-management skills. In June 1974, he came to watch me bat against Derbyshire in a championship match at Chesterfield. It was a beautiful day, I was in really good form but early on I pulled Alan Ward straight to the fielder at midwicket, Brian Bolus, and was out for four. I was beside myself with disappointment, and after a little while Brian came in to see me. I apologised to him and said I had 'ruined the day'. I will never forget what he said to me: 'Look, you see your colleagues outside. They are not sure if they will make a hundred now or ever again. You will get one, if not tomorrow then the week after. You will get plenty, because you are that good.'

I had just failed and he made me feel ten feet tall. That was his gift: he had a way of cutting to the quick. He saw the situation, understood it and turned it into a positive without making it seem small. It must have been unbelievable to play for him, as he gave players absolute belief in their abilities.

There were times when I was down and not playing well; most sportsmen have those moments. Only geniuses such as Donald Bradman, Bobby Jones, Pelé and Jack Nicklaus live on a constant high. Most of us are just talented with moments of insecurity, we need people like Brian Clough with the personality, knowledge and intuition to pick us up. It is not simply a question of saying a few words of reassurance, it is saying the right thing and knowing what to say and when to say it.

Brian's greatest skill was understanding people and putting round pegs in round holes. He did not tell players to improve on their weak points or negatives, he just wanted them to do the job he thought they were good at so he could put the jigsaw of the 11 players together.

I once asked him why he had picked Alan Hinton. He was the Derby County left-winger, who was a bit timid and did not tackle well. Remember, in those days it was a rough game. If you were a shy individual or a skilful winger, you got out of the way of the rough stuff and stayed on the wing. Hinton appeared a bit frightened of tackling, but Brian told me: 'Listen. I don't pay him to tackle; I pay him to pass the ball on to my centre forward's head and he is bloody good at that.' It stuck with me. It was Brian's job to find someone else to do the tackling, he saw what a player could do and asked him to play to his strengths.

I used to love going into his office to chat about football. His assistant Peter Taylor would be there as well; he was like a lovable cockney spiv, fast talking, funny and amusing. I remember when Brian bought David Nish, a midfielder from Leicester for £225,000, which was a lot of money in 1972, and played him at left-back. I couldn't understand why he had paid all that money for a midfielder and stuck him at left-back. Peter Taylor used to love those conversations. 'Here, sign him up as a coach, Brian,' he would say, taking the mickey. It is well documented he later fell out with Taylor, but Brian said to me: 'I loved Peter because he made me laugh every day I came into work.' He deeply regretted they fell out.

We sometimes even talked about possible signings. One day in his office in 1979, Brian said to me. 'I want a left-footed left-back.' He said he fancied Frankie Gray from Leeds, Eddie's brother. I didn't agree, and said I thought he was a winger and not a very good tackler. There was I telling one of the great managers how to do his job. Ludicrous really, but I could get away with it because he was my friend.

A few weeks later, I went off on tour with England. I came back months later and went to one of the end-of-season matches at Forest. Afterwards we went back to his house as usual. He was cooking me dinner, popping in to the sitting room chatting away with Barbara and me, and eventually he said: 'Oh, by the way, that left full-back I bought – our supporters voted him player of the year.' There was of course no 'by the way'; he had been waiting to tell me he knew more about football than me.

Like most successful men Brian was flawed, he was not perfect. There was talk he took backhanders, but I have no knowledge of that. However, the one injustice he has suffered is the suggestion that when he managed Leeds in 1974 he was an alcoholic. In *The Damned United*, author David Peace writes about his alcoholism during that period of his life, but it was not correct and Barbara and the family were really hurt by that.

I was his friend and admirer, but I am not blind to the fact he did become an alcoholic at the end. The pressures got to him after so many years in the job, but that was later on, not in 1974. Peace was unfair and should be ashamed of putting that in his book, even if it was supposed to be a work of fiction. Many people do not realise it is fiction, and read it because they think it is a true story about Brian Clough. Mud sticks and people out there believe Brian was on the booze when he was Leeds United manager. As a public figure, you have to live with the mistakes you make, but it really hurts you, and your family, when people write untruthful stories.

When he joined Leeds United in July 1974, I was one of the first people to see him. He was announced as the new manager on Wednesday 31 July. Yorkshire had played a three-day match at Lord's, which finished the day before, and I had netted at Headingley on the Wednesday morning and then drove to Elland Road to see him. I naively thought I would be able to pop in and have a chat, thinking there would be nobody about. When I arrived at Elland Road, there were press men and television crews everywhere. I went up to a window to talk to a secretary who was taking messages for Brian. I was in a queue of journalists hoping for interviews and she was writing all the messages down. I asked if I could see him and was told to wait. She had written all the names of the people wanting to see him and took a long list to his office. Eventually, she came back and told all the television and media men that he was with the chairman and too busy, but added: 'Mr Boycott, can you wait? He will come and get you.'

I went into his office and sat down with him for half an hour, that is how close we were. He had just arrived, taken training for the first time and seen the chairman. He had a piece of paper in front of him and he had already worked out the average age of the team, and some of the playing staff were getting old. Johnny Giles was nearly 34, Billy Bremner was approaching 32 and Norman Hunter was coming up to 31, while Terry Cooper was 30 and eventually moved on that year. He knew he needed an injection of youth without breaking up the team, and he had no sense of foreboding about the job; he was positive and confident about his own ability. When he was asked by one of the Leeds players: 'What can you do for us that we have not done already?' he answered: 'Do the same again and do it better.' He oozed ambition and drive.

Later on, he never said a lot about his time at Leeds United.

It was such a painful experience that he did not want to be reminded about it, but occasionally he would let slip the odd remark. I know he felt that behind his back Johnny Giles had played a part in his downfall. When Don Revie left, he had recommended Johnny to the Leeds United board as his successor. I'm guessing being overlooked can't have gone down very well with Johnny, and I know the feeling well because when Mike Denness got the England captaincy over me I was not best pleased. So he definitely started with a sceptical and wary team.

Another factor was not having Peter Taylor as his assistant to watch his back did not help. In their partnership, it was always Peter who stayed with the players and he could smell trouble or problems looming before they got out of hand. Brian felt that without Peter around, the players were left with more opportunities to plot. Peter was the fast talker, a lovable rogue, quick-witted with great one-liners and funny asides that kept the players on their toes and laughing. At stressful times he could lessen the tension and break the ice.

Brian believed that sometimes when he walked into the Leeds dressing room, the conversation suddenly stopped in its tracks, and he had a feeling the players had been talking about him and not in a nice way. When there is an atmosphere in the room you can sense it, we have all had that experience. What you have to remember is this successful Leeds United team had adored the previous manager, Don Revie, and in the past Brian had been openly critical of aspects of their play, such as fouling, having a poor disciplinary record, haranguing referees over decisions. One player in particular, Peter Lorimer, was an example of all he deplored. He was a very talented footballer, but Brian believed that far too often he fell down too easily to persuade referees into giving penalties.

Brian actually felt Revie had assembled a talented bunch of players who didn't need to do those things, as they were good enough without the gamesmanship, but his previous comments had caused resentment and anger. Maybe deep down some of the staff felt if they got on with this new guy, they were in some way being disloyal to their former manager. The club should have been aware Brian was going into a hostile environment, because everyone knew his views on Revie. Typical of the man, he had such self-belief in his own ability that he thought he could turn it around. He exuded confidence and thought managing the Division One champions was where his talent should be seen. He had spent six months in relative obscurity at Brighton, working with players who were not very good, and so this was an opportunity he could not turn down.

While he was working at Brighton, Barbara and the kids had stayed in Derby, which he had found very difficult. He liked being at home, he hated travelling from Derby to Brighton and here was a chance to be in the limelight again closer to home. He loved being on stage when it was football, but then when it was not football he wanted a quiet home life.

Leeds were playing in the European Cup as well. He had won the First Division at Derby and had a taste of European football with them, so it was natural he wanted another go. He had bought and sold players at Derby to make a successful team; he had trained and managed them well. He knew he could do it again. His self-belief was so strong, he believed that if the Leeds United directors had the gall to pick him as their manager, then he had the balls to take it on.

They sacked him after 44 days on 12 September 1974. The first thing he did was get the best solicitor he could find to negotiate his pay-off, his deal included a new Mercedes car and £98,000, which was a lot of money then, and enabled him to pay off the mortgage on his house. Immediately after Brian was sacked, he appeared on a television programme with Don Revie, by now the England manager. Revie gleefully tried to bait Brian by asking how he thought he could improve on the Leeds team that had lost only twice in a season. Typical of my friend, quick as a wink he answered: 'I could have gone through the season without losing one match.' That was the man summed up.

I once asked if he would be interested in managing my team, Manchester United, this was just before Alex Ferguson got the manager's job in 1986. I had started following Manchester United in 1962 after they signed Denis Law. He had been my favourite player ever since I first saw him play as a scrawny kid at Huddersfield Town, who were in the First Division and Bill Shankly was the manager. I used to go to the home games with my uncle Jack, and would ride in the sidecar of his motorbike to Leeds Road, Huddersfield's ground in those days. Denis was the same age as me and at 16 was the least likely footballer you have ever seen in your life. He had his collar up and sleeves down over his hands as if he was freezing to death. It was a rough game then, with a heavy ball, horrible pitches and hard tackling. He looked as though he didn't want to be there, until the ball came and then suddenly he came alive – he was like lightning.

I followed his career, and when he joined United from Torino I started going to Old Trafford. I used to stand on the terraces every fortnight in lot number 13 in what is now the Sir Alex

Ferguson Stand. I would get there early so I could stand right on the halfway line. I queued up with my sandwiches and flask of coffee for two hours before kick off, just to watch Denis and in doing so I fell in love with Bobby Charlton and Manchester United.

Anyway, when I asked Brian, he said he would have crawled up the motorway on his hands and knees to manage United, because he thought they were the biggest club in the country. Here was the most successful manager in England, winning the title with Derby and Nottingham Forest and two European Cups, but he was never offered the Manchester United job. In between Matt Busby retiring and Alex Ferguson taking over, Manchester United had five different managers but throughout that dismal period the best manager in England, Brian Clough, was never approached to take over the biggest club in the country. Extraordinary.

I asked him what he would have done if he had been appointed Manchester United manager. He said he would take all the players and staff around the trophy room, show them the cups and then close the cabinets up for good. 'We have to make our own medals and trophies now.' He was not showing disrespect to Matt Busby's legacy, he just knew the club could not live on memories.

It is what I told Yorkshire players in 2012 when I became the club's president. I told them the club has a great history but to forget about that. I said we want to win the championship in our 150th year in 2013, but you can't do that unless first you get out of the Second Division in 2012, which they did. I told them they had to make their own history. I was trying to use what I learned from Brian Clough: keep the message simple.

Brian knew how to handle the players. Sport is full of young, healthy, talented, cocky and confident kids, and you need to be strong to keep them in line because in their environment they are the heroes and can easily get too big for their boots. He gave them a structure. Discipline and time-keeping were paramount, they got fined if they were late. No swearing or arguing with referees or linesmen was allowed; he was the gaffer, he made it very clear he ran the club, full stop. They all knew if they stepped out of line too often he would not pick them.

His whole ethos about football was: don't complicate it. If you select the right players, if you train them the right way, manage them well, then they will be fine out on the park. He never had long tactical talks. Once at training he saw Kevin Hector, his centre forward, taking corner kicks. He said: 'What are you doing, young man? I pay you to get goals as my centre forward and you will not do that taking corner kicks. Now get in the penalty area.'

When you put it like that, you wonder why others were not as successful. The fact was, anyone could say something like that, but it was his knowledge and character that carried it off and made him special.

I remember a little Scottish centre forward he had at Nottingham Forest called Ian Wallace. At one stage, he had not scored a goal for weeks. Brian once told me that every Friday Wallace used to take Barbara some duck eggs, because Brian liked them for his breakfast. Peter Taylor said to Wallace, with Cloughie in earshot: 'We need a goal, I don't care if it is off the back of your head or the back of your arse, but we need a goal and those duck eggs won't save you unless you get one.'

Together Brian and Peter were magical. They spoke

common sense and got to the heart of the matter, but also made you laugh as well. Brian once explained football to me like this: 'You get the ball, play it on the floor, not in the sky, then you pass it to someone with the same coloured shirt, you play in their half more than in your own, and you put the ball in their net more than they put it in yours.' It sounded so easy, but we all know in reality it is not that simple and is bloody complicated, just like batting. Great people can break down sport into its component parts, otherwise you become so wrapped up in technique that you forget the real object is to hit or kick the ball.

When I coach cricket, I sometimes look at a player in the nets and think I could tell him ten things to work on, but if I do it will overload his brain and he will not be able to hit the ball. The clever thing is to choose a couple of things and pick him up as a person. That is what Clough did; as so often with great leadership, he had an instinctive gift. Michael Vaughan was a natural leader, he was born to it. Brian Clough was not coached to be a manager, it was natural. If people go to a cricket academy and learn strategies there, they will all come out like clones, thinking the same way. What you find in people like Brian and Michael is originality.

Brian could pick you up, but he could put you down as well. I saw his team win 5–0 once, and the players were full of joy in the dressing room, but he put his head around the dressing room door and said 'you should have got nine' and left them. He didn't want them getting too carried away.

Once they were losing badly at half time and all the players thought they would get a telling off. He did not appear in the dressing room at all, but just before they resumed the second half he popped his head around the door and said: 'My fault, I picked the wrong team.' That gave them something to think about and they went on to win the match.

Many people make excuses and blame others. He did not do that. Brian bought Gary Megson from Sheffield United for £176,000 in April 1974. There was a summer break and then pre-season training, but Gary never played a match for Brian. He was sold to Newcastle in September 1974 for £132,000. It seemed very odd, as Gary was a hard-working midfielder. When I asked Brian what happened he said: 'When you make a mistake, the best remedy is always to admit it as quickly as possible – and get rid.' He did not blame anyone else, but took responsibility for the mistake. He did add it was better for the boy to be playing football rather than being stuck in the reserves.

There was also a very generous side to Brian which I saw on several occasions. In 1980, when I moved to my house in Woolley, he rang me one day and said he was on his way over with a mate. He pulled up in his car with a trailer attached to the back. In it were eight gorgeous dwarf conifers and that mate turned out to be his gardener. While we had coffee in the lounge, Brian's gardener planted the trees. They were Brian's housewarming gift to me. Many people only knew of Brian's outspoken, abrasive side, but that was not the real man. When Nottingham Forest won the European Cup in 1979, he rang me and said he was popping over. He brought me a cut-glass replica of the European Cup they had just won.

Brian and I had similar backgrounds. We both came from poor mining areas, he in the Northeast and me in West Yorkshire. With not a lot of money coming in when we were kids, we couldn't afford to play anything other than football and cricket. Tennis and golf were middle-class sports and you had to have a lot of brass to join a club or buy the equipment. We had a football or cricket bat and ball and played in the streets with our mates. Perhaps it is one reason why we bonded.

Immediately after I scored my 100th hundred, in an Ashes Test match at Headingley in 1977, I telephoned two people; one was Michael Parkinson, the other was Brian. When I rang Brian's home, Barbara said he should have gone to a committee meeting that afternoon. In those days, Nottingham Forest was run by a committee, but she had to phone the club and tell them he was not moving because 'my mate is batting'. He sat and watched the whole lot on television and missed the meeting.

He loved a chance to play cricket, and one of his most enjoyable moments was when he got me out in a Lord's Taverners match at Lord's in 1975. The match was a special fixture in those days and would feature a mix of proper cricketers and celebrities. I played alongside Denis Compton, Ken Barrington, Tony Lewis and Richie Benaud. I remember hitting the first three balls of the match, bowled by Ted Dexter, for four. I had made over 50 when Brian came on to bowl, I smacked a couple of his off-spinners for boundaries but then chipped one back and he had me caught and bowled for 68. He was over the moon. He knew I had done it on purpose, but he was thrilled to bits. It was a lovely moment.

I don't know anybody who worked with Brian that did not have their lives changed by him in some way, most of them for the better. His former players talk about a strong-minded, brilliant manager. He must have done something right if they all say that.

In the end, the pressure of management was too much. I knew something was wrong in October 1992 when I went to see him in his last season at Forest. I watched his side play a dull 0–0 draw with Sheffield United. At the time, everyone was saying Forest were too good to be relegated because they always played lovely football, but it was rubbish; they were a shadow of Brian's attractive teams of the past. I saw him in his office after the game and he looked terrible. His nose and face were red and blotchy due to the alcohol; he was lifeless and not the Brian Clough I knew. I came away knowing they would be relegated, as he was not in any fit state to manage a team. Brian had thrived on energy and vitality and had not been afraid to make decisions. Now the force had gone out of him, it was like waiting for the guillotine. The alcohol made him inactive, he had lost the drive to go and buy players. I suppose it is what alcohol does to you in the end.

I saw him a few times after he retired, he loved growing sweet peas and spending time in his garden, but football had left a hole. He was not well, but kept it very private within the family.

In the summer of 2003, I was recovering from my tongue cancer and wanted to see Brian, so I contacted Barbara. Talking to Barbara I could tell he was poorly and I needed to see him. In January that year, Brian had undergone a liver transplant and Barbara wanted to get him out of the house, so his daughter Elizabeth agreed to drive them both up to my home for lunch. I was going overseas to commentate in early September and Barbara had confidentially kept me informed of his health and treatments he was having at the time. It was a lovely sunny day when they came to Woolley, and we sat in our conservatory chatting away. When I asked Barbara if she would like a drink, Brian piped up: 'I'd like a glass of white wine.'

During lunch he emptied his glass and asked Rachael for another. Rachael saw the look of disapproval, or what could have been disappointment and dismay, on the faces of Barbara and Elizabeth. But he was not the sort of man to confront even as ill as he was then, so Rachael said no problem, took his glass to the kitchen, filled it a quarter of the way up with chardonnay and topped it up with water. He took one mouthful and the sly old fox knew exactly what she had done and why. He just looked her in the eye with that naughty smile of his and nodded, but he never said a word.

Some weeks later, while I was still in Singapore commentating for ESPN, Rachael was at home when the phone rang very late at night. It was Nigel wanting to speak to me to let me know his dad had died and the family did not want me to learn about it in the media.

Nigel rang Rachael a few days later, asking when I would be back home in England, because Barbara and the family wanted me to speak at his memorial service. I was still doing studio work for ESPN in Singapore on the India v Australia Test matches, but I am so pleased that the family thought enough of me to hold the service when I could be available, and I thought so much of him that I suggested I would fly back for a few days. I arrived home on 19 October and the memorial service was held at Derby County's ground, Pride Park, on Thursday 21 October 2004, my birthday. It rained cats and dogs, a miserable evening, but 14,000 people came to pay their respects and I was one of the two speakers, along with Martin O'Neill.

It was sad, the end always is, but life is not about dying, it is about what you achieve while you are alive. He left lots of wonderful memories, his teams played fairly and he won trophies. He was larger than life, an interesting man and exceptionally talented both as a player and manager. Now when I think about Brian, I see him at Derby when he was so boyish, young and full of energy, he was like a whirlwind. I wish he had been my manager as well as a best friend, as he would have helped me make some better decisions because he just had a gift for seeing things so clearly.

As a man I loved Brian's company and admired his professional achievements. I wish he was still here.

CHAPTER 8

THE SLEDGING CURSE

There has been an enormous rise in the use of sledging in the modern game and sadly the authorities have failed to crack down on foul-mouthed players. It has reached the stage that sledging has become a way of life for today's cricketer, who sees it as being as normal as strapping on his pads or polishing the ball. If the ICC continue to ignore this rising bad behaviour and sledging, then eventually there will be a fight on the field and a player will clock someone. There is testosterone flowing during the pressure moments of a Test match, and players won't always take a backward step when they are confronted.

The Australians are the worst culprits. Baiting Englishmen has become a national sport for them. The players, public and media see us as fair game, but that should not be the case. Yes, the Ashes is a traditional sporting contest between two nations, but nothing more. It means a lot, but it is not about fighting each other. If I remember rightly, we fought two world wars side by side. We are friends and allies, but on England's last tour to Australia the players knew they were on enemy territory.

The tone was set by Michael Clarke and Darren Lehmann. The captain and coach of Australia have a lot to answer for, because they should set an example. Ask people in the armed forces. Guys at the top set the standards and you have to follow them. The discipline is there. It should be the same in sport. But Clarke resorted to foul-mouthed abuse as soon as the series started, and Lehmann set the ball rolling even before England set foot in Australia. It was all very distasteful.

The first Test at the Gabba marked a new low. Two Australian players, David Warner and George Bailey, behaved appallingly and Clarke was picked up on the stump microphone giving the public an insight into the kind of abusive language players throw at each other these days. Clarke purposely walked up from second slip and said to England's tailender, James Anderson, that Australia would 'break his fucking arm'. It was a horrible comment.

These players think they are being clever, hard men, but it is crude, offensive and dragging cricket through the dirt. As soon as a new player breaks into the team, he starts the foul-mouthed verbals from day one, as if he has to prove his toughness to the others.

Look at George Bailey. There he was on his Test debut at the Gabba giving Anderson, England's last man, a gob full of abuse from short leg as Australia closed in on a massive victory. Bailey was 31. The public, the selectors, and probably even he himself were not sure if he was good enough for Test cricket, but he obviously felt confident enough to lay into Anderson, one of the best bowlers in the world, because sledging is second nature to the modern player. I know Anderson dishes it out and is no saint. He is a fast bowler who gets stuck in to batsmen verbally, but there was no need for Bailey to abuse a No 11, who was already scared enough trying to work out how he would cope with the pace of Mitchell Johnson.

Instead of showing some proper leadership, Clarke threatened Anderson in the crudest manner possible after the England bowler had stuck up for himself and had a go back at Bailey. Clarke must have thought he was being a clever dick. I never heard him acting so nasty when Australia were being beaten by England in the previous three series. He was the most mild-mannered and likeable guy you could meet, but then I thought he changed once his team started winning. He should remember it is important to win with dignity. If the captain behaves that way, should we be surprised if his players follow suit?

We all know David Warner is not exactly the nicest person on the planet. A fine player, yes, but some of his behaviour, such as attempting to punch Joe Root in a Birmingham bar in 2013, has shown what he is capable of when riled. At the Gabba, he got in on the act in a public way by rubbishing Jonathan Trott in a press conference. He implied Jonathan Trott was scared against Johnson, saying he was 'pretty poor and pretty weak'. While he was not to know that Trott would be going home a few days later with a 'stress-related illness', it was disrespectful of him to make such comments to the media about a fellow professional. England were right to be very angry. What would the Australians have said if the England players had made comments in public about Warner's episode when he threw a punch at Joe Root?

I don't remember any of our guys saying anything in press conferences or interviews. They were told to keep quiet. They did not go public saying exactly what they thought of Warner. All hell would have broken loose if they had called him a 'talented scrubber'.

Warner is just a product of the system and his behaviour was part of a systematic attempt to unsettle England with abuse, and for that Darren Lehmann has to take a lot of the blame. I love Darren. He played at Yorkshire with distinction for a number of years and is probably the best overseas player we have ever had. He is a great guy, a tough competitor and lives for cricket, but he incited the Australian crowds to abuse Stuart Broad on England's tour to Australia and that was unacceptable.

It all stemmed back to the first Ashes Test in the summer of 2013 at Nottingham. Broad nicked a delivery from the left-arm spinner Ashton Agar, which ricocheted off Brad Haddin, the wicketkeeper, and was caught by Clarke at first slip. Broad stood his ground and was given not out by umpire Aleem Dar. He was on 37 and added a further 28 runs to his score.

At the time Lehmann kept his mouth shut and seemed to brush it off until the Ashes were lost. A few days before the final Test at The Oval, he gave a telephone interview with a laddish radio station in Melbourne and basically told the Australian public to abuse Broad in the return series a few weeks later. He called him a 'blatant cheat' and said he hoped the Australian fans would make his life such a misery that he 'cries and goes home'.

The Australian media picked up on it and before the first Test the *Brisbane Courier-Mail* wrote puerile articles on their front page calling on fans to abuse Broad. Lehmann started it and the boozed-up fans in the stands then felt emboldened to carry it on. Broad played all five Tests in Australia and at every ground the crowd sang 'Broady is a wanker'. That was just personal abuse after Lehmann had set a nation to get at one individual. I thought Darren was better than that; he did not have to stoop so low, and it was unnecessary as he later proved that his cricket brain was enough to beat England.

I admired Broad for the way he never complained and showed tremendous character. He is a strong, feisty bugger and I like that. You need to have aggression as a fast bowler, and he ended up being the best England cricketer on the tour despite the abuse. But he should not have had to put up with personal insults incited by the opposition coach. It was disrespectful, but I fear it will happen again and we will reach the point where a player could even be attacked by a fan.

Darren Lehmann was fined only 20 per cent of his match fee by the ICC for the Broad comments and there was no disciplinary measure forthcoming from his boss, James Sutherland, at Cricket Australia. Sutherland was also wishy-washy with Clarke. He should have told him the abuse of Anderson was not acceptable behaviour, especially for a captain, never mind a player, and publicly admonished him. But instead Clarke was fined only about £2,000 by the ICC, a piffling amount for today's multi-millionaire cricketers. Clarke is the highest paid sportsman in Australia, earning around A$2 million a year. Fining him £2,000 was pointless.

There was no immediate apology or sign of remorse, and to

top it all Channel 9 ended up apologising to Clarke for leaving the stump mic open, instead of turning it off, and getting the Australian captain in trouble. In my opinion Lehmann and Clarke should have been banned for the next two Ashes Tests and if it happened again, I would double the suspension to four matches. Hit them with a punishment that hurts. They have to learn there are boundaries you do not cross.

Six months later, Michael Clarke finally managed to say this: 'I regret the language I used, and I regret that I said it over the stump mic. The last thing I want is for boys and girls watching cricket to be going and playing club cricket and saying things like that to opposition players. I think it's unacceptable that the Australian cricket captain is setting that example. But I don't regret standing up for my team-mates one bit. I don't regret being extremely honest with James Anderson and telling him what Mitchell Johnson's plan was. I don't regret that – I just regret that everybody heard it and the language I used.' It was at best a half-hearted apology, because he seems to think what he said is all right, he's just sorry it was overheard! Maybe someone pointed out the possible repercussions.

If a mother hears her child swearing, she puts a stop to it and explains it is unacceptable behaviour; if she does not, the child, when hearing adults swear, thinks it is clever and does it again and again. Mothers know to put boundaries in place for the child's own good. They could teach our cricket administrators a thing or two about discipline. The ICC should call a summit of all the captains and coaches to tell them it has to stop or there will be suspensions. Sportsmen should not be allowed to get away with things on the field that are unacceptable in the real world.

My point about this trash talking is would these guys say it to someone in the pub? Would Clarke have threatened a taller lad like Anderson with breaking his arm? Of course not, because he would have got a bunch of fives and ended up flat on his back.

The modern cricketer buys into the myth that sledging has always been part of the game. Rubbish. There is nothing wrong with intimidation in a cricketing sense. Cricket is a test of people's courage and character. If a fast bowler hits a batsman in the ribs or on the head, fine. Bowlers like Joel Garner, Michael Holding, Colin Croft and Andy Roberts stared, and if looks could kill I would have been dead years ago. Short balls would whistle past my nose or over my head. I had no problem with that; it is part of the game for a fast bowler to rough up a batsman. If you can't take it, then pack away your bat and get a normal job; but I never heard those great West Indians swearing at a batsman.

The batsman has to be good enough, and brave enough, to cope with that. But I batted against some of the best and nastiest fast bowlers who have ever played the game and they did not sledge me. I was also part of a very good Yorkshire side captained by Brian Close, one of the hardest men to play cricket, but he did not resort to personal abuse.

Dennis Lillee and Jeff Thomson would turn the air blue during some overs, you would constantly hear the f-word, particularly when Thommo was bowling, but it was never aimed directly at the batsman, more a sign of his frustration. All he and Lillee ever did was try to knock my block off, but they never sledged me once. If I thick-edged a ball down to third man, they would swear but it was never personal abuse aimed directly at me. The best bowlers rely on their skill to get wickets not their tongue.

Brian Close would intimidate batsmen not by sniping from second slip but by fielding close in and staring at batsmen. One of our tactics at Yorkshire if we had spinners on and took a wicket was that we always made sure we were ready in our fielding positions when the next batsman came in to take guard. Fielders would be very close and bent down, looking at him from a yard away in order to put the pressure on (today players are too busy performing high fives and then congratulating each other in a huddle when they get a wicket). We saw body language as a tool for intimidation, not mouthing off. We were challenging the batsmen, implying we are ready to get you out. I don't remember us saying anything nasty.

Fred Trueman used to come out with funny remarks that would make people laugh when he was bowling. One of Fred's great sayings to a batsman if he nicked one through the slips was: 'Fuck me, you have more edges than a broken piss pot.' And we would all crack up.

One day a batsman kept playing and missing, and Fred said: 'Fuck me, hold the bat still and I will hit it.'

In its way it worked as a kind of mental put-down for the batsman, and in the heat of battle it made us all laugh. Fred would not have taken more wickets if he had resorted to personal abuse and, like Michael Clarke, said: 'I'm going to break your fucking arm.' Fred would have been tickled though to hear the hypocrisy of an Australian, Lehmann, criticising a batsman, Broad, for not walking.

I played 38 Test matches against Australia and I can say they never walk. In fact, Richie Benaud is on record as saying he was taught at school never to walk. Flick back through history and you will find plenty of examples. In 1946–47 at Brisbane during the first Test match after the war, Donald Bradman edged Bill Voce to Jack Ikin at second slip. He stood his ground and was given not out. He was on 28 at the time and went on to score 187.

There was talk before the Test that Bradman was past it and he would retire if he failed in Brisbane. He had been invalided out of the army during the war down to poor eyesight and there was a lot of speculation over his health. But he went on to finish his career with a mountain of runs. Wally Hammond, the England captain, said on the field after the Ikin incident: 'A fine fucking way to start a series.'

When I was playing, I always said you should wait for the umpire's decision. In the second Test of the 1965–66 Ashes series, I caught and bowled Doug Walters in Melbourne. He had scored a hundred on his debut in the first Test and then went on to score a century in the second innings of his second Test. It was very hot and the match was petering out in a draw, so Mike Smith, captain of England, bowled people like me to fill in and give the proper bowlers a rest. Doug Walters hit the ball straight back to me but stood, implying it had hit the ground first and was a bump ball. The umpire gave him not out and so he started his career with two hundreds in two matches.

W.G. Grace is reputed to be the most famous and most frequent non-walker of all time, so I say to people there is nothing new in not walking and Stuart Broad is not alone. The laws of the game say 'in the umpire's opinion', and the Broad incident was actually an example of terrible umpiring.

I could see clearly, sitting in the *Test Match Special* commentary box at Trent Bridge, that he edged it. It was a monumental howler by Aleem Dar. How could he not see the edge from 22 yards away? That decision probably cost Australia the Test match, as Broad's partnership with Ian Bell added another 59 runs and they lost the match by 14 runs. It should have been umpire Aleem Dar copping the criticism, not Broad. In some ways I admire Broad's gall to stand his ground. I would have been too embarrassed to stay, and most of us would have walked off because it was so obvious. The only reason we walk when we nick it to slip is because it is so clearly out. You would look stupid to stand there and wait for the umpire. We are deflated and walk off wanting to get back to the sanctuary of the dressing room.

At the time Broad was accused of breaking the Spirit of Cricket. Nonsense. The Spirit of Cricket is a nebulous theory that is spouted by people who believe everyone should do the decent thing and walk. It has not really been thought through. They may understand and love the game of cricket, but they are living in cloud cuckoo land if they think it will work. The Spirit of Cricket was thought up in the late 1990s by Colin Cowdrey and Ted Dexter and is widely promoted by the MCC, who have the good of the game at heart. But it should be used to regulate standards of behaviour by players not an issue such as walking.

The ICC has its own Code of Conduct, but perhaps it should be renamed the 'Spirit of Cricket' to punish players for disciplinary lapses such as sledging and general bad behaviour. Part of the problem with on-field behaviour is the umpires are too weak. I think I was lucky to play in an era of strong officials who had played the game. Now many of the ICC's Elite Panel (the umpires who stand in Test matches) have played very little international cricket. I always felt when I played county cricket, the ex-players were the better umpires because they knew all the dodges and scams. They too had tried it on when they played the game.

I am not saying good umpires need to have been great players, but at some point they will have shared a dressing room or played against top cricketers and that makes them less impressionable. These days I think umpires are dazzled by the big stars and in awe of them. That did not happen with umpires like Ken Palmer, Dickie Bird and Arthur Jepson, who had all played county cricket for years. With them if it was out, it was out. If a player had crossed the line or started getting lippy, it was dealt with regardless of who it was.

Bill Alley was also a strong umpire. When Ray Bright started verbally abusing me in 1977 as I was scoring my 100th hundred at Headingley, Bill nipped it in the bud. Bright thought he had me caught behind. Rubbish! I never touched it. I wouldn't have got out to Ray Bright, as he couldn't bowl. Dennis Lillee, yes; Ray Bright, no. Anyway, he was obviously upset with me, but Bill spotted what was going on and had strong words with him and Greg Chappell, the Australia captain, and put a stop to it. That was good umpiring. In fact I did not register a word of what Bright was saying, as I never let that type of thing affect my concentration. I used to chuckle to myself when people tried to sledge me: 'Carry on, when I am still here at tea you will need all your energy just to bowl at me.'

Administrators often say they leave it up to the umpires or 'we can only do anything if an umpire reports an incident to the match referee', but that's a cop out. At the Gabba when Bailey and Anderson were having the altercation, on seeing Clarke in the middle of an over walk up from slip, warning lights should have come on. Any umpire with any brains should have spotted what was going on and moved quickly towards the players to intervene before there was a chance of anything happening.

The reason I think this issue is so important and needs dealing with properly is that when incidents of sledging are seen on television by club cricketers and kids, they think it is okay for them to behave that way because the big stars get away with it without meaningful repercussions. As a result, umpires at club level now get more abuse than ever before. It overstepped the mark in the last two Ashes series and threatened to ruin one of the great sporting contests. I know that Australia won the Ashes back, but that does not justify their behaviour. I also recognise that England are no angels and if our players ever stoop so low, you will not hear me supporting them, I will be just as strong in my criticism. It would not be right and I hope our administrators would react better than the Australian board, but I'm not holding my breath.

CHAPTER 9

SAVING TEST CRICKET

I fear for the future of Test cricket more than any other aspect of the game. I would love it to survive for another 200 years, but it is being allowed to die by administrators too busy increasing their own power and too complacent to tackle the problems it faces.

What is going to happen over the next 30 to 50 years? The rich nations will get richer and the poor poorer. In early 2014, the International Cricket Council (ICC) was carved up by the big three – India, Australia and England. It was a power grab sugar-coated by statements saying it will benefit everybody. Rubbish. They scrapped plans for the World Test Championship and marginalised the smaller nations, while making all the right noises about supporting Test cricket. But do they really care?

The biggest bully of them all is the Board of Control for

Cricket in India (BCCI) and they have just made sure they are going to stay top dogs. Giles Clarke, the chairman of the ECB, was party to this coup along with Cricket Australia. As a result we will see more money from the ICC's television rights for the period of 2015–23 flow upwards to the big three, leaving the other countries even more powerless than they are now.

A tour by India is priceless to every other country. Look at South Africa. In January 2014, India pulled out of the Cape Town Test over a silly political spat involving Haroon Lorgat, the chief executive of the South African board. When he was chief executive of the ICC, he tried to curb India's power, so they took their revenge by pulling out of the New Year's Test in Cape Town. It cost the South African board £11 million in lost earnings. Other countries are terrified they might suffer the same consequences if they upset India. Should we blame India for being strong and flexing their muscles? Or do we blame other countries for being too weak?

In an ideal situation, cricket would have an independent body filled with people without a vested interest to run the world game, but that will never happen. Giles Clarke and his colleagues have seen to that. In 2011 Lord Woolf, the former Lord Chief Justice of England and Wales, was commissioned by the ICC to review its governance. He recommended the addition of independent directors to the ICC board to clamp down on decisions being taken with vested interests at heart, but his recommendations were ignored.

Cricket has now come full circle. In 1909 at Lord's, England, South Africa and Australia formed the Imperial Cricket Conference. In 1926, West Indies, New Zealand and India were made full members. Pakistan followed in 1952, Sri Lanka, Zimbabwe and Bangladesh joined later.

In 1965, the board became the International Cricket Conference and until 1993, when the board was renamed the International Cricket Council, England and Australia had two votes each. They had four out of eight votes before they started, so unless the other countries could split England and Australia they always had their way. It was disgraceful and other countries rightly felt it was a repugnant remnant of Britain's white colonial past. The balance of power began to tip India's way when voting was changed to one member one vote that year, and now they hold all the aces because they generate 80 per cent of the ICC's income from television rights. This has led to a greedy push for more influence.

From the last ICC television contract, India received $52 million out of a generated amount of $1.5 billion over eight years. Clearly they deserve more – nobody would argue with that – but not the 20 per cent share they will now have if the ICC sell their rights for their targeted $2.5 billion. Australia and England are hanging on to their coat-tails as an act of self-preservation.

How did they get away with it? Simple. The other countries do not have any leverage. If they had said they were going to refuse to play against England, India or Australia, they would have gone bankrupt within a couple of years. They were threatened and cajoled into signing up. Zaka Ashraf, the chairman of the Pakistan Cricket Board, abstained when they first tried to push through these changes. But when he went home he was sacked by his board. Why? Because India threw Pakistan a bone and hinted they might play them again in international cricket. It is what always happens when India wants Pakistan's vote. Pakistan know they will make a fortune from television rights if they play India, so they sacked Ashraf for trying to do the decent thing.

South Africa were brought into line with empty promises. Haroon Lorgat was not at the ICC meeting in Singapore when this decision was taken due to some dubious charges laid against him by the ICC, for allegedly playing a part in a statement which criticised the governing body over the row with India about the Newlands Test. He was later exonerated but missed the meeting, so the chairman of Cricket South Africa (CSA), Chris Nenzani, went in his place. The BCCI dropped hints they would shift some of the 2014 IPL to South Africa over security concerns in India, as the tournament coincided with the Indian general election. That would net CSA a lot of money and make up for the £11 million they lost over the Newlands Test. They voted for the changes, but the IPL began in the UAE instead.

The smaller nations were powerless, so they voted in favour of the new arrangements. After the power grab by the big three, Lord Woolf summed up the situation perfectly: 'I don't see how if we had this to consider we could see it as anything but a retrograde step. It is giving extraordinary powers to a small triumvirate of three people, and everybody else has got no power to say anything or do anything. To say a sport that has got aspirations to be a world-class sport internationally should not have an independent body at the top seems to me to be very surprising. It seems to be entirely motivated by money.'

Yes money, but also power. The men at the top have ensured they have the key jobs. N. Srinivasan, the chairman of the

BCCI, will be chairman of ICC in 2015. Wally Edwards, chairman of Cricket Australia, will be chairman of the ICC's new executive committee, while Giles Clarke has got the best job of all. He is a smart cookie and he has made sure he will remain chairman of the finance and commerce committee, the most powerful of the lot, negotiating all those lucrative television and radio rights deals. You can wrap it up in Christmas paper if you like, but it is a plain fact that where there is brass, there is power and that is what it is all about. It is not how I understand democracy to work. I know cricket has to make ends meet, but we want to keep the game alive everywhere, with all ten countries playing each other in a meritocracy.

It brings to mind *Animal Farm* by George Orwell. We have three pigs who have re-written the rules to say 'everyone is equal, but some are more equal than others'. The three pigs – England, Australia and India – are going to make squillions of dollars at the expense of the rest. It is a sad day for cricket.

People keep telling me it will be all right, that cricket has always faced problems and survived, but it is different now because for decades our administrators have been blind to the real issues because of the television money. The cash boards are raking in from broadcasting rights is growing all the time, the administrators love the television money, it is easy lolly and they do not have to do anything to sell the game. They just divide up a load of juicy fixtures, with England, India and Australia making sure they play each other the most often, and just wait for the television companies to start a bidding war for rights. But if television ever decides to desert the game and finds something else, then international cricket, and the counties, will be finished. And don't be fooled into thinking television will be loyal to cricket. It doesn't owe the game any-thing. If it finds tiddlywinks or poker attracts bigger audiences, then it will leave cricket tomorrow. It will not hang around.

But at the moment it is a seller's market. You have rival tele-vision stations scrapping over rights and boards flogging them for eye-watering amounts. As I've mentioned, the ICC are hoping to sell their next batch of rights for $2.5 billion. Even in England over the past 15 years, we have had the BBC, Channel 4, Channel 5 and Sky paying ever-increasing amounts to show cricket. Now BT Sport have entered the market and could be a serious rival to Sky for future international rights.

I know our board say the television money helps them invest in blind cricket, deaf cricket, women's cricket, junior cricket, inner-cities cricket and to shell out a few thousand here and there to clubs struggling to raise enough money to give the pavilion a lick of paint. That is philanthropic and very nice, but it does not help the game at the top level, because fewer people are coming through the gates to watch matches. Crowds are dwindling at Test matches around the world, apart from when England are in town. Anybody who fails to see that prob-lem is sticking their head in the sand.

Ashes series are not the issue; grounds are full in England and Australia when these two countries play each other. They capture the imagination of the public and cricket lovers all over the world. It is an iconic series, bringing alive the history and tradition of the game. It is the dwindling interest in Test cricket when other nations are playing that worries me and should con-cern every cricket lover. If we carry on like we have been in recent years, with matches played in front of a decreasing number of spectators, we are going to get to a point when there is nobody in the grounds. It will take time, yes, but it will happen. A game cannot survive with empty stadiums no matter how big the television money; cricket needs bums on seats.

It is not a case of my being pessimistic; I recognise the fact that people pick up the paper to read about cricket or scan the web for scores and listen in their droves to the cricket on the radio. I understand there is as much interest as ever, but turning that into paying spectators is becoming harder and harder compared with years ago.

When I first toured South Africa in 1964–65, the Newlands Test was full, chock-a-block, you couldn't get a seat. It was the iconic place to be at New Year. These days, unless England are playing, you can walk up on any day to any Test match and pay at the gate. In Cape Town, except on weekends, they are lucky if it is even half full with maybe 10,000 people in the ground. There are empty seats galore. However, when England tour South Africa, it is like a home Test match for us because there are so many British tourists and Barmy Army people there on holiday.

It is the same situation when England play in Barbados: there are more English supporters on holiday with banners bragging about which football team they support than locals backing the West Indies. Without those England fans, you would be lucky to have a half-full stadium.

When I played in the Caribbean in 1968 and 1974, every ground was full; it was a huge event for the locals, who would turn up in their thousands to support the home team. The atmosphere was magical, just amazing. With Calypso bands, people blowing trumpets and conch shells, it was bloody noisy when you were batting, but you should have heard how many decibels the volume went up when they got a wicket. There were no televised matches in the West Indies until 1990, when satellite television started. Even then, the broadcasters were not allowed to show the match on the island where it was being played, as the signal was blocked out to encourage the local population to attend the match.

In India during the 1970s and even up to the 1980s, in Calcutta you could not get a seat during a Test. There would be 100,000 people inside at the game with a further 10,000 outside, some with tickets still trying to get in. All hell would let loose, they would be so mad they would start throwing stones over the wall because they couldn't get in to watch the match. Now you can walk up and sit in any one of 80,000 bucket seats and watch whoever is playing.

Despite the declining attendances for Test matches, India makes more money out of cricket than any other country by a mile and produces 80 per cent of the income of world cricket. Why? Once again, television is the answer. Four or five television stations in India are queuing up for Test cricket and bid figures that are bigger than telephone numbers. In return for their money they want cricket matches – lots of them. As a consequence, because there is too much Test cricket, it is no longer considered a rare event. It is like if you miss the bus and there is another one along in ten minutes, you are not bothered. But if there is only one bus a day, you bloody well make sure you are at the bus stop early so as not to miss it. That is how Test cricket used to be.

The administrators don't seem to care; they just want to put on more matches, which brings in more TV money and keeps the broadcasters happy. Satellite television loves cricket. Why?

It is brilliant because it fills so many hours of airtime. You can have a one-hour show before play, six and a half hours of action, with long breaks for lunch and tea. It has stats and gizmos galore. They have Hawk-Eye, Snicko, and mobile cameras hovering in the air called the spider cam, stump cams and stump microphones and inane player interviews before, during and after play.

In addition, there are natural breaks at the end of every over to show adverts, which in India rake in huge amounts of money. Add in drinks breaks, batsmen getting out and it is perfect for advertisers. Which other sport gives TV that?

Television audiences are up, so the advertisers see it as a chance to flog their goods, meaning broadcasters can charge more for adverts. Everyone makes money, but sod the actual numbers at the ground.

Over-rates do not encourage spectators to come to the grounds either, because they never know what time the match is going to finish. There is too much dawdling around, time-consuming discussions between bowler and captain that take forever. We have endless player huddles in the middle of a game and an amazing amount of drinks interruptions. The slightest bit of drizzle or bad light and they are off.

Twenty years ago, I suggested we should bring in penalty runs to punish teams for slow over-rates. It should not be difficult to bowl 15 overs an hour minimum. I look back at England's tour of Australia in 1970–71, when we bowled eight-ball overs. In the drawn Tests at Brisbane, Perth, Melbourne and Adelaide, where we played out the full hours, we got through the equivalent of at least 100 six-ball overs *in a six-hour day*, the lowest being 494 overs in five days at Melbourne, the highest 505 in the match at Adelaide.

Both sides had fast bowlers: Garth McKenzie, Dennis Lillee and 'Froggie' Thomson for the Aussies and John Snow, Ken Shuttleworth, Bob Willis and Peter Lever for us. No one had a run-up as long as Lever and, as someone said at the time, 'I don't go as far as that for my holidays.' Plenty of batsmen got injured, the temperature was red-hot everywhere, we all got tired, there were drinks intervals and wickets tumbling, but we still got through the overs on time and without any of these stupid allowances.

To stop the dawdling, I believe we should penalise the bowling team 10 runs for every over they are short at the end of an innings or end of the day. That would mess them up good and proper, because it could cost the team a match. Hurt players where it matters, during the match they are trying to win, not afterwards with small fines.

But what did the ICC do? They brought in meaningless fines instead that do not work, because nowadays most of the players are wealthy young men. At the end of the game, the match referee can suspend captains for future Tests, but they hardly ever use this power, except to punish players from the smaller countries who will not make a fuss. All the match referees are ex-cricketers and they do not feel comfortable suspending players. A punishment after the event allows a captain and his players to get away with bowling their overs slowly and indulge in gamesmanship. It is a cheats' charter.

So what is the solution to this problem? In 2005, I delivered the Cowdrey Lecture at Lord's for the MCC. In it, I advocated four-day Tests of seven hours each day, with a guaranteed 15 overs an hour. That's 105 overs a day, 420 in a match. Currently, there are supposed to be 450 overs in a Test, based on 90 overs a day for five days. However, that's only if you are lucky, because on most occasions teams do not bowl their overs at the required rate and some overs are lost. A large per centage of games now finish inside the allotted time, with 75 per cent of Tests completed inside four days, the full 450 overs aren't needed. So I think we need to concertina the game to concentrate the action while losing none of the skills.

Thanks to modern bats, players score quicker now than ever before and you have more wins and losses, even though the over-rate is down to 13 an hour. Players get out because they are playing one-day strokes in Test cricket. They invent shots and take risks in one-day and Twenty20, and then transfer that to the longer format of the game. They score quicker but make more mistakes. It is wonderful, interesting cricket and a great product to watch, but could be wrapped up in four days if modern cricketers were made to bowl decent over-rates.

To me, Test cricket is the heart and soul of the game. Players are judged against each other and those of the past, and that is possible because those basic principles have not changed. But just because it has a history of almost 140 years, it doesn't mean Test cricket should be stuck in the past. I think we should look at the game and ask what can we do to make it better, more interesting and more relevant to today's world and still preserve the character and ethos of Test cricket.

Test match cricket has not changed for years, because traditionalists say it is a sacred cow and they want it to stay the same. They do not mind tinkering with Twenty20 and one-dayers, but Tests? Oh no, they are untouchable. Rubbish, what absolute nonsense!

It is a myth that today we are playing a traditional form of Test cricket that has spanned the history of the game.

Way back in the 1930s there was the occasional timeless Test, which I must say was quite ridiculous as the longest lasted for ten days, when England played South Africa in Durban. That match was abandoned as a draw only because England had a two-day rail journey to Cape Town to catch their ship home. Previously, the usual format was three-day Test matches, in the late 1930s it became four days and eventually they settled on five.

Through the 1960s and 1970s, when I played, we had a rest day in the middle of a Test match; the game would always start on a Thursday and we never played on the Sunday. What did we do on a rest day? Nothing. Often during a Test match in London, being the only northerner, I would be on my own. Players from Essex, Kent, Sussex, Surrey and Middlesex all went home on Saturday night to spend the next day with their families. A lot of the time, Michael Parkinson and his wife Mary would come to the Tests in London and take me back to their house in Bray and I would stay with them.

But cricket realised in the late 1980s that rest days were a thing of the past, fans were happy to go to the cricket on Sundays because life had changed and the Sunday observance laws relaxed. Now Tests can start on any day of the week. The Ashes series in England in 2013 even started on a Wednesday, instead of the traditional Thursday.

Even the length of an over has changed. Many years ago, there were three- or four-ball overs, and as I've mentioned in Australia they used to have eight-ball overs until it was standardised to the present-day six balls.

My point is that crowds are dwindling, but the men currently in charge appear blind to the problem and unable or unwilling to recognise it needs new ideas to encourage spectators back. Sometimes you have to be brave to embrace change and gamble.

On that England tour to Australia in 1970–71 we were 1–0 up in the Test series when the Melbourne Test match was abandoned without a ball being bowled due to rain. When it was announced the Test match had been called off, we agreed to play a one-day game instead and nearly 40,000 turned up, without prior tickets, and paid on the gate. The outfield was slippery and, not wanting to get anybody injured and jeopardise our chances of winning the Ashes (which we eventually did 2–0), we simply treated the game as we would a competitive exhibition match. So the first one-day international was played by accident. The first ball was bowled by Graham McKenzie, and I was the first batsman to receive a ball. I was also the first batsman ever to be out. There were not many rules specifically for that new format – we didn't have four men in the circle, coloured clothing or powerplays, and there was no strict interpretation of wides.

In fact, at that time nobody had even thought of one-day international cricket or day/night cricket. We didn't take that match seriously, as for us Test cricket was everything. Little did we know that this one-off fixture would revolutionise the game.

Over 20 years ago, I wrote that we should try day/night Test cricket in the hot countries and use coloured clothing. We should give the public a product that fits in with modern life. At the moment it is too tempting to stay at home. By watching on television, you do not have the inconvenience of travelling on a bus, tram or train to go to the match. Some will take their car and need to find a parking space, more often than not they will have quite a long walk to the ground and then have to queue up to get in. Sometimes there is the added frustration of a long wait while bags are searched on entry. After watching the day's play, you have most of this inconvenience again to travel home. This is something that the top officials and administrators of the game rarely experience. Maybe they should try it sometime!

People are also worried about taking time off work to watch cricket, because jobs are hard to find and even tougher to keep these days. Everyone seems to have to work harder for less money. We have to recognise that is what is happening in the real world and that as a consequence cricket is suffering.

I mentioned day/night Test cricket again in the Cowdrey Lecture. At the time Malcolm Speed, the chief executive of the ICC, pooh-poohed my idea, patronised me and condescendingly said: 'Well, that's just Geoffrey.' I thought he was a stupid prat! He just summed up some of the game's narrow-minded administrators.

It took the ICC another seven years to agree it was a good idea and give permission for countries to go ahead with day/night cricket, but not one country has been brave or adventurous enough to try it yet. They make excuses about the dew and a white ball, but that doesn't seem to matter when they all fall over themselves to have day/night one-dayers.

In countries where Test cricket is struggling, such as New Zealand, the UAE (where Pakistan now play), Sri Lanka, West Indies and South Africa, day/night Test cricket is the way forward, using the cerise pink ball invented and successfully trialled by the MCC, who have led the way on this issue. The ICC make up all sorts of pathetic excuses not to use it, I can only guess because it was not their idea in the first place. I know they are concerned about the viability of a pink ball lasting long enough during a day's play. But if they really had a strong desire to change Test cricket, they would come up with a plan. For example, why not use a different pink ball at each end so it would have to last for only 40 overs; it does not have to be 80 overs before it is changed. In 1948, when England played Australia, they changed the ball after 60 overs. It was a bit stupid on the part of England, mind you, because Australia had great fast bowlers in Ray Lindwall and Keith Miller and England lost the series 4–0.

In my experience, the ICC do not want any advice from anybody and have paid the MCC lip service because they are jealous to death of their reputation in the game. MCC have a huge standing and respect from when they ran world cricket and are still the caretakers of the laws of the game, like the R&A in golf. It appears there is a resentment towards the MCC by some at the ICC, but the old fuddy-duddies who used to run the game are long gone, the club has changed and the ICC should embrace the fact that the MCC could offer alternative leadership and ideas such as pushing for day/night Test cricket.

Playing at night-time is what sold Packer cricket. The first year of Packer cricket was a flop from the public point of view. In 1977–78 he held Super Tests between Australia and the Rest of the World and got just 14,000 people through the gate on day one. Over the three days in Sydney, only 24,000 turned up and Kerry Packer was shocked. Then one of his guys came up with the idea, after watching baseball in America, to use a white ball, coloured clothing, black sightscreens and play at night. Suddenly it took off and the grounds were full.

Anyone who lives in Australia or South Africa knows when it is hot you want to get up early and go to work. It is not like freezing your balls off in an England winter when you don't want to get out of bed. They go to work early and finish at three then go to the beach or play golf. If Tests started mid-afternoon, then they could pick up the kids after school and make an evening at the Test a family outing. That way you are giving the public a product that fits around their lives. And if we have more kids coming through the gate, we should also give them what they want.

I am a traditionalist and I want to see Test cricketers wearing white. But I am old, young kids love coloured clothing, so the kit could be predominantly white with some colour on it and the players' names on the back. Children love to wear their favourite player's shirt and think they are superstars like their idol. All the jazz that goes with Twenty20 could be transferred to Test cricket, as long as we do not mess around with the fundamentals of the game.

I am not advocating radical changes in the format of Tests. I don't want to see the pitch shortened from 22 yards or a fourth stump added – that would be silly. It would also be unnecessary, because the cricket is so entertaining these days at Test level that if we market the game properly and play it at times when people can watch it then it will survive. The game has always evolved, if there is forward thinking and a strong desire then you can do anything.

Then we come to the problem in England of cricket not being shown on terrestrial television. Many families cannot afford to buy satellite, so they are denied the opportunity of seeing any form of live cricket on television and can't go to the matches because it is too expensive, with the best tickets costing about £100, meaning some pay more than a pound to watch an over. I am not anti-Sky. I started my commentary career with Sky and worked for them for six wonderful years. I loved it. They are brilliant at showing cricket, but I would only sell a portion of our cricket to satellite and some to terrestrial.

The ECB were seduced by Sky's money and say it props up the game and among other things keeps the counties solvent. But it is a vicious circle. The counties are not stupid and know they are storing up danger for the future by not having cricket on terrestrial television. They are aware that vast swathes of the next generation will not grow up, like I did, thinking cricket is our summer game. But they dare not vote to give cricket back to terrestrial television because the reduction in their money would finish off certain counties.

The ECB insisted a few years ago that all the Test grounds should have better drainage, floodlights and recommended the need for a certain amount of covered seating. This all costs the grounds concerned huge amounts of money, which most can only raise by borrowing from the banks. They then have to make enough money to pay back those loans and cover the interest. They are in trouble because of these debts, so whenever television comes in and offers lots of money, the counties are happy because it helps ease their financial problems. They will vote for the chairman at the ECB who can get the big, fat TV contracts.

The county officials are trapped in a catch-22 situation. Take Yorkshire as an example. I joined the board in 2005. On a turnover of £7 million per year, after running costs we had about £1 million surplus, and out of that approximately £700,000 was needed to service the loans. Now that interest payment has gone up to £1.2 million, so in eight years Yorkshire have to find an extra £500,000 a year, just to stand still.

It is down to necessary investment in the ground. Yorkshire built a big pavilion and got a gift of £12 million from Leeds Carnegie University, but there was still the cost of kitting it out and its ongoing maintenance. Now the club has to install those floodlights by the end of 2019, otherwise the ECB will not allocate any more international cricket to Headingley. Those floodlights will cost £1.8 million and the ECB will furnish £700,000 towards them, but that still leaves the club having to find over a million pounds. There is a spider's web of debt, as each county is desperate for money every year just to stay afloat.

Many of our Test match grounds base their borrowing and forward planning on holding a match involving England, otherwise they are in financial trouble. It means all are reluctant to rock the boat with the ECB and do not complain about the lack of cricket on terrestrial television, but they should because their own attendances are being hit, too.

When I played in the 1960s, we would play matches all over Yorkshire but now it has had to become centralised, because of costs, taking the game away from those who do not live in the big towns or cities. Counties now play at their main grounds and live day-to-day on the £2 million-plus handouts from the ECB. That is the pot generated by England rights sold to television, plus sponsorship and perimeter advertising. Even the other counties that do not have an international ground are in debt and need their share of ECB money to survive. But the problem is I can't see county clubs surviving for the next 20–30 years simply on the central handouts.

There have been suggestions that some counties should amalgamate, but how do you say which one stays or goes? It is like having twins and keeping only one: who is going to make that decision? There will be huge resistance and all are scared even to contemplate it. Instead, it will be down to market forces who survives, and some will go out of business – I don't know which ones, it could be Yorkshire for all I know. When I played for them in the 1970s, we had 13,000 members, now the club are lucky to attract even half that number. More spectators used to come to watch me have a net before start of play than now turn up at some county matches.

How long can the television money keep the 18 counties afloat? They are all in debt and the debts are getting bigger, so the pot has to keep getting bigger. Administrators will tell you they care, make all the right noises but a lot of politicians do that as well and we don't believe them either. Some administrators don't care what happens in the future, because they know it will not happen on their watch as they will be dead, retired or will have moved on to another job. When it all goes wrong, it will be someone else's problem to deal with, not theirs.

CHAPTER 10

ASHES DISASTER

In the summer of 2013 England won the Ashes with ease, but a few months later supporters were dumbfounded when Australia gained revenge with a stunning whitewash on their home soil. England fans were left asking: how did that happen? Well, there were many reasons which combined to produce a result that ripped apart English cricket, costing Andy Flower his job as coach and the sacking of Kevin Pietersen.

England were stunned by an Australia side that wanted to win more than they did. Australia were desperate to regain the Ashes after a period of English dominance and for many Australia players it was their last chance to taste Ashes glory. If Australia had lost at home and conceded the Ashes for a fourth consecutive time, they would have been crucified by their media. We have seen how the Australia press give England stick, but it is doubled when they turn on their own

team. The Australian public would also have given the players hell. It would have been an impossible time for the likes
of Michael Clarke and senior players such as Shane Watson
and Brad Haddin, who would have been forever tainted with
Ashes failure.

This burning desire to win was in contrast to England, who
thought because they had beaten Australia three times in suc-
cession they would be able to go Down Under, defend the
Ashes and make history by being the first English team to win
four series in a row. In other words, they were complacent. But
Andy Flower had failed to spot his team were in decline, or did
not want to believe that players who had performed well for
him in the past were fading away.

England did not rate the Aussie batsmen; many thought
Chris Rogers was past it, Watson was always getting out lbw
and Haddin was over the hill. They only really respected
Clarke, and were probably a little bit wary of David Warner's
aggression, but felt the others offered no real threat.

England beat Australia in the winter of 2010–11 under
Andrew Strauss on their own pitches quite comfortably, and
then won 3–0 in the summer of 2013 without playing particularly well. Our players got sucked in to believing their own
publicity and thought they could just go over there and do it
again. Everything would be all right on the day. They were
completely wrong and had been blind to the signs that had
been building for a year. When England batted in New
Zealand in March 2013 and against Australia in the summer
that followed, they failed to compile big first-innings scores. It
is the first innings that controls a Test match; if you can make
a large total then, you can dictate to the opposition.

We did not do that. England struggled against New Zealand because our batsmen were making elementary, silly mistakes due to over-confidence. They were getting themselves out and were lucky to escape with a draw, clinging on by one wicket in the final Auckland Test when New Zealand should really have beaten us.

Following on from that, England appeared to thump Australia 3–0 but the result flattered them. England should have lost the first Test match at Trent Bridge, but were lucky Stuart Broad was given not out off his glove, a poor umpiring decision that cost Australia the match. Australia should have won the third Test at Manchester; they set England an impossible target of 332 to win in the fourth innings and they were 32 for three when it rained on the last day, causing the match to be abandoned. The series should really have been 2–2.

England would have retained the Ashes, but such a result might have made the team and coaching staff sit up and take notice. A dose of reality would have done them some good and they may have addressed the issues which became major problems in Australia.

The appointment of Darren Lehmann immediately before the Tests in England started was a surprise, but it changed the dynamic between the two sides. I know from first-hand experience of him at Yorkshire that he is a very ebullient, confident, aggressive, in-your-face type of individual. His arrival certainly made me think the Ashes could be interesting. But in England Darren had inherited Mickey Arthur's squad and had no say or input with the Australian selectors as to the individuals already picked for the tour or those left out. His only real change was to bring in Steve Smith, which became a good selection. Smith was languishing on the Australia A tour to England, but repaid Lehmann's confidence with a century in The Oval Test before making two more hundreds in the winter return series.

Mitchell Johnson had not been selected to play the English summer against England, but Lehmann chose him for the one-day series and it proved to be a masterstroke. With that selection Lehmann outflanked his opposite number, Andy Flower, who has to accept the blame for overlooking the threat Johnson could pose in the winter. Andy was no longer directly involved in the coaching of the one-day side, having given that up the previous year to Ashley Giles. It meant he did not watch Johnson carefully enough in the one-day series and neither did the batting coach, Graham Gooch. If I saw what was happening – why didn't they?

They failed to spot that Johnson was bowling really fast and straight. He caused problems for our batsmen by getting the ball up quickly with lots of lift from just short of a length and was very accurate. He was hitting them on the glove and making them duck and weave. The only reason Johnson did not take a hatful of wickets is because in one-day cricket, unlike Tests, there is hardly anybody around the bat to take catches as the fielders are spread out to save runs. In Australia three years previously, Johnson had, to say the least, been really poor. He'd sprayed it everywhere and was not a danger to anybody except the wicketkeeper, diving all over the place to save his stray balls down the leg side. Apart from one good Test in Perth, when it all clicked for him and he took nine wickets in the match, he was fast but wild.

The Barmy Army wrote a song about him:

He bowls it to the left, he bowls it to the right,
That Mitchell Johnson,
His bowling is shite.

They were singing that in good heart with England winning and when he was bowling poorly. He reacted badly to all the jeering from the Barmy Army and lost his confidence. He later admitted the Barmy Army song rattled him and he would even sing it to himself at the top of his bowling mark, which shows how much they had got under his skin.

There is no point bowling quickly if you cannot control the direction. Sheer speed alone does not get wickets and Johnson's career was in decline. But I always thought he could end up having the last laugh because raw speed, when harnessed properly, wins matches. Before he returned for the one-day series in England, Johnson worked for some time with Terry Alderman and Dennis Lillee, two great bowlers from his adopted home state of Western Australia. They lengthened his run and got his leading arm higher. He was back in the groove. He hit Jonathan Trott on the helmet and on the gloves a number of times and a few other batsmen were made to look uncomfortable.

If Andy Flower had taken the time to watch that carefully, he would have realised there was a big problem brewing but he failed to notice Johnson had suddenly rediscovered his touch. A coach does not bat and make runs, or bowl and take wickets, his job is to watch, plan and prepare.

He should have seen the improvement of Johnson and noted what damage he could do in Test matches on hard, bouncy Australian pitches when he is allowed to bowl an unlimited amount of overs, rather than the maximum of ten in one-day cricket. Add in slips, gully and short leg, and suddenly Johnson becomes a real threat, particularly as modern batsmen are not comfortable with the ball zipping around their noses. Today's players are simply not used to facing genuine pace. The days of the West Indies having four big, nasty, quick bowlers are long gone. A lot of England's work should have been done before they left for Australia.

In 1990 Graham Gooch was an England player when Mickey Stewart, the head coach, asked me to work with the England batsmen to prepare them for the upcoming tour to the West Indies. Goochie had endured a miserable summer getting out cheaply a number of times to Terry Alderman during the Ashes series. I knew they were not going to play any spinners or face many nice juicy half volleys. They would be facing fast bowlers from both ends banging it in short.

I worked with the batsmen in the nets at Headingley with two cameras to film the action. One was positioned at point, the other behind the bowler's arm. We had a big quick bowler called Tony, who bowled in the Yorkshire leagues, come in to help. I told him to bowl off 20 yards, bang it in short and knock their blocks off. That is what he did, because bowling two yards through the crease gave him the same pace you would face in Test cricket. Our players would come up for sessions every two weeks and very quickly they were grumbling like mad in the changing rooms about all the short stuff I was giving them.

Nasser Hussain had a beautiful off drive, inside out through the covers, but I stopped him after four balls and said: 'Listen, you are four for three. You have nicked all four to the slips.

They have caught three and you might be lucky that one has gone between fourth slip and gully for four.'

I would keep stopping the session and we would study the video together and then go back for more practice. I showed the players how to duck and weave and defend well, a process that would wear the fast bowlers down. If you can't defend you are never in. Eventually they became comfortable with all the short balls and went to the West Indies and won the first Test. The second was abandoned and they would have won the third Test in Trinidad, but were cheated out of it by West Indies bowling their overs slow and bad light.

Had I been in charge before England left for Australia, recognising the threat of Johnson, I would have insisted that the England batsmen did some work in the indoor nets to get used to the speed and the left-arm angle Johnson creates. They may have sent Tymal Mills from Essex and Harry Gurney from Notts, two left-arm seamers, to bowl at them in the nets in Perth at the start of the tour before the Test series, but it was too late by then.

Having left-arm seamers for practice helps you get used to Johnson's angle, but it does not prepare for his extra pace and hostility. Instead of bowling line and length, Goochie should have remembered how I had prepared them for the West Indies tour. Mills and Gurney needed to bowl through the crease and inflict the threat of physical injury on our players. That is the only way to get mentally prepared for what is coming, the more you face short-pitched stuff the more accomplished you become at it; suddenly it does not frighten you anymore. Conquer the fear of getting hurt and you are halfway there.

A fast bowler tests your character by bowling short and making you duck and weave. If you survive the barrage, he will eventually pitch one up and then you hit it. In between times you have to play the quicks well to send them a message. Fast bowlers are unstoppable when they get on a roll. But what you have to remember is that fast bowlers usually bowl only in short spells, perhaps four or five overs at a time, so they can make the most of their energy in explosive bursts. Your plan should be to break their spell down in your mind to four overs, 24 balls. Probably six of those balls will be bouncers down the leg or off side. You can duck and weave and not really play at those balls. Then we have 18 balls left between two batsmen, which is really only nine balls each. In other words see him off. Surely Goochie was telling his batsman this. If not, then he was not doing his job properly.

In other words, you try to lessen his impact. But if you have not done your preparation properly, then you do not know how to see him off and you have no chance. For me Andy's failure to sort that out was a huge factor and the stats bear it out. At the end of the series Johnson had 37 wickets at 13.97. In the last 25 years or so, that is the best by a fast bowler.

You have to go back to 1881–92 to match his performance. In a ten-year period, George Lohmann of Surrey, a seam bowler, played 18 Test matches and took 112 wickets at 10.75. That was on uncovered pitches of poor quality when it was easier to take wickets. Now it is much harder for bowlers. Most historians and many ex-players who are students of the game regard S.F. Barnes as the greatest bowler ever. He played 27 Test matches for England and took 189 wickets at 16.43. Johnson bowled on modern, flat decks and still his record matched the

great bowlers of the earlier eras. It was a remarkable performance, but we helped him along the way by lacking a cohesive
strategy.

What you have to do at Test level, and I know a bit about it
having played a lot of great fast bowlers, is be able to work the
ones and twos. You have to have soft hands and an ability to
turn the wrists so you can deflect the ball in to little gaps. This
frustrates bowlers into trying something new, which then forces
them to bowl you a hittable ball. That is your life-blood against
great bowlers. It keeps you going through the hard times, and
takes the pressure off.

Andy should have known his history. Fast bowlers win Test
matches, particularly Ashes series in Australia. In 1932–33
Harold Larwood put Bodyline into operation and did all the
damage, even cutting down the great Don Bradman's batting
by half. In 1954–55, on Len Hutton's tour of Australia, Frank
Tyson won the series with help from Brian Statham and Trevor
Bailey. There were a number of occasions when Keith Miller
and Ray Lindwall destroyed England, with big Bill Johnson
also a real threat as back-up. In 1974–75 Australia blew us away
with Lillee and Thomson.

History tells us when you have a great fast bowler, you have
an ace to trump anything the opposition have. No contest.
Gooch was a close colleague of mine. He was an opening partner, a terrific batsman and a really good guy. At the end of the
Ashes series he was right to say: 'We all need to have a good
look at ourselves after this performance.' I am glad Graham
Gooch was honest and said everybody had to share the blame.
But was he giving them the right advice or was it a case of them
not listening? If he was giving them poor advice, then he was

failing in his job. If they were not listening, then either the players or the coach has to go.

All through Australia I watched my friend Goochie working with our batsmen. I saw him giving them a lot of throw-downs with the sidearm throwing aid that dog walkers use to pick up a ball and hurl it long distances for the dog to fetch. That's all well and good, but it is not how I see the batting coach's job. The guys loved the fact that Graham was prepared to do the donkey work and took time to help them in that way, but my brother or any member of the Barmy Army could give throw-downs using that stick. For me, coaching is studying the technique of the batsmen under you, helping them tidy up in defence and talking to them about where and how to play certain bowlers. It is about explaining to them that on different pitches against certain bowlers some scoring areas are risky. Point out the scoring areas that offer higher reward for lower risk. In other words, at the top level it is about teaching the art of scoring runs and arming batsmen with the know-how to exploit weaknesses in the bowlers.

There was no shame in losing wickets to Johnson, but what really annoyed me was England had no plan against Nathan Lyon, the off-spinner bowling on flat pitches around the wicket to our right-handers. In eight Test matches, three in England and five in Australia, he took 28 wickets at 30 and we did not improve one iota against his bowling. He is a decent spinner, but he is not Jim Laker and he does not bowl a 'doosra' that can confuse you like Muttiah Muralitharan or Saeed Ajmal. He is an orthodox finger spinner who bowled around the wicket, and that should be straightforward for Test-standard batsmen, but our guys stayed back, crease-bound like flies caught in a spider's web. Our right-handers did not move. They were too scared to use their feet and go down the pitch. They were stuck in the crease, waiting for a bad, short ball to cut. It was like he was bowling hand grenades to them all the time and they were fearful the ball would explode.

In Test cricket you get very few bad balls from a good spinner, so England were reduced to playing sweeps off the stumps, which are fraught with great danger if you miss the ball, especially with the Decision Review System (DRS) giving spinners a lot more lbws these days. The other option is to try to hit him over the top and clear the in-field, but that is very risky if you take the shot on when you have not been in very long. You have not had time to judge the surface, the turn and flight through the air.

The job of the coach is to talk to batsmen in the nets and work out how to counter someone like Lyon. If you talk to better players around the world, or even to Darren Lehmann and ask him what he told the Australia players, you will find out what their policy is towards spinners. On modern, flat pitches if it does not spin then a good batting team should not allow an orthodox finger spinner to tie up one end. He should be batted out of the attack, which is exactly what Australia did to Graeme Swann. When it turns then it is different, you have to be more patient.

After seeing how our batsmen struggled against Lyon in three Tests in England, we should have worked on getting to the pitch of the ball and driving it to mid off and mid on for ones or twos. Cut out the risky shots and take the easy runs on offer. If our guys had picked him off down the ground, the scoreboard would have ticked over and Lyon would have become frustrated by the fact they were playing him easily. OK, you would not be smacking him around, but he would start to experiment and give you the odd poor ball to drive or hit off the back foot through the covers.

But for that to happen, our right-handed batsmen needed the confidence from working on their technique to get the feet moving rather than becoming bogged down. It is like playing chess. You move the pawns first to get in a good position to bring your big guns, the bishops, knights and rooks, into play. Finally you can start moving your biggest piece, the queen. To play chess well, you need to be able to think and plan ahead. It is the same for a batsman in Test cricket. It is about strategy, but instead we allowed Lyon to dictate to us in eight Test matches. All the batsmen were at fault, and nobody escapes criticism apart from the young boy Ben Stokes, who made a marvellous century in his second Test at Perth. But as for the rest, it was a tour of shame.

I could not believe opening batsman Michael Carberry's footwork. He was rooted on the back foot to the quicks, and only came forward to play a flashing off drive. His problem, and this would have been an issue in England as well, was he never got his front foot past the batting crease. Whenever he played forward in an attempt to smother the ball, he was still stuck on the batting crease, so he was miles away from the pitch of the ball. I am sorry but that kind of fundamentally poor footwork will always get him in trouble against top-class bowlers. If he is going to wait for a four ball to play with a flashing off drive, then he needs enormous patience when batting against top-class attacks, and Australia gave England very few bad balls to whack. It is not like county cricket where bowlers make more mistakes.

Joe Root was no better. He lost his footwork and became almost scoreless, frightened to play an attacking shot. In my opinion, he was picked too early by England. At the time various selectors asked me for my opinion and I told them that one day he will be a superb player and play for many years for our country. I saw him at Yorkshire and I felt that when he got in he had the composure, confidence, concentration and wide range of shots to make superb centuries, but he struggled against the new ball early on and was not yet ready. He had one good season for Yorkshire, who were in the Second Division at the time, and was then thrust on to the international stage.

In only 16 Test matches, before being dropped for the Sydney Test, he was shunted up and down the order from No.1 to No.6. He has played one-day and Twenty20 cricket for England as well, so I am not surprised that someone like him, lacking in first-class experience, lost his footwork in Australia. When he played forward to the seamers, he never moved his foot out to the pitch of the ball. He was stuck on the crease every time. He is good enough to correct this problem through some quality time in the nets, but not while he keeps playing Twenty20 cricket. He needs to get some good coaching and play first-class cricket without having to slog the ball around in one-dayers.

Root is young and still learning, but Alastair Cook is one of the best in the world and Australia's planning and preparation for our captain were a lesson to England. They identified his strengths and exploited his weaknesses. Cook lost confidence and his footwork because Australia kept the ball off his pads, which has always been his bread and butter shot. If it is on his legs pitched up, then he tucks it away comfortably. If it is short-ish on his hip, he pulls it and he cuts anything short and wide on the off side. But Australia gave him nothing on his legs or any short balls to cut. They bowled it full and across him all the time. It did not matter to Australia if the ball was wide and he didn't play at it, because it meant he was not scoring runs. He was not able to get going and they kept bowling it wide to tempt him, because they knew it would play on his mind that he was not scoring.

The off drive is fraught with danger against quality fast bowlers with the new ball such as Johnson, Ryan Harris and Peter Siddle. By cutting off his normal area of scoring, Australia forced him to try shots he was not comfortable with and the result was inevitable. It ate away at Cook's confidence and in the end you saw a bloody good batsman out of form. In Adelaide he even hooked at Johnson and got caught at fine leg, something he never does. They scrambled his brain to such a point he was playing at balls wide of off-stump without moving his feet. Australia were pulling him left, right and centre.

I would have explained this excellent Australian strategy to him and told him to stick to his game plan and not go outside his comfort zone. This would require more patience than he had ever had to use in the past and would mean scoring slower against the new ball. But he needed to win the battle against the new ball even at the cost of scoring slowly, then once he had worn the bowlers down, and the ball got older, he could gain momentum. This would not be easy or eye-catching, but it was a better option than playing poor shots and being dismissed cheaply.

Off the field it was just as bad for England. Very few people knew or suspected Jonathan Trott had a problem. After he went home Flower admitted they had been managing his illness for some time. He said: 'I was first aware that Jonathan struggled with these things from our first contact as player and coach. He's been managing it from the start of the tour and there was no reason to suggest that this Test should be any different.'

Now hang on. If you have got some kind of depression or mental health issue, which a lot of people do not understand, and I admit I am one of them, does it not mean you have a ticking time bomb on your hands? At some stage it was going to go off. England have had experience of this before, so they have no excuse. Marcus Trescothick, a bloody fine batsman in one-day cricket and Tests, had his issues which have been well documented. Mike Yardy, a moderate player, came home from the World Cup in Sri Lanka in 2011, again with the coaching staff saying they were 'managing' his situation.

We have had two episodes before, so they should have known at some stage Trott's problem may become so great he would not be able to carry on. Until then, Trott had had continued success and this was his first real crisis. There was always a danger his condition would explode, which is more likely to happen when you are under pressure, such as when you have been hammered in the first Test of an Ashes series away from home. England lost badly in Brisbane, and Trott played Johnson poorly, having struggled against him in the one-day series a few weeks previously. It was stress and pressure. It is the name of the game for top sportsmen. You cannot avoid it; it is the nature of our job. Test match cricket has always been about whether you can handle the pressure.

Having an individual with a stress-related illness begs the question of whether he should have been in the team in the first place. England will say he had a lot of success in the past, but it seems to me that it is when people are not doing well that the stress takes over. Yardy had been dropped and was struggling before he went home with illness. It appears that it manifests itself in failure, and bad performances exacerbate any existing problems. You never see players going home with depression illnesses when they are scoring lots of runs or taking wickets.

England then made a mess of replacing Trott. They unwisely promoted Root up the order, when he did not have the technique to cope with the quick bowlers, and waited until the final Test before finally batting Ian Bell at three. Mind you, he did little better than Root.

Bell is a guy with everything. He has so much talent; he is a modern-day, right-handed David Gower. He is so elegant, batting is effortless and he has superb timing with a wide range of shots on front and back foot, but I get the impression he does not use his brain, and just plays naturally. If it comes off he looks great, if it doesn't he just shrugs his shoulders and moves on to the next knock. Sadly, England are not blessed with many quality batsmen who can replace Bell, so he gets away with nonchalant dismissals, such as his first baller in the second innings of the Melbourne Test, when England were looking to build on a first-innings lead and actually had a chance to win the match.

Bell came in at 86 for three and England were wobbling again. What did he do? First ball he spooned a catch to mid off. He just punched it head high; it was the most thoughtless shot you could imagine. I hope the coaching staff gave him hell for that, but even if they did it must have fallen on deaf ears.

Ian came in at Sydney in the fifth Test with England strug-gling in the second innings. Johnson had destroyed us for four Test matches and was on a roll again. Bell had hardly been at the crease when he tried to uppercut very fast short balls from Johnson. He did not play himself in or try to see off Johnson. His team were in trouble, but he played his own way. He missed the first uppercut, finally made contact with one and scored a four through third man. Australia then set the trap by putting a fielder at third man. What did Bell do? He tried it again. Luckily it went for six over the fielder's head. I was asking myself: what was he thinking? If Bell had been caught he would have looked stupid and a mug like his team-mate KP in Perth. This was the type of thoughtless batting that cost us the Ashes.

Then we have to look at the bowling. David Saker, the fast bowling coach, admirably admitted that he was at fault for Steven Finn's problems. He said: 'It's disappointing and I take quite a bit of responsibility because my job is to get him play-ing well for England and that hasn't worked the way we would have liked.'

That is a start. At least someone was bold enough to put their hand up and admit they made a mistake. I applaud Saker for that. We all make mistakes, but this was a big one because I believe Steven Finn is the best fast bowling prospect we have had for years. They ruined him with all the fiddling about with his action and delivery. He had been taking four and a half wickets per Test with an average per wicket of 29.40, which is acceptable for the modern game. You cannot take wickets like they did in the 1950s, 60s and 70s; nowadays it is harder for bowlers like Finn because the pitches are covered. Modern bats hit the ball further than ever before and the ball flies over the super-smooth outfields, while boundaries are a lot shorter too.

My view is we just let him bowl. Tell him to get the ball from his end, down to the other end and take wickets and stop filling his head with advice. His habit of knocking the stumps over at the non-striker's end with his back leg has led to a slump. When the ICC decided that in such situations the umpire had to call a no-ball, Finn felt he had to change his technique. But who the hell cares if he clips the stumps at the non-striker's end and there are five or six no-balls called per day? Those runs will make no difference, but the wickets he takes can win Test matches. England spent too long concentrating on altering all sorts of things, his run-up, approach to the crease and the point of release, that he forgot how to bowl.

He spent two and a half months in Australia working with the bowling coach, but in the end they did not dare pick him, even for the one-dayers. England should be ashamed about what happened to Finn, and Andy Flower should never have allowed it to go so far. It was pathetic. They should have sent him home at the end of the Ashes series to rest and recuperate and then picked him for the Lions tour to Sri Lanka, where he could have bowled away from the spotlight and rediscovered some confidence. Instead they compounded the problem. Saker left Finn in a mess and Ashley Giles, the one-day coach, then sent him home saying he was 'not selectable'. The lad had been out there having nets for two and a half months and he was now 'not selectable'. Enduring that embarrassment must have been hugely demoralising for the kid.

Steven was one of the three giant fast bowlers picked for the tour, in the belief they would scare the life out of Australian batsmen. It was one of the biggest selection blunders in modern English cricket. Andy was part of the selection process, along with Geoff Miller (the former chairman of selectors), Ashley Giles and James Whitaker, who has since been promoted to chief selector. They were all responsible and must share the blame. In fact, while England were being hammered, Geoff was picking up a gong in the New Year's Honours List, unfortunate timing to say the least.

Boyd Rankin was not good enough or fit enough, Finn had been cocked up by the coaches and Chris Tremlett was a yard down on pace. The mistake with Tremlett went back further than the Ashes tour. Andy Flower was one of the selectors who did not pick him for the fifth Ashes Test at The Oval in the summer. That was a mistake. If he had played we would have seen he had lost pace, which was exactly the message we were getting from people who had seen him bowl in county cricket.

It was three years since he had done well in Australia. That is a very long time for a fast bowler. He had also suffered a number of injuries since then and Andy should have tested him out before taking him on such a big Ashes tour, but instead England picked Chris Woakes rather than Tremlett. Woakes is a nice county cricketer who would have done well years ago when Test matches were played on uncovered pitches and there was a bit of grass to help seam bowlers. He can bat, too. But today's pitches are better prepared, have better covering and marvellous drainage so they are flatter than ever before. There is not so much joy for medium pacers like Woakes. You need genuine pace and he does not have it. He played at The Oval because Flower wanted to look at the young spinner

Simon Kerrigan, which left them needing Woakes's batting ability.

But Kerrigan was embarrassing and Cook did not dare bowl him. He did not use his front arm at all in delivery and looked like a club bowler. That was a monumental blunder and a harbinger of things to come in Australia. The selectors, and Andy, should be ashamed of themselves for those two calls.

With Tremlett and the experiment of picking three giant fast bowlers failing, England needed their senior spin bowler, Graeme Swann, to perform but his retirement in the middle of the series in Australia was a bitter blow.

I watched him very carefully in the three Test matches he played and I could see the ball was not coming out of his hand the right way when he bowled. He has always had flight and guile with good spin. In Australia, he was always going to have few opportunities to spin the ball because of the harder, flatter pitches, so flight and control were vital. Spinners have to bowl a number of balls in the same area, three or four, and then try something different to tempt a batsman with a wider delivery or one flighted with more air. They alter their line and length to take a wicket, but it was quite clear to me Swann could no longer do that.

He could not land it where he wanted. I could see what he was thinking. Every time he tried to tempt the batsman, it failed. The ball was not landing on the right length or on the right line. His control had deserted him. On top of that, the Aussies had a great plan to target him. They did not allow him to settle and tie them down. Remember, England's cricket for a long time had been based on three fast bowlers who could alternate and stay fresh while Swann bowled a lot of overs at one end. Swann's excellent bowling over a number of years allowed our seamers to rest between spells. He would seal up one end by being both a wicket-taking bowler and someone who could also strangle the run rate. It meant the opposition hardly ever got on top of him and the quicks very rarely had to be over-bowled.

Swann was not the same after his elbow operation in the spring of 2013. OK, he had a successful summer against Australia that year, taking 26 wickets at 29, his best series return, but the pitches were so doctored in his favour he could not fail. His problem with his elbow was covered up by those slow, low turning surfaces. Even though he did not have the same flight and guile, he could extract turn and Australians are poor players of a spinning ball. He perhaps thought any problems with his elbow would clear up by playing more cricket, while the opportunity to be in an England team that could win four Ashes series on the trot was too tempting to pass up.

But the magic had gone, and it was noticeable when he retired after the third Test in Perth that he admitted his elbow had never been the same after the operation earlier that year. I am glad he was honest and gave up the game when he realised he could no longer perform. It must have been a terrible decision to have to make. He must have been so deflated when he realised his zip had gone forever and he would never get it back. At that moment I can understand why he walked away and could not face bowling another ball. You just want to run away, hide and get out of the limelight.

I'm sure it hit him hard. Australia coming at him on pitches where it did not turn must have made it worse. I believe Andy Flower and Alastair Cook tried to talk him out of retirement, but his mind was made up. He was smiling on television when he gave his last press conference, but deep down Swann would have been hurting terribly. It must have been tearing him apart to know he was not the bowler he used to be and he was getting slaughtered like he was in Perth, when his last over was smashed for 22 by Shane Watson.

It was fair enough that he decided he could no longer play, but it would have been better had he stayed on with the tour. It was obvious Monty Panesar was going to play in Melbourne and he perhaps could have done with some advice from Swann. If Swann had helped carry the drinks, it would have been a great sign of togetherness; instead he wasn't given that option. Graeme says Andy Flower told him if you can't play then you have to go home. Swanny had his wife and two small children out there on holiday, so was stuck trying to find flights and accommodation. Kevin Pietersen helped him out and spoke to a friend in Dubai, who fixed them up with a motel. It's not surprising he departed with a wisecrack about players being 'up their own arses' and handed the Aussie press another stick with which to beat England.

Swann had been a star player for five years, during which time all the reserve players had carried drinks for him. It would have shown a lot of character to stay on and help the team in the background, and then announced his retirement when he went home. He would have earned more respect if he had seen the tour out. It is not as if he would have got in the way. There are so many backroom staff with an England squad these days that it is like a mini-army touring the world.

Under Andy England over-complicated professionalism. There were about 16 backroom staff in Australia. How do you get

16 backroom staff in the dressing room? If I had been a player, I would have been telling a few of them to get lost and give me some space. If you have coaches for everything – analysts on lap-tops showing you where opposition players hit the ball and a psychologist telling you what you should and should not be thinking – then players stop working things out for themselves.

They were even told what to eat. Before the series started, the Australian press got hold of an 82-page document sent to all the Test grounds in Australia by the ECB to tell them what food to prepare for the players and send to the dressing room at the end of play. Somebody at the ECB had decided foods such as mungbean curry, piri-piri breaded tofu, goji berries and quinoa was good for the players. The menus were designed by Chris Rosimus, the ECB's performance nutritionist. He wrote in the booklet: 'Some ingredients within this book will not be in season when you come to use them. If availability is an issue, please do not use an alternative or omit from the recipe. Please feel free [unless specified] to serve the sandwiches on any vari-ety of bread you wish. However, a preference would be whole wheat, seeded or rye varieties. For any meat used in sandwich fillings, please do not use processed meats, only freshly cooked meats will suffice.'

What a load of rubbish. Can this Chris Rosimus bat or bowl? Does he take any wickets or score any runs? Has he stood in the field all day for six hours in searing heat? That 82-page document made the team a laughing stock before a ball was bowled. The Aussie media had a fine old time deriding us before we started. It was embarrassing and unnecessary. Whoever thought that was a good thing to send to Australia wants his head testing.

If it was Andy trying to be very professional, then it was misguided. If he did not know about it, then he should have denounced it immediately so the team did not get ridiculed in the media. It does not matter if the person who wrote the booklet got upset. I don't know why he had been employed in the first place.

There have been a lot of great cricketers who have lived on eating hamburgers and smoking cigarettes. Look at Shane Warne. He is the best example of all. I love his bowling, his character and everything about him. I wish I had played against him. What a fabulous cricketer and personality. He loves hamburgers and ciggies, but his diet did not stop him taking 708 Test wickets.

And then we come to the team psychologist, Dr Mark Bawden. Apparently he was with the team during the warm-up games in Australia until the first Test in Brisbane. No offence to the guy, but in a team sport players should be talking things over with each other and working things out together, that is what a team is for. The best motto is the three musketeers' 'All for one, and one for all.'

I would not let a psychologist near my team. I first heard he was on the tour while commentating for *Test Match Special* with Simon Mann, my BBC colleague. I asked: 'Why do they need a psychoanalyst?' Simon explained perhaps he helps the players relax before a big event.

I said: 'Jesus, before going in to bat, I didn't need to be relaxed and calm. At the moment of playing in a big game, I want my senses to be sharpened. I want everything in my body alert and ready to move fast. As soon as I go into bat, I will be dealing in fractions of seconds against fast bowlers trying to knock my block off or get me out. I need to move quickly. I need to have feet that are dancing and moving on my toes, because the ball is coming at me at over ninety mph. Calm? Low? Sleepy? No thank you.'

When you play top-level sport you need to have nervous energy; apprehension is good for all of us. The best players are all nervous. Before a big match and going out to bat, if someone tells you they are not nervous then they are either a liar or an idiot. It is about controlling that nervous energy in a positive way.

The best example I can give is my old friend Dickie Bird. I played with him at Barnsley when I was 15. He is five years older than me and he was the star. He used to come to me before going out to bat shaking like a leaf. He would say: 'Put my gloves on for me, Gerald.' I would remind him that my name was Geoffrey, and he would say: 'Right, put my gloves on, Gerald!'

He was that nervous he could not perform. He was OK at club level, but in county cricket his nerves got the better of him. But then he became the best umpire I ever played under. He could control his nervous energy to make the fewest mistakes and lots of good decisions. It helped him handle players brilliantly with a great sense of humour, and not in a schoolmasterly way.

England's reliance on sports psychologists goes far deeper than just the senior side. The ECB's performance psychology team, for that is what they are called, is five strong. They have James Bell working with the Under-18s team, Simon Crampton with the England women's academy and Bawden with the England side. Amanda Gatherer is the clinical psychologist and Dr Wil James the national lead, whatever that means.

When you read this, it is amazing. If the ECB and Andy believe this psychologist stuff is so important, then why did Bawden not stay with the team for the whole tour? Mark Bawden is quoted as saying: 'We very rarely talk about winning. It's pretty unhelpful, really.' He also goes on to say: 'No, we wouldn't talk about losing.' I read that and could not believe my eyes. When you play sport it is competitive; winning and losing are the outcomes, they are what it is all about. But he is saying they do not want to focus on the end result. They want to concentrate 'on our processes'. Sorry. This is mumbo jumbo.

I can't judge Bawden on his successes, because we do not know who he has been dealing with. But presumably I can judge him on Trott, and his advice did not prevent Jonathan crumbling. I do accept the medical profession has moved forward and taken huge steps since my playing days, but I know after 50 years of playing and watching cricket that the best players never needed all this help. Years ago, it was seen as a weakness if you had to go to a 'quack', as we called psychologists, and we would not want to go see one because of the stigma. If you were struggling and out of form, lacking confidence, dispirited or your demeanour was down, your team-mates would say 'pull yourself together'. We actually thought playing top sport was about being mentally strong and not just about ability.

Look at Mark Ramprakash: he was technically excellent, a lovely boy and a beautiful player. He had exquisite timing on the front or back foot, he scored more than 100 hundreds and made runs galore in county cricket, but could not cut it at Test match level. Why? The answer has to be between the ears. I don't know how true this is, but I heard that one time after he was dismissed in a Test match, he was in the toilets bashing his head against the door.

The contrast is David Steele. Watch him and you would call him an ugly duckling compared to Ramprakash. He mainly played on the front foot, had a dogged defence and was a tough nut to crack. He had limited ability but was up for the most difficult challenges, he stood up to Jeff Thomson and the West Indian quicks, Michael Holding, Andy Roberts and Wayne Daniel. You would love him in your team.

I once heard Jack Nicklaus, the great golfer, being interviewed. He was asked which was his favourite club to play with. He pointed to his head and said: 'The one between the ears.' He summed it up wonderfully. In an individual sport like golf or tennis, I can see that maybe the psychology side helps, but I do not see why England paid for a psychologist to come on tour up to the first Test.

If a player wants to see someone privately then fine, the ECB can sort out a session and pay for it. Today's players are programmed into following orders. When you are batting and bowling, you have to work things out for yourself or you ask your batting partner for advice; Broad and Anderson sometimes field at mid off when they are bowling together, so they can talk to each other. The best players ask questions and have an inquisitive mind. In the middle of a match, Plan A may not work so you need to be able to think quickly on your feet and try a Plan B. If that does not work, think quickly again and make a Plan C.

Good cricketers have to be able to adjust. But if you have been told what to do so often and programmed to follow orders from people, then you are in trouble. At the crease you can't pick up a telephone and speak to the coach, you need to use your brain and I was always taught a thinking cricketer is a better cricketer.

Andy organised every detail of the players' lives, thinking that would make England a better team. In other words, he took professionalism to the extreme. He may have preferred that when he played, but players are not computers. They are individuals in a team framework, each guy has to have space to be himself. It is up to the captain and coach to make sure he plays for the team. Mike Brearley was excellent at allowing individuality to thrive. The big phrase he used was: 'Is it really a big deal what the individual does if it does not harm the team ethos?'

In a team environment, laughter is important. It relaxes everybody, and when players are feeling good there is lots of banter and teams play better. It releases tension and stress. All you have to do as a captain is have lots of laughter in the morning, but 10–15 minutes before the start of play say: 'Right lads, let's switch on.'

Apparently when Darren Lehmann took over the Aussie set-up, he decided that each morning a different player would tell a funny story. You can imagine the ribbing a player gets if he tells a bad joke. I think when you have too much organisation and too many backroom staff you become a robot. The disciplined, work ethic is OK, but only to a point. If there is too much it becomes over-bearing, tedious and repetitive. Players become wooden tops waiting to be told what to do. They go through the motions and it is not enjoyable anymore. They do not look forward to playing cricket and their performances decline as a result. England's Ashes tour was a great example of that happening. By the end nobody could be excused for the way England played.

I was so unhappy with what I saw. There is no shame in being beaten, but it is the way you lose that counts. You have to fight to the end, but by the time of the fourth and fifth Tests in Melbourne and Sydney the England players were mentally shot. It was embarrassing; it looked as if they had given up. When Steve Waugh was captain of Australia he coined the phrase 'mental disintegration'. When a team is beaten in the head and they have given up on the prospect of winning, then it is all over. No amount of talent can make up for that mental state. That is exactly how we looked during the final two Tests.

Captains and coaches have a limited shelf life. You can only talk to people for so long before there is nothing new anymore. Players have heard it all before and the message goes in one ear and out the other. They are not really listening. Andy Flower had had some success, but he had reached the end of the road.

Soon after the Ashes series, he was told if he went quietly the ECB would find him a safe job. Two months later that safe job turned out to be titled 'Technical Director of Elite Coaching', with the focus on developing leadership skills and exploring technical innovation in coaching. It entails working with the next generation of England players and coaches, and he will also look to enhance the relationship between the county coaches and the England set-up.

All I can say is this is yet again another example of the ECB having more money than sense. They waste it by making up jobs and having more unnecessary backroom staff. One minute they cry out they need as much TV money as possible, then they throw it around like confetti. This would not be happening if ECB officials had to spend their own money. So, after the worst defeat England has ever suffered, not just in terms of the result but the embarrassing nature of the team's capitulation, we have the man who was in charge now teaching our future coaches and players how to do it. Do the ECB not see the irony in that?

It makes me fear for the future. The next generation of players will grow up not thinking for themselves. The new head coach of the England team, Peter Moores, has to address this and make the atmosphere more inclusive and less of a school classroom.

CHAPTER II

KP THE ENIGMA

When England sacked Kevin Pietersen in the aftermath of the Ashes whitewash, the public were split. Many were mystified why the team's best player had been made a scapegoat when others had been more culpable for the thrashing by Australia, such as the captain Alastair Cook, the selectors and the coach Andy Flower.

Pietersen was England's highest runscorer in Australia, although that wasn't a particularly hard thing to achieve given their rotten performances, and a player who thrilled the public with some of his daring strokeplay. Many cricket lovers just wanted to see him bat and did not care about dressing-room politics. They paid their money and enjoyed being on edge when KP was at the crease. I know, because I loved watching him bat too. He could change a game in a flash. At the back of the mind was always the worry he would play a daft shot and get out, and for that reason nobody wanted to go to the toilet or to the bar while he was batting. Everybody watched with anticipation.

But it would be wrong to think Kevin was the sacrificial lamb for the Ashes whitewash. This massive decision by England was not taken with one series in mind. It was based on cricketing reasons and issues of discipline. In many ways England had only themselves to blame. They were too soft on him, allowing him to play stupid shots and throw his wicket away too many times without consequence. That came back to haunt them in Australia.

On other occasions, Kevin let himself down with his hubris and arrogance which culminated in the crisis of 2012, when he was caught texting his mates in the South African team. Alastair Cook fought hard to persuade the ECB to give Kevin another chance, but he lost patience with him a year later and was instrumental in sacking him.

The disconnect between Pietersen and the ECB began with his first sacking by England in 2009. The relationship never recovered. It changed the whole dynamic between star player and his employer. I felt for Kevin when he lost the captaincy. It was a messy, shameful period, dealt with in a ham-fisted way by our administrators.

Up to that point Pietersen had been a talented player who had not caused England any trouble, other than for his occasional hairstyles, and he had been managed well by a strong captain in Michael Vaughan. When Michael Vaughan resigned from the captaincy in August 2008, after the defeat at Edgbaston in the third Test of the series against South Africa, and Paul Collingwood, captain of the one-day team, also stood down, Kevin was made captain.

England wanted one leader across both major formats of the game, and he was the only player pretty much guaranteed his place in Test and one-day cricket so he got the job on that basis. There were reservations over whether his personality could stand the test of captaincy but they were ignored. They gambled. He started in typical Pietersen style, with a hundred in his first Test and a win over South Africa at The Oval.

But trouble was brewing. Pietersen had to work with Peter Moores, who had been appointed as head coach, replacing Duncan Fletcher in April 2007. The ECB rushed into his appointment, immediately promoting him from his job running the England Academy in Loughborough to be head coach of the senior side only a day after Fletcher resigned, and it was a disaster waiting to happen.

Pietersen's first tour as England captain was to India in 2008–09 and it was marred by the terrorist attacks in Mumbai. The England team left India and went to the UAE for a holding camp to decide whether or not to return to India. Pietersen was instrumental in persuading the players it would be safe to go back, winning a lot of goodwill in the process.

It was a strong stand to take, but the tour did not go well on the field and at the end of it Pietersen was asked for his thoughts on how to improve matters. It was at that point he suggested the sacking of Moores and his assistant, Andy Flower. In the case of Flower, it was a fateful call by Pietersen, who would spend the rest of his England career working under a man he had wanted sacked. After the tour to India, Pietersen spent Christmas and the New Year period on holiday with his family in South Africa.

Behind his back all hell was breaking loose as news of his

demands appeared in the *Daily Telegraph* on New Year's Eve. Pietersen looked arrogant because he was calling for the sacking of two senior coaches, even though he had been captain for only three matches. Both Moores and Flower had been appointed by the ECB and had strong backers higher up the command chain, yet here was Pietersen saying they were not good enough for the job. Kevin had misjudged the mood badly.

He expected to return to England at the end of his holiday to meet with Hugh Morris, then the managing director of the England team, to plan the future. But before he returned home, the ECB's executive board decided to sack Kevin and Moores. Somebody leaked that decision to the media and it became an absolute mess. Hugh was hoping to meet Kevin when he returned and tell him face-to-face he had been sacked, but because somebody could not keep their trap shut and leaked it, Morris realised it would be hugely difficult for KP when he arrived home for his meeting. The press would be waiting at the airport and he would be walking into an ambush. Morris tried to salvage the situation by telling KP over the phone he had lost his job.

It was a humiliating time for Pietersen. He had gone from asking for the coach to be removed, and believing he would have a say in the naming of his replacement, to being sacked over the phone himself. KP was persuaded to officially 'resign' in order to save himself from a great deal of embarrassment, but I am sure the hurt and pain of being dismissed never left him. It probably lingers even now and he will be bitter about it for the rest of his life. Once Kevin lost the captaincy, somebody had to grab him quickly and ensure his priorities were playing for England by giving him the opportunity to justify his talent, but suddenly he was an outsider as the team found a new spirit under Andrew Strauss and Flower.

Results improved and they won the Ashes that summer, a victory that looked impossible a few months earlier at the height of the Moores–Pietersen crisis. The turnaround vindicated the decision to sack KP and Moores. With Strauss's success in the role, Pietersen knew his chance of being captain again had gone.

Just a month after he was sacked as captain, Pietersen was bought by the Royal Challengers Bangalore for $1.55 million, opening the door to riches in the IPL. Now disaffected by English cricket, he knew he could earn vast sums of money playing in India for six weeks in Twenty20 where it doesn't matter if you get out playing a brainless shot. But the problem for Kevin was that international commitments cut his time in the IPL and impacted on how much money he could earn. His loyalty was split. Within a couple of years, matters came to a head.

Flower played a big part in this. The ECB had a retainer in Pietersen's central contract and could limit his time in the IPL. They wanted him back for the early home Test series in May, which clashed with the IPL. It meant Pietersen could play in the IPL for only three weeks, severely limiting how much money he could earn. It was a very uneasy compromise. KP wanted it all, but had forgotten that playing for England had helped him become a star. You can't have your cake and eat it. You cannot have a central contract, play in the juicy series against Australia, South Africa and India and yet skip other international cricket to play in the IPL. Real life does not work like that.

He wanted to play in a full IPL and then come back to play for England when it suited Kevin Pietersen. No employer would accept that in any job or profession. Finally the situation boiled over when KP announced his retirement from one-day cricket in the spring of 2012. He wanted to play only Twenty20s and Tests, but England would not allow that, saying that he could not pick and choose, but had to play all forms of one-day cricket or none at all, so he retired from one-day cricket.

It must have looked to his bosses at the ECB like childish behaviour. He was taking his bat home and sulking because they would not let him play in the IPL for as long as he wanted. Such a situation does not come to a head without plenty of meetings and discussions beforehand. It became wearying and irritating for England to have to spend so much time dealing with just one player, particularly as they had recently been beaten 3–0 by Pakistan and were planning for a series in the summer against South Africa that would decide which team was No.1 in the Test rankings.

Move on to Headingley in August of that year and he played a brilliant innings in the second Test against South Africa, scoring that fabulous 149 against the best seam attack in the world at the time. But then the story emerged he had been sending SMS messages that were apparently critical of Strauss and Flower to 'close friends' in the opposition dressing room. ECB officials were furious with him and many wanted him out forever. You just do not rubbish your captain to the opposition.

There is no excuse for that behaviour. If you are making derogatory comments about your two bosses to the opposition, it is traitorous. It always seemed that Pietersen said or did something silly when he felt his batting was unassailable.

Success went to his head. It was unheard-of in my day. We did not have mobile phones or the internet, of course, but they just provided Pietersen with the means to cause trouble.

The culture during my career was to keep everything within the dressing room. In the early 1960s at Yorkshire under Brian Close and in the 1970s playing for England with Mike Brearley as captain, we all had our say in the dressing room. You could have your moans and groans about anything – other players or tactics – and strong feelings were sometimes expressed. The captain took it all in, then made a decision and we all followed him; whether we thought he was right or wrong was then irrelevant. It did not matter because he was the boss. It certainly was not discussed outside the dressing room, it stayed in-house and was never revealed to our opponents.

We all knew deep down that if you betrayed that trust, the chairman of Yorkshire, Brian Sellers, would sack you. There were no employment laws or unfair dismissal actions in those days. You were out on your ear. I do not think the England selectors would have picked you again either, and we did not have central contracts with England to fall back on. You were invited by the TCCB to play one Test match at a time, so it was easy for the selectors to get rid of you whenever they wanted.

If England had sacked KP over the texting issue, nobody could have defended him. Michael Vaughan is a big supporter of Pietersen's, but he said: 'They could have moved him on and nobody would have batted an eyelid.' After weeks of meetings and speculation, England took him back. I know the chairman, Giles Clarke, other ECB officials and coach Flower did not want him back. Strauss was hurt, but he had resigned and left the scene.

Cook was the new captain and he was the one chiefly responsible for getting KP back in the team. Presumably he had wanted him because as a new captain he thought Pietersen would help him win matches and cement his position. Alastair must have believed he could get the best out of Kevin and build up a good relationship. When a captain wants a guy back, then he gets his way. Cricket puts great emphasis on the captain. He is the guy who leads the team for six hours a day in the field and makes all the big calls. When a captain stands up for a player, or the opposite and says he has to go, then he usually gets his own way.

For the Ashes tour of 1970–71, Ray Illingworth promised Basil D'Oliveira he would pick him in the squad. Illy had made the pledge earlier in the year after England's tour to South Africa in 1968–69 had been cancelled because the South African government refused to accept a squad which included Basil. When Raymond sat down to choose the squad for the Australia tour, various committee men did not want him in the team. Raymond said he had promised Dolly he would be in his squad, and if the selectors decided not to pick him then he could not go as captain, it would be breaking his word. Basil went to Australia and played in all six Tests.

In the end the buck stops with the captain. He has the most authority and Cook swayed the others, like Illy years before. Pietersen was reintegrated. It was an uneasy truce at first. Every movement KP made on the subsequent tour to India was scrutinised. I wrote at the time: 'A leopard does not change his spots.' Then KP played that wonderful innings in Mumbai. His 186 in the second Test was the best innings I saw him play for England, because for the first 70 runs he batted carefully

KP THE ENIGMA | 237

and in an orthodox fashion on a turning pitch. At some point in the 70s he exploded and it was marvellous to watch. It turned the series and England went on to record a magnificent victory.

There was no more talk of Pietersen being a troublemaker. Matt Prior tweeted a picture in the Mumbai dressing room holding up a sign which said 'reintegration complete'. Cook's decision to bring him back looked vindicated, but I said to myself: 'Give it time.'

A year later and it was over. We cannot say for sure what went on in the England dressing room in Australia. We can only guess and speculate from bits of tittle-tattle we hear. Instead, we have to look at the facts. England lost badly and Pietersen played some awful shots as England paid the price for letting him bat in his own style for far too long. I was a supporter of his talent and I am honest enough to say I could never have played some of the innings he produced. But I also would not have played the irresponsible shots that often cost him his wicket.

He got away with playing the way he pleased for most of his career because England were winning. From time to time he made telling contributions with superb innings but any time he failed or played a silly shot, he would always absolve himself of any criticism by saying 'that is the way I play'. In other words, take it or leave it. That is OK for a while, when results are going your way, but it grates when the team is losing badly as they were in Australia. The silly shots were magnified and gave the impression he did not care and that the team's situation was not his problem.

I was critical of some of his poor shots in Australia; there were some absolute howlers. I called him a 'mug' and I stand by it now. With his team in trouble, he made some mind-boggling decisions. It started in the first Test at the Gabba. In the first innings Australia set the trap by stationing two short midwickets, KP took on the challenge and was caught clipping to one of those two fielders. In the second innings he fell for another sucker punch, hooking a short ball from Mitchell Johnson to long leg.

Then in Adelaide in the second Test he was again caught at midwicket exactly where Michael Clarke had put his fielders, it was stupid. My BBC *Test Match Special* colleague, Jonathan Agnew, summed it up well. 'We just want him to bat with responsibility,' he said. We wanted him to assess the position of the match and try to play accordingly. Even if he failed, and was bowled by a snorter or dismissed in some other fashion, then at least he would have been getting out playing for the team and the match situation. But too often he did not do that.

There was no excuse. Kevin played his 100th Test in Brisbane at the start of the Ashes series. He had been an international player for nearly a decade. You expect your senior, experienced players to give a lead, so it was either a case of he couldn't do it or wouldn't do it. But the worst was yet to come. In the second innings of the third Test at the WACA, with his team trying to save the game, he hit the off-spinner Nathan Lyon for six over long on. Australia dropped a man back on the boundary and Pietersen was caught trying to repeat the shot. It looked as if he did not give a damn that the Ashes were about to be lost.

What I know from having played international cricket and being in an England dressing room is that when one of your team-mates plays a howler of a shot there is a deathly silence. Then someone will spit out what you are all thinking and swear. Everyone is muttering: 'What the hell was that?' If it happens regularly, then I do not see how any captain or coach can criticise other batsmen for playing poor shots. How can they tell youngsters or new kids like Ben Stokes what is expected of them if a senior player like Pietersen is getting out in stupid ways? All the kids have to do is turn around and say: 'What about KP? He does what he wants and nobody says anything to him.'

My other point is if the captain and coach had admonished Kevin in the past, but he ignored them, then it was even worse behaviour on his part because he had clearly not listened. If that was the case then it was insubordination. Trust had broken down, which cannot be good for team unity and eventually it wears the management down. People get fed up and irritated and they start to think: 'Is it worth it? Do I want this problem anymore?' You start wondering if the pluses of having a player like KP in the team outweigh the negatives.

Pietersen mixed brilliant innings with irresponsible shots throughout his career. He was close to Vaughan, but let him down in his final Test. Vaughan was fighting to keep his job and Pietersen had a chance to set South Africa a tough last-innings target. But he got out on 94, trying to hit a six to bring up his hundred, England collapsed letting South Africa win and 48 hours later Vaughan had resigned.

On Flower's first tour in charge in the West Indies, incidentally Pietersen's first innings after losing the captaincy, he fell in identical fashion for 97 in Jamaica. He again tried to reach his hundred with a big six, this time off the left-arm spinner Sulieman Benn. His hubris got the better of him, because at that time people were just starting to talk about his habit of getting out to left-arm spinners, so he tried to show them he had no problem. Technically, I never thought he had an issue against left-arm spinners. He made it an issue by trying to bash them, to show us all he was not bothered by left-arm spin. His ego got him out, not his technique.

The daft shots in Australia were not the product of just one bad tour. It was a weakness that has stained his legacy as a batsman. You cannot argue against Pietersen being one of the best attacking batsmen in the modern era, but he will not be remembered as a great player because there were times when he couldn't or wouldn't grasp he should have played more for the needs of the team. Being cocky and confident with a touch of arrogance is part of the make-up of a great batsman, but too many times when the team needed him to play carefully, he let hubris get in the way of common sense. Once this happened time and again in Australia, the other baggage he brought with him began to weigh heavily on the management once again. When the tour ended, a meeting was held at Lord's to discuss Pietersen's future.

Flower had already stood down and he should not have had a say in Kevin Pietersen's future, but I am confident he will have been asked for his views. The only ones gathered for the actual meeting to discuss the Ashes tour were Paul Downton, the new managing director of the England team, James Whitaker, the new senior selector, and Alastair Cook. What is important to remember this time is that Cook must not have stood up for Kevin. We'd all heard a year previously how he had swayed opinion to bring Kevin back into the fold, and once again he had the power to wield a stay of execution, but presumably decided to let the axe fall.

There is no way Downton and Whitaker, both new to their jobs, would have gone against the England captain, particularly after it had been decided Cook could keep his job despite the 5–0 defeat. Alastair was very lucky to still be captain, partly because there was no obvious alternative, so in such a precarious situation he was not going to rock the boat by blaming the ECB or the management for the Ashes failure.

Kevin was different, though; he had no friends at the ECB. There would be no point keeping Cook as captain and then ignoring him if he said Pietersen should stay in the side. A couple of weeks earlier, Ashley Giles, the coach of the one-day and Twenty20 team and selector, had stated Pietersen was a 'million-pound asset' when he was asked about his team for the Twenty20 World Cup in Bangladesh. As soon as Flower stood down as coach, Giles went on record to say he wanted the head coach's job. If he had really wanted KP in the World Twenty20 team you would think he would have made his feelings known to the new managing director and chairman of selectors. But Giles can't have been very persuasive or he was talked around to the others' views. If Cook and Giles had been strong about retaining Pietersen, he would have survived but they abandoned him and he had played his last innings for England.

If Michael Vaughan had been captain throughout Pietersen's career, he would have managed him better and been strong enough to nip any problems in the bud, but Strauss, Giles and Cook are all mild-mannered and soft-natured people. They indulged him for a quiet life, because of his match-winning talent, and were never going to handle KP firmly in a million years. They allowed him to do his own thing on the field and play his own way with no discipline. The situation snowballed and was bound to end in tears.

When it did it was a nasty time for English cricket, as Pietersen's friends mounted a public-relations campaign against the ECB, who were slow to react. It was led by Piers Morgan, the former editor of the *Daily Mirror*, who is a friend, confidant and admirer of KP, but I don't think he did the lad any favours by tweeting comments and making statements supporting him and criticising the cricketing authorities. Piers, like anyone else, is entitled to his opinion and to give his views, but because he was known to be so close to Kevin, it gave the impression that KP was feeding him information and Piers was his mouthpiece.

I had a similar situation happen to me in the winter of 1983–84 when Yorkshire sacked me as a player. A known supporter and close friend of mine at the time, Sydney Fielden, was trying to be my mouthpiece and, because he was so close to me and shared my company, he knew many private and confidential matters. Unbeknown to me, he was speaking to the Yorkshire committee and the media and anyone else who would listen, giving the impression his words were coming from me. I only learned of it later and discovered how it had put the backs up of some members of our committee. People like Syd and Piers think they are helping you, but it can be counterproductive, and I think this is what happened with KP and the ECB.

Kevin was restricted in what he could say, due to him being under contract to the ECB, and rightly or wrongly people got the impression that this was Kevin's way of getting around it, particularly when tweets emerged criticising Matt Prior. The two men had clearly fallen out, but conducting a public spat on

Twitter did little for Pietersen's cause. Nasser Hussain summed up Pietersen astutely after his final sacking: 'History tells you with Kevin that he hasn't really got a foot to stand on whether it be back in Natal; or Hampshire or Nottinghamshire; whether it be Peter Moores or Andrew Strauss or Alastair Cook or Andy Flower – wherever he's been he's been a problem.'

Some believe in cutting out the virus and moving on while others say you should just man-manage your best players. But the people running England were fed up with dealing with Pietersen and could not handle him any longer. They looked at everything that had gone on in the past and decided the previous five years since the captaincy issue had been characterised by too many meetings and acrimony around Kevin.

What he wanted and what he did took up too much time. People put up with it when the team was winning and KP was batting well, but against Australia in England in 2013 he averaged 38.80 and 29.40 in the return series. Some will say those figures are better than most of the others, but England needed more from a player as good as Pietersen to justify all the aggravation he caused. In the end, he was not worth the bother if he was producing figures that were comparable with the rest. England were humiliated in Australia and heads had to roll. Jonathan Trott and Graeme Swann had gone before the tour reached the fourth Test and Flower later resigned.

There was a new team to be formed under a new coach and, having decided Cook would stay, it was time for a fresh start and they did not want to rebuild the team around younger players while worrying if Pietersen would be a malign influence on impressionable young cricketers. It was time to move on.

Pietersen has always been charming when our paths have

crossed and he speaks well about cricket in the media. He has never been caught up in an off-field scandal involving booze or fighting. He is a consummate professional in the way he prepares for matches and works on his fitness. He always signed autographs for kids and even posed for pictures with fans while fielding on the boundary, but clearly there are deeper issues.

The late Tony Greig wrote that there were similarities between myself and KP in that we were both mavericks and unusual individuals. Things certainly seemed to be always happening around us, like when we both briefly held the captaincy of England. He had the distraction of the terrorist attacks in Mumbai and I had the Pakistan Packer players' dispute in Karachi. Instead of being able to concentrate on the captaincy and the cricket, the other issues become all-encompassing. It is a nightmare trying to juggle the players' and the ECB's wishes. Also, our wicket was always the most prized by the opposition bowlers and the media always knew they would have a story if they could get our name in the headlines. We both had a name that captured the imagination, and always being in the headlines for cricket or other things can cause jealousy from other players.

The oddest thing is, for different types of players in different eras, our Test records are almost the same. Pietersen played 104 Tests, scored 8,181 runs at an average of 47.28 with 23 hundreds. I played 108 Tests, hit 8,114 runs at 47.72 with 22 hundreds, but I never slagged off my captain or team-mates to the opposition while playing with them. When it was put to Mike Gatting in Melbourne during the Ashes tour that KP and Geoffrey Boycott were the same he replied: 'Both like batting and know their averages, but Geoffrey never gave his wicket away and wanted England to win. Kevin gives his wicket away and is indifferent to England winning.' England never lost a Test match when I made a century.

Pietersen was sacked at 33, and still has cricket left in him before he retires. He will make more money than anyone currently in world cricket. KP will be rubbing shoulders with superstars of Indian cricket who earn many millions from their IPL contracts and endorsements. He will be ranked alongside the likes of Mahendra Singh Dhoni, the current Indian and World Cup-winning captain, who earns more money than any other cricketer.

Now KP is available to play the whole of the IPL, he will be able to receive his full fee as he can now stay for the duration of the tournament. He will have immense 'pulling power' and be a target for product association and a brand ambassador. He is also free to 'have bat, will travel' and play all the Twenty20 cricket competitions around the globe. He can have the choice of the 'Big Bash' in Australia around the Christmas and New Year holiday period or the South African Twenty20 series called the 'Ram-Slam' tournament in January and February. He has a deal with Surrey and, if the dates are right, he could in future fit in the Caribbean Premier League. There is a Twenty20 in Bangladesh, although they may have to pay him a fortune to go out there.

He will get astronomical sums for a 'kiss and tell' book due out later this year in which he is sure to settle scores with old team-mates, the ECB and the media. He will give his side of what went on with Flower, Strauss and Cook. Financially he is going to be so much better off than if he'd had his wish and stayed on playing cricket for England in the hope of scoring

10,000 Test runs, as he was quoted as saying. Television stations will be keen to have him commentate on any England matches, it will catch the imagination of the public and media. He will be in demand and become very wealthy.

The bitterness over England will remain, but Pietersen's career will go down as proof that you can be an individual in a team, but you can't just be an individual because it is a team game. It is that simple.

CHAPTER 12

PLOTTING
A WAY BACK

If England are to have any chance of reclaiming the Ashes in 2015, they have to nullify the threat and impact of Mitchell Johnson by being a lot smarter to reduce his wicket-taking ability. If our batsmen try to take him on then there will only be one winner and it will not be Alastair Cook and his mates. No team in the history of cricket has won the war against genuine fast bowling by going toe-to-toe with the quicks. History shows that occasionally a batsman will play a fantastic innings – one that takes your breath away and is thrilling and memorable to watch – but they do not win the Test series for his team.

In the first Test of the Bodyline series of 1932–33 at Sydney, Stan McCabe hooked his way to 187 not out, but it was a fleeting success against Larwood and Voce as England still won by ten wickets. You can always guarantee that at some stage in a series, the big fast bowler will dominate and he will win a couple of matches.

During the Ashes series of 1974–75, in the first Test at Brisbane, Tony Greig scored 110 for England against Lillee and Thomson, but they still lost. In the series Lillee and Thomson took 57 wickets between them in the first five Tests and Australia easily won four, with one drawn. In the sixth Test match at Melbourne, Thomson was injured and did not play. Lillee broke down, bruising his right foot and left the field after bowling only six overs. As a consequence, Australia were without any fast bowlers and England won their only Test match of the series, with Mike Denness and Keith Fletcher scoring centuries.

In 1976 when England played the West Indies at The Oval, Dennis Amiss had been struggling against fast bowling and been left out of the first four matches. He made a fantastic 203 against Andy Roberts, Michael Holding and Wayne Daniel, but England still lost the match by 231 runs. Most people remember this match because Michael Holding took eight wickets for 92 runs and six for 57 on one of the flattest pitches of all time.

Allan Lamb was an excellent player of fast bowling, and in 1984 versus the West Indies he made 110, 100 and 100 not out in consecutive Test matches at Lord's, Leeds and Old Trafford, yet England still lost all three matches badly to the fast bowling of Joel Garner, Malcolm Marshall and Michael Holding.

And finally, Kevin Pietersen made a superb century against South Africa at Headingley in 2012. At the time, they had the best fast bowling attack in the world and the match was drawn, but England still lost the series 2–0. So you see, fleeting brilliance with the bat thrills and entertains at the time, but it normally only delays the inevitable.

It is possible Mitchell Johnson will be injured and unable to play next year. He could revert back to his old ways of spraying the ball all over the place, but I think that is highly unlikely. He has found such confidence and a way to be aggressive, bowl fast and take wickets, so England have to plan for him being fit and in form. They have to find a way of combating him; it does not matter if we do not score off him, but we can't afford him taking another 37 wickets at 13 each. If he does then the Ashes series will be over before it starts.

If I remember rightly, a Test match lasts five days, although you wouldn't know it by watching us in Australia. During the last Ashes series, the Tests in Brisbane and Melbourne finished in four days, Sydney in three days, Adelaide one hour into the fifth day and Perth finished at lunch time on the last day. Scoring quickly is lovely, but when you are not able to do that then it is better to score slowly than not at all. It falls to all the batsmen to improve. The England batsmen have to learn to be more patient and keep their wickets intact, exhaust Johnson and make him work harder by bowling a lot of overs for little reward. They need to plan, prepare and above all execute better.

England's batting succumbed too easily and too quickly in Australia, meaning the opposition bowlers were never tired but the England bowlers did not get the same chance to put their feet up, because before long they were strapping their boots on and were out there bowling again. It was a complete contrast to three years previously, when England's batsmen made high scores, giving their bowlers lots of rest. They need to get back to that scenario.

With back-to-back Test matches, it is exhausting for a bowler if he does not have enough rest so it is imperative to keep the Australians in the field for longer by posting decent totals. The England batsmen have to understand they need to get smarter, they have to box clever like Muhammad Ali against George Foreman in 1974. Foreman had knocked out 37 of his 40 opponents before he took on Ali. He was world champion, much bigger and stronger than Ali and punched harder. Ali realised there would be no point trying to slug it out with Foreman, it would be a no-win situation. It is exactly what I am saying here with Johnson, they need to adapt to the situation.

Ali always had fast hands and quick feet but he could not out-punch George, so what did he do? He did his homework and realised this big heavy man had never gone more than a few rounds because he had always knocked his opponents out early in his fights. So Ali thought he would tire him out by staying on the ropes, letting George throw punches that kept hitting his arms which eventually exhausted Foreman. Then Ali took his chance and knocked him out, afterwards they coined it 'Rope a Dope'.

The new England head coach, Peter Moores, needs to impress on his batsmen a better strategy is needed, rather than playing virtually a shot a ball against Johnson. Not only is a plan needed, but it then has to be implemented well. Occasionally a guy like Johnson will bowl on a slow pitch that takes the sting out of his bowling, but that happens infrequently now in modern-day Test matches. The technology and know-how about preparing pitches have improved beyond recognition. We can't just produce slow, low pitches to nobble Johnson. The test for England is to sort the problem a different way.

I know the World Cup is before the Ashes and England have

never won it. It would be tremendous to win it this time, but which is the bigger prize? Is it winning the World Cup in March of 2015 or beating Australia and getting the Ashes back? Ask fans which they would prefer, yes we would like to win both, but the Ashes are the jewel in the crown. They always have been and hopefully always will be.

Alastair Cook needs to keep in mind that winning generals take all the honours and are feted, but losing generals get the sack, and he was lucky to retain his job after the shambolic Ashes tour. In order for him to keep the captaincy, he and his batsmen have to get back to scoring totals of more than 400 in the first innings of every game. It is not absolutely vital to score 500, but 400 runs puts them in a position of strength from which they can then have a big say in the course of the game.

Even if the opposition also goes on to make a big total, there is still more chance of saving the match. It usually takes up three days for two teams to score around 900 runs, leaving only two days for a further two innings. Whether you win or lose the toss, you will not be beaten very often if you score totals of more than 400 in your first innings.

Bowlers love it when their batsmen have put runs on the board. Ask any bowler, if the batsmen have given them a platform to work with they are more relaxed so bowl better. It is amazing then how much scoreboard pressure is put on the opposition. But make low totals then you will be the team under pressure all the time, tensions creep in and the other side get a sniff of victory.

Our England batsmen need to get back to basics and get rid of all these one-day shots: reverse sweeps, scoops and paddles. It is madness to be playing them in a Test match. In the first innings of the second Test match in Adelaide last winter, Joe Root, batting at No.3, got out for 15 playing a scoop shot off the off-spinner Nathan Lyon. Why did he think he needed to play a scoop? There was plenty of time left in the Test and England needed to build an innings. They were facing an Australian total of 570 for nine declared and the pitch was good for batting. It was crazy.

Hooking is another shot fraught with danger, pulling is a much better per centage stroke. When the ball bounces chest high, it is much easier to control it playing a pull. Once the ball gets throat and head high, it is harder to keep down. We have all made the mistake of hooking those balls, myself included. You can make that mistake once, but you can also make sure you don't do it again.

When I used to play against West Indian Malcolm Marshall, the greatest fast bowler ever, he would see me in the car park before the game and, with a big smile on his face, shout: 'Are you hooking today, Boycs?' and I would shout back: 'Not if you're bowling.'

In February 2014 in the second Test at Port Elizabeth, the South Africans showed how to bat against Mitchell Johnson. In the first Test at Centurion, he had blown them away. Graeme Smith was out hooking, players were hit on the head, and too many played indiscriminate shots. It was as if they hadn't watched the Ashes series. They were taken by surprise and Johnson took 12 wickets in the match.

South Africa then did their homework and, unlike England in the previous Ashes series, they occupied the crease, batted slowly with care and a lot of patience to make a total of 423 runs. They took Johnson out of the equation and he got one for

70 in the first innings and two for 51 in the second. It may not have been spectacular batting, but it worked, and by taking the time to put a good total on the board they won the match. The South Africans realised that if Johnson takes a bag-full of wickets at a low cost against you, there is no way you can win a Test match; you have to play him out of the game.

God knows how any of the modern batting teams would have got on against the West Indian quicks in the 1970s and 80s when there were four of them coming at you all day long and there was no respite. Sadly, I think too many of them would rely on sledging to try to talk their way out of trouble, which would be a recipe for disaster. I hope Peter Moores improves standards of behaviour on the field and doesn't sink to Australia's level next year. England should be the first to set their own standards and cut out the lip.

They need to be bigger than the other teams, let the verbals go over their heads and concentrate on playing well. That would wind the Aussies up more than anything else. It will take a lot for that to happen, because England have lost experienced players who could show a lead. Andrew Strauss, Kevin Pietersen and Jonathan Trott have all gone, leaving a more callow team but also a vulnerable batting line-up. There is time for that to change, but the selectors have to show some decisiveness and give new players a chance.

They have four series scheduled between the Ashes contests, but that involves only 12 Test matches (seven of which will have been played by the time this book is published) so it is important the selectors do their job well, identify guys who they think will make Test match players and then give them the opportunity to play in all 12 Test matches to gain as much experience as possible. It will be crucial who the selectors choose.

Losing KP and Trott has left a huge hole in the middle order. If Jonathan makes runs for Warwickshire, can England resist the temptation to bring him back into the team? He was a fine player with a good Test record but what if he returns, the pressure gets to him and he has to go home ill again? England would look like chumps. They say they have managed him once, but it will be risky to try it a second time. Five months after leaving the Ashes tour he gave an interview to Sky, and blamed his breakdown in Australia on 'burn out'. But he collapsed again after just one match for Warwickshire and I can't see how England can trust him again in the heat of Test cricket. If he gets back into the England team and plays the same amount of cricket again, how will he deal with all that travel and playing? Will the stress come back again? Will he run away again?

Those are the serious questions I would ask if I was a selector. Also, did he rush back to play county cricket because Warwickshire had given him a benefit and he knew if he played it would help swell his fund? Or was he just kidding himself? The boy had tears in his eyes at times during that Sky interview. It was all very raw for him. If he faces the Aussies again, they will not be shy with their onfield comments; in other words he will get plenty of sledging.

Jonathan Trott didn't play Johnson well in the ODIs in 2013, and in the first and only Test he faced him, Johnson dismissed him both times for 10 and 9. Anybody can fail, but in the 28 balls he received he looked very uncomfortable. He has always shuffled across the crease, but I noticed when playing Johnson he was shuffling across the crease and moving forward *before* Johnson had let the ball go. That's OK until the bowler bangs it in short of a length, gets lift like Johnson does and because of his pace the batsman has not got enough time to transfer his weight onto the back foot. If you are coming forward to a speed merchant before he delivers the ball, his eyes will light up and you are asking for one or two in the mouth. That's what he got and he was in trouble. It's vital to stay back until the bowler has let the ball go, only then should you decide to come forward or go further back.

Trott's absence means Ian Bell should move up to No.3. If he stays down the order, England will have to have a new inexperienced batsman at No.3 as well as a likely new opening partner for Cook, given Carberry's struggles in Australia. Facing the new ball with two unproven guys is very chancy. If Bell goes to bat at three, then he has to knuckle down and cut out the mistakes; somebody has to be firm with him, because it is not how quickly he scores or how dashing he looks at the crease, it is how many runs he makes. He must battle through the difficult periods with some patience rather than taking the bowlers on or trying to smack spinners over the top.

When bowlers are having a good period, he has to play through it and cannot always attack; he has to show a lot more maturity now Pietersen is out of the frame. Joe Root has been up and down the batting order since he came in the team, so England could finally give him a settled spot at No.4. The kid has immense talent and the character to be a top batsman for England for many years.

I do not think he is ready for opening the innings. I tried to tell various people, the selectors and the ECB, that he was not ready to open against high-quality bowling. I had watched him at Yorkshire in 2011 and 2012, and I spotted he had a bit to learn early on in his innings with his footwork against the new ball. He struggled getting his feet moving. If he gets in, he makes hundreds and looks terrific, but England did not listen.

The sudden departure of Andrew Strauss, retiring earlier than expected, left England with a big hole to fill at the top of the order and they were desperate for an opening batsman. England got sucked in to believing that because he scored runs for the Lions he was a ready-made opening batsman. He may well be one day, but it takes time. Test cricket has better and faster bowlers with a new ball in their hand and they are far more dangerous than county bowlers. When he opened in 2013 against Australia in England, he made one half century and a big hundred at Lord's after he was dropped on 8. In total, he had seven failures. That is not a good return for an opening batsman. If Australia had caught him when he was still in single figures at Lord's before he went on to score 180 it would have looked a lot worse.

The other problem is England fell in love with him to the point where they were picking him in all forms of the game. Wow! You would think we had Brian Lara and Sachin Tendulkar all rolled into one. In my opinion, picking him in all forms of the game has not helped his development. As a lovely, technically correct batsman can you see him as a Twenty20 crash-bang-wallop merchant? I can't. Slogging? Cross-batted shots? Using brute force to hit boundaries? Sorry, I do not see Joe Root as that kind of player. Not now, not ever. I believe this was misguided.

I watched him on television playing in a Twenty20 against

Australia in Melbourne. He came in, played a cover drive, one off his legs and then had a big slog and the ball went up in the air to backward point. How does that help the development of a 23-year-old kid? Many of the best Twenty20 players in the world are average Test match cricketers. Look at Kieron Pollard. He hits it everywhere in a Twenty20 game, but does not get picked in Test cricket for the West Indies, because he does not have the defence, technique or patience required.

Twenty20 is slog cricket and entertainment, but it is not the best preparation for an orthodox young batsman trying to learn how to build an innings. There are very few technically correct batsmen who do reasonably well in Twenty20, because T20 is not about orthodox batting. The few who have done well in Twenty20 playing orthodox shots are a lot older than Joe and have learnt their trade. They have been very successful over a number of years and understand their game. The best example is Mahela Jayawardena, the Sri Lankan batsman, who is magnificent in Test cricket but was able to transfer that to other forms of the game. In T20 you have to hit every ball for runs and it breeds bad habits for Test cricket, so that you then start doing it in any form of cricket without thinking.

As a young kid, Joe should be allowed to develop his game without the pressure of having to strike boundaries. England should get him back to playing orthodox cricket, because it is possible he could be as good in Test cricket as Jayawardena. At the moment, having a regular spot down the order where he can start his innings away from the new ball, is the ideal position for him. Given time, Joe will probably move up to open the innings, but leave the lad alone for now, let him develop.

Matt Prior should be our wicketkeeper in the next Ashes

series. He is a wonderful player and he has always been a positive influence batting down at No.7. But in 2013 his strength was his weakness. He tried to play shots, get on top of the bowlers before he got himself in. Now he is a very senior player and he has to show, like Bell, a bit more patience and common sense. The youngsters will be looking to Bell and Prior for guidance.

The batting coach has to work hard with our tailenders, because in Australia they were hopeless. All tailenders like playing medium pacers and spinners, because there is no physical danger, but however good they are at that, they are all shit-scared of fast bowling. The fear of facing Johnson just blew their minds before they reached the middle. They are not expected to score runs, but there is an expectation they will make Johnson and other bowlers spend lots of energy and effort on getting them out. Psychologically, Johnson's presence had damned them before they entered the arena. That is the fear of getting hurt and they need help in order to conquer it.

The coaches need to teach them how to defend and that should not be too difficult, because in the last 30 years everyone has been wearing a helmet with a grille, chest pad and an armguard, which reduces the chances of getting hurt. But if you stand there frightened of being hit, then you have no chance of staying in. They might as well not bother going out to the middle, because in Australia it was embarrassing. The Aussies rolled over the tail so quickly that it gave them a huge psychological lift.

Monty Panesar has to be our spinner. I don't have any doubt in my mind that he is our best spin bowler now Graeme Swann has retired. The worry for me is that Cook does not know how to manage Monty. He is a guy who thrives on confidence. It is going to be a test of Cook's man-management skills as captain to get the best out of Monty. He has to make Monty believe he wants him in the team.

Alastair gave me the impression in Australia that he did not trust Monty's bowling and there were times when I thought he should have bowled more in the two Tests he played in Adelaide and Melbourne. Instead, the captain threw the ball to someone else. England then dropped him in Sydney for Scott Borthwick, the young leggie who is not even a frontline spinner for his county Durham, but just happened to be out in Australia playing club cricket. Now if Monty gets an inkling that the captain does not believe in him, then he crumbles. It is an absolute must that Cook shows Monty he loves him and makes him feel fantastic. No negative vibes whatsoever or you lose him as a bowler.

Shane Warne will be negative about Monty to help his own Australian side and say he has played so many Tests for England but bowls with the same pace and same trajectory every time. I don't give a toss about what an Aussie says; forget any criticism and focus on the facts: he has taken over 150 Test wickets and helped England win matches.

Perhaps a young kid will emerge to displace Monty, but the next Ashes series will be a harsh environment for a spinner. We know Darren Lehmann, Michael Clarke and his team will use the same tactic as they did against Swann. All the batsmen will go after whoever is the spinner and try to knock him out of the attack. A young player could crumble under such pressure, but Monty has been in the situation before.

It looks as if England have unearthed a talented all-rounder in Ben Stokes. He has pace with the ball plus some ability with the bat, but England have to play him in every Test match now to gain experience. He has a lot to learn. He is still raw with the bat: he scored a good hundred in the second innings of the third Ashes Test at Perth, but then in Melbourne when we were trying to save the game he was caught at mid off trying to hit Nathan Lyon over the top on 19. That is when a coach has to get hold of him and say: 'OK, you got a hundred in Perth playing shots like that when you had seventy, but it is not a smart shot to be playing when we are trying to save the game.' That is the learning process which comes about from playing Test matches and talking to more senior people.

As with Joe Root, I would prefer to see him not playing in the Twenty20 format and be allowed to develop his cricket in Test matches and 50-over games only. These kids have no time to breathe, to collect themselves and take it all in. They play every minute at the top level living in a 'goldfish bowl' with no respite. Each of the three formats demands a different way of playing, a different understanding of what is needed and I think it is just too much to ask them to assimilate all that. England want them to run before they can walk, but their development needs to be paced. It is no surprise to me when these youngsters cannot maintain a high level of performance. The frustrations creep in.

On England's tour to the West Indies in March 2014, Ben had five failures with the bat. The frustration boiled over and he ended up breaking his wrist after punching a locker in the dressing room following a first-ball dismissal. A young player's development is like snakes and ladders. Up the ladder and down the snake, it's a roller coaster ride. Nowadays television

makes young cricketers instantly famous, money comes pouring in, and they think they have made it. The adrenalin and
testosterone is pumping. It is a fantastic, but also a difficult
time in their career.

Good coaches should understand that young players' performances will go up and down and their emotions will
fluctuate. It's a natural learning curve, so it is up to the coach
to occasionally take them out of the spotlight for a break.
Stokes can be a handy back-up bowler next summer, but
England's main strikeforce should revolve around Steven Finn,
who will hopefully be back to his best, and Stuart Broad.
Jimmy Anderson and Graham Onions will be crucial swinging
the ball and Chris Jordan from Sussex has pace. There is always
room for somebody with genuine pace and Liam Plunkett
might come into the reckoning.

Anderson has been our best bowler for years, playing in all
formats of the game. As he gets older – he will be 33 during the
next Ashes series – there is a need to keep him fresh and lessen
his workload. He has been bowling for a long time and played
a lot of cricket after more than 12 years at the top. It would be
wise now to retire him from all forms of one-day cricket and
save him for Tests only. He can still produce marvellous deliv-
eries; the ball he bowled at Trent Bridge to Michael Clarke in
the first Ashes Test of 2013 was a beauty. He brought Clarke
forward, beat the bat and hit the top of off stump. Honestly, if
he had bowled that to me ten times, he would have got me out
ten times, although I would like to think I'd have nicked it and
not missed it like Clarke! If Anderson can bowl balls like that,
then you want him as fresh as a daisy, not travelling around the
world playing one-day cricket.

On English pitches with the Duke ball, Onions can be very dangerous. I don't know why England ignored him in 2013, as he had fantastic figures for Durham, but for some reason they did not trust him. They have Onions and Anderson for swing, Broad and Finn for seam but they need some pace. Chris Jordan is young, raw and worth a punt, because young bowlers can develop very quickly and I was delighted that our selectors took a chance and gave him a few Test matches.

For me, Tim Bresnan is not a match-winning bowler in Test cricket and I would play him only in one-dayers. He is a good, strong guy and he will bowl a lot of overs. I can see why Flower and Cook liked him, but I prefer wicket-taking bowlers like Liam Plunkett, as they win Test matches.

Stuart Broad is a superb cricketer and was our best bowler in Australia. He has a big heart and the stomach for a fight, but you want him ready and fresh. He has had problems with injuries in the past and this will only get worse as he ages, so the selectors have to manage his workload carefully. It is a problem resting bowlers and keeping them fresh, but you cannot win every series and every World Cup by playing the same players. It is impossible. If you want them to be fit and ready for the Ashes, then you have to rotate and give bowlers time off.

Modern international teams have become like Premier League football clubs in recent years, they play so much we need large squads. Slowly and surely we are now seeing cricketers being rested. There is a need to prioritise with most players and decide what is their best format. For example, Broad is the Twenty20 captain, a major player in 50 overs and Test matches, but while he might want to, it is not good for him to play every match. He will be knackered and pick up an injury. There is so much international cricket it is becoming a real problem for selectors to juggle players around.

England's run-up to the 2015 Ashes is a trip to Sri Lanka in November and December, where it is hot and hard for quick bowlers, a one-day tri-series in Australia in January and February, then the World Cup in Australia and New Zealand followed by three Tests in the West Indies in April before the English summer of two Test matches against New Zealand and then the Ashes.

They are going to have to manage resources very cleverly to keep our key guys fresh and fit for facing Australia. If they try to win every match and series with the same players, it will blow up in their faces. Yes, it is good to win, but for that to happen they will have to move players around. That takes skilful management and the one area of genuine worry for me is the leadership of Alastair Cook.

He is not the type of guy to criticise a player and tell him off, but occasionally as captain, he is going to have to face up to players. He has to show them he is the boss and not just because someone has given him some stripes to pin on his arm. That alone does not make you a leader. Leadership is about gaining the respect, trust and confidence of the rest of the team. Nobody can teach that; it comes naturally. There is no captaincy textbook or school.

You learn by watching others while growing up and asking questions of your elders. But even that is not enough, it is instinct; you have to feel the nuances of the game as they happen. It is about the ability to see an opportunity before it happens and to be strong enough to act rather than prevaricate or be too cautious. A lot of ex-players feel Cook's major problem is that he is too pedestrian, he waits too long before making his move and he follows the ball with his field placings. You have to be two steps ahead of the game in your thinking and I don't think Cook will ever get it. He is a nice lad and a top batsman and he will always be just that. He is not a gifted leader.

OK, Alastair had a dip in form in Australia, but that has happened to all of us and his runscoring will return. But the problem for Cook is that he will always be compared to his Australian opposite number, Clarke, who is very sharp. I accept people say: 'If not Cook, then who?' A lack of alternatives is a bigger problem for England to solve. But one day if Cook does not grasp it, then someone else will come on the scene and they will be made captain. You can't stick with a captain because he is a nice lad and a good batsman. He was lucky to survive the 5–0 in Australia, but the ECB realised they did not have anyone else to turn to. The only other candidate was Bell and he thinks even slower than Cook.

The best captain I played under was Ray Illingworth. If he saw an opportunity, he would move fast. What helped was that Raymond played a lot of his career on uncovered pitches, so he grew up expecting the unexpected. We played two three-day matches a week and every pitch was different. Then, if it rained on the pitch, it changed in character so you had to adapt to new conditions. Captains had to think ahead of the game. We also had to fit four innings in to three days, so time was always your enemy and you had to be smart to get results.

Perhaps we were lucky to grow up in an era when we had to think on our feet. But the modern-day player does not understand the challenges we faced. They think if you play on a pitch that has been rained on, the ball would fly past your head but that was not the case. It would seam, swing and turn on some days. On other occasions after rain it would do nothing, the ball would go straight and keep low so captains had to be good at judging situations. You had to keep a sharp brain all the time. Cook lets the game drift and rarely shows any imagination.

England may have the players to beat Australia, it is just whether they have the brains to go with the talent. Beating Australia is what the public demands. If we play as badly at home as we did in Australia and lose abjectly 5–0, there will be the biggest outcry cricket has ever seen from the public and the media. All hell will break loose. There will be a lot more losing their jobs than just Andy Flower, Kevin Pietersen and Graham Gooch. It will be an intriguing series.

ACKNOWLEDGEMENTS

A special thank you to my wife, Rachael, who has been very influential in how this book has turned out. She was my sub-editor throughout, checking my copy, providing advice and utilising her excellent memory to ensure my recollections are honest. Without her care and attention to detail, I could not have accurately recalled my difficulty with cancer, which forms an emotional part of this book.

Thank you Rachael, you were brilliant.

INDEX

(the initials GB refer to Geoffrey Boycott)